Mission, Race, and Empire

Mission, Race, and Empire

The Episcopal Church in Global Context

JENNIFER C. SNOW

OXFORD
UNIVERSITY PRESS

Oxford University Press is a department of the University of Oxford. It furthers
the University's objective of excellence in research, scholarship, and education
by publishing worldwide. Oxford is a registered trade mark of Oxford University
Press in the UK and certain other countries.

Published in the United States of America by Oxford University Press
198 Madison Avenue, New York, NY 10016, United States of America.

© Oxford University Press 2024

CIP data is on file at the Library of Congress

ISBN 978–0–19–759894–8

DOI: 10.1093/oso/9780197598948.001.0001

Printed by Sheridan Books, Inc., United States of America

*With gratitude for my wife, Tita, who introduced me
to a world larger than I had imagined;
for our son, Taal, who shows us all the love and joy in the world;
and for my students, who have shown me why this work is so important.*

Contents

Mission, Race, Empire

Why the Episcopal Church?

The Episcopal Church provides a particularly underexamined aspect of the modern formation of "globalized Christianity." Examination of the history of the Anglican Communion has largely focused on the national churches deriving directly from the Church of England and the British Empire. Yet the Episcopal Church, perhaps the oldest postcolonial Anglican church, has a significant and distinct relationship to the development of the global Communion. Multiple national churches and a national church incorporating multiple cultures arose from the political expansion of the United States, for which the Episcopal Church often imagined itself as the national spiritual leader. The Episcopal Church internally has been deeply shaped by its colonial missional history, with innovative theologies and internal polities directly related to the territorial and political adventures of the United States.

The challenge in grasping this history is that it is not fully an "internal" history of the denomination alone, nor of "mission" alone, if mission is thought of solely as external to the denomination's central momentum. It is a history that is intertwined with the political history of the United States and indeed of modernity, with the imperial expansion of the North Atlantic nations over five hundred years, with the development of contested racial ideologies and identities; it is a history that shaped and is shaped by the rise of global Christianity and its networks. To discern these underlying forces requires a history that sees both social and disciplinary boundaries as constantly being created and transgressed, that attends to the permeability of boundaries as the central organizing point of the investigation. And this focus on the creation, transgression, and permeability of boundaries leads directly to a historical examination of *mission*, *race*, and *empire*.

Mission, Race, and Empire. Jennifer C. Snow, Oxford University Press. © Oxford University Press 2024.
DOI: 10.1093/oso/9780197598948.003.0001

Mission, Race, and Empire

For this investigation, I define "mission," an incredibly multivalent term, as *the church incorporating others beyond its current boundaries.* Among Christians, mission is not only a set of practices of "outreach"; understandings of and practices of mission are also related to a faith and social identity. Thus investigations of mission will consistently run up against self-conceptions, identifications of boundaries of the self or institution, and efforts to transgress or police these boundaries.

Mission has been involved in establishing and policing boundaries between groups and approved or improper ways of life, complicit in cultural destruction and colonial expansion. Yet mission has also been a way in which individuals and groups have attempted to challenge the limits of race and empire in human relationships and political life. Missionaries—those who self-consciously set themselves to cross boundaries and incorporate "others" into a community of faith—sometimes attempted to ameliorate oppression; advocate for the colonized; shift internal commitments to "correct" theology, liturgy, and communal practice; and deny any ultimate, fundamental reality of racial distinctions. Members of communities experiencing the effects of race and empire in the rise of colonialism could also use mission as a creative response to changes in cultural life, developing new religious and cultural worldviews that would in turn reshape the practice of Christianity.

"Empire" is another hugely powerful and symbolic concept. Here I define it simply as encompassing both direct political domination of one cultural or racial group by another and the less obvious methods by which cultural and economic hegemony by one group over another is established and maintained, which is sometimes also called "colonialism." The "great century" of Christian missions coincided with the high eras of American and European global expansion, leading historians to ponder the ways in which church and colonialism have been mutually shaped and the contradictions and complexities in this relationship.

The Episcopal Church, among American denominations, has a very particular connection to the history of empire. The Church of England—the established national church of Great Britain, with the monarch as its head—was planted wherever the British Empire went, including the early English American colonies. Following the American Revolution, the colonial Church of England became the Episcopal Church, the first of many national churches arising from the creation and stuttering dissolution of the British

Empire. The Episcopal Church then became entwined in the new American imperial project as part of American expansion—not always as a direct agent of political power, but following the political power which opened new fields for mission.

As the Episcopal Church developed in tandem with empire in the modern era, it also developed in tandem with ideologies and practices of "race." Modern racial ideologies and categories did not preexist modern European expansion, but largely arose in response to the experience of dominating other cultural groups through enslavement and colonization, and were intertwined from the beginning with religious and cultural marks of group identity. The earliest documented importation of kidnapped Africans to a life of enslavement in English North America occurred in Jamestown in 1619, an English colony firmly within the orbit of the Church of England. The colonial church in the Caribbean and the North American mainland colonies developed theologies and practices of Christian slavery, buttressed by racial practices and distinctions within the life of the Christian community. As slavery was carried over into the new political formations of the United States, so too were these racially based exclusions in the life of the new Episcopal Church. Racial ideologies continued to shift throughout the nineteenth and twentieth century, sometimes in direct opposition to religious understandings of mission and relationships between human groups. When the Episcopal Church struggled—and it was very often a struggle—to reach beyond whatever its boundaries were in a given moment, either demographic or territorial, it was thus crossing boundaries created by race or empire.

Disciplinary Complexities

As this book is intended to document the creation, policing, and crossing of boundaries, unsurprisingly it crosses disciplinary boundaries as well. Within each of the main disciplines here of American history, missiology, and global Christianity, engaging the history of the Episcopal Church through the lens of mission, race, and empire provides a revisioning or engagement of central issues in the discipline.

Modern studies of mission history and world Christianity have emphasized the agency of local "converts" and the importance of "contextualization" and "indigenization," as well as the intertwining and interdependency, the mutually transformative relationships, that exist throughout the colonial era between metropole and periphery. The United States itself is originally a colonial periphery, and its transformation into its own metropole can be traced in the history of the Episcopal Church in particular. However, mission studies have not adequately investigated this mutual interdependency and shaping in terms of the internal theologies, identities, and practices of the "sending churches." Contextualization is usually assumed, however nuanced, to be something done by the "younger churches" as they take on Christian faith and relate it to their local contexts.

I argue that the "sending churches" are equally, if not more so, transformed by the experience of missional practice and relationship, and that this is also a process of contextualization. Examining the history of the Episcopal Church, an American denomination historically dominated by white elites, as transformed through its mission experiences and relationships demonstrates that contextualization is equally relevant and important in the churches of the Global North, not only the Global South. This history demonstrates the importance of looking for missional dynamics *within* "white" and Global North churches, not only in "cross-cultural" or international mission projects. The Episcopal Church provides a uniquely interesting field for this investigation, as unlike most Protestant denominations it made "church" and "mission" organizations identical from the early nineteenth century on, and it constituted itself as both a "domestic" and "foreign" missionary society, identifying missions within the United States and missions outside as equally part of the church's (often weakly performed) missional mandate.

In terms of American history, this book makes a small contribution to ongoing studies of American imperial expansion and colonization, to racial and ethnic studies, and to understanding the relationship between religious and political history. Much of the work I draw from here is relatively recent and focuses on one particular arena, for instance, Gerbner's *Christian Slavery* for the seventeenth century and Hollinger's *Protestants Abroad* for the late twentieth. I also draw from outstanding recent work on slavery and Christianity in the Atlantic world and on sexuality and gender in global Christianity. It may be premature to attempt to put all of these times and places in relationship with one another in a single narrative, given that so much excellent work is currently being done in particular areas, but I argue that they do need to be related to one another in order to fully understand the dynamics of this complex colonial inheritance. I hope that in making the attempt I may encourage more historians to excavate and analyze this history.[1]

In terms of internal Episcopalian denominational history, the work provides two major demonstrations for scholars and Episcopalians themselves. The first is that shifting to a lens of mission completely recalibrates the central points and figures of the church's life. Individuals that were previously somewhat marginal are now in the spotlight; the church's internal diversity and dynamism are demonstrated by focusing on the stories and relationships of those striving to live out their mission in a complex and pluralistic society. Internal shifts in liturgical practice and theological self-understandings are now seen in a different relationship to one another, influenced by international events and ecumenical global relationships rather than solely originating within the United States at General Convention. Finally, the contemporary controversies and schisms of the Episcopal Church and the Anglican Communion can be understood both as bearing the weight of colonial history and as part of a massive shift in missional understanding that comes into global Christian life in the mid-twentieth century.

I am a white Christian Episcopalian lesbian who teaches at an Episcopal seminary, a laywoman as well as an academic. This places me firmly within a specific missional camp of global Christianity, that of the ecumenical or *missio dei* stream. It is worth noting that this is an insider history in the sense that I am not impartial about mission, race, and empire, about the importance of this history to the church, and about how we who identify as Christians understand ourselves and our purpose and our relationships in the world. I believe that our contextuality is deeply shaped by the scars of colonialism and racism and that to look at this history honestly is required. An honest examination can lead, among other things, to a shift in understanding the nature and purpose of "mission" for members of the church.

This history traces both the errors and the unexpected successes of mission. I hope that providing a missional history will encourage Episcopalians to continue this necessary work of developing missional theology and practice in relationship with the global church. In this, I am encouraged by two Native American leaders, George Tinker (Osage) and Vine Deloria Jr. (Standing Rock Sioux). Both of them, when examining and telling the stories of colonialism, mission, and race in the church, emphasized the need for the church to look honestly at this history and to develop a meaningful theology to address it.[2] This book is intended to be a small contribution to that effort.

The Organization of the Book

The book is organized into three major sections, which represent three eras of missional practice. While there is some overlap around the end of one section and the beginning of the next, the sections are roughly chronological. Part I covers 1600–1800, Part II 1800–1920, Part III 1920–2019.

Part I: Christianizing the Colony. This section examines the origins of the Episcopal Church in the expansion of the early British Empire and the earliest Protestant understandings of mission, which conflated (from a modern point of view) conversion and "civilization." Coming from the English Civil War and the memory of religious violence throughout Europe, European settlers in general came to the colonies with an extraordinarily limited toolbox with which to reach beyond religious and cultural boundaries. Mission lacked conceptual tools and successful practices, as well as finances and funding. The general goal of missions was to make converts "English" in language, culture, and economic life, thereby incorporating them into "Christian civilization." Yet from the beginning, it was clear that full incorporation on equal terms would never be possible. The religious practice of the colonial church valued a stable hierarchy and social order as religious goods, and thus could not adequately challenge the social and political order in the case of those who were enslaved and those who were being forced from their land and to abandon their communal traditions. This paradox led to a near paralysis in mission work in some cases, and to contorted efforts to justify conversion that would not have socially equalizing effects in others.

Following many losses and negotiations in the American Revolution, and still battling the perception that the church represented loyalty to the monarch of England, the new denomination suffered a period of exhaustion in the late eighteenth and early nineteenth centuries. It was during this period that the newly structured Episcopal Church began to incorporate free Black congregations, but these churches were not permitted to take part in diocesan governance as equal members, thus continuing the tradition of racial distinctions inherited from the establishment of slavery as an institution in the early colonies.

Part II: Church-Planting, Civilizing, and Christianizing. While the model of "Christianize and Civilize" continued to thrive and develop (as well as be complicated and contested) through the nineteenth century, a new model of mission came on the scene with the rise of competing denominations in a disestablished voluntary system. Episcopalians worked both to strengthen their denomination internally and to expand their denomination, often at the expense of Catholics and other Protestants as well as in mission work among the "heathen." During this period, the leadership of the church reorganized itself to place mission, theoretically, at the center of church life, by making mission work identical with the work of the church in the establishment of the Domestic and Foreign Mission Society, and created the new model of a missionary bishop to establish the church in new territories during the expansion of the United States to the Pacific Coast. Throughout the long century, the Episcopal Church expanded among African Americans and Native Americans in the United States, as well as in Latin America, West Africa, Oceania, and Asia.

Part III: *Missio Dei*. As in the larger global Christian world, Episcopalians experienced shifts in understanding and practicing mission between 1910 and 1950, including increasing critiques of the church building and conversion models of mission, the fundamentalist/modernist split, and the loss of confidence in Christian civilization epitomized by two world wars. However, much of this change simmered beneath the surface until the early 1960s, when the internal missiological tensions came to a clean break between the older and a new model of mission, *missio dei*: the idea that the mission of God was in the world, not in the church. The older missional model as building, sustaining, and nurturing churches and congregations sat uneasily with the call to be "prophetic," the "church for others," and embroiled the Episcopal Church in controversies both internally and globally about issues of race, gender, and sexuality.

PART I
CHRISTIANIZING THE COLONY

The initiation of English colonization in North America took place in the context of the contest of empires: the Catholic Spanish and French against the Protestant English, whose empire was only a thing of patriotic dreams at the beginning of this period and which was wracked by the American Revolution at its end. In between, English colonists and those sponsored by, enslaved by, or governed by them settled the Caribbean and the eastern coast of North America, establishing a settler society that depended upon slavery as well as the displacement of indigenous American peoples.

The Church of England came with these colonists—in some places as an established church, in others as a minority religious preference—and for the first time since the Protestant Reformation, this religious institution needed to develop theories, methods, and practices of expansion, sustainability, and incorporation. Incorporation of all people into the church near birth, through infant baptism, had been a matter of fact and even automatic in Christian Europe, with its cultural expectations established in medieval Christendom and its boundaries of religious difference policed by violence and law. Even as the Protestant Reformation took hold and shifted the patterns of European religious life, still England remained part of "Christendom." It was a society that presumed Christian religious identity and belonging, and the national established Christian community, the Church of England, was supported by law as well as custom.

In the new context of the colonies, the Church of England struggled to work out its mission. The habits of Christendom were not adequate to developing practices of incorporation, expansion, and sustainability, and the church did not do these things according to a thoughtfully developed plan with a strong and compelling theological ground. The church in the colonies used the tools that it inherited to patch and paste together an institution with historical memory of the power of the metropolitan church, imagining itself as the center of English civilization and English values in the colonies, and

seeing English Christianity as the glue that held together all of English culture, which could incorporate those who were neither Christian nor English
into the ordered English life. Theological and organizational developments
arose in response to the difficulties of the local context, not least the American
Revolution

Following the Revolution, a compromise between missional agendas led to
a creative tension between competing views. "High church" values included
a focus on the foundational nature of the bishop for the church, with strong
ties to the monarchy and a value placed on more elaborate rituals and sacramental piety. The "low church," as it developed in the colonies, placed more
value on lay and clergy shared leadership and upon scriptural authority, with
practical effects upon personal, ordered moral life. These two visions had
their roots in the divisions between Protestant and Catholic in the English
Reformation but developed differently within the new American context
due to the missional history of the different colonial regions. Both visions
shared an emphasis upon social order, specifically the ideal of the hierarchically ordered life of the English parish. The mission of the English church, as
these colonial church leaders saw it, was to bring English civilization into the
American wilds, both forest and urban. To Christianize and civilize were in-
separable, and surely was attainable.

In terms of choosing which stories to focus on in this section, I have
given more attention to those stories that have been less well integrated
into existing Episcopalian historiography, including the Atlantic context,
Jamestown rather than the Massachusetts Bay Colony, the mission to the
Iroquois. I have given relatively little space (considering the vast existing historiography) to the rise of Methodism, the "Yale Apostasy," the involvement
of Church of England members in the American Revolution, and the "bishop
controversy," both within and outside of the church. This is not because these
things are unimportant to the history of the Episcopal Church, but there is a
great deal of excellent scholarship on these topics already, and thus they require less attention in this work, which views the denominational history in
the global context of race, empire, and mission.

Chapter 1 focuses on Roanoke and the missional program at Jamestown,
the first successful English colony in North America, particularly in terms of
relationships with the local Powhatan people and the origins of enslavement
of Africans from 1619.

Chapter 2 examines the increasing efforts to creatively adapt the church's
mission to a new geographic, cultural, and racial context through the work

of the Society for the Propagation of the Gospel with enslaved people and with the Mohawks prior to the American Revolution, as well as innovations in church structure and practice that adapted to new social organizations within the white colonial communities. These practices led to regional differences in the colonial church that would continue to play out in the nineteenth-century "churchmanship" controversies.

Chapter 3 traces the ways in which the church adapted to a postcolonial situation after the American Revolution in re-creating its polity and in accepting—partially—the first free Black Episcopalian congregation into the new American church.

1

Original Empire

Introduction

For the English[1] in the sixteenth and seventeenth centuries, to be Christian
was not only to hold the hope of eternal salvation but to partake of a community of practice that encompassed all aspects of life: economic organization, agricultural and scientific technologies, social values, gender and sexual
practices, artistic endeavors, political structures. Racial distinctions and
the separate concept of "culture" were not analytically developed, and race,
culture, and religion were considered to be all one. Religion was not only
"God-talk." It was the life of a complex society, within which each person,
each social role, was veiled with sacred significance and surrounded by political imperatives. Thus, for the earliest English colonists in North America,
bringing forward the first feelers of what would become the British Empire,
their religion as "Christians" could not be separated from their efforts to develop and sustain a community in a new context nor from their efforts to
relate to the metropole—the "home" of England—and their new neighbors,
who were non-Christians or "heathen."[2]

Because all social life was subsumed under the banner of religious identity,
the practice of mission—reaching out to intentionally incorporate people or
groups into the Christian community—did not differentiate between religious belief and everything else it meant to be an embodied, social being.
Mission worked through "civilizing and Christianizing," changing simultaneously both the daily social world and the inward spiritual one. The two
transformations could not be separated in either concept or practice.

In examining how English Christianity intertwined with race and empire,
this chapter will focus on the earliest English expansion around Jamestown,
in what is now called Virginia. This was, of course, not the only English
colony in the Americas in the seventeenth century. However, Jamestown was
first, and for the eventual trajectory of what would become the Episcopal
Church its practice and experience is more basic. Looking at Jamestown
clearly demonstrates the tensions between ideals of the integrated, peaceful,

Mission, Race, and Empire. Jennifer C. Snow, Oxford University Press. © Oxford University Press 2024.
DOI: 10.1093/oso/9780197598948.003.0002

hierarchically ordered Christian community and realities of communal violence and exploitation in the settler colonial society and the evolution of
practices of mission through trial and error.[3]

The English use of indentured servitude, a practice of the home culture that grew cancerously in the colonial context, developed quickly into
a dependence on slavery. In the case of African enslaved and indentured
people, "Christianizing"—being baptized and adapting "English" ways—
originally served as a resource for autonomy and freedom. The English colonial authorities gradually removed Christianizing and civilizing from
the possibilities available to Africans in a systematic effort to ensure that
the enslaved population would always remain separate from that of the
"Christians," developing a Christianity that supported slavery theologically
and practically. This "Christian slavery" model transmuted by the eighteenth
century into racial categories of free and enslaved, with the "Christianity" of
enslaved people always seen as spurious or dangerous to develop.

In the case of Native Americans, by the end of the seventeenth century
in Virginia enslavement was not purely about labor but was also about
colonists taking their land, erasing the land-based and communal practices
of their culture and replacing them with Christian/English practices.[4] The
destruction and removal of Native American people and of their cultures/
religions was thus part and parcel of "Christianizing." The land needed to
be "Christianized" (divided, owned, farmed), just as the Native Americans
needed to become "civilized," simultaneously leaving behind their economy,
culture, and religion, which were all intertwined, in favor of being Christian/
English.[5]

The Virginia colony has often been compared to the New England colony
as purely commercial, without a commitment to Christian mission beyond lip service to justifications for conquest. Yet the claim that the Virginia
colonists did not engage in "mission" only highlights modern assumptions
about mission, or what it looks like, without considering its specific historical context. Seeking evidence of missionary activity in terms of mass
baptisms or religious orders in the Catholic mode is clearly unfruitful with
a Protestant Christian church. Yet seeking evidence of later Protestant styles
of missionary work—publishing tracts and translating Bibles, preaching, offering Bible studies, learning native languages, establishing schools, running
hospitals, sending individuals or married couples to live with non-Christian
groups—would also show little or nothing in the earliest expansion of the
Church of England. The Virginia colonists did not engage in "mission" in

these terms because those practices did not yet exist. That does not necessarily mean that the idea and desire to "convert" the natives and establish a Christian community were not important and meaningful in the colony's justification and history. It was just that the colonists, even the religious professionals, quite literally did not know how to do it. In this earliest era, it was imagined that non-Christians would somehow become Christians through an unspecified method of communal proximity to the English—and there was always the danger of the process working in the other direction, as Christian Englishmen were drawn to Native American life or simply forgot their Englishness in the colonial space. The English settlers, too, would need attention to their Christianity and civilization as time went on.

Church of England/Church of Empire?

What would become the British Empire began in the post-Reformation context of violence and defense against religious and political enemies, particularly the Spanish, in the sixteenth and seventeenth centuries. The two Iberian empires of Spain and Portugal, both resolutely Catholic, divided the world between them according to papal dispensation in 1493, and grew extraordinarily rich on the gold and silver of South America, and the slaves and spices of Africa and Indonesia. England, meanwhile, struggled with its complex and shifting political and religious identity, too inwardly engaged to look outward except for self-defense. Spain and France, Catholic nations and persecutors of Protestants, became the great enemies, and the shadow of Spain's golden wealth and international power always loomed behind the internal religious politics of England.[6]

Individuals active in the first efforts to establish an English presence on North American and Caribbean soil were originally soldiers, sailors, and legally established pirates (privateers) engaged in attacks on Spanish and Portuguese shipping. If the English could not find gold themselves, or find a wealthy but gunless civilization to conquer in support of true Protestant religion, then stealing it from the Catholic Spanish was the next best thing. Chasing Spanish ships in the Caribbean brought English captains such as Sir Francis Drake into the Western Hemisphere, and the wealth they brought back to England encouraged more such adventures. The early efforts toward colonization in North America arose out of these privateering ventures—the need to claim land away from Spain's grasp, to create a base for privateering in the Western Hemisphere, and to ideally find either indigenous wealth or a path to the East.

Because the monarch of England was the Supreme Head of the Church of England, the establishment of colonies by England would always involve, in some way, the extension of England's national church. Sir Francis Drake brought a chaplain with him on his travels and held a religious service on the soil of California in 1579. Yet the nature of this extension was originally unclear. Spanish expansion of their empire had included both missions and baptisms of thousands of Native Americans and Africans. Unlike the Catholic empires, however, Protestant nations such as England no longer had access to the religious orders of celibate priests and monks who could dedicate their lives to this work of baptizing and teaching new converts. The monasteries and convents had been dissolved, and clergy were married members of their local communities.

Among Protestants, the idea of "mission" in terms of converting non-Christians was originally unformed and without much energy. In a theological context where perhaps not everyone would be saved, or where God's eternal plan was manifest over human beings' paltry efforts, the idea that the salvation of other people depended upon Christians' intentional projects made little sense. European Christians, of course, were familiar with the idea of non-Christian cultures even before the "discovery" of the New World, particularly the Jews who lived in European nations and the Muslim nations of North Africa and the Near East. European Christian relationships with both groups were often hostile and violent, ranging from cold tolerance to banishment, exploitation, murder, and war. In the post-Reformation era, the Catholic Church reinvigorated its preaching and mendicant orders with a goal of reclaiming the Protestants for the church and adding new Catholics from the newly discovered lands given by the pope to Spain and Portugal. Most of the energy of the Protestant Reformation, by contrast, went into fighting Catholicism or creating new forms of Christian community among those who already called themselves Christian, rather than imagining ways, means, and reasons to "convert" those who were not.[7]

Thus when the Church of England accompanied the colonists to the "New World" from the 1580s onward, there was little conceptual furniture to bring along in terms of "mission." The habits of European religious warfare would incline toward violence when encountering religious-cultural difference; the habits of European Christendom would incline toward simple cloning, transplanting a religious world with all its practices, ritual, polity, infrastructure, and assumptions from one soil to another.

Conversion and Conflict: Roanoke and Jamestown

Manteo and Roanoke

In 1584, Sir Walter Ralegh sponsored two explorers to reconnoiter the North Carolina coast. One of the explorers reported, "Wee found the people most gentle, loving, and faithful, void of all guile, and treason, and such as lived after the manner of the golden age."[8] They brought two Native Americans back to England as demonstrations of their achievements, Wanchese and Manteo. Manteo learned English and taught his own language to the scholar and philosopher Thomas Hariot, who developed a phonetic alphabet to record his findings. Inspired by their reports, and with the idea of creating a base for further explorations in search of the City of Gold as well as for preying on Spanish shipping, Ralegh sponsored a new expedition to Roanoke.[9]

The charter for the original 1584 expedition, given by Queen Elizabeth, included instructions to ensure that the practices of the Church of England were obeyed in the new land and that natives should be inculcated therein, giving Ralegh and his heirs and assignees the right to "correct, punish, pardon, govern and rule" in ways that did not contradict the laws of England, "and also so as they be not against the true Christian faith, now professed in the Church of England." The charter does not make mention of converting the people of the "heathen and barbarous lands," only of governing, yet the governing is closely connected to the church. This connection of civil to religious governance in order to "live together in Christian peace, and civil quietness with each other" hints at the type of "mission" which would be brought into the new imperial endeavor.[10]

The return to Roanoke in a 1585 expedition included Manteo, Wanchese, and Hariot, as well as the artist John White. Hariot's careful observations and optimistic view of Virginia became the basis for the first book written by an Englishman who had actually visited North America and inspired further efforts to establish a permanent foothold in Roanoke. Hariot's ability to converse in the Algonquin language, and his positive relationship with his teacher Manteo, led to his report that the natives lacked technology such as the English had (particularly military technology) but show "excellence of wit" and certainly, upon seeing the "knowledge and craft" of the English, would "desire our friendship and love, and have the greater respect for pleasing and obeying us. Whereby may be hoped if means of good government be used, that they may in short time be brought to civility, and the embracing of true religion."[11]

Again, the close ties between legal power, governance, and true religion are clear. In a community marked by "Christian civility," this relationship would not be one of equals; a conception of society as hierarchically ordered has "obedience" as a central virtue. The method by which this peaceful integration of the indigenous people with the English would come about appears to be simply through awe and the desire to learn about English "knowledge and craft," perhaps reflecting Hariot's own experience in showing Manteo his scientific equipment and books in England. Hariot envisions no other effort as necessary to obtain Christian civility in the new land. However, the natives were also already being slain by the epidemics that had come with the English: even in small numbers, the settlers' presence devastated local communities, and their need for food and other support led to increased tensions and violence. When the colonists left, Manteo accompanied them back to England.[12]

After this attempt failed, in 1587 Ralegh tried once more to plant a colony. The pilot had been directed to bring them into Chesapeake Bay, but he refused and forced the passengers to disembark again at Roanoke. The little group of families, accompanied by Manteo, would have to try to reestablish a new home in this place where they had already been driven out. The history of all of Roanoke is notable for the presence and constant activity of Manteo. While Wanchese was disenchanted with the English and led an attack against the colony, all of the scanty sources available agree that Manteo remained an active friend to the Roanoke community, to the point where he aided in attacks against natives seen as hostile and was not recognized by his own people when he came back in the company of the English.

On August 13, 1587, Manteo was baptized, by order of Ralegh himself. The baptism on Roanoke was clearly seen by the English as being very significant in their hopes for establishing a stable community in North America, one with—at this point—imagined peaceful alliances with local leaders. The English believed that Manteo had considerable status among his own people, as possibly the child of the *weroance*, or leader, of the Croatoan. The English, at his baptism, made him lord of the local villages, thus bringing him into the religiopolitical world of England marked as a respected peer.

The archives do not tell Manteo's own inner history. It is impossible to say what baptism signified from his point of view, if he saw it as a "conversion" in the modern sense. Manteo's baptism may or may not have had much to do with a specific religious experience, desire for salvation, participation in liturgical services, or ability to read the Bible. A baptism service for adults was not available in the Book of Common Prayer at this time, and so the service for infants may have been adapted. The baptismal rite would have required Manteo's sponsors to make statements about his belief in Jesus and salvation.

Manteo's baptism does seem to mark the way in which he aligned himself permanently with the new English community. From the point of view of the English, upon being baptized, Manteo was understood as desiring to become "English" himself, which was a religious category as much as today it would be considered a racial or cultural or political or linguistic one. The report of his baptism, before Governor White's departure to return to England for desperately needed supplies, strongly indicates the importance of baptism to incorporation in the English social-political community.[13] As the English understood it, Manteo's baptism showed the possibilities of Native Americans becoming loyal partners and participants in an English society—on English terms.

The colony at Roanoke did not survive. The first English child born in North America, Virginia Dare, had disappeared with her parents and all her people when Governor White returned from his supply mission three years late, in 1590. White consoled himself when he found "Croatoan" carved into a tree, trusting that little Virginia and all Roanoke's survivors were somewhere safe, in the care of Manteo and his tribe.

Jamestown

With the death of Queen Elizabeth and the accession of King James I of England and VI of Scotland, a new group of private investors, inspired by Hariot's optimistic description of Virginia, began once again to develop plans for a new colony. James provided the Virginia Company with a charter with somewhat more attention to religion, imagining that the purpose would be "a Work, which may, by the Providence of Almighty God, hereafter tend to the Glory of his Divine Majesty, in propagating of Christian Religion to such People, as yet live in Darkness and miserable Ignorance of the true Knowledge and Worship of God, and may in time bring the Infidels and Savages, living in those parts, to human Civility, and to a settled and quiet Government."[14] Again, the connection (so obvious to the English as to need no comment) is made between civility, governance, and Christianity.

This time the colonists aimed for the Chesapeake region and ended up on a marshy island near where a great river emptied into the bay—surely a potential path to the East—led by a group of gentlemen idlers and a professional soldier of fortune, Captain John Smith. The colony (which had very few women, and thus little chance of permanence at the outset) encountered vast and shocking mortality almost immediately from nutritional deficiencies, malarial fevers, bad water, and exposure. In addition, explorations into the interior encountered a strong Native American "empire" linking dozens of villages belonging to several different Algonquian-speaking groups over a large area called Tsenacommacah by the Powhatan people, under the paramount leadership of the *weroance* Wahunsunacock, whom the English called King Powhatan.[15]

The Powhatan lived in small groups in an intimate relationship with their local land and water base, engaging in hunting, fishing, and small-scale agriculture over a large territory. The inhabitants of Tsenacommacah were well aware of territorial boundaries, but their relationship to territory was so different from that of the English to land that their positions were initially mutually unintelligible. To the English, land was to be owned by individuals and "improved" for industry, agriculture, and cattle, marked for ownership by permanent buildings and boundaries. An individual's status depended upon their ownership of land; those who did not own land would only ever be servants, submissive to those who did. To the Powhatan, land belonged to the group as a whole and was to be used with great respect and care to provide food and spiritual sustenance. The Powhatan therefore saw the English as people who could provide beautiful or useful or powerful trade goods but did not fully grasp—at first—that in allowing these sickly, starving people to live on marshland near the river they were in any way losing their own access and use.

The local tribes had encountered Europeans before. The Spanish colonies and explorations in Florida and the Carolina coast had left many Europeans permanently or temporarily among Native American communities, and in 1571 a Paspahegh who had been captured by the Spanish in 1562 returned to his home. The Spanish had baptized him, taken him to Spain, and expected him to help lead a Jesuit mission in the Chesapeake, calling him Don Luis. Don Luis, however, ended by returning to his own people and leading an attack on the Spanish. As it happens, his home village was one of the first encountered by the Jamestown colonists. When Captain Smith first explored the area after landing, he also encountered a village that had recently been raided by Europeans who had killed and stolen some of their people; they eventually decided that Smith was not responsible for this, as he was not tall enough.

Both natives and English encountered each other warily under a veneer of friendliness, and with a certain amount of deception; both were familiar with violence and were suspicious of the other group's intentions. However, the violence each group was willing and ready to use was different. The local Algonquin nations used war skillfully and almost surgically, for the specific purposes of gaining resources, often women and children, status, and vengeance, but also to expand territory and forcibly incorporate new groups. The empire of Powhatan had been inherited and grown through battle, and Powhatan may have initially approached the English as people that could be so incorporated.[16] This attitude toward war was not always intelligible to the English, who from the beginning encountered surprise attacks from those they had thought friendly and the Powhatan practice of torturing certain captured warriors to death. Smith's first exploration up the Chesapeake ended in the deadly ambush of all his men and his own capture, to which he responded by spinning lies about the purpose of the English and by threatening total destruction if he were harmed; later, Captain John Ratcliffe, one of the colony's early leaders, who had been relieved of his responsibilities because he traded with the natives on too generous terms, was ambushed, captured, and tortured to death. The English, for their part, were from the beginning quite ready to threaten and kill women and children in pursuing their desperate need for the natives' food stores. Thus an early raid included the destruction of a village and the murder of all people except for the "Queene" and her children. On the way back to Jamestown, the English threw the children into the river and "blew out their braynes," and then killed the "Queene" herself with a single shot. The captain responsible for all this no doubt felt himself merciful, as his orders had been to burn the "Queene" alive.[17]

As Karen Kupperman and others note, while the English would have been familiar with various gruesome punishments and styles of execution in the English legal system, and thus not completely shocked by the Powhatan execution of enemy warriors, the willingness of English settlers to kill women and children was a new aspect of war for the Powhatan. Ironically, the most seasoned mercenary of the original settlers—John Smith—seems to have been able to avoid massive bloodletting while he was the main negotiator with the Powhatan, though he was wary and deceptive and willing to threaten and extort with shows of force. The greater violence against the Powhatan began after his departure due to injury in 1609.

At the same time, this violence was interwoven with peaceful relationships. Powhatan and the English traded "sonnes," young people who would learn one another's language and act as cultural interpreters. The natives shared their food stores with the sick and starving English; while Smith and others were not shy about violently extorting what was not voluntarily offered, it seems that quite a lot was indeed voluntary, given as gifts or traded for goods. Smith credited Pocahontas, Powhatan's young daughter, with engineering much of this, but in the early years of Smith's contact she was only ten or twelve and could not have done all this herself without the support of her father. Smith and other observers describe the child Pocahontas visiting the settlement regularly and playing actively with the young children of Jamestown (of which, as the years went on and the Virginia Company engaged in the forcible recruitment of orphan children for colonization, there were quite a few).[18]

The religious life of Jamestown ideally centered around the twice-daily prayer led by Robert Hunt, and later other ministers such as Alexander Whitaker and Richard Bucke. It does not seem possible that ordered religious practice was a high priority for the early English, who were dying at unbelievable rates and could sometimes barely get out of bed due to illness, despair, and starvation—yet building a church was one of their first projects. The survivors of the initial years of dearth met a new expectation in 1611 with the martial law imposed by Captain Thomas Gates and enhanced by Sir Richard Dale. "Dale's Laws" imposed heavy penalties, including death, for missing religious service (or running away to the Indians, stealing food, refusing to work, etc.). While some scholars believe the laws were not enforced as written—and indeed could not have been wholly enforced, given the lack of religious infrastructure—the survivors of this period described the death penalty imposed in creative and terrible ways on the unfortunate colonists.[19]

Dale's Laws do demonstrate clearly the intertwining of authority and social expectations of order and accountability with religious life. The theory of conversion by cultural proximity could work both ways; Englishmen could "convert" to "savagery," leaving behind civility and governance, and this danger was significant particularly in the starving times, when at least one Jamestown colonist cried that there was no God. Thus to run away to the Powhatan was to become apostate as well as treasonous, and earned the death penalty under Dale's Laws.

While the English probably had little energy to actively convert anyone while they were trying to find clean water to drink or avoid cannibalism on the James River, they did inherently understand their religion as bound up in all other aspects of their lives, just as the Powhatan did. The English talked to the Powhatan about their God and their Bible and their monarch and their compasses and guns and ships all in one breath; it all went together. Similarly, the English observed and tried to understand and describe the Powhatan religion in their own terms—an old woman counting repetitions on a stick is like someone saying a Pater Noster; the offering of tobacco to "the Sunne" is like morning prayer; the Powhatan religious leaders are "priests" who care for the "temples."[20] Yet there were aspects of Powhatan religious life that had no clear parallel in English religion, and these were described by the English with bewilderment and condemnation—particularly the *huskanaw*, sometimes called "making black boyes," which was probably a puberty initiation ritual into adulthood. Much of the *huskanaw* was secret and not to be viewed by strangers, but some English believed it included an ordeal leading to death for some young boys.[21] When discussing religion with the Powhatan, those with the most interest in conversion would often mention "not making Black boyes" or ceasing to practice the *huskanaw* as an important part of becoming Christian. The natives, for their part, would sometimes express interest in learning about the English God but would quickly "move to the discourse they better understood"; undoubtedly the English religion was just as impenetrable to the Powhatan as the Powhatan to the English.[22]

Pocahontas and John Rolfe

The first Anglo-Powhatan War erupted soon after the English touched Virginia soil. Many English (and their guns) were captured by Powhatan, and in an effort to get people and weapons back, in 1613 Captain Samuel Argall kidnapped Pocahontas, the daughter of Powhatan, and held her to exchange for the missing colonists and their weapons. In the complicated world of intertribal hostilities and the conflict with the English, kidnapping and giving or taking hostages was a regular practice. Nonetheless this was an enormous betrayal of Pocahontas's trust in her English friends. Pocahontas herself had been an intercultural broker from an early age, moving back and forth between Jamestown and her people, and her kidnapping was abetted by leaders of another tribe, the Patawomeck. Perhaps for these reasons, Powhatan's response to his daughter's kidnapping was not to attack the English. He sent back only a few prisoners and rusty or broken guns; the English demanded more people and the remaining weapons, which they refused to believe could all have been lost or destroyed, as Powhatan claimed. Pocahontas herself spent this time either in Jamestown or Henricus, the new town fifty miles upriver.

While in captivity, Pocahontas was tutored in Christianity by Alexander Whitaker, the "apostle to Virginia," and received Christian baptism from him. Whitaker was notable for his excitement about the work of "planting" Christianity in Virginia, a colonist clergyman with exceptional educational and family credentials (an important aspect of social status in England) who had gone to Virginia specifically because he felt called by God to do so, rather than out of poverty or because he had no other career options. He was the author of the sermon "Good News from Virginia," written in 1612, when the violence of the first war was still at its height, and in it he begged for more "Christian adventurers" who could share the light of the gospel with the natives. As in the earlier English writings about colonization, his encouragement blended governance, "civility," and baptism:

> Wherefore my brethren, put on the bowels of compassion, and let the lamentable estate of these miserable people enter in your consideration: One God created us, they have reasonable soules and intellectual faculties as well as wee; we all have *Adam* for our common parent: yea, by nature the condition of us both is all one, the servants of sinne and slaves of the divell. Oh remember (I beseech you) what was the state of *England* before the Gospell was preached in our Countrey. . . . If we were once the masters of their Countrey, and they stoode in fear of us (which might with few hands imployed about nothing else be in short time brought to passe) it were an easie matter to make them willingly to forsake the divell, to embrace the faith of Jesus Christ, and to be baptized.[23]

Whitaker's open hint that a "few hands" to bring the natives to stand "in fear of us" would be useful to encourage conversion indicates that violence was not beyond the pale in missionary methods. The willingness of the Powhatan to be baptized was not very evident in 1612, but at last with Pocahontas in captivity Whitaker succeeded, sometime in 1614. After her baptism, Pocahontas explained that her "true" name had been Matoaka, after leaving behind her childhood name of Amonute. Pocahontas was only a nickname. This was confirmed later by the Powhatan priest Uttomakin, who explained that they had not told the English her true name previously lest it be used to have power over her. Now that her name had been changed in baptism to Rebecca, it was safe to make known her earlier name.

In understanding the life of Pocahontas, we are dependent upon the reports of the English colonists, who had an interest in her conversion, framing it as voluntary despite her captivity. Yet this part of the story argues for a "conversion" that meant something significant for the newly named Rebecca. The change of name, at least for Powhatan chiefs, indicated a change in one's total orientation and purpose in life and in society; thus, for instance, before engaging in significant acts of war a Powhatan chief would take a new name. Matoaka-Rebecca's willingness to share her previous name and to ascribe power to her new one indicates that, like the English, she saw baptism as a meaningful shift in identity. She was not the first Virginian native convert; there are hints throughout the archives that other Native Americans in close contact with the English had been baptized or were called "Christian." Rebecca, however, is the first individual whose name we know and about whom we can infer something about the meaning of this change.

The English seemed unaware of this parallel between Powhatan religion and Christianity, possibly because—as members of the Church of England—they had been baptized as infants. They had only one name. They did not need to choose their religion or their practice—it was imposed by custom, family, law, and culture. They did not need, in short, to think about what it meant to choose to be Christian.

In any thinking about conversion and baptism of non-Christians, what Protestant English most desired was to avoid being "Spanish"—that is, to avoid imposing a violently enforced baptism on people to whom it would mean nothing, who were not "English" in their ways. The critiques of Bartolomé de las Casas against the Spanish describing their brutal atrocities against the "Indians" in "Christianizing" them were well known in England, and in creating an empire to rival the Spanish the English intended, at least on paper, to do much better. From the earliest period, those who desired or thought about the conversion of the natives had emphasized the need for kindness and open conversation in making natives Christian, ignoring the violent realities on the ground.[24] Thus, Rebecca's "voluntary" conversion (which occurred when she had been kidnapped and held captive) was an important turning point for the English. She was not only a convert; she was a "voluntary" and powerful convert—a "princess" as the English understood the Powhatan hierarchy—demonstrating that close observation of the glories of English Christian ways would indeed sway the natives to convert.

In 1614, one of the first colonists, John Rolfe, wrote a letter to the governor of the colony expressing his passionate desire to marry Rebecca, detailing the ways he had struggled to understand his own desire, emphasizing that this was not a desperate "carnall desire" in a man who had no other choice in women, but a desire that had been with him for a significant amount of time and which to him seemed to have a spiritual basis. The implication is that, though she had already been baptized, Rebecca was not yet Christian and that marrying her would help her become Christian. This points to one of the as yet unexamined aspects of the conversion process for the Church of England: that becoming Christian might begin at baptism but didn't end there. Being a Christian meant living in a Christian society, not only attending service regularly but making one's daily life align with the expectations of English moral culture. Thus marrying Rebecca would not only make Rolfe the happiest of men, but he believed that it would truly help her to become Christian, to become English.[25]

Rebecca and Rolfe did indeed marry and lived together on Rolfe's plantation near Henricus; they had a son, Thomas. Rolfe himself, with the help of his new wife, was quite busy planting and developing the first seeds of "Virginia tobacco," literally the seeds of the colony's future. Their marriage, approved by Powhatan, led to the "Peace of Pocahontas," a time of truce between the English and Powhatan, when violence mostly ceased and the English began to expand their plantations into the hinterlands along the rivers of the Chesapeake, taking more and more of the crucial land and water access of the local tribes. The seeds were thus planted for the future path of Virginia: plantations with cash crops and the ultimate removal of the Powhatan from their ancestral land.

The College of Henrico and the Second Anglo-Powhatan War

The conversion and marriage of Pocahontas gave a great impetus and sheen of excitement to the efforts to convert other Native Americans as part of the justification for establishing the new colonies in North America. For the first time, the theory of mission of the English church (such as it was) had been publicly confirmed: living in close contact with English people and being taught about the Christian religion in the context of English ways of life would naturally lead to a desire for baptism and becoming fully English— with English clothing, housing, farming, buying and selling and owning and planting.

Thus, Rebecca's journey to England in 1616, and the publicity around her visit, coincided with a new and determined effort to make this theory of missions real through the establishment of a college for Native American children at Henricus. Pocahontas had been a child when she first encountered the English, and the preference for young people in the work of cultural and religious transformation was encouraged indirectly by the Powhatan "priest" who accompanied her to England, Uttomakin, who responded to attempts at Christian instruction by saying, "I am too old and set in my ways; talk instead to the children." Clearly an increased and intentional attention to children would provide the way to bring Native Americans into the Christian fold. The plan included financial support for families who would take Native American children to live with them—according to English custom, this probably entailed some kind of servitude—as well as the establishment of a college at Henricus. Land was set aside to support the new college, tenants were recruited, and funds were raised in England to support the venture. The new director, George Thorpe, was sent in 1619 to begin the work.[26]

Thorpe's attitude toward the project was nothing short of ecstatic. An early Powhatan visitor to England, one of Pocahontas's retinue, had converted in Thorpe's protection, became literate in English, died in England in 1619, and was buried in the local church.[27] Thorpe saw the Powhatan as intelligent and morally good and criticized his fellow colonists for abusing them with words and actions that would never encourage them to embrace a Christian life. Following in the path of Hariot, he believed that kind usage and sharing the technological gifts of the English would easily lead to baptism and peaceful unity:

> I doubt God is displeased with us that we do not as we ought to do, take his service along with us by our serious endevours of converting the Heathen that Lie round about us and are daily conversant amongst us yet there is scarce any man amongst us that doth so much as afford them a good thought in his hart and most men with their mouthes give them nothing

but maledictions and bitter execrations, being thereunto falsly carried with a violent mispersuasion (grown upon them I know not how) that these poor people have done unto vs all the wrong and injury that the malice of the Devill or man can afford, whereas in my poor understanding if there be wrong on any side it is on ours, who are not so charitable to them as Christians ought to be, they being (especially the better sort of them) of a peaceable & virtuous disposition. . . . [T]hey begin more and more to affect English fashions and will be much allured to affect us by gift, if the company would be pleased to send something in matter of apparell & household stuff to be bestowed upon them. . . . I am persuaded it would make a good entrance into their affections.[28]

He himself opened his home to Powhatan visitors and discoursed with them regularly, including Opechancanough, Powhatan's brother and successor as paramount chief. According to later reports, Opechancanough visited Thorpe regularly and seemed open to conversion, saying that it was clear the Christian God favored the English and was stronger than the gods of the Powhatan. In line with the belief that English material culture and habits would open the way to conversion, Thorpe had an "English house" built for Opechancanough, with which the chief professed himself delighted.[29]

Not everyone was so sanguine about this project of conversion and civilization. Another Virginia minister, for instance, wrote at the same time as the college was undertaken that the Powhatan should not be trusted, nor would they ever convert unless their priests were all killed—a work that the English should rapidly undertake.[30] Another colonist argued similarly that kindness and openness to the natives would only lead to the destruction of the English; they would never find English life attractive or be able to comprehend the Christian faith.[31]

Regardless of whether they thought doing so would convert the natives or whether they didn't give it much thought, the colonists closely associated with the Powhatan in their daily lives. One colonist wrote about this period, "[W]e were all of one nation." Powhatan people lived in English homes, worked on English plantations, traded the products of their hunt and garden to English colonists, guided English explorers, and ate at English tables.[32] They were not social equals, and often were in servitude, yet in the English understanding hierarchy and servitude were natural aspects of a good Christian society, and native servants and enslaved people would not have been seen as outside that society. At least some were baptized and attended English religious services. If this were the work of conversion, it went forward well.

All of these reports are shadowed by hindsight. In fact, while visiting Thorpe regularly and learning about all the projects of conversion and civilization underway, Opechancanough had been working to plan an attack on the English colonists, who had begun spreading along the James and other rivers, taking the land of the Powhatan. The English believed that they were taking or trading for land that was "unused" or "waste land," since it was not fenced or farmed, but of course this was not how the Powhatan understood their ownership or use of the land. Gradually, the indigenous people were being pushed back and away from the land they needed to survive, spiritually and physically. In preparation, Opechancanough and another chief changed their names. The English did not notice.

On March 22, 1622, at a prearranged signal, according to English reports, Powhatan men sitting at table or at work or walking in the fields with English colonists rose up against them with whatever was to hand, taking them by surprise and killing 347 men, women, and children—approximately a third of the colonists at that point. The attack would have been even more effective had the colonists at Jamestown itself not been warned at the last minute by a "servant" of one of the colonists. According to tradition, this person was a Native American boy, a convert to Christianity, who lived with a colonist and viewed him as a "father."[33]

For Thorpe and the colonists at Henricus, far upriver from Jamestown, the warning came too late. Henricus suffered high casualties, and Thorpe was one of those killed. According to later reports, he too had been warned by a servant living with him, but he refused to believe that the Powhatan would hurt him; the servant ran, but Thorpe stayed.

In death, Thorpe became an unwilling symbol, used to demonstrate just how misguided it was to trust the natives or hope for their conversion. Reports on the events used Thorpe's example to show that the attack had been the colonists' own fault—not because they had taken Powhatan land and undermined their culture but because the English had been too trusting, too open, had not defended themselves properly, had imagined that there could be friendship between the two peoples.[34] A deliberate war of extermination began, killing hundreds of the Powhatan and members of other nearby tribes, including many women and children. One attack by poison killed over two hundred at one time. The colonists practiced a scorched earth policy, burning or stealing the harvests of the Powhatan and destroying their villages, thus forcing the survivors into flight or servitude. Opechancanough himself survived to lead another attack on the English twenty years later, in his old age, and was murdered in custody after his capture in 1646.

After the initial flush of genocidal retribution, the English were of two minds about the Native Americans. There were many—perhaps most—who argued that all the Powhatan should simply be destroyed; others argued that they should be treated with respect and kindness in the hope that all could live together in explicitly Christian peace. Contacts between the local tribes and the English continued over many years despite the wars; Native Americans worked as servants in English houses, traded for goods and food with the colonists, and occasionally were baptized. The Virginia House of Burgesses, the local government of the colony, passed several laws trying to safeguard the rights of Native Americans to their own land, including set- ting boundaries beyond which English could not pass—creating the first reservations—and making it legally difficult for a native to sell or alienate land to an Englishman, recognizing that the loss of land pushed the local tribes into attacking the English out of desperation.

Meanwhile, John Rolfe's tobacco experiments meant that, for the first time, Virginia had something worth selling to the metropole. While immedi- ately after the 1622 attack there was another wave of mortality of new recruits due to poor planning in England, nonetheless with the rise of tobacco the struggling, starving colony of Virginia could at last become self-sustaining, even rich. Tobacco, however, was a problematic plant. It exhausted the land and required many workers. Indentured servants were promised land upon their freedom; wealthy burgesses needed land when theirs could no longer support crops. There was only one way to get this land: ensure that the indig- enous people were no longer using it. Thus legal efforts to protect the Native Americans, including those who were allies or under the protection of the English colony, were regularly ignored or undermined, even by those who had made the laws. The local tribes were pushed farther away, relocated re- peatedly, or sold into slavery.[35]

The vision of "Christianizing and civilizing" the natives ultimately depended upon both the destruction of native culture and the willingness of English colonists to accept native converts as full members of the com- munity. The English had not imagined that the natives would simply prefer to remain the way they were when confronted with an English way of life; their theory of mission imagined that "Christian civilization" was naturally, irresistibly attractive. And while the English succeeded in pushing the native peoples from their land and even in erasing some communities completely, their desire to truly incorporate native converts weakened as the rise of racial and religious distinctions based on servitude and skin color strengthened.

Conversion and Servitude: Enslaved People in Jamestown

In 1619, John Rolfe noted that "twenty and odd Negroes" had been sold from a ship coming into Jamestown's port at Point Comfort, the first record of Africans being sold into slavery in the English colonies of North America. They would have joined many other Jamestown "colonists" who were indentured servants. Servitude and mastership were an essential and familiar part of English life, and indentured servitude became the foundation of the early colony. Indentured servants, including children, were sent to the colony for terms of five or seven years, during which they would repay their passage fee and the care of their masters with service—working in the fields, hunting, fighting, and whatever else their masters required, often with little food or clothing or shelter or protection from exploitation. The authority of the master over both enslaved people and indentured servants was nearly boundless; the treatment of either was likely to be horrific; and many indentured servants, given the high mortality of the early colony, effectively were enslaved for life.[36]

The African enslaved people who were brought to Virginia in the earliest period may not have come direct from Africa but may have been brought from enslavement first in South America. They were likely to already have had experience in the Americas and to be able to speak a European language. Some may already have been baptized and arrived with "Christian" names, such as "Antonio a Negro." Thus they were able to understand and sometimes work strategically with the conditions of enslavement in their new context to achieve a level of autonomy and even, for a few, legal freedom, civil rights, and wealth. Antonio, for instance, became Anthony Johnson, a free man with his own plantation. This made slavery in the earliest years of English colonization very different from what it would later become, as the colony moved from a society with slavery as one among many economic arrangements to a slave society, completely structured by and dependent upon slavery.[37]

In the drive toward freedom and autonomy, enslaved Africans used all the resources culturally available to them, including seeking baptism and status as Christians. The Catholic empires generally saw baptism as completely irrelevant to civil status, and Native Americans and enslaved Africans were usually baptized without any tensions around whether they would thereby become free or have the same rights as European Christians, nor with much emphasis on any preparation for baptism in terms of cognitive under-standing or religious experience.[38]

For Protestants, the situation was not originally so clear. The earliest Protestant experiences with African and Native American enslavement showed a distinct discomfort with the idea of keeping Christians as slaves. Aside from the precise theological meaning of baptism, which continued to be debated among the different internal wings of the Church of England, the sense that baptism was connected to belonging to a community, to worshiping together, to having political rights and a place in a social order, was very strong among English Protestants. Indentured servants were un-free labor but were nonetheless Christian and members of the community, with some legal rights and protections and claims upon their masters, a def-inite beginning and end to their servitude, and the religious obligations of sacrament and sabbath, just as their masters had. This penumbra of social belonging and status seems to have led to uncertainty about whether enslave-ment was appropriate or possible for Christians. While it was never the case that baptism automatically led to freedom, in Virginia some African slaves were able to sue for their freedom or that of their children at least partly based on their baptismal status. The continuing appearance of baptism in court cases for freedom demonstrates that it was relevant to the discussion for both free and enslaved people, both to those suing for freedom and to the powerful slave owners who handed down the decisions, even if no one was quite clear about why.[39]

One result of this was that slave owners became reluctant to permit the baptism or religious instruction of enslaved people. Those who desired to in-struct and baptize enslaved people embarked upon an effort to decisively sep-arate baptism from civil freedom. This began with Virginia's legal enshrining of hereditary slavery, first through court cases, then through law in 1667:

> Whereas some doubts have arisen whether children that are slaves by birth, and by the charity and piety of their owners made partakers of the blessed sacrament of baptism, should by virtue of their baptism be made free; It is enacted and declared by this general assembly, and the authority thereof, that the conferring of baptism doth not alter the condition of the person as to his bondage or freedom; that diverse masters, freed from this doubt, may

more carefully endeavour the propagation of christianity by permitting children, though slaves, or those of greater growth if capable to be admitted to that sacrament.[40]

Even with this law, however, some enslaved people continued to use baptism to sue for freedom, and slave owners remained cautious about allowing baptism for enslaved people. In this shift is the beginning of a particularity about access to baptism, especially for enslaved adults: they must be "capable," and the insinuation is that they are not likely to be so. There is also an ongoing sense that Africans seeking baptism are doing so for spurious reasons or "advantage."[41]

Church of England minister Morgan Godwyn, drawing upon his experience in Virginia and Barbados, worked with these new ideas to develop a theory and practice of slavery that completely divorced Christianity from freedom, from the point of view of both enslaved people and masters. All Christian freedom, according to this theory, was wholly spiritual and not political or physical in any way. While castigating slave owners for their brutality and lack of care for the souls of their slaves, Godwyn wrote that there was no need for them to be concerned about their interests in educating for religious life; indeed, a slave who was baptized would be a better, more obedient and submissive slave.[42] As will be examined in future chapters, this ideology of Christian slavery would continue to develop in tandem with a racialized ideology of servitude throughout the eighteenth century, along with particular varieties of Christian practice and Christian mission. It would provide the base for a society where Christianity would differ significantly by race and class, and where Christianity would be used to buttress these distinctions and social boundaries.

Summary

Seventeenth-century English colonists look fairly terrible to a modern moral eye. They took land, stole property, killed and enslaved people, and deliberately destroyed their culture and religion. Because of these activities, one might judge that either the colonists' Christian religion meant nothing to them or was extraordinarily defective.

Seeking to give serious attention to mission in Jamestown demonstrates that, at least for some of the English colonists, their Christian commitments were meaningful enough to attempt to restrain and judge as immoral many of the activities associated with colonization, settlement, and enslavement and to put colonial and metropolitan energy and resources toward the end of incorporating indigenous people into the English Christian world. This was always the weaker voice in controversy, yet its impact can be traced through the image of the ideal colony, the emphasis on integration and assimilation, education and conversion, that the Powhatan might become English.

Some English theorists of colonization had advised that, if necessary, extermination and total destruction of the indigenous people would be acceptable to plant a Christian nation on North American soil. They were "bad people, having little of humanity but shape."[43] This idea reappeared regularly, particularly after periods of violence. Yet at the beginning, extermination was not seen as desirable, not seen as the best way, if it could be avoided. Voluntary conversion, "becoming English," would be better.[44] The imagined colony was one where indigenous people and English colonists lived together in peace and harmony "as though we were one nation," where the two groups became one through religious and economic transformation. The imagined colony, at the beginning, did not include slavery, but nonetheless was founded upon the stability of hierarchy and "subjection," which were seen as religious and social goods. Even though Christians in Europe violated one another's territorial boundaries and took European Christian lives and property in massive wars quite regularly, order, stability, and peaceful cohabitation was the hoped-for end of conversion to Christianity. The mission of the English church was to bring this about. But over this imagined peaceful world of Christian civility planted in an innocent land loomed the bloody reality of colonization.

Was this desired end even possible? As Opechancanough may have understood—as Powhatan stated, only four years after Jamestown was founded—once the English were "planted," unwilling to be incorporated into the indigenous tribal groups (as individual Europeans had been for decades), the English manner of land use and the constant renewal of colonial immigrants led to land theft and, with the loss of land, the destruction of the Powhatan economy and culture.

It is possible for a twenty-first-century reader to imagine that the English established a colony and incorporated the Powhatan peacefully into it without culturally assimilating them—imagining a community that included both English Christians and Powhatans holding to their own religion, yet where both groups were respected and their religious practices honored and permitted by a secular government. However, the concepts and practices of a culturally and religiously pluralistic community were unavailable to the English colonists. These ideals of multiculturalism and religious pluralism evolved only slowly over the next centuries, partly as a result of the experiences of missionaries and their reflections on the value of other religions and cultures, partly as converts of non-European cultures brought their voices into the conversation about what Christianity truly is, partly as a result of the competition between Christian groups in the North American English colonies and the development of the legal and customary structure that could support disestablishment and a division between church and state. For the seventeenth-century colonists, this was not an imaginable option.

It is also possible to imagine that the English did not attempt conversion or value it, and instead simply destroyed or enslaved the Powhatan without attempting to "Christianize" them. The Powhatan and other surviving indigenous people would then become a permanently socially separate, dominated group, unable to participate in the full life of the settler community. This is a far more imaginable possibility, since the end result is similar to what actually occurred, both to the indigenous people and to Africans brought into the colony unwillingly.

This end result demonstrates a loss of commitment to the original colonial vision for a peaceful, hierarchical, stable, and all-encompassing Christian community. The ideal was replaced by an enormous expansion of English cultural and religious hierarchy and practices of servitude into permanent colonial boundaries between slave and master. As we will see in the next chapters, in ensuring that the servant class would remain in servitude throughout the generations, participating in the Christian practices of the English colonists and their descendants was made more and more difficult for indigenous people and Africans.

Instead of imagining a single community, there would be two: the "Christians," who would be coded as white and civilized, and the dangerous "heathens," the African enslaved people and the indigenous people. The Christianity of the planter class would develop various practices to deny Christian community to the enslaved and conquered. Legal and cultural ideologies of racial distinctions would support distinctions in religious access and belonging. Those who supported the work of mission would try to develop ways to work around these distinctions, to undermine them, or in resignation would focus only on strengthening the proper Christianity and civilization of the colonist/settler groups.

The inability of Christian mission to truly incorporate all members of the community in Jamestown, or to restrain the murder, exploitation, and enslavement of human beings in a colonial context, was very clear in England's earliest colonial endeavors in North America. For these reasons, perhaps, there should not be colonies. But this uncomfortable thought was far, far in the future for the English church.

2

Converting the Colony

As the English colonies in North America developed greater stability in the eighteenth century, members of the colonial Church of England attempted to remake the old patterns with new social, cultural, and geographic materials, not realizing quite how impossible this task would prove. By the opening of the American Revolution, the colonial church had developed in ways quite distinct from the "home church" in terms of polity and practice as its leaders and members worked with a new geographic context, the lack of a bishop, the development of a slave society, competing Christian denominations, and conflicts with Native Americans, while attempting to establish British orderliness in this new disorderly world.

Challenges to Establishment

The religious situation on the ground in early Virginia reflected the impracticality of transplanting unexamined the English ways of organizing religious and communal life. The colony's expansion in a scattered, nonurban form, with few major towns and great dispersal of the people to separate plantations and farms, meant that the geographically bounded parish would suffer from the inability of people to regularly attend services. The minister who resided in one place and expected the people to come to him would be greatly disappointed, regardless of the force of law requiring the people to attend and obey. In this new context, either there would need to be a great many ministers, or ministers must be willing to peregrinate between locations. In addition, the Church of England as an institution, depending upon the pre-existing structures and financial practices of Christian England, had no clear way to send clergy or to support them in this new ground. As one scholar notes, throughout the colonial era Anglicanism in North America was a "money pit" for the Church of England.[1]

In addition to money and towns, the new colony lacked a bishop. The Church of England held to the pre-Reformation pattern of a "threefold

Mission, Race, and Empire. Jennifer C. Snow, Oxford University Press. © Oxford University Press 2024.
DOI: 10.1093/oso/9780197598948.003.0003

ministry" of clergy, including deacon (usually a short-term, transitional status), priest, and bishop. Bishops set the Church of England apart from more thoroughly Reformed Christian communities, such as the Congregationalists of New England, who denied that a bishop was a scriptural necessity. Bishops also tied all the hierarchy of the church tightly into the governance of the nation through the monarch and Parliament. Only a bishop could confirm a Christian, thus admitting them to communion; only a bishop could ordain clergy. And these could be done only in person, through a ritual of laying on of hands.

Yet throughout the entire colonial period, the Church of England failed to provide a bishop to the colonies, due largely to internal politics. Bishops in England being political as well as religious authorities, certain parties in Parliament did not care to create more of them. The Bishop of London became the religious overseer of the colonies almost as an afterthought, but the Bishop of London had many things to do and certainly could never spend the time to visit the North American churches. Throughout the colonial period all those who would be clergy in the Church of England would have to sail back to England for ordination. In addition, there would be no one nearby with the authority to inspect their work, to install them in their churches, to support their discipline, or to ensure that each congregation was well served.

Thus in pursuing its mission in a new land, the Church of England needed to solve problems that had never existed previously. Insofar as mission consisted of replicating the practice of the Church of England, somehow the missing bits of the pattern needed to be replaced with local materials: What would replace the bishop and the "living," legally placing clergy in a permanent position of authority in a congregation? How would clergy be paid, disciplined, trained, and ordained? In a dispersed community, how could the practice of regular prayer, instruction, and sacramental life be continued? Without an ecclesiastical court and the various political and economic powers that a clergyman held in England, how could the responsibilities of discipline and support for the poor be managed? In those colonies where the Church of England was not "established"—supported financially and legally by the local government—how could the ideal of the parish, including all within its bounds without regard to personal religious commitments, be sustained? Where enslaved people were part of the community, how could they be incorporated into the parish (while simultaneously ensuring that they remained separate, thus maintaining order and social hierarchy)?

The Society for the Propagation of the Gospel

In 1684, the Bishop of London reinvigorated a medieval practice for the colonies: the office of commissary. The commissary was someone who could do some of the work of the bishop, particularly in terms of visitation of congregations, and report back to the bishop on the situation in the churches. The commissary, however, did not hold any of the sacramental power of the bishop; he could not ordain priests or confirm laypeople. The first commissaries were James Blair in Virginia and Thomas Bray in Maryland. Blair remained in the colonies for his entire life, shaping the nascent church in Virginia and establishing the College of William and Mary, of which he was the first president. Bray was in the colonies only for a very brief time before returning to England, but his influence upon the imperial history of the Church of England is much greater.[2]

Bray, a precocious practical theologian who had written a catechetical work for children before being chosen as commissary, laid out his ideal of mission in a sermon titled "Apostolick Charity" preached in 1697, before visiting Maryland in person. He envisioned "righteousness," meaning "the whole of religion," as requiring three things: turning from "dead works" of the devil, growing in knowledge of the truth of God and Christ as revealed in scripture, and obeying "God's holy will and commandments," transforming an evil or disordered life into a good and orderly one. This could only be a long-term catechetical process. Bray's vision of the work of mission is worth quoting at length:

> And now it will be easie to understand, what it is to *Turn many to righteousness*. And in the highest and most exalted sence of the Phrase, it is to Reduce whole Provinces under the Obedience of God. It is to rescue that unhappy part of Mankind, which have for so many Ages past, labour'd under the Tyranny of Satan; it is to reduce them to the just and happy Government of their rightful Lord and Master Jesus Christ. It is to instruct those Dark Corners of Earth, in which the Light of the Gospel has not yet shone, or but very dimly: It is to enlighten them with a full and bright Knowledge of their Creator, Redeemer, and Sanctifier. And it is lastly, to render them obsequious *servants* to a just and holy God, *whose Service is perfect Freedom.*[3]

The centrality of obedience, knowledge, and order in Bray's vision reflects the mission of the Church of England in seventeenth-century Virginia, as does the sense of hierarchical relationships, of servitude as the proper relationship to the divine (and thus of servitude as potentially a blessed state). The work of conversion is not only about individuals and their religious experiences or commitments, but also about creating a righteous and peaceful society. Bray clearly sees that not only avowed "heathens," who live in total ignorance of God, require instruction and conversion. The "Conversion of Christians" also requires more laborers in the field.

As ignorance of God was the root of the problem, only knowledge could be the cure. Bray argued that the churches in the colonies required access to religious literature—how could the ministers of the colonies do their work properly or effectively without adequate theological reading?—and established the first religious literature organization of the English Church, the Society for the Promotion of Christian Knowledge. The Society raised funds to establish religious libraries in the colonies, ensuring that every minister in the Church of England would have proper theological training available as they "read for orders" and engaged in their life of ministry and preaching.

In addressing the issue of providing clergy, and providing for them, Bray founded the first missionary society of the Church of England, and the one which was most closely associated in the future with the hierarchy of the church and its loyalty to the monarch: the Society for the Propagation of the Gospel in Foreign Parts, or the SPG. In 1701, the SPG became the Church of England's missionary action arm. Within the North American colonies, from the Caribbean to Canada, wherever the Church of England was not fully established, the SPG supported missionary clergy to inculcate religious life according to the proper values and rituals of official English Christianity.[4]

The SPG was blessed by the monarch and provided with a royal charter, and at various times was funded by royal letters and collections among the parishes and dioceses of England. Predating the evangelical missionary societies by almost a century, the SPG was tightly tied to the monarchically centered, episcopally ordered vision called the "high church" party in England. The Archbishop of Canterbury was always its president, and soon after its founding its membership included every bishop in England and Wales, as well as a large portion of clergy and supportive laymen. The funding for the SPG's work in supporting the salaries of colonial clergy came from these donations, from bequests, from royal bounty specifically designated for colonial ministers, and even at times from the Secret Service line of the royal budget. Thus the work of the SPG was deeply entwined with the extension of English political power and the vision of a uniquely English-ordered

Christian society. As Bray wrote, "[E]specially is this a Care and Concern incumbent upon such a Church and Nation as ours. A Church so pure in its Doctrine, and so Heavenly in its Worship, as in that respect is the fittest in the World to be a Model to the New Acquisitions which shall be gain'd to the Church of Christ."[5]

For Bray and other members of the "charter generation" of the SPG, the first priority was missions to the Native Americans and enslaved Africans, but as the eighteenth century wore on, greater attention and resources were given to the "Conversion of Christians."[6] Bray's report on the status of religion in the colonies at the beginning of the eighteenth century painted a dire picture for the Church of England. Many colonies had few or no churches for the Church of England, where a minority of "orthodox" settlers were surrounded by dissenters (such as Puritans) and "enthusiasts" (such as Quakers) and even Roman Catholics. Those colonies which did have churches often did not have enough of them for their population, and certainly not enough ministers.[7]

In pursuing Bray's strategy of providing educated, "orthodox" clergy for the colonies, the SPG soon decided to focus its limited resources on those colonies where the Church of England was not fully "established"—that is, where clergy were not paid through government taxes. Thus the SPG clergy were sent largely to the middle colonies of Pennsylvania and New York, to the New England colonies of Connecticut, Rhode Island, and Massachusetts, and occasionally to the Carolinas. Virginia, and for the most part Maryland, had an adequate establishment and could recruit and pay their own clergy. These regional differences in Anglicanisms—one version fully dependent upon establishment, the other able to function in a pluralistic society; one combined with governance, the other working in coalition with or even against local governance; one interwoven fully in secular social life, the other more about spiritual sustenance as an option among many, competing with others for allegiance and support on semi-equal terms—provided both opportunities and challenges for the future church.[8]

Virginia: The Establishment

The Church of England was most fully established in Virginia, where it played an enormous role in day-to-day governance through the institution of the parish. In England, the parish was the congregation with a resident minister, which incorporated all people within its (generally very small) boundaries.

In Virginia, as the population spread far, wide, and thin, the parish became much larger and often incorporated multiple congregations and chapels of ease, all of which were served by a minister who would visit them all regularly in turn. Because the minister visited only occasionally, regular Sunday services were often led by laypeople. Only the minister could baptize or offer communion, which therefore might occur only a few times a year; however, in terms of frequency of communion, this did not distinguish Virginia from the practice of the Church of England at that time.[9]

The minister, respected and necessary and unique as his position was, did not hold the power in Virginia that he did in England. Without a bishop to induct a clergyperson into a permanent living, Virginia developed the English institution of the vestry far beyond the home church's practice. Vestries, an organization of respectable laymen who supported the rector in fulfilling the church's social responsibilities, in Virginia became much more active and powerful vis-à-vis the clergy. While The system was supposed to include induction of the minister by the colonial governor, but by the time the colonial governor attempted to exercise this prerogative, the colonial vestries had already decided they would have none of it. The vestry generally identified and hired their own clergyperson (licensed by the Bishop of London) and kept him in a technically probative status, so that they could fire him if he proved unsatisfactory. It appears that this rarely actually happened, but nonetheless the status of a clergyperson in Virginia was far less secure than that of a minister in an English parish.[10]

The vestry had other powers too. The parish was the unit of local governance beneath the county level, and the laymen elected to vestries (always men, and almost always from prominent local families) were involved in collecting taxes, walking the bounds of properties, settling disputes, bringing people to court for various infractions, and more, in addition to managing the finances of the parish and all its congregations and identifying clergy when necessary. The parish wardens had even greater responsibilities, particularly regarding family life, and essentially acted as social workers visiting those in trouble, identifying those in need of charitable support, and removing children from families where they were being abused or neglected to place them in families where they would supposedly be cared for, be educated, and learn a trade (a practice called "binding out," similar to the indentured servitude of the earlier colonial era). The parish taxes supported the clergyperson, but also all the social welfare and disciplinary work of the vestry and warden; thus the parish taxes were often larger than any other tax on Virginians.[11]

As noted, in England the church was the center of social discipline. Once the colony became more sustainable after the early Jamestown years, the discipline of the people, particularly around the sexual issues of fornication, bastardy, and adultery that had been the particular purview of church courts in England, was served by a blend of civil courts and religious authority. Despite the efforts of James Blair, the first Virginia commissary, no ecclesiastical courts were set up in Virginia. Beginning in the seventeenth century, a hybrid system arose whereby such "crimes" were brought to civil court, while sometimes the punishment—for Christians—would include standing in a church to do penance. Those who were not Christian—that is, many enslaved people and Native Americans—were forced to pay fines or extend their periods of servitude.[12]

This differentiation in punishment for sexual infractions among the community between those who were Christian and those who were categorized otherwise reflects other ways in which this transplanted church shifted its practices from the home culture. In England, the ideal was a parish church that included all individuals in its geographic area. All were equally expected to attend services, say the prayers, partake in sacraments, accept admonition and discipline, and listen to instruction. In this new context, distinctions were now made in participation in the church. Not all would receive instruction; not all would participate in sacraments, including baptism; not all would attend services.[13]

Sacramental life also developed differently in Virginia, as well as in the Caribbean and the Carolinas, with an emphasis on home-based sacramental service, particularly baptism and marriage, for white elite families. It is not clear whether this was an outgrowth of the dispersed nature of the plantations—baptisms and marriages were occasions of community celebration and feasting, and if the church was not close by, clearly it would be more convenient to do this in the mansion house—or of the growing social distinction in the plantation colonies between the wealthy and the poor, and particularly between the white community and the African enslaved and free community. For poor whites and free or enslaved Africans, both marriage and baptism were more likely to take place at church. In the island colonies, enslaved "mulattoes" would sometimes be baptized in the planter's home, likely because of their parentage.[14]

New England and Middle Atlantic:
The Missionary Context

In the New England and Middle Atlantic colonies, SPG missionary clergy found themselves in the very different situation of being a minority church, even if one favored by the English government at home. In Massachusetts and Connecticut, the established church was Congregationalist. The creation of "conforming" congregations—that is, church worship that used the official Book of Common Prayer in the style of the Church of England—was controversial and seen as a direct attack upon the Congregationalist establishment. Yet there had been, all along, a few individuals or families who preferred Prayer Book worship to the theocratic congregationalism of the Puritans, and as the colony shifted from charter to royal governance, the colonial governors and other British officials began to insist upon it, at least for themselves and their families, soldiers, and employees.[15]

Thus there were groups of people throughout the colonies who lobbied the SPG for clergy. In an effort to steward limited funding, the SPG began to prioritize sending clergy to places that promised at least some support for their clergyperson, and where small congregations had already gathered and committed to participation. Instead of sending missionaries out into the field of "heathendom," or even into the field of colonial frontiers, where little financial support was likely, the SPG often ended by sending its missionaries into the heartland of colonial Christendom, offering not a new faith but an alternative version of an existing one. The theological and polity distinctions between the Church of England and competing versions of Christianity tended to be highlighted and emphasized. In particular, the Church of England missionaries emphasized the importance of the threefold order of ministry: deacon, priest, and most especially bishop. The congregation became, in a sense, more modern—a group of the theologically likeminded choosing their preferred form of worship among several on offer.[16]

In 1722, the SPG and the Church of England trumpeted a particularly important victory over Congregationalism with the Yale Apostasy. The rector (or president) and several faculty members and students from Yale, a Congregationalist school for preparing Congregationalist ministers, spent significant time in study with the SPG missionary in the area, Reverend George Pigot. They publicly announced that they were convinced of the fundamental requirement of episcopacy—the supervision of the order of bishops over priests and deacons—and questioned the validity of their own ordinations as clergy, which had not involved a bishop. Upon resigning their positions, several then sailed to England for episcopal ordination, and sailed back (minus one who had died of smallpox) to become SPG missionaries themselves. The centrality of episcopal ordination and supervision in the sense of the mission and purpose of the church for these clergy, and for the church in Connecticut, became especially important after the Revolution.[17]

Pennsylvania and New York were much more religiously diverse, and SPG missionaries jumped in not as competitors of particular established Christianities but as simply another contender in a crowded ring of Dutch Reformists, Roman Catholics, Quakers, Moravians, Lutherans, and other dissenting groups. Thus while the churches in Connecticut and Massachusetts sharpened their theological emphasis on the episcopacy—the main difference between themselves and the Congregationalists—the SPG missionaries in the Middle Atlantic colonies worked with whatever local materials came to hand, growing congregations from colonial officials' requirements, royal orders, English immigrants, and those disaffected with other kinds of Christianity. Rather than authority, SPG missionaries in the Middle Atlantic colonies worked through persuasion.

Where SPG missionaries did go into the backcountry and away from "civility" in established towns, they might have a hard time of it. Charles Woodmason, for instance, was sent into the western frontier area of North Carolina and left a journal describing his endless frustrations with the uncouthness of the people, the horrors of the climate and food, the hundreds of miles of riding between settlements, and the constant and creative persecution of Irish Presbyterian immigrants (or, as Woodmason put it, "the scum of the earth"). Enforcing "civility" without the support of an established church and governance proved impossible.[18]

"Spiritual Freedom": The SPG and Enslavement

In the seventeenth and eighteenth centuries, slavery as a system was accepted by nearly all European Christians as biblically and legally justified, especially for prisoners of war. Europeans enslaved one another during the wars of religion and were enslaved in turn when captured by Turkish corsairs. Captain John Smith of Jamestown, for instance, had been enslaved by pirates and had escaped after killing his owner, according to his own account; Elias Neau, who would later teach enslaved Africans in New York City in the early eighteenth century, was himself enslaved by the French due to his Protestantism and spent five years as a galley slave before being redeemed.[19]

The exponential growth of the slave trade from Africa, however, expanded to encompass far more people than this occasional European experience, and changed in character as slavery became a fundamental economic and cultural practice in colonial societies. Slavery became not some low-probability accident that could happen to anyone in the wrong place at the wrong time, but something that a vast category of human beings were destined for from birth, something that could not be escaped, that one's children would inherit, that would last forever. The possibility that it might not last forever, that enslaved people might become free, became more and more terrifying to masters as the decades wore on and as their own economic and cultural prosperity depended upon continued racial slavery.

This white anxiety over the possibility of slave revolts, and the challenge to racially defined cultural dominance of skilled, intelligent, prosperous, and free African people, shaped the Christian theological and practical response to slavery in this era. The majority of English Christian writings on slavery until the late eighteenth century defended the biblical and legal basis for slavery, argued that baptism should not lead to freedom, and although there might be criticisms of "bad" slave owners who abused their slaves, the fact that slavery itself was abusive by its very nature was not seriously acknowledged.[20]

At the same time, converting the "heathen" African slaves was an important way in which the slave trade was morally justified. From its inception, the SPG was particularly interested in evangelizing Africans, both slave and free. The SPG's vision of mission and conversion placed an emphasis, constantly, on *voluntary* conversion even in the context of slavery. It would have been completely possible for masters to baptize every slave they owned and take them to church every Sunday, but this was never what missionaries wanted or preachers exhorted. The goal was for masters to *allow* enslaved people to be educated in religious matters and to have them *request* baptism (and indeed to prove themselves worthy by being able to recite the Lord's Prayer, the Creed, and sometimes the catechism). The incongruity of desiring and valuing voluntary spiritual commitment in the context of a system of total control was never acknowledged.

The SPG itself became a slave-owning institution less than ten years after its founding and imagined that its inherited Caribbean plantation, Codrington, would provide a showpiece of Christian mastery, demonstrating the way in which slavery could be beneficial to Christian life. Unfortunately, the SPG's efforts to provide chaplaincy and catechetical services to their members' slaves were undermined by the reality of making a plantation profitable. Not only did the vast majority of the Codrington enslaved people refuse Christian instruction and baptism when it was (rarely) available, but the running of the plantation even, at times, exceeded the local norm in brutality. As antislavery sentiment strengthened among some Christians in the late eighteenth century, the SPG resisted. The slaves of Codrington were not freed until 1834, in the general British emancipation.[21]

Many enslaved people in the Caribbean plantations lived for only a few years after being brought there, and there was a great imbalance between men and women. Thus newly enslaved people were always being brought to replace those who had died. Remembering their own African religious lives and speaking in their own languages, there was little attraction for many of them in the Christian practices of the masters, and little time for SPG missionaries to gain access to teach them. Since masters would not allow religious instruction to cut into working hours, slaves resisted catechism at least partly because it cut into their very limited time to care for themselves, work their own vegetable plots, and socialize with other enslaved people. The SPG missionaries in the Caribbean and Chesapeake often gave up trying to reach Africans, justifying this by the resistance of masters (which was quite real), and instead focused on trying to inculcate the ideals of benevolent Christian slavery among the white owners.[22]

The benevolence of the Christian master was the constant goal of SPG missionaries (and indeed of Anglican clergy who were not SPG missionaries). Enslaved people were described as members of the "family"; thus missionaries deliberately ignored the enormous abuse and exploitation heaped on these particular "family" members. Many clergy throughout the English colonies in North America owned slaves personally, sometimes as part of their "glebe," or publicly funded financial support. They struggled with the endless contradictions of owning people absolutely, depending upon their constant work for financial prosperity, being willing to separate families in order to gain wealth, and yet desiring a voluntary submission from the enslaved person to both the master and Christ.

The benevolence of the master was supposed to be balanced by the submission of the enslaved person, but neither benevolence nor submission was real. For the master, benevolence began and ended with permitting religious education, Sabbath keeping, and baptism, and perhaps refraining from particularly grotesque physical abuse; it never extended to respecting a slave's personhood, will, or relationships. This contradiction affected not only clergy but laypeople. For example, Elizabeth Foote Washington of Virginia tried desperately to live up to the ideal of the Christian mistress, requiring her slaves to join her for morning and evening prayer, and recorded her sense of failure that they hated to do so and tried to avoid it wherever possible; she even took the radical step (for a devout Church of England laywoman) of adapting and rewriting parts of the Book of Common Prayer for her household devotions, thinking this might be more attractive to the enslaved people of her "family." Reverend James MacSparran of Rhode Island described his frustrations and inability to enforce Christian sexual mores about monogamy and marriage upon his slaves, but simultaneously refused to acknowledge or protect the integrity of their relationships, selling them and their children away from one another.[23]

Nonetheless, SPG ministers and other clergy recorded that enslaved people and free African Americans did approach them for baptism, or brought their children for baptism, and attended classes, participated in worship, and even took communion despite the many obstacles in their way. SPG missionaries reported that Christian masters were reluctant to let their slaves be baptized because it made them "saucy" and increased their sense of self-worth and what was due to them. The missionaries argued that this was surely not true, and that a Christian slave would be even more submissive and helpful than an unbaptized one. Yet it is quite possible that the emphasis on the equality of souls before God involved in the Christian catechism—which was, after all, the basis upon which the SPG argued for the baptism of the enslaved—did encourage enslaved people to resist more strongly. For the enslaved person, responding positively to Christian teaching when it was offered thus might reflect submission to the master's demands and expectations, but could also reflect seeking spiritual autonomy, finding meaning and strength in the Christian teachings, and developing the immensely powerful tool of literacy and reading and interpreting scripture and Christian doctrine in ways that cut against the vision of Christian mastery.[24]

The desire of enslaved people to be free was seen as a danger by SPG clergy and non-SPG masters alike. The danger of Christian social-spiritual equality had to be averted by changing the religious education desired for Africans, particularly by avoiding literacy (especially dangerous) and even adding to the baptismal promises for African people a statement that they did not desire freedom through baptism. This uncertainty about Christian slaves had its roots in English legal-religious debates. It was not clear for many years whether a slave could be Christian, or whether a Christian slave must be set free in English law, and despite colonial efforts beginning in 1667 in Virginia, the metropolitan/imperial legal system did not clarify this in a way that would make masters comfortable.[25]

In the Carolinas, early SPG missionaries described an African population with significant interest in Christianity. Many of these enslaved people were brought from the Kongo and were likely experienced with Kongolese Catholicism—a form of Christianity with significant differences from English Anglicanism but with similar emphasis on the spiritual power of ritual and sacrament, including baptism and communion, that would make the teachings of SPG missionaries such as Francis Le Jau familiar and perhaps exciting or comforting in this alien, abusive world of slavery. Le Jau described Africans pressing against church windows during worship since they couldn't fit (or weren't allowed) into the building. In 1710, he offered to spend half an hour after the service teaching slaves and was excited to have fifty enslaved people remain to hear him. Another South Carolina clergyperson reported to the SPG that his congregation consisted of nearly half Africans, half whites.[26]

Many enslaved people were drawn to books and the possibility of literacy which missionaries might offer. However, the desire for literacy was connected with the fear of slave revolts, and missionaries who offered it were castigated as risking the "safety" of the "community." When Neau became the SPG's first missionary to enslaved people in New York City, he organized a successful school to which slaves came in their free time, often after dark, to learn to read from SPG tracts, sing hymns, and read the Bible as well as learn the Lord's Prayer and the Creed. Neau realized that his school was in great danger following a 1712 slave revolt in New York. Only two of his students were involved in the revolt (and were executed with nineteen others), but popular opinion held that Neau's school and his teaching literacy to the slaves was at the heart of the problem. The rector of Trinity Parish, William Vesey, under whom Neau served, was uncomfortable with the enslaved catechumens coming to worship, and owners refused to permit their slaves to be catechized or baptized. Despite his own personal experience with slavery, Neau urged the SPG to support colonial laws stating clearly that baptism would not lead to freedom for enslaved people. The New York law that was eventually passed stated not only that slaves could not be freed but that the children of slaves would also be enslaved—something which had not previously been legally explicit.[27]

These early engagements of SPG missionaries in work among African enslaved and free people fade after the early eighteenth century, as slave populations grew in southern colonies. As the SPG withdrew its efforts from evangelizing Africans to focusing on the civilizing and Christianizing of white colonist communities, another missionary society based in England attempted a new type of evangelism project—this time, buying enslaved people in order to have their "work" be that of evangelism. The Associates of Dr. Bray bought two young slaves—but did not free them—in the expectation that they could do this work of catechizing enslaved people in the Chesapeake both more effectively and more cheaply than white clergy missionaries. Little is known of the life of Harry and Andrew, but one can imagine the contradictions and frustrations required in being the slave of a missionary organization, forced by the masters to study and teach the Christian faith to others. One of the two young men was eventually evaluated as unsuccessful and was sold away; the other taught at a school for slaves for twenty-five years before being institutionalized for madness. The experiment was briefly repeated, also unsuccessfully, in Codrington.[28]

African Anglicans, even enslaved, knew enough about the workings of the church and the nature of its relation to the metropole to be able to strive for freedom not only through baptism and petition to the courts but also through direct efforts to communicate with the authority of the Bishop of London. Bishop Edmund Gibson, took his duties as the bishop of the colonies seriously. In 1723 he sent out a questionnaire to SPG missionaries and colonial clergy asking various questions about the ways in which mission was being undertaken, including to the slaves and "heathen" Indians. But even before it was possible that this letter had reached the colonies, an anonymous enslaved person or group to write a desperate letter to the bishop begging for help in 1723:

and most honoured sir a mongst the Rest of your Charitabell acts and deed wee your humbell and poore partishinners doo begg Sir your aid and assisttancce in this one thing which Lise as I doo understand in your LordShips brest which is that your honour will by the help of our Sufvering Lord King George and the Rest of the Rullers will Releese us out of this Cruell Bondegg and this wee beg for Jesus Christs his Sake who has commaded us to seeke first the kingdom of god and all things shall be addid un to us

and here it is to bee notd againe that wee are commandded to keep holey the Sabbath day and wee doo hardly know when it comes for our task mastrs are has hard with us as the Egypttions was with the Chilldann of Issarall god be marcifll unto us

here follows our Sevarity and Sorrowfull Sarvice we are hard used up on Every account in the first place wee are in Ignorance of our Salvation and in the next place wee are kept out of the church and our matrimony is deenied us

and to be plain they doo Look no more up on us then if wee ware dogs which I hope when these Strange Lines comes to your Lord Ships hands will be Looket in to

and here wee beg for Jesus Christ his Sake that as your honour do hope for the marcy of god att the day of death and the Redemtion of our Savour Christ that when this comes to your Lord Ships hands your honour wll Take Sum pitty of us who is your humble butt Sorrowfull portitionors.[29]

The letter was discovered in the archives by a twentieth-century scholar, but whether or not the Bishop of London ever saw it, he did not take action to advocate for the enslaved Anglicans in Virginia.[30]

Despite the acknowledged and real opposition of white masters to providing religious education and opportunity to their slaves, there is enough evidence of Africans' interest in Christianity in the colonial era to require an explanation of why the Anglican missionaries so thoroughly failed, at least in terms of numbers of converts. One reason was certainly the support for the system and practice of slavery from the SPG itself and from all leaders of the Church of England in America during the colonial period. For all the SPG's stated desire to Christianize enslaved people, SPG missionaries themselves were individuals largely isolated from the metropole except for their biannual correspondence with the secretary, who needed to forge relationships with local slave owners to survive and prosper. As time went on and local culture, particularly in the southern colonies, developed into a full-blown slave society, along with the racialization of slavery and legal marginalization of all nonwhite people, missionaries became less able to critique slavery or to put effort into evangelizing the enslaved against their masters' wishes.

The Successful Mission: The Anglican Mohawk

The second priority for the SPG had originally been the Christianization of the Native Americans, including the Haudenosaunee of upstate New York, a confederation of tribes known to the colonists as the Iroquois. New Netherland made its final move from Dutch to English control in 1674, by which point some tribes in the Hudson Valley had already accepted baptism from Dutch Reformed dominies, while to the north and west French Jesuits from Canada were working to convert Native Americans to Catholicism. The allegiance, political and religious, of the Haudenosaunee was of great interest to both the British and the French. The Iroquois were considered the most warlike and organized of Native American peoples, and they controlled the trade routes for fur into English areas. The aid of the Haudenosaunee could balance the French power in Canada and enrich the English; their hostility would strengthen the French and weaken the English position in North America.[31]

Thus even before the founding of the SPG, English leaders had tried to encourage contact with the Haudenousaunee, including having the English military chaplain in Albany take responsibility for visiting the Mohawk, the easternmost of the confederation's tribes. At this time, many of the inhabitants of Mohawk villages were not originally Mohawk themselves, but had been adopted (through capture in war) in order to replace the many who had died through epidemics. The Mohawks lived mostly in two villages in upstate New York and were depleted not only through war and sickness but through missionary work. The Jesuits who converted Mohawks encouraged them to move to "reserves," Catholic Christian villages in Canada. Mohawk leaders who opposed this drain upon their people, and who feared falling entirely into the French sphere of influence, looked to the English as a balance to power. The Mohawks, Keepers of the Eastern Door, led with the Covenant Chain, a relationship of "linking arms" (from the Haudenosaunee point of view) or "treaty" (from the European point of view), which was maintained and "brightened" by regular council consultation, the exchange of wampum, and the giving of gifts from the Europeans. While the Covenant Chain had originally been established between the Haudenosaunee and the Dutch, when the English took New Netherland it easily moved from a Dutch-Haudenosaunee to an English-Haudenosaunee relationship. From the Haudenosaunee point of view, the English and the Dutch were not very different and could easily substitute for one another.[32]

For the Haudenosaunee, relationships between peoples depended upon gifts, memory, and respect for tradition. Diplomacy worked through gifts and the regular "brightening" of the chain through holding councils, which lasted for many days and during which the English were expected to lavishly host the visiting Iroquois—leaders, and often entire family groups—and which ended by giving the Iroquois gifts to take home as well. The English found the diplomacy of the Haudenosaunee expensive, opaque, and frustrating, but the continual sharing of resources, repetitions of promises, and transparent, public decision-making were crucial to positive and respectful Haudenosaunee relationship.[33]

The visit of the "Four Indian Kings" to England in 1710 fit well into Haudenosaunee understandings of diplomacy, though it was orchestrated by English leaders in the colonies. Four Native American leaders spent several weeks in England, feted and publicly celebrated and formally presented to the queen. They requested that she send Anglican missionaries to them in order to balance the French Jesuits who were converting and taking away their people. The queen was delighted to agree, and the SPG swung into action. At the queen's order, a chapel was built for the Mohawk in the village which the English called Fort Hunter and which the Mohawk called Tiononderoge.[34]

Missionaries visited the Mohawk off and on for the next few decades, with mixed results (due largely to the varying temperaments and abilities of the missionaries, who were also made responsible for the English church in Albany). More than once, a successful missionary to the Mohawks was called to become rector of Trinity Church in New York City, leaving the Mohawks without instruction or sacraments until a new missionary settled in. While the first SPG missionary in the early 1710s despaired that the Mohawks continued to dance, drink, and divorce despite all his efforts, by the 1720s a majority of the Mohawk tribe considered themselves Christians, members of the Church of England. Baptism had become a central spiritual event in Mohawk life, celebrated with feasting and demanded of missionaries. Missionaries described the people as reverent beyond any other group, including white colonists, in their respect for worship; one noted that Mohawk families came some fifty or sixty miles, from winter camps, to participate at Christmas.[35]

In some ways, Anglican styles of worship fit well with Haudenosaunee culture. The formality of liturgy and the Book of Common Prayer matched what the Haudenosaunee expected of a sachem, a wise leader dedicated to the peace of the people whose strength lay in eloquence and formal, careful use of words. Compared to other forms of Christianity available

to the Mohawk, Anglicanism was in some ways more flexible and culturally accommodating; unlike the Jesuits, the Church of England did not
want the Mohawks to move to Canada, and unlike the Presbyterians and
Congregationalists of New England, the Anglicans were more accepting of
dancing and drinking.

The expectations of English "civilization" matched less well. The
Haudenosaunee, like the Powhatan in Virginia, lived by hunting and gathering as well as horticulture. Though the Haudenosaunee certainly had their
own understanding of land as territory, it did not match that of the English.
Haudenosaunee men found the colonial authorities' expectation that they
should learn to farm to be completely unfathomable and dangerous. Men
were warriors and hunters; women gathered and planted. If men planted, the
tribe would be vulnerable to attack. Because of these different understandings
of gendered labor, colonials saw Haudenosaunee men as lazy, letting women
do all the work. The Haudenosaunee who ceded land to settlers understood
this as entitling them to a perpetual share in the fruits of the settler's farming;
thus where settlers saw Indian beggars and thieves coming to steal their harvest or farm animals, the Haudenosaunee understood this as the appropriate
perpetual payment for the use of the land, which correspondingly lessened
Haudenosaunee ability to hunt and fish.[36]

Unlike the hierarchical and centralized understanding of power in English
culture, Haudenosaunee valued dispersing power among many competing
factions, thus increasing individual freedom. Consensus, relationship
building, thoughtful and eloquent argumentation, community memory,
lavish generosity, and extended conversation were valued. Giving orders was
not acceptable, and those who attempted to do it were seen as ridiculous, or
even dangerous to the community.[37]

The most effective British relator to the Haudenosaunee was not a missionary but Sir William Johnson, the Irish-born Anglican English agent
settled at Johnson Hall on the Mohawk River. With his partner and mother
of several of his children, Mohawk leader Molly Brant, Johnson developed
a respect for and skill with Haudenosaunee diplomacy that strengthened
their connection with the British in the 1760s. Haudenosaunee culture supported women's leadership, and Brant exercised this effectively
throughout her life, providing care for a huge circle of Mohawks and other
Haudenosaunee after the American Revolution and working closely with
Johnson on Haudenosaunee-British relations. Johnson negotiated the
Treaty of Fort Stanwix in the 1760s, which was supposed to ensure that

Iroquoia was closed to all future white settlement in return for other land cessions, which the Haudenosaunee made in areas belonging to "props of the longhouse," weaker or dependent tribes in Delaware, Pennsylvania, and the Ohio Valley.[38]

Brant's younger brother, Joseph Brant, became a leader in the political and religious life of the Anglican Mohawks. Johnson sent him to a school for missionaries in Connecticut led by Congregationalist Eleazar Wheelock, and Joseph considered missionary work himself but was far more attracted to the Anglican forms of worship. He taught the Mohawk language to a white Presbyterian, Samuel Kirkland, who later evangelized among the Oneida, but he himself started a collaboration with the local Anglican missionary on a translation of the Book of Common Prayer into Mohawk, a work to which he would return throughout his life. Johnson himself did not want Brant to become a missionary but a warrior and leader. In this, Brant would more than succeed.[39]

Mohawk lands, the closest part of Iroquoia to white settlement in the Hudson Valley, were under constant pressure by colonization. The village of Tiononderoge was claimed by the city of Albany under a supposed 1686 cession, and the Mohawk had great difficulty in repelling settlers and claims. The Mohawk attempted to lease their lands to settlers rather than sell them, but this was frustrated by settler intentions and the colonial leadership's understanding that leasing would allow the Mohawk to retain more power than selling. Joseph Brant traveled to England in order to press the case of the Mohawk against the colonists, demanding that the English government protect the loyal Mohawks. While he was feted and admired, his request was only partially met; the British government attempted to stop the colonization of the Mohawk lands but was not able to enforce the border of the Fort Stanwix treaty against local white leadership in Albany. The effort to do so added to the strained relationship between the British imperial government and local white colonists. The colonial desire to expand into the fertile Haudenosaunee lands was frustrated by British efforts, however ineffective, to maintain a good relationship with the Haudenosaunee. As with slavery, here we see the difference between metropolitan imperial views, which could critique slavery and colonial expansion and mistreatment of natives as examples of the moral coarseness of colonials, and colonial settler views, which saw both as justified and crucial to survival and the imperial legalities as a plot to keep the colonials poor and weak.[40]

The Mohawk remained loyal to the British, whom they believed—thanks to Johnson's representations of the British government—would protect them against the loss of their land to settlers. During the Revolution, Joseph Brant led a group of white Loyalists and Haudenosaunee in support of the British army, called Brant's Volunteers. The Oneida, due to the influence of Presbyterian Samuel Kirkland and their suspicion of the Mohawk, supported the patriots and attacked Mohawk villages. Thus the Revolution became an intra-Haudenosaunee war as well. Eventually, almost all Haudenosaunee supported the British thanks to General John Sullivan's attack on Iroquoia, where the Patriots destroyed over forty Haudenosaunee villages. Colonial soldiers were impressed by the fertility and prosperity of Iroquoia and looked forward to occupying it when the war ended.[41]

At the end of the American Revolution, the Anglican Mohawks fled to Canada, led by Molly and Joseph Brant, to establish new villages there in areas given by the British. Joseph visited England again, to protest that the British had given away Iroquoia to the United States in a shameful treaty without thought for their native allies, and demanding compensation for the suffering and loss of the Mohawks. The embarrassed British government provided some monetary funding for the Mohawks to begin their lives again, though of course not adequate to what had been lost. Joseph established Brantford near Niagara, trying to gather all the scattered Haudenosaunee into one place, and built an Anglican chapel where the Book of Common Prayer and gospels could be read in the Mohawk language, though they were sometimes without a clergyperson. He blended English and Haudenosaunee cultures, including building an English-style house, wearing a combination of Haudenosaunee and English clothing, and performing a Haudenosaunee style of leadership using generosity and diplomacy (though he occasion-ally veered toward the hierarchical European style, much to the annoyance of other Haudenosaunee). The Anglican missionary sent by the SPG, John Stuart, ministered in one of the new Haudenosaunee villages.

In the end, the most successful mission program of the Church of England among Native Americans had succeeded in tying the Mohawks closely to the British Empire—ironically, in the hope of retaining the lands they were forced to leave due to British weakness. However, the hostility of colonists to the Mohawk people, even those who were willing to become Christians and adopt European modes of dress and economy, meant that the possibility of a strong Native American presence in the new Episcopal church in the post-Revolution United States was foreclosed for many decades.[42]

The Beauty of Orderliness

The question that the eighteenth-century colonial Church of England asked might have been: What might an Anglican church without establishment, without bishops, without "civility" become? Instead, most missionaries attempted and failed to re-create the Church of England. The SPG clergy in the New England states longed for a bishop who never came. The colonial leaders in the Middle Atlantic states tried unsuccessfully to re-create a full Anglican establishment in the face of the most pluralistic Christian society yet to exist. The missionaries to the Mohawk and the backcountry settlers struggled to inculcate a way of life both impractical and undesired by their listeners, and to reconcile the Christian empire with the destruction of indigenous people and exploitation of enslaved Africans and impoverished whites. The vestries of Virginia congratulated themselves on the wealth, power, and governmental centrality of churches that, as the eighteenth century continued, became the actual voluntary spiritual affiliation of fewer and fewer of the white and African-descended people around them.

What the eighteenth-century colonial Church of England had in common across all of these situations and local contexts was an emphasis, above all, on order: order in worship, order in society, order in sacraments, order in the proper organization and qualifications for religious leadership. Spiritual and social order went together, belonged together, and were guaranteed by the written word in the Book of Common Prayer.

Those who troubled this sense of order to the greatest degree were thoroughly marginalized: African enslaved and free people and Native Americans. Enslaved people could be baptized only if their masters permitted it and could participate in religious life only in a limited fashion; they were barred from leadership and gradually separated from the white community by deepening racial hierarchies and sacramental restrictions that were supported by clergy in the name of order and safety. The Mohawk Anglicans were never included in the religious life of the white colony in nearby Albany; separated by language, culture, and colonial rapacity, they were excluded from religious companionship and equality. When the Revolution ended, the Mohawk Anglicans were politically disinherited and literally exiled.

The distinctions between the established churches and the SPG-supplied regions would become extremely important during and following the American Revolution in developing the foundations of the Episcopal Church. It is fascinating to imagine how this new version of Anglicanism—the first postcolonial Anglican church—might have developed differently had the Mohawk and African American Anglicans been able to bring their views of the church's nature and mission to the debate table. Had the Anglican church been able to truly ask the question that could never be asked, envisioning a church without a bishop, without establishment, without "civility" and "orderliness" as its missional bases—the church may have taken a very different course. Without these creative contextualizations, the material from which the new church could build was limited to what could be imported from England: the episcopacy.

3

A Conventional Religion

As the North American colonies moved toward revolution and independence, the Church of England needed to deal with new missional challenges. One was competition from a new form of religious life that grew out of the Great Awakening, both in England and the colonies: Methodism. Second was the growing tension with the metropole. Unlike other Christian groups in the colonies, the Church of England was directly connected with the British government, and its clergy were all obedient, in theory, to both a distant British bishop and a distant British king. As tension became armed rebellion, the colonial church had to reinvent itself, developing new forms of church governance that both reflected the new, democratic ideals of the new nation and connected with the older, hierarchical ecclesiology of the English church—a balancing act that was both shaky and dynamic.

Finally, after almost two centuries of expressed desire to do so, the new church had the opportunity to incorporate free African Americans who had voluntarily chosen the church, with the petition of St. Thomas African Church to join the Episcopal Church in the Diocese of Pennsylvania. However, the missional orientation of the new denomination, fixed on membership in a democracy of white property-owners, including the owners of slaves, could not easily accept the full participation of Black Christians, whose missional orientation focused on justice, racial equity, and freedom for enslaved people.

A Lack of Enthusiasm

What religious historians call the "Great Awakening"—a series of revivals and religious uprisings throughout the British colonies—began in the 1730s among New England Congregationalist churches but quickly spread, along with controversy, among many Christian denominations. The new religious pattern was characterized by emotional preaching aimed at an emotional transformation in the hearer—first a sense of sinfulness and despair, then a

Mission, Race, and Empire. Jennifer C. Snow, Oxford University Press. © Oxford University Press 2024.
DOI: 10.1093/oso/9780197598948.003.0004

sense of salvation after accepting Christ's sovereignty and power to save. This sense of salvation would then enable a complete transformation of a sinful life. In addition to the emotional transformation of the conversion experience, people might have bodily experiences—shouting, "jerking," trembling, weeping.

A similar movement toward dramatic conversion and amendment of life took place in England, often associated with the "holy club" at Oxford that included John and Charles Wesley, as well as George Whitefield. These young English students, who would soon be ordained in the Church of England, were eager to strengthen their faith through participation in small groups of accountability, ascetic prayer practices, and scripture study. Both Wesleys and Whitefield were sent as missionaries of the Society for the Propagation of the Gospel, the mission organization established in 1701 by Thomas Bray for the Church of England, to the new colony of Georgia as missionaries soon after their ordination. All three became known (and unpopular) for instituting strict regimens of prayer, Bible study, regular fasts, scrupulous attention to the rules of taking communion, and other religious practices that, while part of the Church of England's total repertoire, were not generally expected of laypeople to this degree. The Wesleys separately left Georgia in uncomfortable circumstances (John Wesley had denied communion to a previous romantic interest who had married someone else, a situation that may or may not have been technically legitimate but that certainly was a source of scandal). Whitefield was inspired to found an orphanage, Bethesda, and became known for his energetic sermons and gradual move away from the liturgical requirements of the Book of Common Prayer.[1]

The Wesleys did not have their own "conversion experiences" until after leaving the colonies, but their early commitment to strict practices of common prayer and study combined with the new "enthusiasm" and their organizational skills to develop a new movement within the Church of England, called "methodism." Whitefield inspired John Wesley to preach outdoors, but he himself was the one who became the Great Itinerant. In seven journeys to the colonies, he preached to entranced crowds of thousands both in churches and in the outdoors, and drew additional interest from his willingness to engage in highly public controversies with local clergy people, particularly members of his own Church of England. In New England, he engaged in public debates with local clergy on the nature of the church and baptism as well as denying the necessity of episcopal ordination, the very doctrine closest to the heart of the local churches; in New York City, the rector of Trinity Church denied him the pulpit; in Charleston, South Carolina, the commissary denied him communion and attempted to suspend his orders. (Not being a bishop, the commissary found himself unable to enforce his proscription.) In each case and many others, Whitefield not only delighted in the fray but was eager to forward and publicize it in the service of drawing more crowds to hear his preaching, to experience the new birth, and to thus be saved.[2]

The Wesleys and Whitefield preached the need for a new birth, arguing that those who had not experienced the conversion were "dead in their sins," and those clergy who did not require it and incite it in their parishioners were lax and without zeal. The Church of England, both in Britain and in the colonies, found such a view troubling. The ideal of the parish encompassing all people, however truncated this inclusion had become in the colonial situation, did not allow for a vision of the church of the elect. Christians should not expect dramatic, sudden spiritual shifts, but a slow growth in holiness through regular participation in the spiritual and social life of the community—family, town, parish, kingdom—sharing in its legitimate sacraments and obeying its laws. While there was room in this scheme for dramatic emotional transformation centered upon an individual's inner spiritual life—for which reason the Wesleys and Whitefield were able to remain priests in the Church of England until their deaths—it was not expected or required. For the Wesleys and Whitefield, and for their Methodist followers, it was.

Preaching in the fields, licensing lay preachers and "exhorters" who could even be slaves or women, provided a way the new enthusiasm could spread quickly and effectively among those who had not been attracted by or welcomed into the Church of England's structure and practice. The emphasis on personal experience meant that this new source of spiritual authority and comfort was not limited to those with an education or means to attend regular formal services and catechism. The huge public gatherings, and the classes organized by Wesley's system and the leaders he sent from England, meant that people of various social classes and distinctions were physically close and emotionally intimate in ways that had never been the case previously.

While some younger clergy were willing to allow Whitefield to preach or sponsored Methodist societies, in general the colonial church found enthusiasm highly disordered and, for that reason, dangerous. The Church of England colonial pulpit generally viewed the revivals disdainfully and with disgust. In 1743 New England, Reverend Timothy Cutler, one of the "Yale

Apostates" who had converted under the guidance of the SPG, described total social upheaval, what today might be called charismatic experiences (trembling, shouting, "jerking"), along with mixtures of all ranks of society with results detrimental to social order in the last degree: "[O]ur presses are forever teeming with books, and our women with bastards."[3]

New methods of the revival spread enthusiasm and Christian ideas among thousands of enslaved people who had had only limited access to them previously, and allowed those with conversion experiences and charismatic skill to become preachers and exhorters themselves. But the basic dynamic of colonial Christianity regarding race and slavery did not shift. Whitefield preached to slaves and encouraged others to do so, and also publicly condemned the abuses and brutality of slave owners. Yet he himself supported slavery and was instrumental in bringing slavery into the Georgia charter, which previously had forbidden it. Like other white men, Whitefield was both influenced by the anxieties around white mastery and the potential for slave revolts and convinced that the economic feasibility of the colonies required slave labor.[4] One of his great successes, the conversion of the Bryan family, led to an outpouring of excitement on the Bryan plantations for teaching and preaching to enslaved people, their own and others'—but the Bryans did not free their slaves or advocate for their freedom. Thus while enthusiasm originally broke down some social barriers and offered enslaved people a more flexible and creative way to engage Christianity, it did not immediately change the majority of white Christian opinion of slavery as legally and biblically justified; congregations in all denominations arising from enthusiastic religion soon became segregated even if they had not been so at the outset.[5]

For the colonial Church of England, the experience of the revivals added to the sense of both competition and uniqueness. SPG missionaries reported that in some cases they had lost members. One remarked on "those who were not present at public worship"; another said that he permitted Whitefield to use the pulpit because, strategically, this allowed the curious to hear him within the congregation's walls instead of outside at a competing event. They also reported that parishioners who were distrustful of "enthusiasm," who were disturbed by the idea that an emotional experience was required for salvation or that there should be ranks of Christians accordingly, or believed that drinking, card playing, dancing, and other colonial pastimes should be condemned by the church, began to find the Church of England more congenial.

In rejecting enthusiastic religion, the colonial Church of England also rejected the practical methods that helped to spread it: permitting individuals to preach and teach based on their own spiritual experiences rather than extensive education and episcopal ordination; preaching outdoors; and preaching and teaching among groups of socially marginalized people. These choices had long-term consequences for the mission of the church in terms of expansion beyond its core supporters.

A Tale of Two Bishops

In the years leading up to the American Revolution, the distinctions between the regional expressions of the colonial Church of England were united by one overriding reality: the lack of a bishop. Without a bishop, there could be no ordinations of priests; aspirants would have to sail back to England, a dangerous and expensive trip. Nor could there be confirmations of laypeople, traditionally the rite of passage by which young people became religious adults, eligible to receive communion. Without a bishop, there could be no oversight of clergy work; no discipline of ineffective, scandalous, or abusive clergy; no consecration of parishes; no higher authority to mediate between a clergyperson and his parishioners or to set clergy within parishes. Without a bishop, those who had joined the Church of England because of their respect for episcopacy found the church spiritually incomplete as well as practically impaired.

However, the Anglicans of colonial America could not simply raise up a bishop for themselves. In order to exercise valid episcopal authority, the bishop would have to be a clergyman consecrated to the order of episcopacy by three other bishops within what was called apostolic succession—the belief that bishops had received consecrations from others in a direct line going back to the apostles. Thus, a colonial bishop would have to be consecrated by English bishops.

Colonial Anglican requests for a bishop came largely from the New England and Middle Atlantic regions, as well as from leaders in England itself. Upon the death of Bishop Edmund Gibson, the Bishop of London and overseer of colonial churches for twenty-five years, the new Bishop of London refused to accept his responsibility for the colonies. Recognizing the impracticality of overseeing the colonial establishment in addition to the busiest diocese in England, Bishop Thomas Sherlock requested that a bishop, or more than one, be created for the colonial church. Colonial clergy wrote many pamphlets, the tool of choice for social action at the time, and sent official requests to Parliament and to the SPG requesting bishops. None of these requests was ever fruitful—not because the Church of England didn't think that bishops were important, but because the creation of bishops was not strictly in the purview of the church. The intertwining of church and state in England meant that the monarch and Parliament had to create these bishops, and for political reasons one or both of the parties was consistently unwilling to do so throughout this period.

These political reasons included the visible and vocal dislike of bishops by the majority of American colonial leaders. Colonists who were not members of the Church of England, and even Church of England members in places with a colonial establishment, such as Virginia, were far less excited about a potential bishop. Within the pre-revolutionary context, this was known as "the bishop controversy." Patriots demanding more independence from Britain saw the bishops as just another means of introducing imperial control—not unreasonably, as one of the rather tone-deaf arguments offered by SPG clergy in support of a bishop was that Church of England members were more loyal to Britain, and that bringing over a bishop would help keep the colonies in line. They also argued that a bishop for the colonies could be purely spiritual, without authority over anything but church matters and members. However, since a bishop without political authority had never existed in English memory, and could not easily be imagined as a reality, most colonists assumed that "spiritual" authority would very quickly warp into official British power. Anglican leaders in Virginia also saw the bishop as a threat to the lay-led establishment that had developed in the absence of episcopal authority. In terms of colonial policy, it was clear that introducing a bishop would inflame passions against Britain already running high.[6]

As the tensions between British control and local leadership became more pronounced, Anglican clergy and sometimes laypeople were targeted as loyalists by those supporting revolution. Anglican clergy were visibly connected to English power, had taken oaths of loyalty to the monarch as part of the ordination process, and were required by the Book of Common Prayer to pray for the monarch in public services. While a good number of clergy, particularly in Virginia, supported the Revolution and simply dropped the prayers, many others, particularly those in the New England and Middle Atlantic region supported by the SPG, were vocal opponents of the patriot movement. They refused to drop the prayers for the monarch, or simply stopped all public services in protest; they were also often targeted by mobs who destroyed their property and beat them. Some of these leaders, such as Samuel Seabury, a clergyman in Westchester, New York, wrote pamphlets decrying the Continental Congress and the patriot movement and recommending loyalty and a rejection of violence.[7]

In addition to the clergy, a good portion of the Church of England laity identified as loyalists and disapproved of the Revolution. Both Methodists—members of the classes and societies organized by the Wesleys—and regular members of the Anglican establishment often felt close ties to Britain and rejected what they saw as the violence, social disorder, and irregularity of the patriots. As the patriot movement became a full-fledged war against Britain, growing numbers of these laypeople and clergy fled their homes for areas that remained loyal to Britain, particularly Canada. After the Revolution, as noted previously, the Anglican Mohawks were exiled to Canada as well, and their SPG missionary, John Stuart, followed them after three years of imprisonment in Schenectady. The Church of England lost thousands of clergy and laypeople to the loyalist exodus.

Not all Anglicans, of course, were loyalists. Historians have long noted that Anglicans played an important role in the patriot movement, even a majority role of the official leadership. These Anglicans, however, mostly came from Virginia—the heart of the fully established and locally independent, lay-led version of the Church of England that had developed since the settlement of Jamestown. George Washington, for example, was a vestryman in his local parish. In Pennsylvania, between the southern establishment and the northern colonies of New York and New England, William White, rector of Christ Church, Philadelphia, took on the chaplaincy of the revolutionary Congress.[8]

Along with other clergy who supported the Revolution, White considered the problem of the church's continued existence in a new situation. The Church of England had always been a national church, connected explicitly to the monarch and the government. How could the church adapt to a new system where government was democratic, not monarchical, and where there might be no bishops at all, even ones in London?

White's plan did not consider how the church would be financially supported. While the church was not fully established—that is, not fully supported by the government—in most of the colonies, the idea that all churches would be fully disestablished didn't occur to him, nor to the vast majority of church leaders. That the church would lose as well the financial support of the SPG wasn't addressed in the concerns about the future which White tried to answer. The existence of a church without any government support at all, even minimal support, was a completely new idea, one which came to the fore only in the debate about rights, responsibilities, and individual religious freedom as the Revolution ended and the new nation was established.

White was initially concerned only with internal questions on ordination of clergy, which meant the issue of the bishop. *The Case of the Episcopal Churches Considered* assumed that the armed struggle between Britain and the American colonists would drag on for many years, leaving the struggling colonial Church of England in limbo. Yet by 1782 the church was already in crisis; White reported that there were only three clergy left in Pennsylvania, thousands of laypeople and dozens of clergy had fled to Canada, and public services had been interrupted. In this situation, he argued, the church could not afford to wait until peace had been made and it was possible to obtain bishops from England (should that even be possible). The holy mandate to preach the gospel and provide the sacraments must take precedence—and therefore the church should initiate a reorganization immediately, with an expressed intention and desire to obtain bishops, but meanwhile relying on what was locally available: priests and laypeople.[9]

White's vision of the church involved "presbyteral ordination"—that is, priests ordaining other priests—rather than "episcopal ordination." While episcopacy might be the best way to organize the church in an ideal situation, it should not get in the way of the basic work that the church needed to do. White clearly saw the episcopacy largely through a lens of functionalism, not spiritual validity: it had much to offer in the right circumstances, but where those were absent, the church nonetheless had to fulfill its mandate.

Organizing the church with a commitment to episcopacy in general, and a plan to obtain the succession in the future, White was mostly focused on the practicalities of not waiting forever to begin the work and on the possible anxieties people might have about the powers of a bishop. He did not address the sacredness of episcopacy or the need for an apostolic succession. The episcopacy as described in the Thirty-nine Articles—the only firm and specific doctrinal statement of the Church of England—was acceptable to scripture but is not described as required or foundational.[10] He also argued from history that those who had been ordained without a bishop in times of English upheaval, or who came from Continental ordinations, were not then required to be reordained during the English Reformation, but only to appear before a bishop and assent to the Thirty-nine Articles.[11]

Readers might certainly be forgiven if they assumed White in fact thought the episcopacy largely unnecessary to the mission of the church in any deep theological sense, and such readers immediately expressed their terror of White's radical plan. These protests came largely from the SPG strongholds of Connecticut and New York. The clergy of Connecticut wrote a strongly worded collective protest to White, making the opposite argument: that without the episcopacy, the church was essentially spiritually incomplete, not merely functionally hampered. The episcopacy and, more than anything else, episcopal ordination were in fact required by the gospel, and therefore saying that one could pursue the gospel mandate without it was inaccurate. Crying that there was a necessity to do without was a false trail—after all, they hadn't actually tried to get bishops from England yet.[12]

Other protests came from loyalist New York, including from John Stuart, the SPG missionary to the Mohawk Anglicans, and Charles Inglis, the rector of Trinity Church in New York City. Inglis reprobated the scheme of beginning a church organization without bishops but also argued that involving laypeople in any aspect of the church's decision-making—including electing a bishop, one of White's innovative suggestions, but also disciplining clergy or discussing liturgical choices—was improper. Only clergy should be involved in the governance of the church.[13]

The Connecticut clergy did not wait for White's response but came together in a clergy-only meeting (deliberately excluding laypeople from the discussion and vote) to choose a potential bishop from among them. Their first choice, Jeremiah Leaming, refused because he believed he was not capable of guiding the diocese. Leaming deferred to Samuel Seabury, although privately he later said that had he known Seabury had so many enemies he would have accepted the election. Seabury, the second choice, immediately set off for England to request consecration.[14]

Seabury brought with him a letter from the Connecticut clergy explaining the need to consecrate a bishop quickly in order to forestall something like White's plan of a non-episcopally based Episcopal Church. Nonetheless, his request was rejected for multiple reasons. Parliament could not dispense with the requirement that the bishop must take an oath of loyalty to the monarch, which was not feasible under U.S. sovereignty. There was also uncertainty about the validity of Seabury's election. For the Church of England, the choice of a bishop belonged to the monarch—to whom did it belong in the

United States? Did it also require the assent of whatever state powers existed now in Connecticut? Why had the clergy of Connecticut chosen a bishop in a secret meeting? What would Seabury's diocese be, and who had set those boundaries, and who would support the bishopric financially?[15]

Despite his determined efforts, Seabury eventually had to give up on the project of consecration from the bishops of England. However, there was another option: the nonjuring bishops of Scotland. This minority group of bishops had refused to take an oath of loyalty to the monarch during a change of regime; they were part of the Scottish Episcopal Church, which was not the established state church of Scotland. For these reasons, they were free (and perhaps eager) to ignore the governmental requirements for consecrating a bishop. Thus Seabury was consecrated Bishop of Connecticut in 1784 by the requisite three bishops in the apostolic succession; in return, he promised that he would advocate for the new Episcopal Church to include the Scottish version of the Eucharistic Prayer in its new Prayer Book. For those who considered apostolic succession the basis for the church's theological mission, Seabury's consecration was the necessary first step to create the new Episcopal Church in the United States.

Meanwhile, the Revolutionary War ended much more quickly than White or likely anyone else had anticipated. Thus White's proposal to just get the church running without bishops turned out to be unnecessary. White worked with clergy from the southern and Middle Atlantic states—in fact, all but those in Connecticut, who refused to join until Seabury had been consecrated and his privileges to preside over convention guaranteed—to develop a new organizational structure and governance plan for the Episcopal Church based on dioceses (gatherings of congregations). Each state was to be a diocese and have its own bishop. There would also be a General Convention once every three years, where every diocese would send representatives to deliberate and vote upon decisions for the entire church. General Convention, carefully designed according to the new ideals of representative democracy for a new nation, would be the connection that created a nation-spanning, if not nationally established, church: the Protestant Episcopal Church of the United States of America.

White's original plan had called for bishops to essentially be first among equals within a group of parishes; they would primarily be rectors of their churches, since there was no way to support a bishop aside from a congregational financial commitment, and their work as bishops would largely be restricted to calling meetings. As Bishop of Pennsylvania, and later the presiding bishop of the church until his death in 1836, White led a large congregation as well as a diocese and church. His "bishop's seat" was a plain cane chair, still held in Christ Church Philadelphia: an ordinary seat which served a functional purpose, one seat among many, a chair no different from that of a layperson. Seabury's episcopacy viewed the bishop in a different light: conventions included only clergy, no laypeople, and it was the bishop alone who made all real decisions. It is worth noting that within his local context of Connecticut, Seabury's "high churchmanship" was not extreme. He had to discipline one of his clergy who excommunicated others for using the newly created American Book of Common Prayer and who argued that the new church was invalid because it still permitted laypeople to participate in General Convention, even though Connecticut wasn't sending any.[16] Nonetheless, Seabury's vision of the episcopacy was substantially different from White's, and this distinction would continue in the postcolonial church, lending energy both to creative engagement and to conflict.

The first two conventions, in 1785 and 1786, were notable for their activity in setting up dioceses, designing a new proposed Prayer Book, voting on a constitution which would include laypeople as well as clergy, and sending a formal request to England to consecrate bishops (White of Pennsylvania, Samuel Provoost of New York City, and David Griffith of Virginia were elected, though only White and Provoost were able to go). They were also notable for Connecticut's refusal to take part. Even after Seabury returned from Scotland with his miter, he refused to countenance participation until White organized a shift in the organization to provide a House of Bishops with partial (later full) veto power in addition to the House of Deputies, which included clergy as well as laypeople; to permit dioceses to send delegations to General Convention which did not include laypeople; and to ensure that the validity of Seabury's consecration was recognized by the remainder of the dioceses. Seabury put some additional spokes in the wheel by ordaining people from other dioceses and occasionally signing his letters "Bishop of All America." But the changes were made, and Seabury was named the first presiding bishop of the church.[17]

Seabury died in 1796; Provoost, the first bishop of New York, resigned in 1801. Only White remained of the three original bishops to shepherd the church into the period of the early Republic. As one historian notes, White was an old-fashioned low churchman, holding neither an evangelical nor a high church view of the church's mission. This moderation and ecumenical inclusivity permitted him to effectively guide the new denomination, settling quarrels and encouraging new leadership. Almost all the leaders of the next period of the church's history had a direct connection with him; some studied with him personally before ordination, though some became evangelicals and some became high church in their own orientations.

The SPG left the new United States. In a curt response to the first Bishop of Connecticut, who had written thanking them for their support for twenty-one years and expressing willingness to continue as their missionary in his new ecclesiastic role, the secretary wrote, "I am directed by the Society to express their approbation of your services as their Missionary, and to acquaint you that they cannot consistently with their Charter employ any Missionaries except in the plantations, colonies, and factories belonging to the kingdom of Great Britain; your case is of course comprehended under that general rule."[18]

The Church of England learned one important thing from the American experience: the importance of bishops to loyalty and to good governance in church and state. The remaining North American British colonies received their own bishop by 1787: Charles Inglis, previously rector of Trinity Church, New York City, and a loyalist who had fled to Canada. The British government would henceforth appoint bishops for British colonies as a matter of course. However, as the Church of England continued to expand globally through its missionary work, this did not fully solve the question of bishops, because much of the expansion did not involve direct political domination for long periods of time. The question of bishops for areas in which the Church of England was spread abroad without direct imperial control remained open and complicated until the mid-nineteenth century.

With all the energy of its revolutionary leaders expended upon reorganization and episcopacy, the new church's mission was focused not on individual conversions but on maintaining and strengthening a polity that at the least included, and for some was founded upon, episcopacy in the apostolic succession. The mission of the church was to be and to provide to all the proper and complete church, offering not enthusiastic conversion experience but a holy polity ordained by Christ himself, from which flowed all social good and sacred blessing. In practical terms, the post-Revolution disestablishment of religion meant that the Protestant Episcopal Church was now competing with other churches for spiritual affiliation but also for financing. In such a context, the church needed to prove that it was, indeed, the right church, that it was distinct from and more desirable than other options. Episcopacy, apostolic succession, liturgical formality, the Prayer Book—all these were important ways in which the new church could pursue its mission.

The divisions between the regional colonial churches—the tax-funded establishment churches of Virginia and Maryland, the pluralistic and pragmatic churches of Pennsylvania, and the SPG-supported churches of Connecticut and New England—continued in the new church as theological distinctions around mission, particularly about the value and perception of the person of the bishop. The gradual hardening of these distinctions in views of church and organization led to the American version of church parties, known as low church and high church, each of which had a distinctive vision of the church's mission.

A Mission for Freedom: The First Free Black Church

The American Revolution provided an opportunity to challenge the institution of slavery among some colonists, who pointed to its disturbingly negative effects on republican ideals, and British loyalists, who pointed to the obvious hypocrisy of a revolution for "liberty" depending upon the oppression of slaves. Abolitionist sentiment became more open in Great Britain, and among some of the white population of the colonists and new United States, leading to the abolition of the transatlantic slave trade in 1807 (Great Britain) and 1808 (United States). However, while the international trade was abolished, slavery itself was not, and in the United States "internal" slave trading continued. It was still legal, after 1808, to buy and sell human beings. Within the United States, slavery continued to grow in economic importance in the Deep South and remained culturally foundational even in states that became less economically reliant upon slaves, such as Maryland. The racial aspect of slavery became more prominent as well. There were no white slaves. Black people continued to be legally bought and sold, and legally free Black people were at constant risk of being kidnaped and sold into slavery, a danger that continued until Emancipation.

In the northern states, gradual emancipation began in 1780 in Pennsylvania, which prohibited the importation of new slaves and made all future children born in Pennsylvania legally free regardless of the status of their parents. However, those who had been enslaved in Pennsylvania prior to 1780 remained slaves for life, unless freed by their masters.

Such was a man named Absalom Jones, born in slavery in Delaware and sold away from his mother and siblings as a child to a man who moved to Philadelphia prior to 1780. His master was a member of Christ Church in Philadelphia, which since 1767 had hosted a school for enslaved and free Black children under the auspices of Dr. Bray's Associates. Philadelphia was a hotbed of republican and abolitionist sentiment, home of Benjamin Franklin and Benjamin Rush, the home of the revolutionary Congress and the capital of the United States from 1790 to 1800. It was also the home of Bishop William White and the location of five of the first seven of the General Conventions of the new Episcopal Church.[19]

Absalom Jones had taught himself to read while a child in Delaware, with a great interest in the Bible. In addition to his work for his master, he also worked to earn enough money to buy the freedom of his wife and to buy a small house, but he himself remained a slave until 1784, when at last his master agreed to accept the money he offered for his manumission. As a free, literate, and relatively well-off Black man—he continued to work for wages for his old master—Jones became one of the leaders of the Black community in Philadelphia.[20]

In 1784, the Methodists separated themselves officially from the new Episcopal Church, becoming the new Methodist Episcopal denomination. Jones and Richard Allen were licensed as preachers in St. George's Methodist Church in Philadelphia. St. George's had been created as a Methodist society in the 1760s and had taken an unfinished church building to be their own in 1769. Work on this building continued with the contributions of its members, including its African American membership, who helped to build a new gallery and lay a new floor in the building. Upon completion of the new gallery, the African American members were surprised to learn that they were all required to sit in it, separately from the white members of the congregation, the first of several significant racially based insults to the African American Methodists. The segregated seating was enforced physically by the white wardens of the church, humiliating the African American congregants.[21]

Meanwhile, Jones, Allen, and other leaders had gathered to organize the Free African Society (FAS), a benevolent group with religious overtones intended to help support the destitute and rebuke the dissipated of the free Black community. Founded in 1787, the FAS included leaders from other denominations, but the ongoing racial tensions within St. George's meant that it gradually became a center of religious life for the Methodist community as well. Jones was elected an "overseer" of the group, whose work included visiting all members to ensure that they were living up to the moral standards of the FAS. Those who did not maintain these standards were rejected from membership in the FAS until they mended their ways. In addition, the group began holding "religious meetings" and even tried Quaker-style silence at the beginning of their meetings.[22]

In 1792, Jones was interrupted during prayer in St. George's by the white wardens, who insisted that he get up and leave the church. He and Allen led the African American congregants out in a definitive, final protest. Now the FAS became the germ of a new religious congregation, and the membership, not wishing for any radical break with Christian tradition, voted overwhelmingly to leave the new Methodist denomination and to affiliate instead with the new Episcopal Church. Ironically, only Jones and Allen voted to remain Methodist. Allen continued to associate with Methodism and eventually, after many frustrations with the white leadership of the denomination, began a separate African Methodist Episcopal denomination. Jones, however, accompanied the majority in their new efforts to become Episcopalian.[23]

It is unclear why the Episcopal Church was the overwhelming preference of the largely Methodist FAS members. Some of them may have had positive experiences at Christ Church's school for African Americans, which included catechism for its students; the negative experiences at St. George's were clearly in mind as well. Given that the Methodist-Episcopal split was so recent, the liturgical practices of the Episcopal Church were probably quite familiar to the exiles from St. George's, and the increased Methodist expectations for a conversion experience and personal religious piety could also be brought with them into their new denominational home. Perhaps the group saw the Episcopal Church as a familiar version of Christianity rather than a denominational shift. The Episcopal Church had not offered the same sort of direct racial insult they had just gone through at St. George's. Perhaps as an Episcopalian congregation, the members of the new St. Thomas African Church, with its building already in downtown Philadelphia, could experience inclusion and respect.

The challenge now was how to organize the official affiliation with the Episcopal Church. The leadership of St. Thomas wrote a constitution which specified that its elected officials, aside from the minister and assistant minister, would always be members of the African race. The minister and assistant minister would have no vote in the church council, and the church would always be able to choose its rector. These specifications were clearly intended to safeguard the congregation's autonomy in the likelihood that their clergyperson was white. The constitution and request to affiliate with the Episcopal Church were presented to Bishop White, who recommended to the Standing Committee that the congregation be accepted into the diocese.[24]

From this point forward, the story is murky, because St. Thomas was not fully accepted into the diocese on an equal basis, and the written record is cagy about why not. The congregation requested that Jones be ordained as their clergyman, and Bishop White recommended that the Standing Committee agree to this, waiving the requirement for literacy in biblical languages. There was a canon requiring this for ordination, but there was also a defined process for waiving this requirement, and Jones was not the only clergyperson who was accepted under this waiver. However, Bishop White simply reported to the Council that he had conveyed the approval of Jones's ordination to the vestry of St. Thomas, as well as the newly formed restrictions on St. Thomas's participation in the diocese: that they should never send a clergyperson, or deputies, or have any vote in the diocesan convention or governance of the church, due to their "peculiar circumstances." The discussion of these restrictions, either between Bishop White and the Standing Committee or between White and the members of the St. Thomas vestry, are not recorded. The nature of the "peculiar circumstances" are not defined. As discussed in a future chapter, St. Thomas would not become a fully equal member of the diocese until the Civil War. Free Black Episcopalian congregations in other contexts, including New York City and in the postbellum South, also struggled for full recognition and inclusion in diocesan conventions, and were denied based on the precedent set with St. Thomas.[25]

Nonetheless, St. Thomas African Episcopal Church now existed, a stronghold of African American culture and leadership in Philadelphia. Jones was ordained deacon in 1795, the first level of the "threefold ministry" of the Episcopal Church. While he was not "priested" (ordained a priest) until 1802—a much longer waiting period than for typical white clergy, who were priested after six months or less—he nonetheless was the first African American to be ordained a clergyperson in the United States.

What did Jones and the people of St. Thomas African Episcopal Church understand as the mission of the church? They did not share in the obsession with polity and episcopacy, or proper order, that shaped the missional views of the high church Connecticut clergy or the low church evangelicals in the next decades. Coming originally from a Methodist formation, but more particularly from an experience of slavery and oppression, Jones defined the Christian mission as the struggle for a truly faithful life for the community, one which strove toward liberation and rested upon the conviction that each person in the community was worthy of this liberation and capable of this faithful life.

Thus, for Jones and for other free Black people in the early republic, the missional ideal of "Christianizing and civilizing" in the context of social order took on a different cast. It was crucial for the Black community to demonstrate to the white community their capacity for living in an "orderly" and "Christian" fashion—not because this was at the heart of being Christian per se but because by demonstrating this the Black community could assuage the fears and anxieties of the white community, and thereby gain their support for the liberation of all Black people. They demonstrated to all the world what Black people were capable of, the good and worthy lives they could live once freed and allowed to participate in society, the contributions they could make to humanity. Jones's work as overseer for the FAS, in organizing the Black community's self-sacrificial response to Philadelphia's yellow fever epidemic in 1793, and his ministry, preaching, and activism all demonstrate his efforts to bring the life of the Christian community into the world of individual Black members as well as in the larger Philadelphia society.[26]

However, this strategy of looking for recognition and acceptance by the white community had its limits; it might even be characterized as a cruel deception. From the white point of view, regardless of the achievements of the Black community, the most important thing a free Black person could do was to be quiet and humble so as not to antagonize white people. But quiet and humility could never be enough, because the white people were incredibly anxious about Black freedom, and even those who counted themselves as friends of the African American community saw the relationship as a paternalistic one, not as a relationship of equals. In the sermon at the consecration of St. Thomas Church, the white guest clergyman, Samuel Magaw, recommended that the Black congregation express their gratitude for being taken from a pagan country, for which they should respond as Joseph did to his brothers who sold him into slavery, and accept the bondage of those still unfree, as this was God's dispensation and intended for good. They should also express gratitude to all the antislavery people and benefactors who supported them; compassionate love toward those still enslaved; humility;

and, most of all, they should not become proud. "It is said, there is a great deal of this among your people, already; and that it is increasing extremely fast. . . . [Y]our friends meet with discouragements on this head." The congregation of St. Thomas should remember their lowliness and say "A perishing slave was my father" to remind themselves not to "cherish the least pride, in your freedom—in dress—in your favorable reception among your fellow citizens, even in this stately building." Finally, they must exercise "circumspection in [their] conduct," as they had enemies watching them to find them failing in expectations of order: peaceableness, truth, diligence, temperance, and "an obliging, meek, friendly conversation. . . . A contrary behaviour will certainly increase their darkness [of those still enslaved] and tend to rivet only closer their chains. It may render the yet existing reproach of your country perpetual." The implication was that free Black people who did not express enough humility and respectability were at fault for the ongoing reality of enslavement.[27]

Trying to be meek, humble, and respectable had strategic limits that were clear to Jones and his congregation even in the eighteenth century. Being "good Christians" and waiting for freedom would never be enough for liberation: the leaders of the church, therefore, must step into the political sphere. Jones led the organization of two formal petitions to the federal government against the 1793 Fugitive Slave Act, which permitted agents of enslavement to search for and kidnap "runaways" in the free states, and the ongoing international slave trade. When the international slave trade was abolished in 1808, Jones preached and published a sermon of thanksgiving for God's action in the world:

Yes, my brethren, the nations from which most of us have descended, and the country in which some of us were born, have been visited by the tender mercy of the Common Father of the human race. He has seen the affliction of our countrymen, with an eye of pity. . . . He has seen the anguish which has taken place, when parents have been torn from their children, and children from their parents, and conveyed, with their hands and feet bound in fetters, on board of ships prepared to receive them. . . . He has seen the neglect with which their masters have treated their immortal souls; not only in withholding religious instruction from them, but, in some instances, depriving them of access to the means of obtaining it. He has seen all the different modes of torture, by means of the whip, the screw, the pincers, and the red hot iron, which have been exercised upon their bodies, by inhuman overseers: overseers, did I say? Yes: but not by these only. Our God has seen masters and mistresses, educated in fashionable life, sometimes take the instruments of torture into their own hands, and, deaf to the cries and shrieks of their agonizing slaves, exceed even their overseers in cruelty. Inhuman wretches! though You have been deaf to their cries and shrieks, they have been heard in Heaven. The ears of Jehovah have been constantly open to them: He has heard the prayers that have ascended from the hearts of his people; and he has, as in the case of his ancient and chosen people the Jews, *come down to deliver* our suffering country-men from the hands of their oppressors. He *came down* into the United States, when they declared, in the constitution which they framed in 1788, that the trade in our African fellow-men, should cease in the year 1808: He *came down* into the British Parliament, when they passed a law to put an end to the same iniquitous trade in May, 1807: *He came down* into the Congress of the United States, the last winter, when they passed a similar law, the operation of which commences on this happy day. Dear land of our ancestors! thou shalt no more be stained with the blood of thy children, shed by British and American hands: the ocean shall no more afford a refuge to their bodies, from impending slavery: nor shall the shores of the British West India islands, and of the United States, any more witness the anguish of families, parted for ever by a publick sale.[28]

Jones's sermon emphasized the connection of God's actions in the world with political action; criticized the "inhumanity" of white slaveholders; rejoiced that so much evil in the world would now end. Theologically, the God of Absalom Jones was an active God that heard the cries of the people and would "come down" to change the hearts and laws of nations in order to preserve the innocent—a very different God from the orderly, distant clockmaker God of the more Deist Anglicans, such as Thomas Jefferson and George Washington. Jones was able to draw on his own experience of enslavement and that of many of the people in his congregation. But Jones also obeyed Magaw's suggestions, reminding the people to not be proud, to thank their benefactors, and to care for all those still enslaved and those who would still be freed. And unfortunately the "publick sale" would continue with the internal trade. Jones, with his congregation, would continue to agitate, organize against the slave trade, and serve the Black community at large out of their own missional trust in God's care for them—and in their own responsibility to take an active part in God's liberatory work. In this sense, Jones and the Black Episcopalians of the revolutionary era were living out a missional attitude that would not become prominent in white-majority Protestant denominations until the later twentieth century.

Competing Missional Visions

African American Episcopalians continued to struggle for liberation through the nineteenth and twentieth centuries, as will be discussed in future chapters. One of the strategically important ways in which they did so was to demand recognition and inclusion at the diocesan level, which was very slow in coming. It is useful, once again, to imagine what the Episcopal Church's missional trajectory might have looked like had the diocesan conventions beginning in 1795 included the full voice and vote of African American Episcopalians, bringing the discourse of liberation and universal human worth, as well as political activism, into the discussion of mission and allocation of church resources that happened at diocesan convention and General Convention.

The creative missional input of the African American Episcopalians was deliberately set aside, and the Native American Anglican community, which could have offered much in the way of alternative structures of debate, decision-making, and ritual making of sacred relationships, was physically exiled. Missional resources to expand creatively and contextually were thus curtailed and cramped. In making these decisions about which mission would be central to the church's identity—or in casually ignoring other options without much consideration—the church was shaped and guided by the needs of empire and the growing importance of racial ideology in its larger social context. Imperially, the American project would depend upon access to land for immigrants and farmers, and this land would be taken from the indigenous people of the continent. Ideologically, these farmers and immigrants were imagined as explicitly white—as stated in the 1790 Naturalization Act, which restricted citizenship to "free white men," thus leaving free and enslaved Black people, Native Americans, and later Asians excluded from the rights and privileges of citizens.

Instead, the Episcopal Church's sense of mission, growing out of the brokered compromises between New England and the other colonies after the Revolution, was focused on proper polity and worship. For the next decades, the missional mandate to "Christianize and civilize" would come to life wrapped in a new mission: to extend to all people a church expressed in proper liturgical practice, organized under the sacred order of episcopacy.

PART II
CHURCH PLANTING, CIVILIZING, AND CHRISTIANIZING

The model of "Christianize and Civilize" continued to thrive and develop through the nineteenth century, sometimes called the "great century" of Protestant missions. Within the United States, this period also coincided with the territorial expansion of the original thirteen colonies to the Pacific Coast, displacing and destroying indigenous cultures, as well as engaging in wars to obtain additional territory.

Mission among racial and cultural groups different from the white majority in the church, both within and outside of the United States, emphasized *assimilationism*, the idea that if "others" would become similar enough to the white majority all would be well. The language of "civilizing," "Christianizing," "tutelage," and "wardship" all supported this ideal. Internally, a new model of mission came on the scene with the rise of denominations in a disestablished voluntary system, focused on denominational competition and the development of new financing and organizational structures.

Chapter 4 explores the church's responses to the religious realities of the early republic. The Second Great Awakening in the early 1800s fired up all Protestant denominations for mission, but the Episcopalians came late to the party. The challenges of western "domestic" expansion set the stage for the creation of the Domestic and Foreign Missionary Society and the crucial innovation of the missionary bishop. This chapter traces some of the central missional personalities of this early period in New York (Philander Chase and John Henry Hobart), the nearly dissolved church of Virginia (William Mead), and the first missionary bishop, Jackson Kemper, in the context of the early divisions between high church and evangelical missional views.

Chapter 5 follows the African American community and the Episcopal Church in the years leading up to the civil war. The debate over abolition and the status of free Black Episcopalians created further tensions between the high church and evangelical visions of mission. The Episcopal Church, unlike most other Protestant denominations, did not split over slavery, but did so during the Civil War itself. Since the denomination never clarified its stance on slavery, white congregations and dioceses as a whole might include people on both sides of the issue, leading to a further withdrawal from political engagement among most (though not all) Episcopalian leaders. This chapter traces the work of Alexander Crummell and free Black congregations in the North, as well as Episcopalian work among Black enslaved congregants in the South.

Chapter 6 compares two new missional fields, the expanding eastern city and the new territory of the West Coast. William Augustus Muhlenberg and William Ingraham Kip provide a way to engage the missional challenges and shortcomings in this era, particularly in terms of incorporating culturally and racially diverse people, and the limitations of the vision of the central General Convention, which was responsible for providing guidance and resources for missional work.

Chapter 7 addresses further the response of the Episcopal Church to territorial expansion and violence against Native Americans. During this era, American expansion throughout the continental United States led to the last "Indian Wars" and the closing of the frontier. This chapter examines the complex relationships between Episcopalian white leaders and Native American leaders in this period through the stories of Jackson Kemper, Enmegabowh, and Henry Whipple, exploring the complicated balance of agency, partnership, paternalism, and resistance.

Chapter 8 moves the history of the Episcopal Church from the debates over slavery to the reality of freedom for African Americans. : After the Civil War, Black Episcopalians left the church in droves, and the church attempted to respond to this with various models of missionary intervention and control. This chapter traces the work of Black Episcopalians both in the northern churches, struggling for inclusion and respect in their dioceses, and in southern churches, with special attention to George Bragg and James Solomon Russell, as well as James Holly's effort to create a fully Black-led church in Haiti.

Chapter 9 traces the ways in which the heavily assimilationist model of mission expected of Black and Native people in the United States was carried out in overseas territories gained near the end of the nineteenth century and the beginning of the twentieth, with a focus on the annexation of Hawaii and the Philippines.

4

The Great Innovation

The Challenge of Disestablishment

Following the American Revolution and the brief experiment of the Articles of Confederation, the very first constitutional amendment in the Bill of Rights provided for two radical innovations, which taken together are called "freedom of religion" or sometimes "separation of church and state." Scholars of religious history identify the first right as *disestablishment*, that the government should not support any religion or denomination, and the second right as *free exercise*, that the government should not constrain people's ability to worship in any way they desire, or in no way at all. Taken together, disestablishment and free exercise created a *voluntary system* for religion in the new United States, a completely new system for religious life and institutions.

The new voluntarism meant that religious groups needed the freely given support of their members to maintain themselves financially, and that they could not rely on any state requirements, even indirect ones, to encourage people to affiliate with any given religious group. For some groups who had always been in the religious minority, such as Quakers and Baptists, this was an experience of freedom. They would no longer have to pay taxes to support a minister of a denomination they did not belong to. Voluntarism also meant that religious organizations had to compete for the affections and interest of the people. For the Methodists and other evangelical groups emphasizing public preaching and an exciting conversion experience to draw in newcomers, this shift did not greatly change their way of life and organizing.

For the new Episcopal Church, particularly where it had been deeply woven into the fabric of governance, the voluntary system was utterly disorienting, leading to a near complete collapse between 1776 and 1800. This collapse was most extensive in places that had been more fully and deeply established, particularly in Virginia, but was evident to some degree almost everywhere in the new United States. In 1811, with two new bishops-elect to be consecrated, the church's dependency upon episcopacy almost

Mission, Race, and Empire. Jennifer C. Snow, Oxford University Press. © Oxford University Press 2024.
DOI: 10.1093/oso/9780197598948.003.0005

derailed it—only two American bishops had attended the previous General Convention, and a consecration required three. A retired bishop had to be brought on board in order to consecrate his own successor.

In order to respond to this new context and system, where every church was a "minority" church that would have to compete for funds and members, the new Episcopal Church would join the fray as one denomination among many. Between 1800 and 1835, the church developed two competing strands of missional vision and practice, high church and evangelicalism, joined together with two adaptive innovations: the missionary bishop and a churchwide Domestic and Foreign Missionary Society, which counted every Episcopalian as a member. With this new framework of missional theology and practice, the Episcopal Church belatedly joined the denominational scrum for the population of the western United States and set the pattern for its expansion in ways that would track with Manifest Destiny, the violent and rapid expansion to the Pacific.

The Exhausted Old Low Church Mission: Virginia and Pennsylvania

After the American Revolution, early Episcopalian concern for mission was eclipsed by the reality of a weak and poorly funded church without strong leadership or new ideas. The General Convention of 1792 had proposed a central committee for missional expansion along with the new settlers beyond the Alleghenies, with a state-based fundraising structure and a treasurer and committee connected with General Convention. In an address that was to be read in churches on a specific Sunday dedicated to raising funds for mission, Bishop William White and Reverend Samuel Magaw (who would give the inaugural sermon at St. Thomas African Church a few years later) noted that converting the Indians was something to be hoped for, but the greater need was to provide the church to the growing white population in the "West," the territory beyond the Allegheny Mountains and the newly obtained territory of Iroquoia in upstate New York. These settlers were already Christian, but the church needed to do its work to provide them with a Christian ministry.[1] In 1795, however, this plan was dropped in favor of greater autonomy of each diocese to fundraise and lead mission as seemed best in their own locality. The ability of the different dioceses to undertake their own mission fundraising obviously differed significantly, and this plan, as could be predicted, largely encouraged funding to support mission within a diocese rather than beyond it in the newly settled areas.[2]

In the southern United States, particularly Virginia, the church that had sustained daily life and social interaction in each county and parish collapsed without the financial support of the parish tax, and the fact that it had not attracted the majority of white colonists for some time became painfully obvious. Churches were taken over by other denominations or collapsed; clergymen left their pastorates. Prior to the Revolution Virginia had between ninety-six and two hundred congregations scattered through its parishes; by 1801, it still had fifty-eight clergy on the rolls, but many of these were "relics" from the colonial era and were not able to adjust to the new conditions of a disestablished church.[3]

When young William Meade offered himself as a candidate for ordination to Bishop James Madison in Williamsburg, Virginia, after graduating from Princeton in 1811, it was a subject of public amazement. No young man within memory had considered the church as a career. After his examination, Meade went with Madison to the Williamsburg parish church, which was "in a wretched condition, with broken windows and a gloomy, comfortless aspect. The congregation which assembled consisted of two ladies and about fifteen gentlemen, nearly all of whom were relatives or acquaintances [of Meade]. . . . [He] was put into the pulpit to preach, there being no ordination sermon." Around this time there was a rumor that the bishop had secretly "renounced the Christian faith," and conversations during Meade's visit to the College of William and Mary included such topics as the existence of God and whether the Christian religion was beneficial or detrimental to humanity. By 1823, when Meade was fundraising for a new seminary in Virginia, U.S. Supreme Court Justice John Marshall told him that it was really almost unkind to encourage young men to enter the ministry, as the church was gone beyond recovery.[4]

The parish of Abingdon Church in Gloucester County demonstrates the difficulty of the transition to disestablishment. The parish had been established around 1650 and the first church built in 1660. The church flourished throughout the colonial era. In 1724, the minister reported to the Bishop of London that there were three hundred families in the parish; about two hundred in attendance at church; services every Sunday morning, on Good Friday, and at Christmas; communion three times a year with sixty to seventy communicants; a house and glebe about four miles from the church;

a living of sixteen thousand pounds of tobacco per year; and a free school in the parish with five hundred acres of good land, three slaves, cattle, and household goods, as well as a professional schoolmaster in addition to the minister. The church was rebuilt and improved in 1755.[5]

In 1776, the Virginia House of Delegates ended taxation for the support of the church. The last entry in the church's register was made in 1780. Since the wealth of the Virginia church had been established by taxation, much of it reverted to state control in the early republic. In 1802, the state legislature confiscated church lands and other property, including Abingdon's glebe lands, and from 1818 on the church building was used by Methodists, as legislation required that an Episcopalian church building be available to all denominations if it did not have a regular minister. It was not until 1826 that the church had a minister again, and it was not until 1830 that a vestry was elected and recorded a meeting. Throughout the 1840s there were ongoing conflicts about which denomination "owned" the church, as the Methodists continued to claim it.[6]

Abingdon Church was luckier than many in Virginia; the church building itself was not destroyed, and when a new deacon arrived in 1826 there were still at least a few families who wanted to be part of an Episcopalian congregation. Bishop Madison was not so different from most of the parish clergy of Virginia who lived through the Revolution. Clergy whose skills had consisted of liturgical leadership, careful and scholarly preaching, pastoral visits, societal respectability, and soothing of elite tempers, with an assurance that the "best" part of white Virginian society would appear in church and run its social service programs because they were supposed to do so, now had to develop completely different skills: preaching that could draw in those otherwise disinclined to attend; inventing schemes of voluntary fundraising among members and communicants for their own salary and the care of the church and parsonage, which in the past had been paid by the parish taxes; developing apologetics that would demonstrate the superiority of Episcopalian worship and polity to that of competing Christian groups as well as atheists, skeptics, and deists; and attempting to soothe the distaste of many nonelite Virginians for the church of the wealthy and powerful planter families, who for their part tended to disengage as the church lost status. The ministers of the post-revolutionary Virginia church were unable even to maintain their own congregations, and certainly couldn't muster the energy and develop the new skills required to engage in expanding the church in the new disestablished reality.

The experience of disestablishment in Pennsylvania was less stunning and disastrous than in Virginia, as the Episcopal Church there had begun its existence as a minority church and had always had to compete with others and to maintain itself through self-funding. Nonetheless, the funding structures that existed were minimal and suffered in the financial upset of the Revolution. Traditionally the churches were funded through "pew-rents" from the members, but these were in arrears for almost twenty years after the Revolution at Christ Church Philadelphia.[7] Keeping the congregation solvent was the first concern of every rector, and Bishop White must surely have spent a good amount of energy simply keeping his congregation functional and the church building repaired. In addition to the responsibilities of the presiding bishop until his death in 1836, White continued as the Bishop of Pennsylvania and the rector of the United Churches, a three-congregation amalgamation in Philadelphia—the rectorship being his only paid position. White had been the youngest of the post-revolutionary bishops, at thirty-nine, and led the church until he was eighty-eight. He certainly had no shortage of energy and excitement for the church, but this was expended largely in his position as rector and as leader of many Philadelphia humanitarian organizations and schools. As bishop, White held back from a strong leadership position, visiting congregations only when asked and invited. Both because of his own sense of the minimal and functional role of the bishop and because of his worry that a strong episcopal hand would be cause for alienation of those who believed strongly in democracy, White did not stride out in front of the church as a missional leader.[8]

In Philadelphia itself, the church was thriving, with new congregations fully staffed, provided with organs and Sunday Schools. In one case, a congregation was even established specifically to attract a notable preacher, built within a year and the minister paid a salary during construction. In rural areas, however, congregations struggled for years to build a church and could not offer salaries that would attract the few ordained clergy that were available.[9]

Beyond the limits of the city, the diocese struggled to provide clergy even for those who requested them and wanted to found a congregation, while within the city, wealthy churches sprang up seemingly overnight. The strategy for mission, such as it was, was to respond to calls for clergy from Episcopalians who wanted, and were willing to support, a congregation and clergyperson. Even with this very limited target, the diocese fell short and could not respond to many calls, particularly those in western Pennsylvania and western Virginia, Kentucky, and Ohio, beyond the Allegheny Mountains. The conditions of travel at this time made the mountains a formidable obstacle; Bishop White didn't personally cross them until the 1820s, encouraged by his young assistant at the United Churches, Jackson Kemper.[10]

Kemper had been deaconed by Bishop White in 1811. Like Meade, the novelty of a young man being ordained drew attention and brought a certain amount of excitement to the church, leading to the establishment of the Society for the Advancement of Christianity in Pennsylvania in 1812, and Kemper's leading role in it. As a deacon he went on the first missionary journey for the diocese, visiting rural congregations in Pittsburgh and beyond. Throughout his travels he stumbled upon people attempting to maintain an Episcopalian faith from their childhood without prayer books. In visiting one such community, he noted that the people had found many creative places in which to worship, but "they seemed to be utterly ignorant of the liturgy." Everywhere he went, he found small congregations, or groups of Episcopalians who wanted to become congregations, but lacked the money for a building and lacked the wherewithal to attract a clergyman.[11]

On this journey Kemper met with a Presbyterian who had become an Episcopal minister ordained by Bishop White, Joseph Doddridge. Doddridge confirmed to Kemper what he himself had observed in his travels, that many of the immigrants into the western territories came from "church folk" in Virginia, Maryland, and eastern Pennsylvania, and were being lost to "sectaries" (meaning Methodists, Baptists, and Presbyterians) not because of doctrinal preferences but because the "sectaries" and Catholics were there in force, providing churches, preaching, and sacraments to people who actively wanted them, while the Episcopal Church was conspicuously absent. Clergy appeared, when they did, nearly by accident—such as the clergyman from Kentucky who came lonely to General Convention in 1814—or because they themselves, like others, were on the move. The Episcopal Church had not given adequate thought to these people in their new situation, and was losing them for lack of care and attention.[12]

Doddridge had suggested to White that a bishop be consecrated for the churches beyond the mountains, and White was supportive but was uncertain that a "suitable person" and financial support could be found. In 1811, General Convention considered the idea, but when Bishop Madison of Virginia died without a successor in 1812, the plan fell off the table. Doddridge later wrote:

I then lost all hope of ever witnessing any prosperity in our beloved Church in this part of America. . . . The vestries were not reelected, and our young people joined other societies. Could I prevent them, when I indulged no hope of a succession in the ministry? . . . I entertained no hope that even my own remains after death could be committed to the dust with the funeral services of my own Church. . . . How often have I reflected, with feelings of the deepest regret and sorrow, that if anything like an equal number of professors of any other Christian community had been located in Siberia, or India, and, equally dependent on a supreme ecclesiastical authority, had been so neglected, that a request so reasonable would have met with a prompt and cheerful compliance! . . . Had we imitated at an early period the example of other Christian communities—employed the same means for collecting our people into societies and building churches, and with the same zeal—we should by this time have had four or five bishops in this country, surrounded by a numerous and respectable body of clergy, instead of having our very name connected with a fallen Church. Instead of offering a rich and extensive plunder to every sectarian missionary, we should have the first and highest station among the Christian societies of the West.[13]

Kemper worked with the diocese in 1823 in an experimental program to try to at least supply clergy to the many congregations that did not have one of their own, in which ministers of settled congregations would spend two to three Sundays per year visiting and serving those which did not. The ministers would be paid for their traveling expenses by the diocese, but the expenses themselves were quite high, and the program ran out of money quickly. Not all clergy were eager to peregrinate away from their comfortable home congregations, and some refused pointblank at the waste of their time or the dangers and difficulty of the travel. But some took up the cause faithfully and reported on old congregations dissolving, taken over by Unitarians, by Presbyterians, begging for clergy, and the possibility of new congregations that would be lost in a few years. One wrote of the situation in the Susquehanna Valley, where many of the people had come from Connecticut and were eager and devoted Episcopalians, who had for twenty years read divine service with a lay reader and would soon become Presbyterian simply because there was no Episcopalian clergyman to provide them with the sacraments and Christian burial.[14]

On hearing that Bishop White might at last cross the mountains to visit western Pennsylvania in 1824 (a visit that ended up being rescheduled to the next year, as White was injured in a carriage accident on the way west), one layman in Meadville, John Wallace, wrote eagerly to Kemper:

> It is Mrs Wallace's intention and mine, to meet you at Pittsburgh, God willing. It is nearly a year since I have had an opportunity of attending divine service in our church and much longer since Mrs Wallace has had it. Those only who are deprived of the benefits of our church, after having enjoyed them, know how great the privation is. To see again our beloved Bishop, and to hear again his voice, is where our opportunity to do so presents, not to be omitted. On reading the other day of the great preparations and eager desire to see the Marquis La Fayette, "I would rather, said Mrs Wallace, see the Bishop, than all the Marquises in the world" in which sentiment I heartily join.[15]

In his travels in western Pennsylvania, Kemper came to some conclusions that would stay with him in what would become a legendary missionary career. First, the West provided a mission field beyond anything the church had had previously, if only the church were able to meet it. Second, inattention to rubrics and liturgical forms would lead to "fatal consequences to our Zion." And third, despite the perseverance, faithfulness, and creativity of laypeople left to their own devices, the energy and health of a congregation depended upon the energy of the pastor.[16]

And other churches were ready to meet the need. Methodists could provide clergy easily from the grassroots, without the extensive requirements of education and episcopal approval of the Episcopal Church; Presbyterians and Baptists could provide clergy relatively easily as well, and as Catholic immigration swelled the Roman Catholic Church was sending religious orders, priests, and bishops throughout the United States and the western territories. For Episcopalians, valuing a high level of education, the clergy faucet was on slow drip. In 1801 Bishop White had developed a standard curriculum of study for potential ministers, who would study with clergymen and work under them in their congregations, a process called "reading for orders," followed by examination by the bishop and ordination. This curriculum was expected to take no less than three years and presumed a classical university education beforehand; it would also be limited by how many individuals a clergyperson could mentor.

Upon completing this program, this university-educated and highly trained individual would be able to read biblical languages, discourse upon theological doctrines, offer communion and baptism, and write sermons. He would be perfectly suited to serve a preexisting congregation that could pay him a respectable middle-class salary with which to support and educate his family in a dignified fashion, but would most likely be reluctant to spend his career in a tiny church (or multiple churches) that struggled to pay him in a rural area distant from the refined urban centers, or to provide catechism and sacraments to those who were not already familiar with and committed to the Episcopalian liturgy and polity. It was a system that could not possibly meet the need.

The dioceses of Pennsylvania and Virginia found their own ways to a new equilibrium as time passed, but energy for new beginnings was low. Bishop White and Bishop Madison both represented what is sometimes called the "old low church" version of the Church of England, holding Enlightenment views that emphasized rationalism, moral action, practical goodness, and social order above all. Bishop Madison's death in 1812 left the tattered diocese of Virginia on life support; the clergyman elected to replace him declined the election, and young William Meade, still a deacon, wondered whether the 1813 diocesan convention would be the last. The low churchmanship of the old church was at its lowest ebb, soon to be transformed into the evangelical Episcopalianism that would revive Virginia, excite Pennsylvania, and lead to a new missional vision in the Ohio Valley. Meanwhile, the high churchmanship of Samuel Seabury was being reinvigorated and reinvented in the North.

The Reinvigorated High Church Mission

Prior to the Revolution, there were five Anglican churches in upstate New York, two of which were for the Mohawk. All suffered greatly in the war, and many of the clergy, including John Stuart, the missionary to the Mohawk, fled from the American Revolution to Canada as loyalists to Great Britain.[17] The first Bishop of New York, Samuel Provoost, was notable mostly for his personal antipathy to Samuel Seabury, his fierce commitment to the patriot cause, and his lack of attention to his episcopal duties due to family troubles and poor health. In 1801, he resigned his episcopacy.

Despite Provoost's obstructive leadership, the church began to recover and to establish new congregations relatively quickly. In Albany, after the departure of the loyalists, Reverend Thomas Ellison became the rector of St.

Peter's Church in 1787; as the SPG had withdrawn their financial support, the congregation needed to raise funds to support him, which they were able to do relatively easily via a subscription from members. Unlike in Virginia, the congregation had some experience in contributing to the maintenance of their pastor—the SPG generally required a congregation to front at least some funds—so the experience was one of shifting from partial to full support. In 1791, St. Peter's welcomed its first episcopal visitation, and for the first time since the church was founded the congregants could receive the rite of confirmation. One hundred forty-seven of them took advantage of the opportunity, including eleven "persons of color," who may have been free or enslaved Black people or Iroquois who had not left the area. Between 1790 and 1810, the Diocese of New York grew from one functioning upstate parish (St. Peter's) to twenty-five congregations and mission stations.[18]

Geographically, New York was not constrained in the same way as Pennsylvania. There was a clear path west, with no mountain ranges in the way. The fertile lands of Iroquoia drew a rush of settlers and land speculators, particularly from the stony fields of western Massachusetts, Vermont, and Connecticut. Many of these immigrants had been members of the Church of England, and as they developed their new towns and communities they also tried to build churches, even when they did not have a clergyman among them.[19] As in Pennsylvania and Virginia, it was the commitment of laypeople with a preexisting attachment to Episcopalianism that led to the growth of congregations. The missionary clergy came after the laypeople were already there, a pattern that would repeat itself throughout the century.

The early Episcopalian missionary work among the new settlers in upstate New York was authorized by a diocesan missionary society established in 1796 and supported financially by the wealthy laypeople of New York City and Trinity Church. Trinity Church had been endowed with land in Manhattan during the colonial era, and its investments and developments provided wealth that could support the growth of the church throughout the diocese. The coffers were not bottomless; by 1820, Trinity had to withdraw from funding actual church building and choose more carefully where to put the mission funds. But there was far more to work with than any other postrevolutionary diocese could boast. And since the Bishop of New York was the same person as the rector of Trinity for the first fifty years after the American Revolution, the coffers tended to be available for such purposes.[20]

Bishop Provoost's 1801 request to resign led the diocese to elect a bishop co-adjutor—in essence an assistant to do the episcopal work, with rights of episcopal succession. When Bishop Co-Adjutor Benjamin Moore had a stroke in 1811, the diocese had to elect a second bishop co-adjutor, John Henry Hobart. While Hobart did not become the diocesan bishop until Moore's death in 1817, when he also became rector of Trinity Church, he essentially ran the diocese from his 1811 consecration.

Hobart was as unlike Provoost as it is possible to be. Studying under Bishop White, Hobart developed away from White's low church position toward a uniquely American version of the high church tradition, one which saw episcopacy not as functionally useful but as divinely required for a valid church. Even before his election as bishop, Hobart made his name as a controversialist, engaging in a pamphlet war with Presbyterians about the divine institution of episcopacy and its corollary, the inadequacy of nonepiscopal churches. Hobart believed that the Episcopal Church most perfectly held the pattern of the early or "primitive" church in the apostolic age, and that this apostolic inheritance enabled it to provide the most ideal form of Christian life and teachings. Because of this, he refused to act in concert with other churches in multidenominational organizations such as the American Bible Society.[21]

The high church party in the Church of England was associated with more elaborate and heartfelt forms of sacramental prayer life, which Hobart also embraced and encouraged. However, where the English high church connected their piety with social hierarchy and loyalty to the monarchy, Hobart instead developed the idea that the church was an "ark of refuge" from the political evils of the world. The church should simply avoid politics at all costs. A church that engaged in politics was no church and could not provide spiritual guidance and care. Hobart took this position to the point of refusing to vote in elections and rejected the evangelical Episcopalian attention to social reform.[22]

Hobart described the Episcopal Church not as a voluntary organization of human origin, but as divine and ordained by God. In this true and apostolic Episcopal Church, "men are *obliged to be members,* as they value their everlasting happiness . . . with enforcements of *rewards and punishments.*" The differences between denominations were thus not trivial doctrinal matters or of personal liturgical taste but questions of absolute right and wrong which connected directly with salvation. This was Hobart's high church missional response to the new situation of disestablishment and denominational competition. In this context, the missional project of the church must be to establish more churches, all of which must also be doctrinally and liturgically correct and led by clergy ordained by a bishop in the line of apostolic suc-cession, in order to provide the primitive Christian truth to all those who were willing to come—which, most likely, would not be all people, since the church was destined to be in the minority in the constant battle against error.[23]

With the wealth of Trinity, an energetic commitment to mission, and a new missional vision, Hobart set the tone for a new kind of bishop: an ac-tively leading bishop, one who visited congregations constantly (whether they asked or not), developed diocesan institutions to train clergy, built and consecrated new churches, supervised and disciplined clergy, and supported missionaries throughout his diocese. Hobart's episcopacy was stunningly successful in terms of expansion. A few years after his death in 1830, the Diocese of New York was officially split into two dioceses, the first time this had been required by the growth of the church, and the first time a state had been divided into more than one diocese.[24]

Hobart's high church vision inspired a generation of younger clergy—not accidentally, as he worked tirelessly to ensure that the first seminary of the Episcopal Church, General Theological Seminary, was placed in New York City and that he himself, as the Bishop of New York, would be its dean and thus choose its faculty, all of whom shared his high church vision. From 1822, when the seminary was moved permanently from New Haven, Connecticut, to New York City, students at General learned to share Hobart's vision of the church's polity and liturgy as a divine institution, and mission as helping to provide the benefits of this divine institution to newly settled communities. And while the high church vision thus expanded through its base in the wealthiest and most influential diocese of the church, the old low church mission was being transformed into something Bishop White could no longer recognize: the evangelical low church.

The Transformed Evangelical Church Mission

In 1795, a young man who had just graduated from Dartmouth College presented himself at the home of Reverend Ellison in Albany. A Congregationalist farm boy from New Hampshire, he had converted him-self to Episcopalianism after reading the Prayer Book in college, and asked Ellison to train him for the ministry. Philander Chase was soon deaconed by Bishop Provoost and began the first of a lifetime of peripatetic missionary journeys, this one over four thousand miles throughout the Adirondacks and western New York, establishing five congregations on the way. Chase also visited Daniel Nash, another Congregationalist convert from Connecticut. At that time Nash was still a deacon; Bishop Provoost had told him that missionary work in the upstate wilderness was a waste of time and effort, a hopeless project, and Nash was so insulted that he vowed he would never accept ordination to the priesthood from his hands. Nash established congregations deeper into western New York than Chase, and lived in a simple, frontier style in a log cabin he had built himself.[25] Both Nash and Chase were examples of the reinvigorated and transformed evangelical movement in the Episcopal Church.

The departure of the Methodists in 1784 from the Church of England, creating a completely separate new denomination and refusing to join with the new Episcopal Church in the United States, meant that the main reservoir of "enthusiastic" religion had separated itself from the Episcopal Church. But not all methodists, or those sympathetic to evangelical experience, went along with them. Those who remained retained the traditional focus of the Church of England on a formal liturgy and social order, but also incorporated sympathy with the emotive center of religious life and a theological commitment to the reality of the "conversion experience," a life-changing moment of spiritual despair turned to joy and assurance that was available to every person and was often associated with prayer meetings, extempore prayers, revivals, exciting preaching, and communal singing. Even a high churchman such as Bishop Hobart remembered his mother's emotionally evocative prayers throughout his life, and his own preaching and piety had a great deal more sentiment and emotional expressiveness than the pre-revolutionary Church of England would have accepted.[26]

Evangelical Episcopalians lived their faith through the liturgy and sacraments of the Book of Common Prayer, but also through more informal means that were sometimes controversial within the Episcopal Church: prayer meetings, small group Bible studies, singing hymns rather just the traditional metrical psalms, and emotional conversion experiences. Evangelicals valued and practiced powerful, emotional preaching that moved people to different levels of religious experience, and distrusted aspects of religious life that detracted from the power of the word to open hearts, including flowers and candles on the altar, elaborate vestments, and "altars" of stone rather than the traditional wooden communion table. Such things were thought to ride dangerously close to worldliness and "popery," or Roman Catholicism.

In addition to these evangelical Episcopalian inroads from the older Great Awakening of the eighteenth century, in the early nineteenth century came a Second Great Awakening, a new round of revivals and spiritual excitement in both Great Britain and the United States. Denominations on both sides of the Atlantic felt the revival call to mission: reforming the society around them and extending the faith among non-Christians in other parts of the world.

For Episcopalians, this new revival spirit transformed the older low church vision from a rational and restrained spirituality into an emotive and committed one, beginning with William Meade's consecration as assistant bishop of Virginia in 1829. Virginia generally moved toward an evangelical Episcopalianism as a result of Meade's devoted episcopacy, but evangelicals could be found everywhere. Pennsylvania became divided almost evenly between evangelical and high church adherents, leading to tension and conflict in the diocese. Even in New York City, the center of Hobart's high churchmanship, there were parishes and congregations known for their evangelical leanings and practices. Connecticut, home of Seabury, was largely high church, but all other New England states developed in the opposite direction.[27]

In 1811, Hobart shared his consecration with Alexander Viets Griswold, consecrated bishop for the Eastern Diocese. As a young priest in Connecticut, Griswold served multiple parishes in addition to farming and teaching to pay his own salary, and was called from farm and field to St. Michael's in Bristol, Rhode Island, where he helped organize the Eastern Diocese plan: all New England states except Connecticut combined into one enormous diocese due to the weakness of the church. The Second Great Awakening was enlivening throughout the New England states at this time, and it was as a bishop that Griswold became a more fervent evangelical, organizing prayer meetings and revivals and encouraging missionary efforts of all kinds among his clergy. Despite the fact that Griswold had to deal with a very different demographic situation than Hobart—the same settlers who were rushing to the earthly paradise of upstate New York were leaving lorn the fields and towns of New England, and there was no Trinity Church to fund his efforts— his thirty-year episcopate increased the numbers of functioning parishes in New England from twenty-four to one hundred, and after his death in 1843 all five New England states were stable enough to become separate dioceses with their own bishops.[28]

Meanwhile, the ever energetic Philander Chase had moved from New York to New Orleans in 1805, sent by Bishop Moore of New York in response to an interdenominational group of evangelical Protestants who wanted an Episcopalian minister. Chase established a parish and a school as well, and then returned to Connecticut, where he pastored Christ Church Hartford successfully for six years. That, apparently, was long enough to stay in one place, and Chase headed out for the new state of Ohio in 1817 with no congregational call, introduction from a bishop, or any means of support. Three months after arriving, he was offered work as principal of a newly founded school and spent his spare time running a farm, preaching, and organizing parishes in Zanesville and Columbus. Ohio held its first diocesan convention in 1818, with two clergymen and nine lay delegates, and chose Chase as their bishop.[29]

Chase's personality and energy, and his initial experiences with General Convention, which withheld consent for his consecration for several months, made him unwilling to wait for permission before engaging in new experiments, nor was he willing to apologize for his innovations after the fact. On the ground in Ohio, Chase became aware very quickly that eastern-trained clergy were rarely able to manage the very different context in the western territories, and that few of them were even willing to try. The potential clergy he might recruit in Ohio did not have the money to spend three years at General in New York City, nor did they have the necessary education to even attempt it. He came to the conclusion—quickly, as he reached all his conclusions—that the solution was a diocesan seminary that would raise up clergy from the local students, one that would offer the traditional subjects of a typical liberal university blended with divinity and that would support itself through farming. When he presented this idea to his fellow bishops at General Convention, White ignored it, and Hobart actively opposed it as a threat to General. Chase wrote in frustration:

> No missionaries make their appearance, nor are there even the most distant hopes of obtaining any from the East. . . . The few clergy we have may keep us alive, under Providence, a little longer; but when they die or move away, we have no means to supply their places. . . . Unless we can have some little means of educating our pious young men here, and here being secure of their affections, station them in our woods, and among our scattered people, to gather in and nourish our wandering lambs, we have no reason to hope for the continuance of the Church in the West.[30]

Chase decided he would make the most audacious move of all: he would travel to England, where he knew no one, and fundraise for his new school.

Hobart was furious—he went to England himself and attempted to forestall Chase's requests—but the English evangelicals were enthralled by Chase's vision of an evangelical school in the wilderness, blending their missional commitments to individual conversion and social reform through education. Chase raised a substantial sum of money and established Kenyon College and Bexley as the divinity school. A student who attended Kenyon from England, and who then spent ten years as a minister in Kentucky, described a bucolic life where the missional vision was truly being lived: students wandering through woods and finding cabins full of farmers, blacksmiths, and millers, all of whom were eager to read tracts, discuss the Bible, and attend services held in the open air.[31]

Chase's own self-directed personality became his downfall; he argued with his faculty in 1831, and when the board of trustees sided with them, he resigned both school and bishopric and retired briefly to Michigan, where, as usual, he preached, farmed, and taught school until his next meteoric shift, but his work in Ohio had set the tone for an evangelical diocese through the next generation.

Tensions between the evangelical and high church missional visions tended to be played out at General Convention and in debates and conflict about funding (as when Hobart attempted to block Chase's effort to raise funds for his western seminary). Believing that General Theological Seminary was too deeply in Hobart's pocket and too intensely connected with the high church vision, evangelicals founded Virginia Theological Seminary in 1823 to provide clergy who shared their emphasis on biblical preaching, emotional religiosity, and individual conversion to the Episcopal Church. Such conflicts would only increase in the next decades, as the Tractarian or Oxford Movement began to draw high churchmen even further from evangelical Episcopalianism and undermined the energy and practical effectiveness of both missional visions. Each faction became less and less able or willing to pool resources, plan together, or support innovative missional experiments.[32]

The Domestic and Foreign Missionary Society

In 1818, evangelical Bishop Griswold of the Eastern Diocese was the only American clergyman who responded to a circular letter from Josiah Pratt, the secretary of the Church Missionary Society (CMS) in England, describing to Pratt the missionary situation and efforts in the United States. Pratt offered two hundred pounds from the CMS to help support a missionary from a new American-based missionary society and asked Griswold to recommend candidates. This correspondence led to Griswold's efforts to organize a version of the CMS for the Episcopal Church, which General Convention authorized in 1820. Like the CMS, it would be a voluntary society, funded and guided by those who subscribed funds to support its work, though it would report to General Convention. The American version, Griswold told Pratt, would be called the Domestic and Foreign Missionary Society (DFMS).[33]

As a voluntary society, it required membership and subscriptions. For the next fifteen years, the DFMS struggled to obtain both, and struggled as well to plan and carry out missional projects. "The first step—and how many times since then has this first step been taken!—was to write a letter to the bishops" asking for funds and suggestions for fundraising. Hobart declared that any fundraising in New York would interfere with his own diocesan efforts; many, including Griswold, didn't respond at all. The request to send agents to dioceses for fundraising was generally seen as a distraction from diocesan needs and undermining diocesan autonomy. Philander Chase, on the other hand, rejected agents visiting dioceses as too timid an effort and recommended instead "personal application to every individual throughout the States," presumably meaning every Episcopalian. Chase was also, against his will, "confined" to the state of Ohio by the other bishops; he recommended that every state and territory without episcopal supervision immediately be provided with at least one missionary, a suggestion that may have influenced later schemes.[34]

Appeals to support the church among the white settler population in the western territories were driven by the reality of denominational competition, which the Episcopal Church, year after year, was clearly losing. According to the 1826 Board of Missions Report, "Much of this destitute land remains to be possessed [by Christianity]. . . . Other denominations are even now taking the field; let it not be our reproach that we are always too late."[35] This reproach was easily made. From its founding, reports of the Mission Society to General Convention had been received with some dismay at the paltriness of what had been accomplished. The lack of personnel was severe, as was the lack of money.

The DFMS's first foreign missionary interest was West Africa, in a very specific sense: it was intended that free Black Americans should emigrate there (along with supervising white clergy) and Christianize the African natives. This scheme was the project of the American Colonization Society, but it was also the Episcopal Church's earliest foreign mission field. Bishop Griswold's first identified missionary prospect, Joseph Andrus, ended up going to West Africa in 1821 under the authority of the Colonization Society rather than the Episcopal Church; he was met and supported there by the CMS and provided with African Christian guides and interpreters, but died before the next spring.[36] Beyond consistent interest in colonization and West Africa, the early foreign missions were haphazard and undirected except by particular individuals who were moved to fundraise for their own projects, bringing Episcopalians to Greece to found schools and in a strange and futile one-man mission to the Ottoman Empire.

In the domestic field, missions to Native Americans were restricted to the Oneida, an Iroquois tribe that had fought on the side of the patriots in the Revolutionary War and were not forced to flee to Canada. It did not take long, however, for them to be dispossessed by the white settlers in upstate New York, and a group relocated to Green Bay, Wisconsin. The Diocese of New York supported the mission and continued to do so when the Oneida went to Wisconsin, sending Eleazar Williams, a Canadian Mohawk, to serve them. Williams may have been the first Native American ordained as a deacon, in 1826, but he later claimed to be the Lost Dauphin and a pretender to the throne of France, leaving his work as a missionary far behind.

After Williams's departure, a white missionary, Richard Cadle, was sent to run the school for the mission in Duck Creek. Cadle brought his daughter along as a teacher, the first single woman supported as a missionary by the Board of Missions. The school served Native children from different nations, including the Oneida, Menominee, Chippewa, and Sac. At least five had been baptized by 1834, receiving "Christian" names, as reported to the Board of Missions. In 1832, the Green Bay mission received the first recorded "mission boxes"—donations of clothing and other materials to the mission, which became a typical way in which women supported mission work.[37]

In 1834, the DFMS Board of Missions sent Jackson Kemper, along with Joseph Milnor, a leading evangelical, to investigate public controversies arising from abusive and unauthorized punishment of several children by the supervisor of the dormitory at Cadle's mission and school. Several Native American children had been whipped severely, their hair had been cut, and then they were whipped again.[38] The pattern fit some of the worst realities of Christian mission and American government work among Native Americans for the next century: boarding schools where cultural assimilation and school rules were violently enforced, abuse of children, and a low standard of living that led to sickness and death. In 1834, it was agreed by all that the punishment was improper, and the employees responsible were fired, but the controversy continued to roil the community.

Kemper's journal demonstrated that he gave great thought to the problems Cadle experienced in the mission field, and what that indicated about how mission was being accomplished (or not). The poverty of the children led to unhealthiness, Kemper noted, as they survived almost completely on salt pork, and since "the cry from Phil[delphi]a [the headquarters of the Board of Missions] was always economy," the mission and its school and dormitories were "scarcely comfortable." In fact the mission could not make economical choices, buy in bulk, or plan ahead for its needs when its financial support was so unpredictable and grudging. Cadle himself would have preferred to simply go live with the "Indians," but he had had to deal with a plan for a school that had been settled before his arrival by the Executive Committee of the Board; in addition, it appeared that Cadle was too "honorable" to deal well with "crafty men" and was often cheated in his efforts to procure needed supplies. Cadle had already resigned from the mission before Kemper and Milnor arrived, frustrated that he was publicly blamed for the abuse which he himself condemned. In Kemper's view, he had overreacted and made a bad thing worse. Cadle, Kemper thought, was overly emotionally sensitive for his position; he did not have the practical, hard-headed common sense that was necessary to adapt a plan to the realities on the ground and learn to live and manage finances in a new way; he was also exhausted and overworked, worn out by the cares of living up to a plan made hundreds of miles away, in a different context, and unprovided with the funding that was necessary to make the plan a reality.[39] Kemper would bring to his next role the lessons learned in how not to run a mission.

In 1835, a committee of bishops and laypeople brought a new and radical proposal to General Convention. The committee had included both leading evangelicals—Bishop Charles McIlvaine, Chase's successor in Ohio, and Milnor, New York's most prominent evangelical rector—and high churchmen, such as Bishop George Washington Doane of New Jersey and Kemper, who had moved from Philadelphia to Connecticut. Yet, according to the story they all told after the fact, every one of them came to the table with the same proposal: to make the DFMS not voluntary but all-encompassing, identical with the church as a whole. Every Episcopalian, by virtue of their baptism, was a missionary, and the mission belonged to every one of them, and every one of them was responsible for it. And in order to ensure that the church in its wholeness would be present in every territory and area of mission, the Episcopal Church would create a completely new sort of clergyman: the missionary bishop, to be sent out into the world without diocese or clergy or congregations, but to organize and ordain whatever God provided.[40]

General Convention was electrified by this eloquent vision, elaborated upon by Doane and McIlvaine, seemingly joining together the two fractious missional visions into one churchwide commitment to missions. As a missional theological statement, the reorganization of the DFMS was revolutionary, far ahead of its time. Voluntary societies were the norm in all other Protestant denominations, and it would not be until the mid-twentieth century that this missional shift occurred at a global level in Protestant Christianity. As a practical matter, it left something to be desired. Funding was centralized but still essentially voluntary: while the Board could ask for money from General Convention or dioceses, there was no guarantee it would get it. The DFMS took up the SPG model of requiring some local support before sending a missionary, which would clearly make it difficult to extend the church beyond an already Christian and already committed audience.

Over the next decades, efforts to raise interest and committed personnel through the *Spirit of Missions* periodical, visits of agents and secretaries to dioceses, missionary pleas directly to congregations, and missionary bishops' preaching in seminaries constantly fell short—dramatically short—of what was needed. Such efforts did not address the bottleneck of clergy educational requirements and did not take full advantage of the commitment and gifts of laypeople. They also did not truly join together the two missional visions of evangelical and high church Episcopalianism. Accidentally at first, or perhaps planned in an informal conversation in committee, the two missional visions were given separate spheres. The high church would be responsible for domestic missions, while the evangelicals were given the foreign field. As tensions heightened during the 1840s over Tractarianism and the rising Anglo-Catholic movement, the two committees were less and less able to work fruitfully together and would often compete for funds or even deliberately undermine one another's fundraising efforts.[41]

The Missionary Bishop

Bishop Hobart's missional view was quite different from that of Bishops Chase, Meade, and Griswold's. Yet they were all a new kind of bishop, one that actively guided and goaded clergy to missional activity, and who regularly visited congregations in person throughout an enormous geographical area. In this active visitation and preaching, using the opportunities and novelty brought by the episcopacy and sacrament of confirmation to draw in new participants and give energy to scattered congregations, they provided a model and organizing principle for future missionary work both in the Episcopal Church and in the Church of England.[42]

That it was an innovation, and an exciting one, is clear. Bishop Doane's purple-prose description of the first election of the new missionary bishops in 1835 leaves nothing to the imagination: "Two overshepherds were to be sent out, the messengers of the Church, to gather and to feed, under the direction of the House of Bishops, the scattered sheep that wander, with no man to care for their souls, through all the wide and distant West. It was an act, in this Church, never exercised before. And yet, upon its due discharge, interests depended which outweigh the world, and will run out into eternity."[43] Francis Hawks, however, declined the election, leaving the Southwest without a missionary bishop until the next General Convention in 1838. Kemper accepted, and was consecrated as the first missionary bishop of the Episcopal Church, bishop to the territories that are now Indiana and Wisconsin and that would later include Minnesota and Iowa.[44]

Kemper, a widower, left his children in the care of relatives and embarked on eleven years of travel in which he was effectively homeless, visiting cities, towns, and isolated cabins in all weather via barely existing roads, staying wherever he was offered or could rent a bed or a floor and eating whatever his hosts provided. Kemper's companions, and his own letters, describe his sleeping in one-room cabins on the floor where snow drifted in, traveling through bitter winter weather and swarms of mosquitoes day after day. According to one companion, the food was often "chicken fixins" or fried chicken, considered uncouth food of the poor in the East but probably a special treat to honor the visitor in a western cabin. Kemper would take the least popular pieces, refusing to ask for a particular part of the bird. After watching him take the leftovers day after day, one clergy friend finally burst out, "Give the Bishop a little breast, for the love of God! It's been nothing but legs, legs, legs for days!"[45]

Kemper's job was to organize parishes and dioceses, consecrate churches, and identify and support missionary clergy. All of this was extraordinarily difficult, and it all depended upon finding pockets of Episcopalians in the burgeoning cities, little towns, and isolated hamlets throughout the West. He needed to compete with other denominations; he and others described the competition from Methodists, who were "everywhere, seeking all," and the "Romanists," who in a town in Iowa were proselytizing young people and offering a nearly free education at a local college which they had somehow wrested from the "Protestants of this place."[46]

His work also depended upon wringing donations from the eastern church, which were slow in coming. Compared to missionaries of other Protestant denominations, he struggled mightily to interest the Episcopalian congregations and dioceses in supporting him. Missionaries and their families suffered from poverty, leading to high turnover and discouragement. In 1845–46, a particularly hard winter left missionaries begging one another for potatoes or clothing; donations from the East became smaller rather than larger, as people believed that the churches should be self-supporting by this time. Congregations in the West, for their part, promised what they could not deliver financially in order to attract a clergyperson—or refused to deliver it, according to Bishop Chase, when they felt that the preaching wasn't good enough or the clergyman fell short of their hopes in some other way.[47]

The sheer fact of social mobility in the western regions militated against Episcopalian expansion in another way: clergy who were in the area tended to move as much as other people did in the West, which was quite often. This led to frequent turnover of clergy in a mission territory. Since the creation of new dioceses and calling of a bishop required a year of residence by a certain number of clergy—not just living in the area, nor being in a missionary capacity, but being a permanently installed minister of a parish—new dioceses might struggle to call a bishop year after year as clergy moved in and out of the territory, and in some years could meet the canonical number of clergy and in other years not. The canons of General Convention were based in a vision of stability in terms of clergy and parishioners which simply didn't exist in this period in many western areas.[48]

In addition, the actual apostolic itinerancy of the missionary bishop, though viewed with pride by the church as a whole, was not very attractive to the vast majority of eastern clergy. A truly itinerant clergy had never been acceptable, even in the colonial era, and though the sharing of a clergyperson by multiple congregations had been common in colonial Virginia, it was seen as an undesirable, improper, and temporary situation in the nineteenth-century Episcopal Church. The educational process and expectations for clergy success in the East would tend to attract and produce individuals who valued and desired ministry in a settled community with settled norms for the religious leader, not a creative, improvisatory itinerancy in a large, dispersed, and pluralistic context. No fewer than four individuals declined Indiana's election as bishop year after year in the 1840s; they had comfortable lives in the settled East which they were not inclined to leave. When a bishop finally agreed to be consecrated for Indiana in 1849, he traveled to Indiana for visitations only in the first years of his episcopacy, much to the consternation of his new diocese. His first goal was to build a cathedral.[49]

Given these challenges, it is not surprising that when Kemper traveled back east to speak to seminarians there about the need for missionaries, he suggested that the men who volunteered be not only doctrinally sound and zealous for the faith but also physically strong, willing to endure hardship in humility, and specifically that they be unmarried. This vision excited a group of seminarians at General, who had been inspired by their high church–style church history course to imagine themselves as monastic missionaries in the mold of the primitive church. The seminarians decided that they would travel west to help Kemper, living together in a celibate community. At least two of the little group were forbidden to go west by their bishops, and another was told by his bishop—also a high churchman—that though he would permit the student to go, the idea was dangerous and ridiculous, and his ministry was more needed in the diocese he came from, not the missions of the West. Nonetheless four of them traveled to Wisconsin in 1841 to live out their experiment in what would become Nashotah House, a high church school and seminary and the beginning of contacts of the Episcopal Church with the Plains native cultures.[50]

Limits of the Great Innovation

The missionary bishop—the bishop as an authoritative missionary sent to cover thousands of square miles of territory—was an extraordinary innovation. It worked, as far as it did, because of the important and respected role of bishops in the Episcopal Church. By creating a bishop for a missionary territory, the church ensured that the missionary territory at once had a voice and a respected representative at the highest levels of church governance, who could bring the needs of that territory to the General Convention for funds and support (though both might be slow in coming). It ensured that the interests of mission would be woven into the life of the church as a whole at its center, rather than as an auxiliary, extra interest. The union of church and mission in the 1835 reorganization of the DFMS solved the problem of bringing missionary territories or "younger churches" into relationship with the church as a whole, which was a stumbling block for many missions in foreign contexts. The mission territory was not relegated to an extra room at General Convention or told to leave its context at the door while the church did important things; it was present in the House of Bishops every three years.

The challenge remained that funds and personnel were at a life-support level, and thus the church missed many opportunities where people would have welcomed a missionary. The story of the expansion into the West and missions among Native Americans has a single constant refrain: the need for men (specifically and always men, since women could not be ordained at this time and the Episcopal Church expected religious leaders to be ordained clergy). The church rejected or undermined potential innovations that could have addressed the need, such as alternative educational paths for clergy, greater reliance upon and respect for lay leaders (as was common in mission work by other denominations and especially in foreign missions, and as had been the practice of the Church of England in the early years of colonization), and a program for itineracy as a valid career path rather than as a disappointing short-term fix. The new organization of the DFMS worked better than what had come before because it did recognize a specific kind of itineracy (for the bishop) and the bishop engaged in public relations far beyond eastern clergy, preaching in public places and private houses as well as publicizing his visits to new communities.[51]

The most effective missionaries embraced itineracy and frontier life, including Kemper and later James Lloyd Breck, one of the seminarians who founded Nashotah and who later moved to Minnesota and California. Chase also clearly had a yen for itineracy, moving frequently and from his earliest life visiting frontier areas and coming to the church as an adult himself; he took his own way and thus offended large numbers of more traditional Episcopalians. Kemper let settled dioceses go to other bishops and at least twice declined an election to diocesan bishop when offered, differing from Leonidas Polk, elected as the missionary bishop of the Southwest when Hawks refused, who settled down as Bishop of Louisiana after three years of a missionary episcopacy. Not until his old age did Kemper accept a diocesan bishopric in Wisconsin, but even then the diocese was huge and still required a great deal of effort for visitations, which Kemper gladly provided.

The church's most impressive expansion, in upstate New York, depended upon what is now called "demographic opportunity" in modern studies and theories of church growth. New people were beginning to create and populate new communities, and they wanted a church as a benefit for their communities and families. They were willing to invest in having one and would respond to a clergyperson who offered to serve them. Nonetheless, even in upstate New York, early post-revolutionary efforts to create churches in rural contexts—simple churches that depended upon itinerant or part-time clergy and the leadership of laypeople—had actually become weaker by midcentury than they were earlier. The same pattern developed in Pennsylvania: the church grew and thrived in an urban setting, but struggled for financial sustainability, lack of clergy, and local relevance in rural areas. The church more and more became an urban phenomenon.[52]

All this weakened the ability of the church to expand beyond its existing boundaries. Yet other denominations sometimes had even worse conditions for their missionaries and nonetheless were able to put more workers into the field' as one scholar noted, in the 1840s the Episcopal Church had a total of 152 clergy in all the territory beyond the Allegheny Mountains, while the Baptists had 150 in Missouri alone.[53] The inability to pay missionaries, severe and crippling as it was, was less of a problem than being able to attract and develop leaders who were willing and able to innovate for their local contexts and were supported in doing so. The Episcopal Church's expansion was also limited by its unwillingness to adapt its liturgical practices, to make it easier to organize new dioceses and provide new bishops, to change the educational requirements for clergy, and to encourage lay leadership, and by its continued and growing infighting and competition between representatives of the two dominant missional strands of the church. All of these limitations were recognized by those concerned with mission practice even at the time and yet were unable to be addressed in the authority structure of the church. The growth strategy of the church, in practice, focused only on providing churches for existing Episcopalians who said they wanted one, and even at this the church fell short.[54]

5

Slavery and Antislavery

In 1836, Isaac DeGrasse had just begun his studies at General Theological Seminary, a candidate for orders in the Diocese of New York. He was surprised to be called in to a private conversation with his bishop, who required him to leave the seminary permanently, with the offer to attend classes without officially enrolling, receiving a degree, living in the dormitory, or fraternizing with other students. DeGrasse wrote in his diary, "Never, never will I do so!" The bishop's concern, as he told DeGrasse, was that, should it become known that a free man of color was attending the seminary, it would "bring the Institution into disrepute," cause southern benefactors to withdraw their funding and students, and drive the other students to "abandon the School of the Prophets." DeGrasse obeyed his request to leave the seminary and study privately, although he refused to attend seminary classes on the humiliating terms offered. He could hardly do other than obey the bishop if he hoped to be ordained, but in his journal he wrote:

> Upon reflection, it is my present opinion that Bishop Onderdonk is wrong in yielding to the "unrighteous prejudice" (his words) of the community. If the prejudice be wrong, I think he ought to oppose it without regard to consequences. If such men as he countenance it, they become partakers with the oppressors. He says, by and by Providence will open the way; but will Providence effect the change miraculously? We cannot expect it. He will, however, effect by appointed means, and these means ought to be resorted to by his instruments—men. And what men more suitable than men high in office, high in public favor, high in talents? Particularly should men commissioned to preach the Gospel, which teaches mercy, righteousness, and truth, enter upon the work.[1]

The Episcopal Church did not divide over slavery, as other denominations did, but it was nonetheless rent by the tensions around enslavement and

Mission, Race, and Empire. Jennifer C. Snow, Oxford University Press. © Oxford University Press 2024.
DOI: 10.1093/oso/9780197598948.003.0006

racism that structured and divided all of U.S. society. The American Colonization Society, an organization dedicated to ending slavery by sending free Black people to Africa, was a favorite charity of many leading Episcopalians and a prominent focus of the foreign missions committee from its beginning. The particular missional vision of the high church pushed against any involvement in or discussion of "political" issues, while the evangelical Episcopalians were split between indifferent or antislavery northerners and proslavery southerners. The African American Episcopalian community in the North and South struggled against racism, discrimination, and the realities of slavery, exemplified in the enforced religious participation of enslaved people in southern churches and the segregation of free Black congregations from diocesan conventions in the northern states. Some nineteenth-century Black Episcopalians supported voluntary emigration of African Americans to Haiti and Liberia, while others in the United States fought, with white allies, to be fully included in the church's governance and permitted to sit in diocesan conventions. The simple conclusion of a seminary student that it is the duty of human beings to oppose what is wrong, and that the leaders of the church should be foremost in doing so, was not in any way obvious to much of the white Episcopal Church prior to the Civil War.

Enslaved African Americans in the Southern Episcopal Church

In the "slave states" of the southern United States, the lives of African Americans were defined by the realities of slavery and the anxieties of the white owners. Often state-level laws made it illegal to teach African Americans to read and required freed slaves to leave the state permanently, as it was thought that a free Black community was a bad example for enslaved people.

Generally, the enslaved African American community was seen as a "mission field" for the Episcopal Church, among whose members were many of the largest plantation and slave-owning families of the South. Southern bishops made a priority of encouraging the Episcopalian slave owners to educate and provide religious opportunities for enslaved people. Bishop Stephen Elliott of Georgia made missions among enslaved people the focus of his first address to diocesan convention in 1847, calling for "missionaries" who would "settle in the midst of them and make himself comprehended among them and minister at their sickbeds, and be with them in their moments of temptation and affliction, and prove himself their friend and teacher, and very soon they will welcome him to their hearts with the same true affection with which they now cling to those who labor among them." Elliott requested planters to employ such missionaries directly on their plantations "so that masters and servants may worship together in unity of spirit and in the bond of peace. It would tend very much to strengthen the relation of masters and slaves. . . . There should be much less danger of inhumanity on one side, or of insubordination on the other, between parties who knelt upon the Lord's Day around the same table, and were partakers of the same Communion."[2] Bishop William Meade of Virginia continually stressed how important this was both for his clergy and for their white parishioners; in his address to the Virginia Diocesan Convention in 1842, he described "a class of the poor of this world abounding in [our] parishes":

> Just in proportion as the ministers of religion shall feel deeply and labor zealously in this cause, will the masters and mistresses be influenced to do the same. . . . It should encourage us to action in this cause, to think that a small congregation becomes quite large when considered as comprehending this class of our fellow-beings. Nor would our ministers be less benefited than their hearers; for in seeking to bless the poor, themselves will be blessed of the poor man's friend. Moreover, a better school there cannot be for learning how to practise that foolishness of preaching by which God is pleased to save men; and he who does not know how to preach the Gospel to the poor, does not know how to preach as Christ and the Apostles preached.[3]

It was indeed the case that small congregations became large; in many of the southern parishes reporting to diocesan conventions, the "servants" or "colored people" were significant numbers of communicants or baptized individuals. Trinity Parish in Newport, Maryland, reported twenty-six baptisms of enslaved or free Black people in 1824 and only one white baptism, and the African American worshipers had "great devotion and regular attendance on Divine worship."[4] Bishop Leonidas Polk, in his brief tenure as missionary bishop of the Southwest, described enslaved people as among the "devout recipients" in Alabama.[5]

For these African American church members, the church entrenched practices of segregation in its worship, education, and sacraments. African Americans were generally required to sit separately from the white worshipers, or to worship at separate times; if they received communion, they would do so after the white communicants were done; their catechizing was separated from whites' due to the restriction on teaching literacy to enslaved people in many southern states; and their masters could refuse to permit them to be married or baptize their children. Certainly there would be no chance of an enslaved person rising to leadership in ministry. Bishop Elliott of Georgia suggested the possibility of creating a permanent diaconate for missionaries among enslaved people; in this scheme, the educational requirements of the Episcopalian minister would be removed in favor of the natural ability of an evangelist. The suggestion was never passed in General Convention.[6]

The Episcopalian clergy themselves were often slave owners and shared the general reticence to permit the full range of church membership and sacramental life to enslaved people, most obvious surrounding issues of marriage and sexuality. Slaves were castigated as being sexually immoral and promiscuous, despite the obvious fact that enslaved people did not have full control over their own sexuality and how it was abused by masters, or whether they would be able to choose a partner of their own. Catechisms designed for enslaved people demanded a high sexual standard of marriage and monogamy, and those who did not live up to those standards would, according to the rubrics of the church, be forbidden to take communion. Yet keeping the marriage vows was not always within an enslaved person's power due to rape and the separation of families. Even the rector of a church in North Carolina, whose commitment to marriage in general must be assumed to have been fairly significant, engaged in cat-stepping around the fundamental issue: when his slave wanted to marry a slave belonging to someone else, the rector worried that when he moved away the marriage would be at risk. He was reluctant to permit the marriage until his father-in-law offered to buy the other slave for him, so the two enslaved people could be together under the rector's mastership. This peculiar sort of "happy ending" does not at all challenge the central issue: that people who were enslaved did not have the possibility of living the ideal Christian life which the rector himself preached, and that all of their relationships of faith, love, and family were constantly at risk and threatened by the institution of slavery.[7]

The constant exhortations and pleas for energy and attention to enslaved people from southern bishops, decade after decade, indicated that many Episcopalian masters were not very excited about providing religious education for slaves. Reverend James W. C. Pennington, an escaped slave and abolitionist, wrote that his master, an Episcopalian, never brought him to church or provided any religious education for his slaves, which seems to have been a general pattern despite the fact that most of the slave owners in that part of Maryland were Episcopalians.[8] In 1839, a group of "gentlemen" from Alabama requested a missionary from the Domestic Committee, claiming, "He can have a respectable congregation of white persons and any number of blacks."[9] Much like the method of expansion in the western territories, this demonstrates not only the assumption that "blacks" would attend the church in large numbers since their white masters would bring them if the missionary wanted them to, but also the typical Episcopalian strategy of gathering a set of committed members before calling a missionary.

For the clergyman called to a plantation church, however, and who genuinely wished to fulfill the responsibility of religious education for enslaved people, creative strategies would be needed far beyond the usual rather passive Episcopalian missionary methods. The journal of the Domestic and Foreign Missionary Society, *The Spirit of Missions*, recorded many examples of clergy attempting to provide religious education to enslaved people in quite creative ways. In the 1850s, the magazine reported an example of self-sacrificial support for foreign missions, with "the plantation Negroes on the Ogeechee River bringing their eggs and corn as a response to an appeal from China."[10] One enthusiastic article in 1844 described a clergyman giving up on the traditional catechism at the audience's lack of interest, and simply sitting down to tell the story of the Bible in short pieces, like an exciting serial, in his own words, and allowing the audience to make comments and questions upon it. He reported that the enslaved audience was excited and engaged and returned week after week to learn what happened next and to apply it to their own lives. The missionary noted, "The very fact that they had something to say, and were permitted to have their part in the services, called forth their attention. . . . I soon saw new faces in the church, and my congregation shortly but steadily increased. In my morning walks I could hear them trying to recall to mind the leading truths in some history they had heard." Supported by the "master and mistress," he also began to teach the enslaved people how to participate fully in the liturgy by learning the responses, the

Creed, and the Lord's Prayer, all from memory.[11] The editor of the magazine, however, did not focus on the important innovation: the informal, dialogical sermon and intent to welcome and support the participation and ideas of the enslaved audience. Instead, the experiment proved the appropriateness of the liturgy for the religious lives of enslaved people, as opposed to the emotional exuberance of Methodists.

In Waccamaw Parish in South Carolina, 90% of the population by 1810 was enslaved people on rice plantations. Reverend Alexander Glennie visited the plantations regularly and was strongly supported by the planters, including one of the largest slave owners in the South, one of the wardens of All Saints' Pawley's Island. In 1855, Glennie held 212 services for the enslaved people on the plantations and 65 for the white people; in 1858, he had 46 white members of the church, and 236 "negro" members, with almost 700 enslaved children "catechized under his direction," meaning by the slave-owning families between his visits. The geography of the plantation South meant that much of the catechetical work of enslaved people was part of the "home devotions" of white women: they would teach enslaved children as part of their responsibilities as mistress. One white woman described her mother's work with the children on their plantation in South Carolina before the Civil War: "It was always spoken of as 'Kate Kism' and was the event of the week for the children. Their best clothes, their cleanest faces greeted Mrs Allston on her arrival at the church. After the lesson, a big cake was brought in a wheel barrow by one of the house boys. . . . Each child went to the barrow and dropping a curtsey, received a slice, then passing the mistress with another curtsey, filed out." The reward of cake and requirement of curtseys point to the general white Episcopalian sense of racial paternalism and use of proper religious indoctrination as part of a hierarchical, orderly society. The charming memory of the author's mother's work elides the horrors of enslavement that every child every day endured—and the direct involvement of the mistress of the house in using Christian education as part of the system of control.[12]

Literacy in catechizing was a source of anxiety, tied to the fear of rebellions. White catechists would sometimes take care to ensure that the book they were reading would never be touched by the hands of enslaved people, lest they feel themselves entitled to its dangerous literacy.[13] Reverend Napoleon Scriven, a missionary on a plantation on the Wateree River in South Carolina, wrote in 1836, "Our experience convinces us that they can be rescued from their moral degradation, and their usefulness enhanced by the power of Religion.

To impress them with proper principles, it is not necessary to put books into their hands, and certainly none to put false notions in their heads."[14]

Slave catechisms would often include teaching the enslaved people that slavery was a benefit to them. These catechisms were adapted from traditional white catechisms not only in form—requiring oral or visual teaching, since it was forbidden to teach slaves to read—but in content. Bishop Meade's own interest in the duty of Christian mastery led to the publication of three collections of sermons for enslaved people; Bishop Christopher Gadsden of South Carolina and Bishop Levi Silliman Ives of North Carolina both produced slave catechisms intended to be used purely orally and preached the importance of obedience to masters, explained as an aspect of the fifth Commandment to honor parents. The emphasis on obedience was thus tied rhetorically to the racial paternalistic understanding that African people, enslaved or free, were eternally "children," needing the strong hand of white "parents."[15]

The strong hand of white guidance was supported by intimations of divine retribution for Black disobedience. A North Carolina slave who earned his freedom, Lunsford Lane, wrote in 1842 that the content of sermons to slaves was generally only about submission and obedience. Lane hinted that this was an idolatrous subversion of the true gospel: "The first commandment impressed upon our minds was to obey our masters, and the second was like unto it, namely, to do as much work when they or the overseers were not watching us as when they were." Lane noted that while he had at one time been drawn to the Episcopal Church, he chose another variety of Christianity when told that it was God's will for him to be a slave for all eternity.[16]

The idea that slavery was a morally unacceptable system of human relationships, and certainly an un-Christian one, was rejected wholesale by southern Episcopalians. Even those who felt that slavery was not the best way to organize society did not believe that slavery itself was sinful—an idea that grew among northern abolitionists in the mid-nineteenth century but was violently rejected by southerners. Bishop Meade of Virginia became more conservative, rather than more critical of slavery, as he grew older. As a young person he had emancipated the enslaved people he had inherited and believed that the church had a responsibility for care and attention to the "servants," but he did not believe that slaveholding itself was morally wrong, nor did he publicly criticize the institution. In his old age, he came to believe that because there was so little welcome for free Black people in the United States, emancipation might do more harm than good; he supported the American Colonization Society as a move toward gradual abolition and the deportation of African Americans as the best solution. Despite his strong racial paternalism, even Bishop Meade's mild requests to treat enslaved people with kindness and recognize their humanity were challenged as too radical by some Episcopalians. Bishop Leonidas Polk of Louisiana, a major slaveholder in his own right, argued that Meade's emphasis on what enslaved people were entitled to from white Christians would lead to enslaved people's insubordination, perhaps even to rebellion.[17]

For those whites who aspired to a more Christian form of mastery, slavery was conceptualized as a beneficial, harmonious system where everyone was cared for and happy in their proper place doing their proper work. Religious instruction was crucial in this: this beneficial system was strongest where slaves were taught the divine sanction for their station by their kind masters. Believing in this beneficial Christian slavery required a huge amount of deliberate blindness about the reality. In 1846, Bishop Ives of North Carolina imagined that, could critics see the happy slaves on the plantations attending Easter services, they would understand that their intimations of suffering, abused slaves were completely false. William Jay, a northern abolitionist Episcopalian, directly challenged Ives: "You well know, sir, that in the choice of their church and creed the slaves are passive . . . and that, had the communicants been sent to auction on Easter Monday, they would each thenceforth have worshipped in the place and manner directed by the 'highest bidder.'"[18]

Free Black Episcopal Churches in the North

For free Black people in the North, life was infinitely better than enslavement, but still filled with obstacles to peace and prosperity. Most African Americans lived in cities, and the cities of the United States began to expand rapidly through immigration, mostly from Europe. The African American urban community became smaller and smaller as a proportion of the population and yet remained highly visible, and a frequent target of violence. Black people were discriminated against in education, attending separate schools from white children and denied access to higher education; in employment, where they were denied licenses to carry on certain businesses; and in terms of civil rights were either not permitted to vote at all or only after paying a tax or proving they owned property at levels far above white people.

While African Americans lived throughout the city, more and more as they occupied the lowest rungs of the economic ladder they lived in unhealthy and poorly kept housing. Urban African Americans who became relatively prosperous as doctors, lawyers, restaurateurs, grocers, and ministers did so at least partly because they learned to work around the many obstacles in their way, including strategically finding white allies and building relationships with other Black people to support their efforts to wend their way through the maze of racial discrimination that made up their world. They dreamed of and worked for a world where this would no longer be necessary, and for this, too, they needed to find allies. In the Episcopal Church, the African American communities found both apathy and enmity, but also occasional allies who helped individuals and churches to respond to and live through racism.

Free Black people were well aware, indeed constantly aware, of slavery as a reality that surrounded their communities, even when it was illegal in their location. Sheltering escaping slaves, supporting civil lawsuits over freedom for enslaved people brought to the free states by masters, observing the slave trade and southern commodity investment in free states, remembering the parent born in slavery or one's own experience of it—all of this was part of the world of free Blacks. As the antislavery movement became stronger and more political, African Americans supported it, organized around it, and celebrated every move toward slavery's ending. While the African American community was internally diverse in economic and educational status, for its urban leaders it was a political community in the largest sense of that word: constantly organizing, seeking solutions that would aid those in need, strategically making alliances and building relationships, envisioning necessary defenses and the steps needed to obtain a better life for all its members.[19]

At the same time, the precarious safety of the free Black community meant that those who were enslaved were not always welcomed by free Black people. This was true in the only African American Episcopal congregation founded in the South before the Civil War, St. James Baltimore, established by the "first great missionary hero of the Black race," William Leavington. Leavington was born in New York around 1795, moved to Philadelphia, and was ordained there in 1824, with the courageous intention of going into Baltimore—a city in a state that had not abolished slavery, and would not until after the Civil War—to begin a school and church, partially supported by Philadelphia donors, for Baltimore's Black residents. Divine worship and Sunday school began immediately, and the church was built in 1827. Some of the free Black community wished to exclude the enslaved Blacks from full participation in the church, but Leavington refused to make this distinction. He wrote:

> Can a wise man with a feeling heart, suppose we, some of whom have felt the yoke of bondage, should draw a line of separation? No, let the day be darkened forever on which we should do it[.] Have we not all one Father? Hath not one God created us? Why should we deal treacherously every man against his brother? The Church is none other than the House of God, and this is the gate of Heaven. We charitably ask the Christian public, shall we be partial in the house of God, and at the gate of Heaven become judges of evil thoughts? No, we will remember them that are in bonds as bound with them ourselves.[20]

The pattern of free African Americans expressing anxiety about association with enslaved people, and wealthier African Americans about association with poorer ones, nonetheless left an ongoing tension in the Episcopalian Black community. Some African American Episcopalian leaders continued the strategy laid by Absalom Jones, emphasizing the ability of Black people to live "orderly" lives, attempting to demonstrate to the white community their worth and value in the world, and admonishing those African Americans who didn't live up to the standards to do so. The congregation of St. Philip's in New York City, the second Black Episcopal congregation founded in the United States in 1809–19, at all times demonstrated to visiting white clergy and bishops orderly decorum and proper Prayer Book worship (which such observers always noted as if it were a surprise).[21]

The rector of St. Philip's, Peter Williams Jr., expanded this strategy into education, setting up schools (often short-lived, due to financial constraints) and social organizations, creating groups that addressed every need of the community, from cultural debate to help for the indigent and orphaned, identifying particularly gifted young people and arranging support for their education from wealthy abolitionists. The end hope of all of these strategies was not merely the success of the individuals who were helped but the demonstration of the worth and ability of all African Americans.[22] For Black Episcopalians, claiming the spiritual and social equality of Black people through a variety of strategies was fundamental to the mission of the church.

Reverend Williams was also on the Board of the Anti-Slavery Society, an abolitionist group, in 1834, when anti-abolitionist riots ripped through

New York City's Black neighborhoods. Along with the homes of wealthy white abolitionists such as Arthur Tappan, Williams's home was attacked, and St. Philip's was completely destroyed by the mob. Afterward, Williams received a letter from his bishop, Hobart's high church successor Benjamin Onderdonk, which instructed him to resign from the board of the Anti-Slavery Society—not, as Williams noted afterward, because Onderdonk himself supported slavery (although he may well have) but because the church needed to stay away from politics. And, as Williams also noted, he himself, while obeying his bishop according to his ordination vows, and resigning from the Board, continued to be an active member of the Anti-Slavery Society and was a delegate to two of its conventions.[23]

Despite this attack on his church and the humiliating obedience to his bishop, Williams continued with his multiple missional strategies: maintaining good relationships with the bishop, the only way in which his church was connected with the diocese as they were not permitted to attend diocesan convention, and developing educational opportunities for Black youth. One of his projects was to help young Black men become ordained as Episcopalian clergy to serve the community, and in 1836 his first protégé, Isaac DeGrasse, was accepted as a candidate for ordination and into General Theological Seminary. Despite his humiliation at Onderdonk's directing him to leave the seminary due to his racial identity, DeGrasse pursued private studies and was ordained in 1838.

The second student of Reverend Williams who attempted ordination in the Episcopal Church was Alexander Crummell. He characteristically came to the situation ready for a battle. Williams chose Crummell for special educational support particularly because he hoped Crummell would demonstrate a "pure African" capability to whites. Crummell's father had been captured in West Africa and enslaved around the age of thirteen; he simply left his master after about ten years, daring him to try to get him back. Boston Crummell and his freeborn wife were abolitionists and community organizers, and their son Alexander spent his youth helping to support the cause.

In his autobiography, Crummell wrote that he was inspired by Williams, despite what he considered Williams's timidity in submission to the bishop: Williams, he said, "charged me never to allow myself to be abused and insulted, as he [had] suffered himself to be. . . . [T]hose in the ministry, should stand erect in their position as men and not allow themselves to be cowed by any power or authority." His life course certainly bore out the need for this advice. Williams's efforts to provide education for Crummell, who was turned away from "white" colleges, included attending the Noyes Academy, an interracial school in New Hampshire that was destroyed by white residents of the community. Crummell recalled watching the white farmers spend two days hitching ninety oxen to the school building and dragging it to destruction. He then attended the Oneida Institute, a radical abolitionist college that accepted whites and Blacks on an equal basis, where he experienced an evangelical awakening and was drawn to the ordained ministry. On graduating from Oneida in 1838, he was accepted for candidacy for ordination in the Diocese of New York. When Crummell applied to attend General Seminary he knew exactly what had happened to DeGrasse two years earlier, and exactly what was likely to happen now.[24]

The dean of General, William Whittingham, stated that Crummell's attendance at the seminary was out of his hands and that he could not be admitted to the school. Crummell then appealed to the board of trustees, which included Onderdonk. Onderdonk became exceptionally abusive, bringing the young candidate to tears. Only Bishop George Washington Doane of New Jersey took his side. Onderdonk also refused Crummell permission to study at a nondiocesan seminary and demanded that he study privately, as DeGrasse had done. Crummell, unlike DeGrasse, refused completely to obey the bishop and was removed from the list of candidates for ordination.

After studying at Yale, again under limiting restrictions due to his race, Crummell was accepted as a candidate for ordination by Bishop Alexander Viets Griswold of the Eastern Diocese; undoubtedly Crummell's own fiercely evangelical piety matched well Bishop Griswold's, better than with the high church Bishop of New York. Crummell then went to Philadelphia in the hope of raising up a new church there. Unfortunately, Bishop Onderdonk's brother was in charge of the Diocese of Pennsylvania, and since Crummell's experience with the Bishop of New York had become a matter of public record, Crummell did not receive a warm welcome in the City of Brotherly Love. Bishop Henry Onderdonk insisted that if Crummell entered that diocese or raised up a new church, he would be subject to the same constrictions as St. Thomas: he would never attend diocesan convention, nor would his congregation be entitled to vote in it.[25]

In Philadelphia, St. Thomas had been denied participation in diocesan convention since 1794 due to its "peculiar circumstances," and in 1843 the Pennsylvania Diocesan Convention, to provide some canonical underpinnings to Bishop Onderdonk's rejection of Crummell, resolved that "no church in this Diocese, in like peculiar circumstances with the African Church of St Thomas, shall be entitled to send a Clergyman or Deputies to the Convention, or to interfere with the general government of the Church."[26] From this point forward, including free Black churches in diocesan convention became a way in which dioceses, bishops, and clergy could express their support for the antislavery movement and the rights of Black people—or, conversely, express their antipathy to both. John Jay's defense of Crummell and embarrassment of Onderdonk in New York City was part of a larger struggle over the inclusion of St. Philip's in diocesan convention and Jay's agitation around slavery and the rights of African Americans both in the public square and in the Episcopal Church.[27]

When St. Philip's was first considered for inclusion in diocesan convention in 1846—something that was simply a technicality for all white churches—the "divisiveness" of the issue led to a committee to report on it. The committee noted, "We deeply sympathize with the colored race in our country, we feel acutely their wrongs—and not the least among them, their social degradation." The report continued past this rather insincere expression of sympathy to state that, as a result of their degradation, Black Episcopalians were not fit subjects for association with those who attended General Convention. In Philadelphia, the 1850 "majority report" on the question of including St. Thomas in diocesan convention included outstandingly offensive language, much of which echoed this line of racist reasoning:

And let us ask, can there be a doubt, with dispassionate persons, as to the incompetency of the parties in question, for the post of advisers and legislators in the concerns of this portion of the American Church? Are they qualified for it, either by education, cultivation, or social position? . . . Are members of this House fully and sincerely prepared to receive the proposed new comers in such way as to exhibit in nothing, a distinction between them and others on the floor. . . . Is there no reason to apprehend that heartburning or jealousy will spring up from imagined, perhaps actual slights, induced by the unconquerable aversion, in many, to the admixture of races physically so diverse and separate, as the Black and the white? . . . [T]he retributive justice of the Almighty, for the inceptive wrong of [Africans'] original subjection [being enslaved and brought to the United States] seems to have travelled with them as a moral plague, and to have rendered their presence the constant source of disturbance and evil.[28]

In New York City, St. Philip's was finally admitted to diocesan convention in 1853, after its incorporation in 1819. St. Thomas was not admitted in Philadelphia until after the Civil War began, despite the efforts of Onderdonk's successor, Bishop Alonzo Potter, to advocate for the church and to challenge diocesan convention on the issue.[29]

Colonization and Foreign Mission

For those white people who were morally uncomfortable with slavery but nonetheless unhappy at the idea of freed Black people becoming part of their community, the answer was colonization. The American Colonization Society offered a "solution" to slavery that split the difference between slavery and racism by advocating for gradual abolition and sending freed people to colonize West Africa. As a bonus, the colonists would then Christianize and civilize the "heathen" Africans, proving that slavery had indeed been beneficial for Africa and Africans. In essence, the American Colonization Society made obvious what was hidden in the "free states" of the North: that African Americans were not welcome in America, regardless of whether they were slave or free.

The American Colonization Society, founded in 1817, included prominent Episcopalians from its inception. Bishop William White was one of its vice presidents in the early years, and colonization in West Africa was one of the earliest foreign mission goals of the Episcopal Church. In his 1820 letter to the Church Mission Society, Bishop Griswold reported that his first suggestion as a missionary to Ceylon, Joseph Andrus, had instead gone to Africa with the American Colonization Society; Josiah Pratt, the CMS secretary, responded that English missionaries had met with Andrus and provided him with African interpreters and guides, though he lived only a few months afterward.

In the same 1820 letter, Bishop Griswold condemns slavery as a social evil: "The pertinacity, with which so large a part of our citizens adhere to the slave-holding interest, precludes the hope of this country's soon becoming what it is so often and so absurdly called, 'a land of freedom.' The next State to be admitted into the Union has a constitution admitting negro *slaves*, but excluding those who are *free*."[30] Bishop Griswold was clearly antislavery, and connected this with the mission of the church, as he made it a topic of conversation with the CMS. He was also a supporter of free Black leadership in the church to some degree, ordaining the young Alexander Crummell after he was rejected in New York. Yet like many white church leaders, he did not seem to grasp the fundamental problem with colonization as a solution.

Most free African Americans, and some white abolitionists, were repulsed by the obvious racism of the colonization scheme and angry at the implication that Black people's "home" was not America after at least as many generations as whites. Nonetheless, some free Black people wearied of the hard and endless work of fighting American racism and imagined freedom and respect in an African-majority society that did not struggle under the burden of white supremacy and the terrors of white violence. Crummell, after his difficult experiences in the United States, was one.

In 1847, after struggling to resurrect DeGrasse's church in Queens, Crummell traveled to England to raise funds for it, supported by John Jay. While in England, Crummell bonded with leading English evangelicals and abolitionists and learned from them about the missions in West Africa; they supported him in finally getting a degree, from Cambridge. He became known as a public speaker, one of his strongest gifts. England was a revelation to Crummell. Like other visiting Black abolitionists, he was welcomed and treated with respect by white people of the middle and upper classes. Here he was at last welcomed as what he had always seen himself to be: an intelligent, educated leader. Rather than return to the United States, he took ship for Liberia in 1853, where the American Colonization Society had been sending African Americans and missionaries since 1817. Crummell believed that as Liberia had become politically independent in 1847, it would develop its own, autonomous Episcopal Church, free of the supervision, racism, and paternalism he had experienced as a clergyman in the United States.[31]

In fact, the white missionary bishop of Cape Palmas, John Payne, had arrived in 1851 and was still working to maintain and develop the Episcopal Church there. The Liberian mission was complicated by conflicts between the African American settlers, the white missionaries, and the native Africans, all of whom had different agendas. Crummell was part of an effort to create an autonomous Liberian Episcopal Church based in the "African" section, farther upriver from the capital, Monrovia, which tended to be the area of settler influence. Miscommunication, personality conflicts, and animosities on all sides undermined this effort, and Bishop Payne put a stop to it with a General Convention resolution requiring that any church becoming independent from the Episcopal Church must be able to financially support itself. The intention for the new Liberian church had been for it to continue being financially supported by the U.S. church until the Liberian economy had developed to the point of being able to sustain its clergy and churches.[32]

These tensions over "native" direction of the church foreshadowed many others in years to come. By the mid-nineteenth century, the CMS in England and the Congregationalist missions in the United States had come to the same conclusion: the future of a mission must always be its euthanasia. The goal was not to control the new churches from a central point but to permit and encourage their independent development in every way. Both Rufus Anderson of the Congregationalist mission organization and Henry Venn of the English CMS described this as a "three self" proposition: that a church should be self-governed, self-sustaining, and self-propagating. It should have its own clergy and hierarchy and its own methods of evangelism—thus without dependence upon missionary personnel from other countries—and its own financial resources.[33]

As it happened, in country after country, there would often be many evangelists from the "native" group; in fact, in most missions around the world, the true work of expanding the church was always accomplished by grassroots "native" evangelists, catechists, and "bible women," who greatly outnumbered the foreign missionaries. But there would often be few ordained clergy, particularly in the case of the Episcopal Church, with its strict requirements for educated ministry. Both Bishop Payne in Liberia and Bishop William Jones Boone in China, among others, noted that it was almost impossible to meet the canonical requirements for ordination in their missionary contexts, and requested General Convention to find some solution, a way to ordain people without the usual educational requirements or to create a perpetual diaconate; neither solution was ever upheld. Often the missionaries themselves were unwilling to leave, even when there were clearly enough Christians to begin their own functioning congregations, arguing that they were "not quite ready" for independence, much of which reluctance was based in racial paternalism. Most of all, the issue of financing was a stumbling block to independent churches arising from a mission field. In economies where there was little money to pay clergy or to develop theological education, financing from the outside mission agency was crucial to maintaining the local network of catechists, evangelists, and teachers and to develop local ways of training ministers in the mold the missionaries had brought. The English and American churches of most denominations—and the Episcopal Church was similar to others in this—were very reluctant to continue financing a church over which they would have no control. Racism and paternalism played their part in rejecting the autonomy of churches founded by mission organizations, as did the desire of many white American missionaries to spend their lives doing the work they loved and believed in, even when this might stand in the way of the "euthanasia" of the mission and raising up local leadership to replace them.[34]

For Crummell, the goal of the Liberian mission was to demonstrate to all the world that Africans were capable of Christian civilization and self-governance. From the example of Absalom Jones and many other African American leaders, he expanded the idea of racial ability to imagine a world stage, where Africans would not only live up to white expectations but would surpass them, bringing the special gifts of the "African race" to the world through their own well-ordered, courageous, and educated Christian lives. In this way, Crummell became one of the founders of the ideal of pan-Africanism, imagining that all those of African descent in the world could be united by their sufferings and could transform the world through their special gifts. Inspired by English abolitionist and evangelical ideals, he imagined that the church would guide development of alternative economies and independent governmental structures in impoverished areas, thus undermining and replacing exploitative colonialism and slave economies. Shaped by a deeply felt and unbending evangelical Episcopalianism, he imagined that the individual life of every African and African American would be transformed into sober orderliness through the strict discipline of the church.[35]

Crummell struggled for years to uphold his dream of the free Liberian church, even working with the detested American Colonization Society on speaking tours to recruit new settlers. But the loss of the possibility of an autonomous church, and vicious infighting among factions in Liberia, led him to leave the mission at last and return to the United States permanently in 1872. When he arrived, he found a changed world: the enslaved people had been freed, the Civil War had begun and ended, Reconstruction was in full swing, and the Episcopal Church was coming to a new sense of mission after years of internal conflict and political division.

White Episcopalian Church Leaders and the Inadequacy of Missional Vision

Within the white clerical and lay leadership of the Episcopal Church in the years leading up to the Civil War, with a few notable exceptions, the issue of slavery was generally seen as untouchable. For high church leaders, there were theological as well as practical grounds for this view. From Bishop Hobart forward, the high church theology had emphasized apoliticism, the church as a sanctuary from the world, which could pronounce only on those things which scripture spoke of. As scripture did not forbid slavery, and in fact seemed to countenance it in both the Hebrew Scriptures and the New Testament, slavery could not be a sin, nor forbidden by the church.[36]

In 1834, following the anti-abolitionist riots, Bishop Onderdonk of New York published Peter Williams's letter, without Williams' permission, agreeing to resign from the Board of the Anti-Slavery Society, and editing it so as to leave out Williams's statement that he would continue to engage in antislavery work. As a dedicated and rigid high churchman, Onderdonk was not necessarily personally invested in the continuance of slavery—although undoubtedly some wealthy New York Episcopalians were—but in his understanding of the church's mission, anything touching on politics must be avoided.

Northern evangelical Episcopalians were sometimes more willing to take political stances, at least partly because American evangelicals in general had long been involved in social reform movements. Bishop Onderdonk's evangelical Episcopalian opponent, layman John Jay, had been a leader in the antislavery movement from his sophomore year in college. As a practicing lawyer, Jay used the courts to defend fugitive slaves. As a supporter of St. Philip's and the efforts to ordain young Black clergy, Jay publicized the stories of DeGrasse and Crummell, challenging Onderdonk to explain his behavior; in 1839 he published his own pamphlet, *Thoughts on Slavery*, which was read on both sides of the Atlantic and made strong distinctions between the English church, which had identified itself with the antislavery movement in both its evangelical and high church forms, and the American church, which Jay described as a "buttress of slavery." Another pamphlet, *Caste and Slavery in the American Church*, was written partly to help fundraise among English evangelical Anglicans for Crummell's financially challenged church in New York. Much of its material was used by English bishop Samuel Wilberforce in his 1844 *History of the American Church*. The American edition had much of the antislavery section redacted or "mutilated" to lessen the impact of the critique, about which Jay was furious and wrote another pamphlet criticizing the church for its obsequiousness to slaveholders.[37] Jay was also active in supporting St. Philip's for inclusion in diocesan convention, just as evangelical Bishop Potter worked to include St. Thomas in Philadelphia.[38]

Bishop John Henry Hopkins of Vermont, who became the presiding bishop in 1865, wrote a series of proslavery pamphlets based on public lectures beginning in 1851, supporting the traditional high church view of slavery as beyond the church's ken to criticize. In 1861, Hopkins was asked by some "gentlemen of New York" to elaborate his views on slavery, which had by this time become even more anti-abolitionist. He came down hard on scripture as the only source of possible condemnation of slavery, and the bishop as the person who could interpret what scripture says—and he interpreted scripture as not ambivalent, but positive, about slavery. He also came out against the Declaration of Independence's claim of equality of human beings as antiscriptural and undermining the gospel:

> [T]heir tendency is in direct contrariety to the precepts of the Gospel, and the highest interests of the individual man. For what is the unavoidable effect of their doctrines of human equality? Is it not to nourish the spirit of pride, envy, and contention? To set the servant against the master, the poor against the rich, the weak against the strong, the ignorant against the educated? To loosen all the bonds and relations of society, and reduce the whole duty of subordination to the selfish cupidity of pecuniary interest, without an atom of respect for age, for office, for law, for government, for Providence, or for the Word of God.

Slavery, in fact, had been good for "the Negro," and even if it was now not the best system, this did not mean it was to be condemned.[39]

Yet in his own mind, Hopkins was not a proponent of slavery. He argued that while slavery was not wrong in and of itself, if desired it could gradually be ended by a state program compensating slaveholders for their monetary loss. His own feelings on the matter, as he saw it, were irrelevant; they could not influence what the church or its bishops were entitled to say or do about slavery. For Hopkins, while it was acceptable to find slavery personally distasteful and to hope that it would someday be abolished, it was not acceptable to say that it was morally sinful, to insist on its abolition, or to critique or punish those who owned slaves.[40]

Hopkins, of course, had indeed ventured into politics with his proslavery pamphlets, despite his high churchmanship and repeated insistence that he had done no such thing. He regularly gave lectures promoting his view, and his pamphlets in various editions became more and more sympathetic to slaveholders and opposed to the antislavery movement, partly because he had developed strong personal and financial ties to several southern bishops. He was deeply offended when accused of supporting the proslavery Democratic Party, though he had given permission to a group of Pennsylvania Democrats to reprint his pamphlet during a contested race for governor. Evangelical Episcopalians in Pennsylvania published an open letter criticizing Hopkins's views and actions as "unworthy of any servant of Jesus Christ," signed by more than one hundred clergy and Bishop Potter, to which Hopkins responded with an outraged tome, denouncing the disrespect of Potter's critique of a senior bishop as well as doubling down on the Christian mastery ideology of slavery and quoting southern slaveholders on how happy their slaves were.[41]

Among evangelical Episcopalians, attitudes toward slavery leading up to the Civil War were largely sectional. In the South, evangelicals such as Bishop Meade took positions not very different from that of high church Bishop Hopkins, claiming that while slavery might be a bad system for a modern nation, scripture permitted it and therefore it was not inherently sinful and the church could not forbid it or criticize slaveholders. Meade was, however, quite willing to make playing cards, drinking alcohol, and attending the theater, also unaddressed by scripture, matters for church discipline. These moral issues were not considered "political"; slavery was. Evangelical Virginia clergy were expected to avoid politics just as much as high churchmen were. When a group of clergymen in Richmond invited congregations to pray about the "national crisis" in 1856, they were criticized for being too political; another group was accused of "a desecration of God's house."[42]

Both Meade and evangelical Bishop McIlvaine of Ohio originally supported the American Colonization Society, and both left it prior to the Civil War—but for different reasons. For Meade, and for other southern evangelicals, the Society was too radical and "political": its stated purpose, however poorly and slowly pursued, was to eventually bring slavery to an end. Bishop McIlvaine and some other northern evangelical leaders had become more antislavery, and it became more and more clear to them that the Society was both racist in its principles and undermined the argument for immediate abolition.

Northern evangelical Episcopalian clergy, such as Dudley Tyng of Philadelphia, his father, Stephen Tyng, of New York, and laypeople such as William Jay and John Jay in New York and Salmon Chase, the nephew of Philander Chase, in Ohio, were outspoken, politically active, and radical antislavery advocates. McIlvaine and Salmon Chase were both "revolted" by the refusal of Pennsylvania to seat delegates from St. Thomas and other churches at its 1843 diocesan convention in the wake of Crummell's visit to Bishop Onderdonk. McIlvaine took the opportunity to tell the Board of Missions about his antislavery views and tried to force the Board to disavow a new proposal in *The Spirit of Missions* to use slavery to fund missions by buying a plantation, in a model similar to the SPG's plantation at Codrington.[43] In 1859, McIlvaine was incensed when he learned that the first Black student at Bexley Hall was forced to wait until white seminarians and then the entire white congregation communed before he was permitted to take communion, though this was typical practice in the Episcopal Church at the time. McIlvaine refused to preach in the chapel the next day; instead, he sat down next to the African American seminarian, in the back of the building, and asked to share his Prayer Book. The bishop brought the student to the rail to commune with him immediately after the clergy.[44]

Salmon Chase was known as the "Attorney General for Fugitive Slaves" because of the court cases he brought against the 1850 Fugitive Slave Act. Both McIlvaine and Chase, a member of Lincoln's cabinet, worked throughout the war to convince Lincoln to place slavery and emancipation at the center of his policies and strategies, and Lincoln sent McIlvaine on an unofficial diplomatic mission to England in 1861 to convince the English not to support the South in the Civil War. He succeeded in connecting the war to slavery and thus brought out English abolitionists, particularly evangelicals, against support of the Confederacy.[45]

Despite all that the Episcopal Church could do to avoid politics, politics happened. The House of Bishops at Convention in 1862 produced a pastoral letter about the war, choosing between two competing versions. Bishop Hopkins's high church version emphasized charity and avoided politics; Bishop McIlvaine's evangelical version emphasized support for the Union and castigation of the rebels. The House chose McIlvaine's version.[46] Yet the pastoral letter did not discuss slavery; its call to break silence and speak upon the evils that had led to the war, and for which the country was bearing the chastisement of Providence, avoided this central issue.[47] Bishop Leonidas Polk was a general in the Confederate Army and had recently invaded Kentucky. Yet the Convention had called the roll for all the absent southern bishops, who had just set up the Protestant Episcopal Church in the Confederate States of America, as though the division of the nation had not occurred. In the next General Convention, in 1865, led by Presiding Bishop Hopkins, the southern bishops were welcomed back without a mention of their absence, quite as if the entire war hadn't happened at all, and the church of the Confederate States, and the reason that church had existed, was only a misty dream.

Summary

In 1850, the vestry of St. Thomas in Philadelphia produced their own response to the majority report of the committee which refused to permit them to join diocesan convention, expressing shock at the report's statement as to the fitness of their complexion for moral and legislative leadership. "We are not surprised at the final result, but confess that we are perfectly astounded" that the reasoning was based in open prejudice rather than scripture or the Book of Common Prayer. The vestry continued:

> *Therefore, Resolved,* That if we were heretofore desirous of being admitted into union with the Convention, we are not now, nor can we hereafter be, (with due respect to ourselves and posterity) while "COLOR, PHYSICAL AND SOCIAL CONDITION AND EDUCATION," continue to be the test of admission or rejection. . . .
>
> *Resolved,* That in the opinion of this Vestry, the expressions that were used by some of the members of the Convention, should be kept from the heathen, lest the Gospel should fail to have its salutary effect upon their minds, they instinctively rejecting the message at the hands of those who justify complexional distinctions in the Church of Christ. . . .
>
> *Resolved,* That the consideration offered, by reminding us that the rejection could not debar us from communion with the Spirit, did not, in our humble opinion, come with very good grace, after having been told, in terms not to be misunderstood, that we were "entirely unfit" to hold visible fellowship with a delegated council of that body, which defines the Church to be a "VISIBLE BODY of faithful men" &c, whose high mission on earth is fulfilled only so far as she is a co-worker with the Spirit.[48]

After the Civil War, and for many decades afterward, the mission of the white Episcopal Church would be deeply shaped by this internal legacy of racial paternalism.[49]

In 1866, Alexander Glennie reported that almost all of his three hundred Black communicants in Waccamaw Parish, South Carolina, had left the Episcopal Church to attend churches led by Black ministers; he resigned in despair. Only one determined Black member remained at St. Matthews Hillsborough in North Carolina, a church that had once been almost a quarter African American: the grandmother of the first African American woman Episcopal priest, civil rights activist Pauli Murray.[50] Throughout the South there was a great exodus as almost all of the Episcopalian freedpeople ceased attending their churches, demonstrating the truth of William Jay's challenge to Bishop Ives in 1846: despite the pretense of Christian mastery that an enslaved person was spiritually free, they had not chosen to be Episcopalians. They were forced to be.

Reverend Phillips Brooks, considered the greatest preacher of the nineteenth century, expressed the great frustration of younger white activist Episcopalians at the General Convention of 1862, writing to a friend, "Its shilly-shallying was disgraceful. It was ludicrous, if not so sad, to see those old gentlemen sitting there for fourteen days, trying to make out whether there was a war going on or not, and whether if there was it would be safe for them to say so."[51] In the end, there was no way to avoid taking a political stance on the issue of slavery, and pretending avoidance was just that. Insofar as it did not take a stance on slavery and the war, the Episcopal Church in essence was taking the stance that the status quo was acceptable, in the fear of controversy and threats to church unity.

6

From Sea to Shining Sea

Two figures in the mid-nineteenth-century expansion of the Episcopal Church from the East Coast to the West, William Augustus Muhlenberg and Bishop William Ingraham Kip, demonstrate the ways in which the Episcopal Church attempted to engage in missional work in new urban contexts as well as in the territorial expansion to the West Coast. Their careers demonstrate both the possibilities and the weaknesses of Episcopalian missional approaches, particularly the challenges in pushing the church beyond its comfortable liturgical and racial demographic.

Kip and Muhlenberg both ministered during a liminal time in the history of American racial ideologies, particularly as regarded religion and mission. Among missionaries, racial paternalism (the idea that there are "stronger" and "weaker" races, and the "stronger" must care for and provide tutelage to the "weak") tended to be the more accepted variety of racial ideology. However, by the 1850s American ideas of race beyond the church were moving away from a basic equality of races, if not opportunity—imagining the major boundary as one of "heathen" and "Christian," a boundary that could be crossed and could theoretically bring the "heathen" to the point of "Christian civilization—towards scientific racism.[1]

Scientific racism saw differences between "races," which were moral and cultural as well as physical, as immutably based in biology and inheritance. These races existed in a hierarchical relationship and in constant competition, with the stronger race (usually the "Anglo-Saxon") destined to dominate and perhaps exterminate the "weaker" races. While Darwin did not publish the *Origin of Species* until 1859, nonetheless ideas of a natural competition between "races" seen as "species" by scientific racists was common. Anti-immigrant rhetoric was frequently based in scientific racism, particularly prominent in the anti-Chinese agitation that led to the Chinese Exclusion Act in 1880. The lack of attention to race by Muhlenberg, and lack of concern for racial injustice and violence by Kip, has to be understood with this shift in racial ideology as the background context.[2]

Mission, Race, and Empire. Jennifer C. Snow, Oxford University Press. © Oxford University Press 2024.
DOI: 10.1093/oso/9780197598948.003.0007

Muhlenberg and the Memorial

William Augustus Muhlenberg was born a Lutheran in Philadelphia, attended Christ Church as a child as well as occasional Quaker and Roman Catholic services, and was confirmed by Jackson Kemper in the first years of Kemper's ministry in Philadelphia. Muhlenberg was passionate about mission. He and Kemper were lifelong friends and correspondents, and Muhlenberg's Church of the Holy Communion became Kemper's home base whenever he was in New York City. Muhlenberg helped identify and recruit young men to accompany Kemper west as missionary clergy, and his short-lived periodical, *The Evangelical Catholic,* regularly published information on James Lloyd Breck's missions to the Ojibwa as well as missions in Liberia and China. For Muhlenberg, however, the western wilds and "heathen lands" were not the sole arena of mission. In 1851, he wrote that there was an area for mission that the church had sadly neglected:

> We mean the field of domestic missions which lies immediately about our doors; we mean the ministering of the Gospel to the souls, and to the bodies too, of the thousands who have no name in the world and are so unknown to the church—the poor and the ignorant, the destitute and afflicted to whom the Gospel was first preached, and who surely have more than a residuary claim on the appointed dispenser of the Gospel. Would that it be our privilege to wake up the Church to a deeper consciousness of her mission in that regard; and to a conviction, also, that only by an earnest discharge of it will men be satisfied that she has a mission.[3]

New York City was known for its beautiful, expensive church buildings, and the Episcopalians for the most beautiful and expensive among them, but these churches—as with almost all other Episcopal churches in the United States—were built by the donations of the wealthy and sustained by the wealthy's "pew rents," guaranteeing their families a seat in the building. The poor might come in the door, but they would have to stand.

In a traditional pew-rent church, only those who rented pews could take part in the governance of the congregation—being part of the vestry, attending diocesan convention, and helping to choose the rector. "Free churches," where pews were open to anyone who came in, were largely missionary charity operations, were not self-governed or funded, and were seen as bearing the stigma of poverty. The Incorporation Act of New York State did not even envision the possibility of a self-sustaining free church: it required that the vestry be made up of pew holders or else that it was a mission church financially sustained by another organization. In order to incorporate Holy Communion, Muhlenberg had to petition the New York State legislature to change the legal structure of incorporation.[4]

Muhlenberg, using his sister's wealth, intended to begin something quite different: a truly economically diverse church, where the wealthy and impoverished attended together and had the same privileges in church government. And to ensure that the wealthy would not have any undue privileges, this new church would not even be part of diocesan convention; its connection with the diocese would be purely between the rector and the bishop, so that it would not have to be under the governance of the wealthy laypeople who ran convention. Bringing rich and poor together into one holy community bound in love: this, preached Muhlenberg as the cornerstone was laid for the Church of the Holy Communion, was Christ's great ordinance of fellowship. The life of the church must "rebuke all distinctions of pride and wealth, which the founder of the church designed should never be provided for here."[5]

Instead of the traditional system of pew rents, the Church of the Holy Communion would be sustained by free-will offerings from all according to their ability, gathered weekly as part of the communion service. Muhlenberg's intention was to develop endowments for the church but to depend primarily on "the offertory," which was itself an important innovation. In 1847 he wrote, "I am endeavoring to get the people to realize the idea of offerings— which in the minds of the majority has no [meaning]. I regard that part of the communion service as invaluable—and a special provision in favor of what we call free churches." Historically, offerings from the congregation were collected only at communion services—which happened only a few times a year—and were intended for the support of the poor, not the church per se. In fact, some clergy in the eighteenth century thought that some people might avoid the rare communion services specifically because they did not want to make an offering for the poor. For Muhlenberg, the shift to weekly communion meant not only a more frequent sacrament but a far more developed attention to the open financial offering as part of the church's life.[6]

In his own church, legally incorporated in a way that permitted significant experimentation beyond the usual pale of diocesan congregations, Muhlenberg could do more or less whatever he wanted, and what he wanted to do was to increase the decorations of the church, set up an altar with a cross and Bible, and wear a surplice and scarf for every service. He celebrated Holy Communion every Sunday rather than monthly or quarterly, and organized Morning Prayer, Litany, Ante-Communion, sermon, and Holy Communion, traditionally all held at once in a multihour service, into smaller, separate versions. He created a boys' choir and emphasized congregational singing of hymns. In order to explain how the church worked, he wrote a series of "pastoral tracts" as guides to the liturgy.[7] All this led to Muhlenberg's being seen as a high churchman or even a ritualist along the lines of the controversial Oxford Movement, though he was theologically a moderate evangelical. For him, all of this experimentation in liturgy as well as in church finance was rooted in one desire: to make the Episcopal Church relevant and welcoming to those who were not already wealthy Episcopalians, and to use all of its gifts and genius, evangelical as well as high church, to bring people of all classes and backgrounds into fellowship with Christ and one another.

The neighborhood of Holy Communion (now known as the Flatiron District in New York City) was a neighborhood of poor immigrants in 1844, mostly from Great Britain and Germany. Muhlenberg used his connections and relationships with wealthy New Yorkers to encourage some of them to join the church, and opened the doors to the local immigrants. As he got to know the people in his new neighborhood, he began to develop church programs to meet their needs, adding a Christmas tree where poor children could receive presents and a parish dispensary to provide basic medical care. This would eventually develop into his vision for a church-run hospital, and with the help of his parishioner Ann Ayres he organized the first religious sisterhood of the Episcopal Church, the Sisters of the Holy Communion, to provide nursing care for the poor. He created a "fresh air fund" to send impoverished families on summer vacations away from the city, an employment society for women, a parish school; he organized a charity for "fallen women" called the Midnight Mission and a free cemetery for the poor.

Muhlenberg was particularly scathing on the church's failure to reach out to the poor and "rude" classes and the implicit understanding among many Episcopalians that theirs was the church of the refined and elite. He was emphatic, as well, that the church must provide bodily care for those who needed it, particularly the poor members of the church itself. In 1850, in a sermon published to raise funds and gather stakeholders for his proposed church hospital, he wrote that the church fails when assuming that the state will take responsibility for the poor. The state was not religious and couldn't provide care to the body and soul together, as the church could and must.

And insofar as the church provided such care only through individual efforts of charity, it was also a failure: the church is communal and must act as a body. To the argument that poverty was unconquerable and that the church couldn't possibly solve this problem, or that poverty and inequality were God's will, he stated, "O wondrous piety! to refrain from interfering with the Providence of God. O discerning Churchmanship! to look at the poor, and to see among them no members of Christ's Body—to recognize no spiritual relation between them and us, as their claim on our sympathy." He somewhat sarcastically proposed that "members of our own communion" at least could be served, as there were not many of them. Passionately—for a man whose great projects depended upon the wealthy—he wrote:

> If it be said that our first care must be for the *spiritual* wants of the poor, let it be granted, and then the question only to be put, what are we doing so extensively in that line, that it may serve as an offset to our apathy in regard to their temporal wants? . . . If we throw open the street doors of the sanctuary, are there not an hundred little doors within to our private apartments, where we should be ill at ease, if "the man in vile raiment" should take his seat at our side? . . . We bid the poor to bring their children to be christened; they do so, and then where do we bid them send their children to be educated according to their christening? . . . Our zeal seems to expire at the font. . . . Is it because until very lately we have been so poor a people? Is it that the command of wealth is a new thing among us, so that hitherto there has been the ability merely to provide for our own pressing wants? Our past poverty?—is that our apology? You smile at the question.[8]

Indeed, New York City Episcopalians had not recently become wealthy, as Muhlenberg, and his audience, well knew. They were and had long been among the wealthiest people in the United States, and with his skill at encouraging their donations Muhlenberg was able to found and fund a hospital as well as many other projects.

Along with Muhlenberg's desire to bring the poor into the church and to provide social and physical support of all kinds to those who needed it, his interest in western missions meant that he was also aware of the challenges of making the church and its long, involved liturgy relevant to those who were not already Episcopalian. His relationship with Bishop Kemper reminded him constantly that the great need was to find more, and more appropriate, clergy for new and different contexts than the current system provided for.

Yet instead of focusing on these problems, the church argued about altar decorations and ritual, a stagnant brangle in terms of missional activity. Muhlenberg found this situation frustrating and futile, in contrast to his own emphasis on "practical Christianity," serving body and soul, and the need to bring the gospel to those who didn't have it, in American cities as well as in "heathen" nations.

With this in mind, in 1853 he gathered together a group of like-minded and well-known supporters from both the evangelical and high church groups and presented a Memorial to General Convention as an attempt to encourage the church toward radical change in its missional practice. Muhlenberg's general and principled practice of charity toward those whose religious practice he might not fully agree with made him popular with both sides of the internal Episcopalian tension between the high church and evangelical "parties," which was reaching a high boil at this point. Thus he was able to gather a group from both sides to sign his Memorial, though the high church signatories tended to be more qualified in their support.[9]

The Memorial requested the bishops to consider strengthening the church in two specific ways: first, by enabling liturgical experimentation, particularly in mission situations, since the liturgy of the Prayer Book was designed for settled congregations of people already Episcopalian; second, by creating an umbrella church organization, which would include the Episcopal Church as it already existed but would also offer Episcopalian ordination in the apostolic succession to those who were called to different gifts in the missional field—preachers, evangelists, itinerants—whose education and theological commitments did not need to be identical to the traditional requirements for Episcopalian clergy. These specially ordained clergy would report directly to bishops, but their work would often be quite different from "regular" Episcopalian clergy. The idea was that this would create a unified, yet diverse Christian church, which held the general commitments of Protestant Christianity; could reach all people of varied cultures, languages, and educational attainments throughout the United States; and was united through the ministry of the Episcopal bishops. In the theological language of Muhlenberg and the Memorialists, this would be true "catholicity" for a unified Protestant church.[10]

General Convention received the Memorial with excitement and alarm. There was something for everyone to like and to anathematize. High church leaders tended to be suspicious of it due to its weakening of liturgical practice and discipline for the "extraordinary" ordinands, while appreciating its emphasis on the importance and centrality of the bishop to Christian unity; evangelicals appreciated the call for liturgical flexibility and extempore prayer, something they had been asking General Convention to permit for years, while disliking the freedom it would give to continued theological and liturgical experimentation by ritualists. Moderates of both camps, however, were excited enough to create a Commission of Bishops to study the Memorial and to gather further information. This Commission, which included both supporters such as Bishop Alonzo Potter of Pennsylvania and detractors such as Bishop George Washington Doane of New Jersey, sent questionnaires to bishops and church leaders and met regularly to produce their Report and Recommendations in 1856. While the nation lurched toward Civil War, the Episcopal Church gave its attention to this attempt to develop a more effective and meaningful missional practice.

The Report itself was most likely written by Bishop Potter. Like Muhlenberg, he had personal experience with other denominations (he was brought up as a Quaker) and shared Muhlenberg's desire to focus on mission and practice rather than on distinctions between church parties. The Report of the Commission critiqued the church's sad record on expansion as "matter for deep humiliation and shame" when compared with the general increase of population and even compared with other denominations. It recommended developing the skill of extempore preaching and encouraging all ministers to do this at least once per day, as well as permitting extemporaneous prayer and adaptation of the liturgy to the incredible diversity of the people who needed to be reached. The Report imagined a preacher who could give the message that was necessary in terms of form as well as content adapted appropriately to the time, place, context, and audience, not simply the prescribed format of a pulpit sermon. The gospel included all the vast range of human and created and eternal life, and thus the preacher should always be able to pick up some thread that would enable listeners to hear and understand, rather than only preaching on predetermined matters of doctrine or morality.[11]

Since one of the main requests of the Memorial was to consider different sorts of education and gifts for ordination, the Report pointed to the apostolic idea of a diversity of gifts for the benefit of the church, contrasted with the narrowness of ministry as the Episcopal Church has accomplished it. Many gifts given to the church were unrecognized and unused, such as the gift of caring for the poor and destitute; the gift of men who were able to administer and govern; the gift of "men whose temperaments incline them to be constantly moving from place to place" with a "frankness and cordiality of manner" that enabled them to befriend anyone they met;. From this last group Potter recommended finding "Evangelists" who can do mission work: "[m]en, whose chief, if not sole employment, it shall be to preach the Gospel in remote and morally destitute parts of the country, or in the neglected districts of our large cities, where the Pastors of established congregations never come, and the preachers at missionary stations but rarely." For these evangelists, and for those who would be ordained to the ministry, adequate financial support was necessary. Few young men were interested in ministry, and of those few, even fewer were being fairly paid for it.[12]

The Report was jam-packed with exciting and practical suggestions along this line to provide a new missional engagement for the church as a whole, none of which involved debates over candles, vestments, or the liturgical phrasing of baptismal vows. In the end, however, almost none of the material regarding evangelists, female ministries, adequate finance, religious education, or youth ministry was incorporated with the official Resolution which the commission offered to General Convention. The final Resolution consisted almost entirely of recommendations to shorten the liturgy and permit extemporaneous or additional prayers.[13]

After all the controversy and excitement, almost nothing was done to change the existing practice: clergy were highly educated and poorly paid beyond the established and wealthy urban congregations of the East, and there would continue to be very few who could be effective missionaries in different contexts. The liturgy was permitted to be shortened in a specific way, but no real attention was given to the suggestion of developing practices of liturgy that would suit different contexts, organizing itinerant evangelists or other orders of ministry, or encouraging extempore preaching and prayer as a necessary skill.

Following this failed attempt, Muhlenberg returned to New York City to continue his rectorship, his leadership of the hospital, and his care for the poor, and to develop his life's final project, the planned Christian community of St. Johnland. Bishop Potter similarly returned to Philadelphia to manage his own hospital project and to continue to agitate for the inclusion of St. Thomas African Episcopal Church and the Church of the Crucifixion in the diocesan convention. The Episcopal Church continued on its preset path, depending solely upon the missionary bishop as missional strategy, and focused on serving the small slice of American humanity which already found it attractive.

The Golden West: Bishop Kip and the Limits of the Missionary Episcopate

The Muhlenberg Memorial wasn't the only excitement at General Convention in 1853. Two delegates had arrived from California, the Golden West, requesting admission to diocesan convention as a new Episcopalian diocese.

California became a U.S. territory in 1848, quickly followed by the discovery of gold at Sutter's Mill, touching off the California Gold Rush and filling the place with immigrants from the East Coast, Asia, South America, Europe, and Australia. Into this cauldron of humanity the DFMS had sent a missionary in 1849, at the request of San Francisco laymen. Jean VerMehr was delayed by the opposition of his bishop, smallpox, and a long journey around the southernmost tip of South America. Thus he arrived after another clergyman, Flavel Mines, had been called without the Board's knowledge. The local Episcopalians decided to solve the problem by founding a second church, and so two parishes were erected in San Francisco, only a few blocks apart, while in most of the new territory there were neither clergy nor churches despite laypeople's attempts to create them. By 1850, as California moved into statehood following heated congressional debate about slavery, several other clergy had arrived as immigrants, military chaplains, and fortune-seekers. They decided to organize a diocese and elected Horatio Southgate, who had just resigned his position as the missionary bishop of "the dependencies of the Sultan" in the Ottoman Empire. (He declined.)[14]

The new "diocese" then sent deputies to General Convention in 1853, which refused to seat them because the constitution of the new diocese had neglected to mention "the pledge of loyalty to the doctrine, discipline and worship of the Protestant Episcopal Church." The Convention may well have decided that the madness of the Californians needed to be brought in line—Flavel Mines was trawling the East Coast telling people that California could choose whatever bishop they wanted, including perhaps the Russian Orthodox bishop who had authority over the previously Russian-owned territories of northern California—and decided to appoint a bishop for California as a missionary district, not a diocese.[15] Despite the fact that

California Episcopalians saw themselves as a diocese, not a missionary district, and had already tried to elect their own bishop, they welcomed their new missionary bishop kindly enough when he showed up at the wharf of San Francisco. Neither missionary bishop William Ingraham Kip nor the Board of Missions nor General Convention really knew what they were getting into.

California was reeling (or thriving, depending upon one's point of view) from the Gold Rush, as hundreds of thousands of immigrants threw aside their settled lives and answered the lure of the gold, which could, so rumor and journalism had it, be scooped up from the very rivers. After the news of the strike at Sutter's Mill reached the East and was confirmed by the president of the United States—only a year after California had been wrested from Mexico in the settlement of the Mexican-American War—San Francisco had become a ghost town as all able-bodied men raced for the placers. Its port was choked with ships sailed to the Bay and abandoned. And a great rush of humanity trampled through the hills and valleys of California in search of the ultimate success, finding at best a minimal and rough survival if they did not die of exposure and sickness, and destroying the livelihoods and lives of indigenous Californians.

The world of California was an alien one to people from the East Coast of the United States, topsy-turvy, without order or towns or anything recognizable. Like Jamestown in 1607, it was cut off from the "motherland" by a dangerous overland journey via train, horse, and foot, or a dangerous sea journey around the Horn of South America, or a dangerous combination of the two through Panama, all of which took months and risked shipwreck, violence, and disease. (Bishop Kip himself was shipwrecked near San Diego on his very first journey to his new episcopate.) The transcontinental telegraph would not reach California until 1861; the transcontinental railroad not until 1869. There was no way to keep in close touch with California, no way to understand what was happening except through the personal accounts of the gold rush immigrants themselves.

Newcomers to San Francisco described an experience of total disorientation. Between the secularization of the Mexican missions in 1833 and the coming of the Americans with the discovery of gold, Yerba Buena was a tiny town trading in tallow and hides, with a ruined presidio and mission buildings, and a population of about a thousand, made up of Californios—Mexican or American settlers—and California Indians. A year later, in late 1849, twenty thousand people lived there; by 1850, fifty thousand. The influx came from China and Japan and the Sandwich Islands, Australia and

New Zealand, Mexico, Chile, Europe, Canada, and the United States. San Francisco became a city with a diversity of languages, cultures, and mores. Local newspapers described Maori from New Zealand as "hideously tattooed," along with Englishmen, Japanese, California Indians, and a cacophony of other Europeans, Latin Americans, and Asians, all understood as being fundamentally different from the white American immigrant. This immigrant population was overwhelmingly male and young—in the 1852 California census, 92% of the white population was male—and overwhelmingly transient, hoping, for the most part, to strike it rich and go home.[16]

While California was seen from afar as the golden land, living in California was hard and expensive. Gold Rush immigrants commented on the exorbitant and unpredictable cost of food and the very high cost of housing. There was no local industry aside from gold mining to provide goods, and no local agricultural base to provide food. The lack of decent housing for men, either in San Francisco or in the mining areas, encouraged frequent devastating fires, lonely deaths among strangers, and a social life based in well-appointed public gambling halls, often by far the finest and most attractive structures in town.[17]

Transience, and the motivation to "get your pile and get out" among most of the Gold Rush immigrants, shaped a society with few rules, disciplined only through violence. Prostitution, murder, vigilantism, and gambling were prominent aspects of early California American life. Some early immigrants found life in San Francisco and California at large attractive precisely because of its lack of stability and traditionally strict religious mores, the excitement and freedom where anything could happen, anything could be done. In 1850 one female immigrant wrote home that she had not attended church in over a year and that it made little difference in life. Gambling or going to church were options open to anyone on a Sunday morning, and people were free to choose without social pressure. The immigrants were also ludicrously well-armed, imagining themselves entering a land without law, where they would be attacked by hostile Indians; one group pulled a howitzer all the way across the continent. With the tools of violence to hand, and the expectation of the use of violence, it is unsurprising that violence was common as a method of solving problems, conflicts, or disagreements as well as for more generalized murder, dueling, and theft.[18]

This was not a situation in which one would generally choose to place a middle-aged, mild-mannered scholar of patristics, an aristocratic and fastidious scion of a wealthy Dutch family from New York who had never lived anywhere but in a city, whose personality generally shrank from any kind of conflict, who avoided politics, admired the "high" culture of Europe, and desired moderation, order, and stability in all things. Nonetheless, William Ingraham Kip was elected and consecrated as the first missionary bishop of California in 1853, and within two weeks was on his way.

Why was Kip chosen? Among items in his favor may have been his bringing a congregation in Albany, New York, to financial and demographic stability and his desire to do some church planting with the help of a local patron outside the city limits. He had written about the history of the Jesuit missions in North America and had also visited Kemper's mission in Wisconsin and praised the virtues of Nashotah House as a system of missionary expansion. He was known as a moderate in the tensions between evangelicals and high churchmen, despite his own high churchmanship, and as a man who respected and valued the order and polity of the church—perhaps this seemed particularly important to the General Convention and House of Bishops, since California seemed so in need of orderliness and appropriate polity. While initially it was believed that California was rich because of its wealth in gold, by the time Kip was elected it was known by the eastern bishops that the California church was essentially financially destitute—and it may not have been an insignificant factor that Kip was personally well-off. As the discussions about potential candidates in the House of Bishops were strictly confidential and without record, there is no way of knowing with certainty.[19] Kip may not have been suited, in personality, energy, or interests, to the unique needs of California as a missionary field and the rigors it entailed, but he would uphold the interests of the House of Bishops, maintain the standards of the Episcopal Church in polity and theology, and, ideally, bring order to chaos.[20]

Unfortunately, Kip embodied nearly perfectly that class of Episcopalian clergy whom Muhlenberg had excoriated as believing, implicitly, if not explicitly, that the church was suited for a certain class of person and that, when push came to shove, other classes of person were not worth the church's investment. Push came to shove quite early on in California, and Kip needed to make hard decisions throughout his bishopric about where to put his energy and the slim resources available to him. In general, he chose to put money and effort into providing clergy for white people who were already Episcopalian.

Bishop Kip envisioned himself as the "first missionary" of the diocese, who should travel from place to place and gather "churchmen" to organize congregations. In the service of this vision of the missionary episcopate, Kip was tireless in journeying to mining and agricultural towns, but he rapidly began to despair of the possibility of keeping the promises he was making to these local groups. He frequently found himself in the position of visiting towns with Episcopalians who were eager to start a congregation and for whom he could find no clergyperson and was able to offer only a license for a local lay reader. Because of the slowness of communication and travel between California and the East Coast, it might take a year or more even to find a candidate, and while they were on the way a potential congregation (or even an entire town, given the vicissitudes of mining) might evaporate. There were not adequate clergy eager for mission work in California, and if there had been, there was no money for them, particularly if they had families; and if they had come out, many of them would soon have given up anyway as being completely unsuited for the work, and the bishop would have to start all over again. As mining towns were replaced by agricultural towns, Kip also had to face the reality that the early congregations established with so much labor and mission funds were now located in shrinking communities, harnessed with the weight of maintaining a church building far beyond their needs. Yet he could not abandon them. Meanwhile there was less money to establish the church in the newer agricultural communities, which would be more stable in the long run.[21]

No one in the East really understood the problems. Kip did not even attend General Convention until nine years after his consecration because of the challenges of travel and the fragility of the situation in California. Even after being formally elected as the diocesan bishop, not just missionary, he continued to ask the Board of Missions to identify and help pay clergy candidates, and was frustrated that the easterners seemed to have no understanding of the difficulties involved in placing and supporting clergy in the land of gold, nor of the vast and rugged geographic area he was responsible for visiting via exploding steamboats and overturning stagecoaches. (At one point Nevada was casually added to his responsibilities, as it was assumed that it was an easy journey from San Francisco.) What little support the Board of Missions offered sometimes led to even more frustration with shifting priorities, resulting in situations where the bishop placed clergy in congregations in good faith and then was denied funding by the Board.[22]

Kip's strategy of focusing on white Episcopalians who were already organizing churches was not that different from the Episcopalian mission strategy in many other domestic mission areas, from upstate New York to western Iowa. California, however, had far more possibilities for radical shifts in welcoming new groups to the church and—although technically without slavery—plenty of opportunities to criticize social evils and abuse of human beings. Another man might have pursued these with at least some ardor, and missionaries from other denominations, particularly Presbyterians and Methodists, did so. Kip, however, seems to have avoided or weakly supported missions among the Asian, African American, Spanish-speaking, and California Indian populations. And while Kip's decisions may have been personally difficult and stressful in terms of where to place his bets among white miner and settler communities, it seems unlikely he lost much sleep over any sort of missionary work among other groups. His interactions with the Chinese and African American communities demonstrate his weak support and general antipathy to mission work among people from other racial or cultural groups, and his lack of interest in the suffering of the California Indians is a profile in apathy. Kip's concern (or lack thereof) for these groups of Californians indicates both a missionary strategy focused on "our proper people," as Muhlenberg might have sneered, and the development of a newer racial ideology among white Americans which identified "the Anglo-Saxon" as the epitome and future of humanity.

The Chinese

On Palm Sunday 1854, Bishop Kip laid hands on his first group of California confirmands, including a woman from China. Kip at this point was hopeful that the Chinese in California, already numbering in the thousands, would be a great mission field, and wrote that "before the altar of our Lord we are all one, and within the fold of the Church, the distinction of race or country are all forgotten." This attitude would not last long. In 1855, Kip wrote in *The Spirit of Missions* that the Chinese, who were suffering poverty, legal oppressions, and race-based violence in the mines and the cities, were to blame for their unwillingness to "mix" with white society. He characterized the difference as both racial and insurmountable, using words which indicate his intellectual acceptance of early scientific racist ideologies. "Between the Mongolian and the Anglo-Saxon races," he wrote, "there is a 'deep gulf,' as impassable as that which at the South separates the white and slave population." The California Chinese were the "vilest offscouring of China" and brought dangers of immigration from the "teeming millions of the East," including opium, liquor, filth, gambling, perjury, violent gangs, and prostitution, "imitating the vices, but not emulating the virtues of the whites." He quoted verbatim from an anti-Chinese "investigation" which recommended driving them out of the city physically, and Kip noted, unsympathetically, that quite a few California towns had already done so.[23]

Back east, news of the Chinese immigration to California led the Board of Missions to develop a missionary program for them, and they decided to send a returned missionary from China, Edward Syle, to serve the community. Kip wasn't consulted about the plan or the choice of man (though there would have been few or none to choose from among Episcopalian clergy with any experience at all of China), and he expressed his displeasure by telling Syle that it was sure to fail, but he was welcome to try. Syle, for his part, was quickly discouraged. The Chinese in San Francisco were of a completely different class—and in fact spoke a completely different dialect—from those he had known in Shanghai. He was disturbed, as well, by their poverty and the way they were mistreated and abused by white Californians, including the recent legislation requiring every Chinese immigrant to pay a head-tax of $50 on disembarkation. But because of the high cost of living in San Francisco, he had to live in Oakland—across San Francisco Bay, at that time with no bridge, from the Chinese community in San Francisco. Bishop Kip tried to support him in his own inimitable way by also giving him charge of a white Episcopal church in Oakland, which provided him with some funds for support but took even more time away from the Chinese.[24]

By late 1855, Kip and Syle together reported to the Board of Missions that the effort should be abandoned. Kip's letter to the Domestic Committee was a masterpiece of passive-aggressiveness, and the editor found it worthy of printing verbatim in *The Spirit of Missions*:

I have been placed in this matter in a very delicate position. To the Committee this enterprise seemed so plain a call of duty, that the Chinese Mission was organized without any previous consultation with me, or I never should have advised its present form. It was commenced at the East, with a zeal which was highly commendable, evidently with the community generally, awakening more interest than all the other Missions in California. I could only, therefore, take it as it was; and after giving you my view of the Chinese, as I did in *Spirit of Missions*, await the result of the experiment. I told Mr Syle, when he came, of my doubts of anything being done in this way, but that of course I should do nothing to damp their zeal or efforts at the East, in the hope that these fears should be unfounded. I therefore should aid him to the utmost; leave him to work out the problem for himself; and then, if failure came, I should have nothing to reproach myself with, or for which I could be reproached by others. . . . The result, however, has been exactly what I anticipated; and I do not think anything has been done to compensate for the amount of labor and money expended by the Committee.[25]

Syle suggested instead that the Chinese, who would soon be thinly scattered over California since the antipathy of the white community would force immigration to cease, be ministered to by parochial clergy and assimilated into their congregations. The Committee gladly seized on this option, which would cost them nothing, despite its obvious shortcomings: since the Chinese were hated by the white community, as Syle had just described, why would they be able to live among white communities and become part of white congregations? Just as practically, how would the local white clergy, already underpaid or unpaid, unable to speak any Chinese dialect, and stretched to the limit, add Chinese missionary work to their portfolio?[26]

Otis Gibson, a Methodist home missionary and advocate for the Chinese, visited Episcopal congregations in San Francisco in 1868 and advised them to begin Sunday schools for the Chinese. These schools would teach English as well as Christianity. At least two churches began programs, Church of the Advent and Trinity Church, and in 1879 Bishop Kip ordained Walter Ching Young to the diaconate. Known in most English sources as Ah Ching, he had attended Gambier College in Ohio prior to coming to San Francisco, where he struggled in his ministry and to support himself and his family. The congregation was never very large, and there were almost no baptisms due to the transience of the Chinese community. Walter Ching Young seems never to have been ordained to the priesthood, and Kip's support was tepid and apathetic at best. By 1891, the ministry was no longer in existence and he returned to China.[27]

In 1887, Kip confirmed his first Japanese Episcopalian, a boy at Christ Church Alameda who had been prepared by St. Paul's Oakland, but it is not clear how he became Episcopalian as the diocese had no record of mission work among the Japanese.[28] The Episcopal Church seems to have done very little in the way of work among the Chinese in California for the remainder of Kip's episcopate, providing a contrast with the Methodists and Presbyterians, who poured resources into this community, not only in terms of preaching and worship but for schools, medical care, and political advocacy, often in the face of extreme hostility from the white community.[29] Kip, by contrast, publicly supported the perception of the Chinese as both dangerous and inferior and joined in supporting anti-Chinese legislation. The church seems to have done and said absolutely nothing about the appalling abuse and discrimination experienced by the Chinese, or the situation of Chinese women sold into sexual slavery, or the burning of Chinatowns, all of which were addressed frequently by Methodist and Presbyterian leaders. This to some degree may have reflected Kip's distaste for conflict and politics, both theological and personal, but the avoidance of conflict in a racially charged context meant that he remained publicly and comfortably on the side of the status quo.

African Americans

While California was a "free state," this did not mean that free African Americans were welcome there—far from it. During the debate on California statehood and its Constitutional Convention, white leaders publicly declared that they desired no slaves, but also no free Black people in California. (They also stated that there was no such thing as slavery, and no need for it, in California, conveniently ignoring the dependence upon "indentured servitude" of California Indians, which was little different from slavery in practice.) The first governor of California, Peter Burnett, insisted that the goal must be to keep free Black people out of California, and during the Constitutional Convention some advocates argued that even the free Black people already in the new territory should be forcibly expelled (following the example of Oregon in 1844, which established a penalty of whipping any free Black or mulatto person who remained within the state's borders). California's white immigrant leaders desired more white immigrants, and only those, to form their new state. Free Black Californians, like California Indians, were for many years denied the right to testify in court, to sit on juries, and to vote.[30]

Bishop Kip's typical desire to avoid conflict joined with his personal discomfort encountering other races and cultures to comfortably permit him to simply ignore the entire problem. When it did intrude on his consciousness, he paid it little attention. He was somewhat opposed to slavery as an institution, but he also believed that slavery could not be ended without serious economic consequences. He foresaw, quite accurately, that there was no way to end slavery while making everyone happy, and that it would lead to a division in society and in the church whenever the subject was raised. His policy, therefore, was to never raise the subject and to forbid others from doing so. During the Civil War Kip personally supported the Union, and his son fought in the Union Army, but he demanded his clergy in California avoid all mention of the war, slavery, or political debates. He understood this lack of a stance on slavery and the war as an attractive feature of the Episcopal Church, as compared with other denominations, and as pastorally necessary in a divided situation since California included both southern and northern white immigrants and was pro-Union by only a very small margin.[31]

Kip's specific beliefs about slavery and free Black Americans, including free Black Episcopalians, mirrored that of many other white northerners. Believing in a hierarchy of races with the "Anglo-Saxon" at the top, Kip thought that Black Americans were unlikely to be "elevated" as a race but was willing to give them the chance. In 1853, just before leaving New York City for San Francisco, one of Kip's final acts in the Diocese of New York was to vote to seat St. Philip's Church in diocesan convention. His biographer notes that this, on the literal verge of his departure, was the sole occasion upon which Kip broke ranks with his parish's lay delegates, and indicates both his desire to avoid conflict whenever possible and, perhaps, some sympathy for the inclusion of Black Episcopalians in the full life of the church. His activity in California, however, did not continue this trend.[32]

In 1863, an African American man named Peter Williams Cassey presented himself to Bishop Kip for holy orders. Originally from Philadelphia, he had been mentored in California by a white priest from Connecticut, Giles Augustus Easton, and organized a school in San Jose in 1862. The school was a necessity for the education of local African American children, as they were denied enrollment in the local white institutions. This became the Phoenixian Institute, an association for education and morals of African Americans in the area, and was associated with a boarding school which welcomed students from as far away as Oregon. Ordained deacon by Kip in 1866, Cassey established an African American congregation along with his school in San Jose.[33]

In 1868, while still a deacon, Cassey also became the central organizer for the budding St. Cyprian congregation in San Francisco, visiting alternate Sundays while still maintaining St. Philip's in San Jose. While Cassey's work was supported at St. Cyprian and later at a second San Francisco mission, Christ Church, by white San Franciscan congregations, he had no support from the diocese and had to struggle constantly for his own living as well as his ministry. Eventually he had to abandon San Francisco as the financial and organizational obligations for two such geographically distant communities were too much. Cassey spent at least $3,000 of his own meager funds to try to purchase a permanent home for St. Philip's and his school.[34] His devotion to his work and ministry must have been exhausting: he was a teacher; managed a household of twenty family members, staff, and students; engaged in pastoral care; tried to find clothing for impoverished community members; and worked constantly to raise money for his church and school.

Cassey was never ordained a priest by Bishop Kip, which would have removed some of the difficulties that Cassey labored under; as a deacon, he was completely dependent upon white clergy to visit and provide communion, and at one point St. Philip's went without communion for two years as a result. St. Philip's was also never listed as a diocesan congregation at diocesan convention. While Kip's biographer notes that this was "the practice" back east, by this point most or all of the northern Black Episcopalian churches had been included in their local diocesan conventions, as Kip well knew. The lack of episcopal support for or interest in Cassey's commitment to ministry and service in a difficult situation is striking, and in 1882 Cassey removed to North Carolina, where he was placed in charge of one of the first African American congregations established there after the Civil War.[35] With his departure, Episcopalianism among Black Californians languished until after the death of Bishop Kip.

California Indians

Like Jamestown before the colonists, California before the Gold Rush was not empty or "waste land." It was inhabited by thousands of Native Americans, speaking over fifty different languages. The diverse California Indian cultures had thrived in a land rich for forage, hunting, and fishing, with little need for agriculture, managing the forests and streams and their bounty through careful use of fire and balancing of resources at different times of year. The development of the mission system by Spain from 1769 to 1833 had negatively affected the coastal tribes and had spread disease as well as the practice of enslavement, weakening the peoples. But much worse was to come.[36]

In Jamestown, English settlers looking to strike it rich traded with, ran away to, fell in love with, killed, and were killed by the Powhatan. At that time the English were still developing an ideology of imperial expansion and figuring out how indigenous peoples could be part of their empire. In upstate New York, the English had brought the Iroquois to fight on their side against the colonists in the American Revolution, engaging them as allies in the imperial project. In California, reflecting the development of more extensive ideologies of scientific racism and the ideal of Manifest Destiny, the Gold Rush settlers began a concerted, public, and completely legal campaign to destroy the native peoples physically and culturally, engaging in hundreds of small- and large-scale massacres of men, women, and children, who were often unarmed and helpless. A frequent pattern was for a few white settlers or miners to identify a *ranchería*, or small village, and attack it at night, shooting first into the houses made of tule rushes and then shooting the survivors as they ran out in confusion and terror. Other massacres were undertaken during indigenous religious rituals or after the whites had herded large groups onto small islands with no way to escape. While the local tribal cultures were not unfamiliar with war among themselves, they were not particularly warlike and did not have the modern armament of the settlers. Most expeditions against the California Indians reported no deaths among the white attackers, and even wounds were rare.[37]

Occasional violent attacks on settlers, immigrants, and miners by California Indians in retribution for these massacres could sometimes include the death of white women and children; this provided one motive for violent expeditions against the natives. For the most part, however, whites went after Indians suspected of taking stock (whether there was proof of this or not) or because white miners wanted the Indians' claims or gold or because the Indians' labor could be sold for profit. California Indian children were kidnaped for legal "apprenticing" in indentured servitude (carefully not called enslavement, since California was a "free state") and their parents murdered. Survivors were herded onto tiny reservations and starved or used as sources of unfree labor, or both. Torture and rape were both common; local ranchers boasted of "Indian hunting" as a sport and displayed the scalps they had taken. The vast amount of weapons brought by the settlers was not enough for all the slaughter, and requisitions for arms and ammunition to kill Indians were filled by the local and federal government. All of this was done in public, organized through democratic processes (among local white miners and settlers), documented in legal requests for financial support, reported in local papers, and often paid for by the federal government.[38]

Bishop Kip's response to this situation, as far as can be told from his public and remaining private papers, was a resounding silence. In his younger years, Kip had been fascinated by the mission work among the Ojibwa conducted by James Lloyd Breck and supported by Bishop Henry Whipple, both of whom were correspondents during his bishopric. During one of his first journeys from San Francisco to Los Angeles and back he even stayed in an indigenous Californian village, writing of the strangeness of life while he lay down to sleep in a tule rush hut, dependent on the hospitality of the tribe.[39]

On an early visit to Marysville, a place with a great many "Churchmen," Kip visited a local village and recorded, "The inhabitants are a remnant of the Digger tribe [*sic*], and are the most degraded Indians I have ever seen. . . . They were lounging about in the warm sun, some of them almost entirely naked, the men with sticks thrust through the lower part of their ears, which adds to their savage appearance. They are dying off fast, and will soon be entirely extinct."[40] In this description, Kip shows his particular personal preferences; for instance, throughout his travels he was both fascinated and repelled by "dirt," which he associated with the "lower classes" of all kinds of people, and which seemed to stand in for everything he found uncomfortable about engaging with people other than those of his own class and race. He also demonstrates how easily he took on the political perceptions of white Californian settlers and miners. There was, for instance, no such thing as a tribe of "Digger" Indians. "Digger" was a demeaning word used by whites to describe all California Indians, regardless of their tribe, and went along with other dehumanizing terms used to report upon the murder of California natives: so many "bucks," "squaws," and "papooses" killed in each place, rather than "men," "women," and "children." The visit Kip reported here took place in the early 1850s, when the actual, physical, murderous extermination of native Californians was regularly taking place. As an avid reader it is unlikely he was unaware of the militias killing Native Americans during his episcopate, which was regularly reported and celebrated in the San Francisco papers. The idea that this "extermination" was destined by providence, and thus that the natives deserved no concern or even mission work since it would be a waste of time, was proffered from the highest ranks of California politics, beginning with its first governor. The idea stemmed from the destined conflict of "races"; that the "Anglo-Saxon" would naturally triumph and destroy all others might make some sad, but it was simply the way the world worked. Kip comfortably embraced this view, including its penumbra of racial hierarchy and violence.[41]

Race and the White Missionary

Despite Kip's rather poor record as bishop, there is no denying his committed efforts in a role for which he was personally unsuited, working himself to exhaustion, supporting his family with his savings as his salary was often in arrears. Muhlenberg spent his own entire fortune as well as the money he received from his sister and other donors on his projects and creative outreach, and died penniless in his own hospital. Yet, bound by their own understandings of mission, race, and the church, they did not succeed in stretching the church's boundaries beyond its core white demographic.

Muhlenberg's Church of the Holy Communion is sometimes credited as the first "institutional urban church," a church notable for connecting social programs to its mission. But of course, St. Philip's, the African American church of New York City and the second African American Episcopal Church founded in the United States, also worked from its inception in 1809 to set up schools, cultural programs, and other support for its members and its community. St. Philip's, too, was separated from diocesan convention. The difference in the high reputation of the Church of the Holy Communion and the paternalistic dismissal of St. Philip's was the race of the members, as well as Muhlenberg's personal and very striking ability to wring money from wealthy Episcopalians for his projects.

St. Philip's and Holy Communion, however, were joined in the person of John Jay II, the aristocratic and combative white abolitionist who supported the inclusion of St. Philip's in diocesan convention, and rented a pew there. Jay was a former student of Muhlenberg's, and Muhlenberg supported his activities. Other students of Muhlenberg were also notable for their abolitionist work, including John McNamara, an Irish "foundling" who was brought up by Muhlenberg, went out to work with Bishop Kemper in Wisconsin, and became known for his radical abolitionist activities there and in Kansas. Muhlenberg himself detested slavery; he helped some enslaved people escape through the Underground Railroad and allowed his hospital to be used as a "station" by one of the sisters. He was infuriated by the Fugitive Slave Act and the *Dred Scott* decision. Yet he did not consider himself an abolitionist, perhaps because of his general distrust of the political system and the fact that abolitionism itself was a political statement. Muhlenberg himself does not seem to have supported St. Philip's financially with his wealthy contacts and fundraising acumen, but focused on the general problem of wealth and poverty, not race, in imagining a sacred community that crossed boundaries.

Muhlenberg's extant writings are very limited, and what there is shows little or no attention to race as a factor in Christian or social life. In this, Muhlenberg (born in 1796) is similar to most early nineteenth-century American missionaries, who placed the line of social distinction between "heathen" and "Christian" rather than "white" and "nonwhite." Alonzo Potter, on the other hand, born in 1800, seems to have envisioned a community that crossed racial lines as a missional ideal. In his early years he was the rector of a mixed-race congregation in Schenectady, New York, and as Bishop of Pennsylvania he worked behind the scenes and developed creative schemes in a effort to have St. Thomas African Episcopal Church accepted in diocesan convention.[42]

Kip, Muhlenberg, and Jay all were at work during a liminal time in the context of American racial ideology. In the early colonial era and the earlier nineteenth century—and continuing into the twentieth for many missionally oriented leaders.

With Kip and Muhlenberg, it is possible to see the limits of the Episcopalian missional vision in the mid-nineteenth century, as well as the missed opportunities to expand both the church's identity and its membership. Bound partly by internal struggles between "high church" and "evangelical" Episcopalians, partly by its unwillingness to experiment with different structures of clergy training and payment, partly by its general unwillingness to get involved with "political" issues such as racism, the Episcopal Church was limited in its ability to develop relationships with and incorporate culturally or racially different groups.

7

Exile and Education

It was Easter Eve, 1880, and around the font of S. Mary's was gathered such a group as, probably, has not been seen upon our Atlantic coasts for many a long day. In snowy surplice and stole stood the commanding figure of an Indian priest. It was the Rev. J. Enmegabowh, the first "red man" ordained to the ministry. Around him were gathered the clergy of S. Mary's and the little surpliced colored boys who acted as servers. Before him, at the font, knelt an Indian girl to whom he was sealing the name of Elizabeth Amelia, as from the baptismal shell he poured the regenerating drops upon her head while, at the rail of the baptistery, stood the old Christian Indian Chief Minnegoshig, the English Sisters of All Saints, the colored Sisters, the young Haytien girl whom Bishop Holly had sent, and a number of the congregation of St. Mary's. It was truly a Pentecostal scene.[1]

In an era in which race and empire were increasingly intertwined with Christianity, this Pentecostal scene was valued precisely because it was rare and seemed possible only with the grace and intervention of the Divine. At the baptism of Elizabeth Amelia, formerly known as Chatry, there were gathered the Episcopalian gleanings from the post–Civil War exodus of Black people from the church and the exiles of the Native American tribes brought into connection with the Episcopal Church as a result of the wars and destruction created by the white settlement of the Plains.[2]

This chapter and the next explore the ways in which the Episcopal Church dealt with the challenge of including and incorporating racial "others" in the period after the Civil War, largely through strategies of assimilation, paternalism, and segregation. In this period racial ideologies in society at large shifted away from paternalism toward scientific racism, an ideology that was largely rejected by the church. The Civil War–era conflicts between high church and evangelicals shifted to Anglican Comprehensiveness in the new Broad Church movement, which was generally associated as well with Social Gospel and justice concerns and which provided a stronger theological basis

Mission, Race, and Empire. Jennifer C. Snow, Oxford University Press. © Oxford University Press 2024.
DOI: 10.1093/oso/9780197598948.003.0008

for the church to become active in political advocacy as well as charitable endeavors among the "unfortunate" and "wronged" peoples.

However, the church's preference for paternalistic assimilationism as a missional strategy meant that even white Episcopalians with the best of intentions toward Native Americans and Black Americans were often still complicit in undermining their agency and well-being—and the growing development of paternalistic segregationism in the southern dioceses would fit easily into the new secular scientific racism. As modern scholars of race and colonialism note, the damage done by assimilationism to minority or politically subordinated groups, even when used as a strategy against the racism of dominant groups and institutions, is lasting and not easily healed.[3]

Assimilation of the Exiles

In 1843 the Domestic Committee of the Board of Missions sent their secretary, Reverend Nathaniel Sayres Harris, on a "journey to Indian Country," the territory west of the Mississippi that was not yet part of any state or U.S. territory, to which the Choctaw, Creek, Cherokee, Seminole, and Chickasaw had been violently removed since 1830 (and to which many other tribes would also be assigned, in addition to the Pawnee, Osage, Caddo, Quapaw, and others who already lived there). On his journey, Harris recorded the ideas he had for an invigorated mission to the "five civilized tribes" as well as the local tribes. Despite having never been in the mission field before, aside from his preordination work as a soldier at Fort Snelling, Minnesota, Harris's journal bubbles over with fully formed ideas for mission strategy, demonstrating the continuity between "civilization" and "Christianization" that Episcopalians shared with most other Christian denominations at the time. Harris's strategy never came to fruition, due to a lack of money and interest from the church at large, but it demonstrates the themes of Episcopalian mission through the early twentieth century, as well as the early, somewhat more culturally flexible white views of Native American cultures prior to the 1860s.

Harris's positive views of assimilation run through his commentary on the Indians he visits with, noting those with neat little farms and log cabins. Unlike later nineteenth-century Indian mission strategists, however, he is not particularly horrified by those who do not wear dresses or trousers, commenting descriptively rather than negatively on those who are naked or wearing blankets, amazed at how little the men seemed to need to wear despite the weather, and how cleverly the women "managed their blankets" in a game of ball. In fact, he criticized a Methodist missionary for insisting that women in their school wear only Euro-American clothing rather than their own native dress, which he felt suited them better and was both more comfortable and more attractive; he also criticized those who he felt crushed the Native Americans' "instincts" or cultural habits instead of helping them to build on their strengths. He imagined how the skills and attention of Indian women to needlework might help them build up an industry of lace-making, an idea that became a prominent strategy in later Oneida and Dakota Episcopalian missions. He has in general nothing but good to say of the Indians themselves, whether assimilated or not: they have suffered and been wronged much, but are not pitiable; they are healthy and strong, innovative and problem-solving, determined and clever. Harris's writing differs from later nineteenth-century commentary on Native Americans in that he does not imagine, for the most part, that they will disappear or be destroyed. For Harris, the tribes have a good future ahead of them, through the door of cultural assimilation, "disappearing" within the population of white farmers to become truly "one people." In this, he echoes far more closely the colonial views of mission and Native Americans rather than those of the later nineteenth century, which become both more explicitly racist and more pessimistic about the future existence of indigenous people.[4]

Education was central to Harris's hopeful vision of the Indians' future. He noted approvingly that the Choctaw had spent all their annuity on schools and that English was becoming the dominant language among them. In particular—and this was something of an innovation on his part—Harris believed that "females" needed special attention, and that mission schools had failed because they focused only on the young Indian boys. Without a "Christian home" to return to, well managed by a faithful Christian wife, how could the young Indian man coming home from mission school retain his Christian ways? "The main effort will be directed, *in the first place*, towards *female* education, the neglect of which I am satisfied has been the true source of former failures in civilizing and Christianizing the Indians. Let the Indian mother be fitted to raise her children, and all will eventually come right." This points to the emerging evangelical Protestant missionary strategy of the "Christian home," which originated in early nineteenth-century Congregationalist and Baptist missions to Hawai'i and Burma, as well as the unexamined assumption that a native mother would not know how to raise her children without such help.[5]

This assimilation, Harris assumed, would require the extinction of native languages in favor of English—but he was corrected more than once by the more experienced Congregationalist missionaries he met, who preached and taught in local languages and worked to translate the Bible into them. Finding missionaries preaching and teaching in Cherokee, he challenged them, "Would it not be better for them, more conducive to the happiness and civilization of the race, to drop their mother tongue as soon as possible, and take up ours? The sooner the various tribes in that Territory become one people, under the operation of our language and institutions, the better?" The missionary told him—as had a previous missionary among the Choctaw— that insisting on English was the old way, but that they had changed their practice "for good reason."[6] Harris may have been convinced enough by this to bring the news back to the missionally inclined; it was clear, at any rate, that later Episcopalian missions to native tribes valued and put great effort into translation and insisted that missionaries learn indigenous languages. However, the idea that assimilation required learning English remained central to many educational efforts later on, particularly those supported by the U.S. government.[7]

Above all, Harris envisioned a completely "native" ministry, beginning (but not ending) with a white Episcopalian missionary bishop who would identify, train, and ordain native people to run their own church. This vision of a "native pastorate," to which a "native Bishop" would be the crown, echoes the evangelical missional strategy of Henry Venn of the Church Mission Society in the Church of England: self-governing, self-sustaining, self-extending. Harris wrote a letter to the Creek chief, who was absent during his visit to Indian Territory, describing his vision of an Indian Church:

It has been presumed, that sending a Bishop to collect and form a Church from the Indian population, and relying upon a church so formed to perpetuate and extend itself, would be most agreeable to you, as involving the least possible number of white men as its agents, and, of course, the least possible occasion of offence on their part. The experiment has never yet been tried of an Indian Church, relying for its ministry, its catechists, its officers of every kind, with one exception, and that only till an Indian bishop could be raised to govern it, upon the materials found among you.

Harris had been a bit forward in making this offer, as he also explained that he would make this proposal to the church if the Creek chief found it interesting. It is not clear whether he ever received an answer, but the proposal for a bishop for the Indian Territory was made to General Convention in 1844, without approval—the only request for a missionary bishop that the House of Bishops ignored that year.[8]

The Indians of Indian Territory never received their own bishop or Episcopal mission and were largely ignored by the Episcopal Church. Harris's grand plans came to naught. However, in the northern plains, missionary bishop Jackson Kemper was pursuing the ideal of a native ministry with zeal, with the help of James Lloyd Breck. Their ideal missional strategy, coming from a high church orientation, was less focused on the Christian home (which required sending and supporting both a male missionary and his wife and children) than on a newly revived monastic ideal, or at least the missional practice of leaving one's children back east with relatives. However, their mission shared the commitment to "civilizing and Christianizing." Salvation for Native Americans, in this world and the next, would come through learning to be, dress, act, speak, love, learn, and work like white people.

This ideal of assimilation was held equally by the U.S. government and church organizations, a partnership that would prove to be particularly damaging, as it provided assimilationism with the power of military violence and the withholding of official food rations—and, for a brief period, gave the church legal power to direct these coercions. As the nineteenth century progressed, increased violence against and displacement of Native Americans meant that Episcopalian bishops—who, according to Episcopalian high church ideals, were bishops to all the people within their territories, Episcopalian or not—needed to choose between the needs of the white settlers and the indigenous people in their dioceses or missionary districts. Some, like Bishop Kip of California, simply assumed that the Native Americans were doomed to extinction, and did nothing at all for or with them. Others, such as Bishop Kemper and his successor in Minnesota, Bishop Henry Whipple, took their calls to care for all of their people much more seriously, depending upon the missional strategy of assimilationism while challenging the abuse, exploitation, and murder of native people.

Bishop Kemper had visited the mission at Fort Snelling, Minnesota, as early as 1843, and even before that a missionary chaplain to the fort, Reverend Ezekiel Gear, had had Dakota in his mission school there since 1838. Kemper was deeply interested in the Native Americans in his immense missionary district, and when Breck found that Nashotah House had become too staid, leaving behind his early missionary monastic ideals for a more typical seminary method, Kemper invited him to Minnesota to begin again on the northern frontier. Breck set up a mission school in St. Paul, and in 1851 a man named Enmegabowh brought his son there to be educated.[9]

Enmegabowh, also known by his baptismal name, John Johnson, was a remarkable man, and his meeting with Breck had formidable effects on Episcopalian mission history. Born of Ottawa parents who lived with an Ojibwa band near Rice Lake, Enmegabowh had attended a Methodist mission school at Sault Ste. Marie and set up a native-led Methodist mission with his cousin and another convert at Lac Courte Oreilles, Wisconsin, in the 1830s. He married Charlotte, an Ojibwa woman from the family of the chief Hole-in-the-Day, and her family required him to remain in Ojibwa territory as a condition of the marriage. Some sources note that Enmegabowh himself had been trained in the spiritual leadership tradition of the Ojibwa, the *midewewin*, before he had become Christian.[10]

In 1849, the Methodists expelled Enmegabowh, perhaps for fighting a white man for insulting Charlotte. He and Charlotte remained with Hole-in-the-Day's band at Gull Lake, but Enmegabowh still wanted a Christian education for his son. He learned about Breck's mission school and requested that the Episcopal Church send missionaries to Gull Lake—at which point Kemper directed Breck to go there. In 1852, Breck and Enmegabowh together established St. John's in the Wilderness, and Kemper consecrated the church in 1853. At this service, Breck presented the first confirmation class of five Ojibwa, including Enmegabowh, to Bishop Kemper, in a bilingual service with Enmegabowh as the translator.[11]

Breck and Enmegabowh together worked to transform the Gull Lake Ojibwa community along "civilizing" lines, encouraging log cabins, vegetable gardens, Euro-American gendered roles, and literacy. Breck was less liberal than Harris in matters of clothing, insisting that converts cut their hair and wear donated clothes from back east, but he and Enmegabowh shared a sense that to become a Christian, Ojibwa must—and would—live differently in many aspects of their daily lives, including religious matters such as keeping the Sabbath, but also building cabins instead of wigwams, farming instead of hunting, going to school instead of dancing and singing the old tales, eschewing alcohol and multiple wives, and seeking "scientific" medical care rather than the spiritual ministrations of the *midewewin*. In 1858, Breck left to establish a new divinity school at Faribault, and Enmegabowh remained at Gull Lake to direct the mission on his own, with the help of Church of England clergy in Canada. In 1859, as one of his last acts before withdrawing from Minnesota and the missionary episcopate to take up the diocesan episcopate of Wisconsin, Bishop Kemper ordained Enmegabowh a deacon.[12]

The new Episcopal Bishop of Minnesota, Henry Whipple, arrived in 1859 from his only other missionary appointment as rector of a "free church" among German immigrants in Chicago. On the way to Minnesota, Whipple baptized a Dakota child in Red Wing; the child's father, Wabasha, would eventually also be baptized and become a close ally of Whipple. Among Whipple's first acts in reaching St. Paul was to accompany Breck to the Ojibwa at Gull Lake. Despite the work that Enmegabowh and Breck had done to "civilize" the Ojibwa Christians, Whipple was still horrified by their "pitiable condition" of near-starvation and was inspired by Breck and Enmegabowh to commit himself to their spiritual and holistic care, even though he wrote later, "I was saddened upon my return, that good men advised me to have nothing to do with Indian missions, on the ground that the red men were a degraded, perishing race."[13]

Whipple's missional method was to visit with Christian Indians and let them do most of the talking and evangelizing to other Ojibwa, but he also preached himself. Like Enmegabowh, and likely influenced by him as well as Episcopalian understandings of conversion, he imagined a gradual enlightenment that would change how the Ojibwa lived. His first sermon in 1859 at Red Lake told the listeners that all men are brothers; all die because of disobedience; all can choose to be with Great Spirit: "Great spirit gives the light to all who ask it—pray—keep praying—avoid firewater—if you begin I promise you . . . God, he will help you and lead you to heaven." He described a "solemn congregation . . . deeply interested."[14] Whipple believed that the "degradation" of Ojibwa life, particularly disease, alcoholism, and extramarital sexuality, were caused largely by contact with white people. Although he criticized Ojibwa religious ceremonies and religious leaders, he believed that there were good aspects to traditional belief and practice that should be supported and built on toward Christianity— a missional strategy held by a variety of Christian missionaries across the globe. Whipple often was contacted by Ojibwa asking him to send missionaries, with the explanation that they couldn't hold to Christian teachings without a missionary to live with them and show them the way—supporting Whipple's own understanding of how missional transformation would work gradually in daily life. Whipple, however, rarely had missionaries to send.

Throughout his episcopate, from 1859 to his death in 1901, Whipple engaged in work for the benefit of Indians as he understood it, including policy, advocacy, intervention, work on treaties, managing annuities, and more. Like William Augustus Muhlenberg and Alonzo Potter, who founded hospitals in urban centers, he saw the mission of the church as caring for bodies as well as souls; he even learned from a dentist friend how to extract infected teeth so he could personally provide this service on his yearly episcopal visitations to villages and reservations.[15]

For Whipple, like Muhlenberg, "Christian civilization" (meaning white Euro-American culture) was basically good, needing only to keep people to ideals of charity and justice to make it a positive experience for all. While he strongly critiqued abuses of the Native American peoples, he did not offer any deep critique of the status quo, or the ultimate source of the abuse: the white settlers' demand for land and resources. In his assimilationist understanding, the future for Native Americans lay in joining the white American demand for land as farmers and participants in the settler economic system. Part of the assimilationist ideal for Whipple was that Indians were essentially good, corrupted by abusive whites. With Christianity and capitalism they could live well and contribute as full members of white society. All the education, training, and cultural transformation provided by or demanded by the Episcopal mission was intended to enable the Native Americans to become indistinguishable in culture from the whites, and thus to enable them to thrive and survive.[16]

Ojibwa Contextualization

Native Americans themselves, Christian and non-Christian, had much more complex relationships with assimilation and with "Christian civilization." For Enmegabowh and his Christian Ojibwa community, Christianity and "civilization," becoming farmers and living in the white man's way, was to save the people who were weakened and disorganized by the conflicts and oppression of the settlers. Enmegabowh reported regularly on his people's faithfulness, hoping to publicize to white people that despite the Ojibwa's adversity they could still survive and thrive and should be respected and their rights defended by those in power. In a skit presented by Ojibwa to the visiting bishop, the white people destroyed the Ojibwa people with firewater and violence, plunging them into destitution and disaster; at last appeared a "pale faced man who sought neither trade nor anything else," followed by an Indian clergyman and wife in white-style clothing, symbolizing the rebirth of the people in a new way of life.[17]

After the disastrous Dakota Uprising (sometimes called the Sioux War), the continuing Minnesota Ojibwa mission was forced to relocate to White Earth Reservation, led by Enmegabowh and white missionary priest Joseph Gilfillan (later the editor of the Ojibwa edition of the Book of Common Prayer). Enmegabowh's efforts demonstrate the close connection between Christian faith, the struggles of the people to survive, and "Christian civilization" in terms of farms, hospitals, and schools among the Native American Episcopalians. A pair of letters published by the Board of Missions in 1876, one from the white missionary and one from Enmegabowh, demonstrate this clearly.

Gilfillan, the white missionary, reflected that while many people believe that Indians were bloodthirsty and ferocious, he had found them to be open-hearted, trusting, a "simple-hearted, guileless people . . . with traits in some respects resembling children." This style of paternalism echoed that of Bishop Whipple, who frequently described himself as a father of the childlike Indians and emphasized the ideal of "wardship" over them, the importance of white people providing care, protection, and teaching of the "red race."[18] He described their devotion, their love of singing hymns, their dignified care of the dead, their keeping of the sabbath and refusal to swear, their raising up of candidates for ministry, in the same breath as their engaging in agriculture and wood-cutting, wearing pants and jackets, beginning to raise cows, persisting in the growing of rutabagas after a terrible plague of locusts. "They are never tired of contrasting themselves with what they were a few years ago, and the way they live now with they way they did then. . . . They also contrast themselves, with great complacency, with the wild or blanket Chippewas who have not yet adopted the habits of Civilization."[19]

For Enmegabowh, pride in the building of the church at White Earth is next to that of the "fine Hospital [that] has been erected near our church, which is a great blessing to my people." The people had worked hard and had successfully raised a good crop against the winter:

> Chief Wright has raised thirty-seven bushels of onions. . . . Chief E. A. Washburn raised over two hundred bushels of wheat. . . . The Chiefs and others who have raised wheat this year are much encouraged, and say they will work harder next year to raise more wheat, and sell the flour. So we are

beginning to live and learn in the ways of the palefaces. If the sharp whites do not take advantage of us and take away our land and country, I do not see why we cannot become independent and self-supporting people in the future. Christianity has taught us these things; the Religion of the GREAT SPIRIT has led us to see the beauty of those things, and to make provision in the future, of both temporal and spiritual things. This is the secret and beauty of the Christian Religion. The eyes, ears, minds and hearts are enlarged more and more for the glory of God.[20]

The success of Enmegabowh's new religion and way of life was admired by some other Ojibwa; he described the pleading for a missionary from another band, far away in Turtle Mountain. He had visited them and heard from the "heathen chief" that the Christian Ojibwa never once missed saying morning and evening prayer and always kept the Sabbath, though they had not seen a missionary in three years.

Enmegabowh's letter also includes a tribute to Whipple, who, despite his assimilative goals and paternalistic viewpoint regarding his "red children," was deeply regarded and trusted by many of the Ojibwa, Christian and "heathen" alike. "The Indians said, again and again, that they do not want any other [denomination] but the Bishop's Missionary. Go among the Indians, wild and civilized, and in their Councils they talk about the Bishop. They love him: no wonder they do; it is his instrumentality that has brought about this great change among us."[21]

Uprising and Exile

When Bishop Whipple arrived in the new state, the groups of Native Americans he first encountered were called Sioux by the white people: the Oceti Sakowin, the seven council fires or bands, speaking Dakota, Lakota, or Nakota. By 1858, forced more and more by white settlement to give up even the reservation lands they were promised, the Dakota depended upon two Indian agencies for survival: Redwood (Lower Sioux) Agency for the Mdewankanton (including Wabasha's band) and Wahpekute, and the Yellow Medicine Upper Sioux Agency for the Sisseton and Wahpeton. Fort Ridgely was across the river about fifteen miles below the Lower Sioux Agency. The trader at the Lower Agency, Andrew Myrick, was known for his corruption and abuse, refusing credit for food and telling them to go eat grass.[22]

In 1860, Dakota leaders Wabasha, Wakinyanwaste (Good Thunder), and Taopi invited Whipple to set up a mission with their people. This was the first mission of any Christian group among the Mdewankanton, according to Whipple. He visited the band when they assembled at the agency for their rations and listened to the leaders' story of what they had been promised, including schools for their children and payment for their land. When they asked him to send a school and a missionary to run it, Whipple promised to do so if he could find "the men and the means." Back in Faribault, he recruited Samuel Hinman, an orphaned young man from Connecticut whom Whipple regarded as a son, to begin the mission for Wabasha.[23]

Not all the Mdewankanton wanted the mission. One group, led by Little Crow, was very hostile to the mission. Their experience with white people had led them to be suspicious of the work of conversion and assimilation, which was the strategy chosen both by the churches and by the government. The government had paid white farmers and craftsmen to teach Indians about farming and trades, and this had led to an internal, hostile division between the "farmer" Indians and the "blanket" Indians. The "farmers," including those who supported the mission, nonetheless tried to balance their culture and traditions against the overwhelming demands of white assimilation and were well able to critique white Christianity on its own terms. For instance, in 1862 Whipple visited the agency and was horrified to see a scalp dance in progress, the end result of a Winnebago attempting to steal horses. When he confronted Wabasha about this, Wabasha agreed that it was inappropriate, but then "slowly blowing a cloud of smoke into the air said, 'White man go to war with his own brother; kills more men than Wabasha can count all his life.' "[24]

Only a few weeks after Whipple's visit, the Dakota Uprising began as the people gathered for their annuity were denied it over and over again. The people had been there since June and were missing the annual buffalo hunt and were angry at the months-long delay, as well as hungry and in need of the promised annuity money which could buy their rations. Four young men went out hunting, were unsuccessful, and found eggs on a white farm, which blew up into an attack on the settlers. They returned to their camp and excitedly told about their accomplishment, encouraging others to go with them and make war on the whites. The chiefs, including Wabasha and Little Crow, argued against this, knowing how it was likely to end. Little Crow even urged his band to turn the young men in to Fort Ridgely. But in the end Little Crow agreed to join the war party, which attacked the Redwood Agency the next morning.[25]

The war party pressured or extorted members of the "peace party" to join them on the raids, and so there was a division in the group between those who were more or less just present at the battle and massacre sites, and who often attempted to save the white settlers, and those who actively engaged in violence against the settlers. Emily West, the single woman missionary who worked with Hinman and his wife, recorded that as she fled she was met by a war party in paint, who were aiming for a nearby farm. They told her to go to the fort, but recognizing her as a member of the mission did not attack her or those she said were under her protection. Taopi, Good Thunder, and Wabasha all tried to dissuade the band from warfare but were overruled by the war party. Little Crow sent to the Upper Agency bands telling them to join, but the Christian Dakota overruled the war party in those bands and defended local settlers from them. According to some accounts, during the period of raids and violence over the next few weeks, the Dakota war party killed some eight hundred settlers, including women and children. After a significant loss to the U.S. Army on September 23, 1862, the most active members of the war party, including Little Crow, fled, leaving behind over two hundred white prisoners, as well as the members of the peace party to take the blame from the furious, grieving white settlers.[26]

After the decisive battle in late September, Henry H. Sibley and the U.S. Army collected all the Indians they could find and put hundreds on military show trials—over forty in one day—and condemned 307 to death. Sixteen hundred prisoners were marched in chains downriver to Mankato. During this journey, the women, old men, and children were attacked by white people bent on vengeance for their losses; one Sisseton remembered seeing a white woman grab a baby from a Dakota woman and smash it against the ground. The baby died a few hours later. The condemned remained at Mankato, and the remaining prisoners were marched to Fort Snelling. They were "camped" within a stockade outside the fort for months in winter; subject to appalling conditions, disease, exposure, and malnutrition, many died. Hinman moved into the stockade with the prisoners, enraging the white population; at one point he was beaten unconscious by whites who broke into the stockade. As he and Bishop Whipple continued their ministry under these conditions, many of the imprisoned Dakota were baptized and confirmed as Episcopalians.[27]

Bishop Whipple, while condemning the violence and mourning the deaths of the white settlers, defended the Dakota as the wronged party, claiming that the government abuse and broken promises were the original cause of the bloodshed, and demanding that a distinction be made between Dakota who had actually engaged in violent atrocities and the vast majority who had either not engaged in violence at all, had actively tried to stop the violence, or had engaged in violence on a battlefield against white soldiers or in self-defense. Whipple traveled to Washington to plead with President Lincoln, demanding a review of the sentences. Upon this review, Lincoln determined that only thirty-eight of the condemned Dakota had engaged in "atrocities" rather than legitimate warfare. Even this much smaller number is dubious; among the thirty-eight hanged on the day after Christmas 1862 some were almost certainly innocent or victims of mistaken identity.[28]

While white public opinion demanded that all Indians be expelled from Minnesota, Hinman continued to minister within the stockade and Whipple visited weekly, to the fury of the white settler community. Many Indian communities who had nothing whatever to do with the violence were forced into imprisonment or exile. In February 1863, Congress approved legislation that ended all treaties with the Minnesota Oceti Sakowin bands, as well as the Winnebago, and expelled them permanently from the territory.[29]

The Ojibwa were able to remain in Minnesota and avoid congressional expulsion because of Whipple's intervention on their behalf; he had publicized the fact that Enmegabowh at Gull Lake had learned of the uprising when Little Crow sent messages inviting Hole-in-the-Day to join. Enmegabowh had walked through the night downriver, pulling his children in a canoe, to warn the local fort that there would be an attack. He also sent messages to the Mille Lacs Ojibwa band, asking them to protect the fort; over one hundred Mille Lacs went at his request. Two of Enmegabowh's children later died from exposure, as Hole-in-the-Day's band expelled all Christian Ojibwa and destroyed the mission at Gull Lake. Enmegabowh's Christian Ojibwa relocated to Crow Wing, near a white settlement, and eventually to White Earth.[30]

Peace Policy, Education, and Assimilationism

"The Lord have mercy upon our men in high places, who, charged with a generous nation's benefactions for a race struggling to emerge from

Heathenism, misapply them. They will need mercy in the day of the Lord." So wrote Nathaniel Harris in 1843, and so thought Bishop Henry Whipple as he began to grasp the ways "Indian affairs" were managed. In trying to defend the Dakota prisoners, Whipple wrote that the cause of the problem was a "bad system of Indian affairs—based on a falsehood that these heathen are an independent nation and not our wards." In Whipple's understanding of racial and cultural relations, paternalistic "wardship" was the appropriate relation, not independence or equality. Moving from wardship to independence would require "Christianizing and civilizing": becoming Christians would save their souls, while living in a way similar to that of the white settlers would save their bodies. Christianity was the assimilative bridge. Whipple's lifelong work for Native Americans thus had two goals: "Christianize and civilize" them, through missions and schools, but also reform the white governmental structure that, ideally, should defend their rights and provide promised goods of food, tools, and teachers. By the late 1860s, these two goals had become one as churches were put directly in charge of government Indian policy.[31]

Even before the outbreak of violence in 1862, Whipple had predicted that it would come. The Dakota were being constantly cheated and starved by the Indian agents who were charged with administering their annuities. These agents were chosen not because of their skill, honesty, or ability to work with the Native Americans, but as beneficiaries of patronage, given by politicians as a reward for support. It was expected that the agents would milk their responsibilities for their personal reward, as was true of all patronage posts. Whipple wanted to reform the "Indian system," which he thought was corrupt and the cause of uprisings because it cheated, abused, and ruined the lives of native people. He wanted a system that would forbid whiskey, protect converts from hostility of non-Christian natives, allow landownership by individuals, and provide agricultural training. While he eventually accepted that the Dakota would have to leave Minnesota because of the hostility of settlers toward them, he insisted that they should be given a good, permanent reservation, protected from exploitation, abuse, and those who traded in alcohol, and taught agricultural skills so that they could thrive on the new lands which would be given to them as individuals. He accepted without much reflection the white understanding of land as a tradeable commodity—lose some here, gain some somewhere else—as a fair solution to conflict over resources, which influenced his advocacy heavily. George Tinker argues that for this reason Whipple was involved in the illegal taking of the Black Hills from the original reservation area given to the Oceti Sakowin: he believed that they would be better off with a smaller reservation because it would force them to remain in one place and farm. He found a treaty fair if it provided good land in trade for the land that was taken—land suitable for a community of farmers, not land which could support a no-madic or hunting community. He did not recognize the ties of the people to a particular land beyond its "use" for agriculture. Conversion to Christianity, with all Whipple believed went with it, was the root of survival for the Oceti Sakowin and Ojibwa. Whipple recognized that this solution—becoming Christian, living in scattered farms and towns as the white people did—was not always attractive to the indigenous people, but he believed it was their best option and would in the end make their lives better as well as providing spiritual salvation.[32]

Whipple's rhetoric also defended the white settlers; the wrongdoing was that of the government, not the settlers themselves, who were as innocent as the Dakota in the situation. However, while it was the government agents, not the white settlers as a whole, who had refused the promised annuities, the white settlers were the ones who had taken the lands of the tribes, denying them access to their traditional sources of sustenance. Whipple did not see this as the true problem behind the broken treaties; he saw keeping the treaties as the solution, and requiring the Native Americans to adopt white ways and get the best out of their remaining land as agriculturalists.[33]

President Grant's Inaugural Address laid out a policy of treating Indians with a goal of "civilization and ultimate citizenship." The Peace Policy, in-spired partly by the advocacy of Whipple and other religious leaders, would essentially be the same as the old policy of reservations and assimilation, but it would be run by religious groups to avoid the problems of graft and cor-ruption of the older system. Denominations would have the right to nom-inate men to be the agents for Indian affairs in their assigned areas. The reservations were divided among thirteen denominations. The long-term goal was to dissolve the reservations when the Indians were educated and able to support themselves, and assimilate the Indians into white society.[34]

It became the official policy of the government to enforce "detribalization," the weakening of communal bonds and ways of life, by breaking up what remained of tribal lands and assigning them to individuals. In 1887 Congress passed the Dawes Allotment Act, very much influenced by the Protestant missionaries and seemingly very much along the lines of Whipple's idea: to essentially force the Indians into dispersed, single-family farming and to dissolve the bonds of camp, tribe, and hunt. Each Indian householder could have 160 to 320 acres of land, and any land not taken by them would be sold at auction to settlers and railroad companies. The Dawes Act, so deeply valued by the white "friends of the Indian," was devastating to tribal communities. They lost more and ever more of their land undermining the cultural organization of daily and generational life, ritual, and family .[35]

Education was almost as central as churches to the strategy of Whipple and his missionaries. The ideal he wanted to provide for the Ojibwa was a mission and school in every Indian village, with "promising boys" sent to the boarding school at Faribault to train for the ministry. The original goal was not to take children away from their parents and families for schooling.[36] However, the assimilative policy became more stringent as the government began taking direct control of Indian policy once again in the 1880s. Governmental strategy moved toward large-scale, off-reservation boarding schools, such as the Carlisle School in Pennsylvania, founded in 1879. These multitribal schools were pan-Protestant and militarized. The off-reservation boarding schools were thought to hasten detribalization by taking the children away from the "bad influences" of their home cultures and families for years at a time and forcing them to speak only English, as without it children from different tribes could communicate neither with one another nor with their white teachers. When education became legally required in 1891, Indian parents began to more strongly prefer local mission schools, as they tended to be on the reservation, even if these schools too were attempting to teach the children to adopt white ways and speak English.[37]

Mission among the Dakota, Lakota, and Nakota had continued during their exiled wanderings, first to the arid land of Crow Creek, where the band continued to suffer starvation, and then, after Whipple's intervention with the government, to a reservation more suitable for agriculture near the Niobrara River in what is now Nebraska. Samuel Hinman accompanied the Santee Band through all of their sufferings, and when they settled in Niobrara he remained with them and continued to prepare young men for the ministry. Paul Mazakute was ordained by Bishop Robert Clarkson of Nebraska to the diaconate in 1868 and assigned to the Yankton Agency in South Dakota. From this point forward much of the work of evangelizing the Dakota was accomplished primarily by Dakota themselves, not the white missionaries.[38]

At the new reservation on the Niobrara River, the survivors developed an Episcopalian Christian Dakota community.[39] Becoming Christian did not erase their identity: they became Christian on their own terms. Philip

Deloria, a Yankton Dakota, converted because his father, a medicine man, believed that the new religion would protect him from a ghostly vision. They were both baptized in 1870, and in 1892 Deloria was ordained priest. Chief Gall, an older leader, would come sit in the chapel and listen to Deloria's sermons, and converted near the end of his life, when one of his wives had died. Gall's conversion demonstrated to the local Hunkpapa that it was possible to be both Lakota and Christian, as he said that the teachings of Christianity were the same as those of the religion of the pipe. Four young Yankton Episcopalian men, including Deloria, organized Wojo Okolakiciye (the Planting Society) in 1873 to encourage young men to engage in farming and to reconcile with those who continued to prefer a nomadic life; the Society endured great hostility but persevered.[40]

By 1868, the missionary bishop of Nebraska and Dakota had become the diocesan bishop of the new Diocese of Nebraska and had chosen to focus his energies purely on the white settlements. Bishop Clarkson desired to be free of the responsibility for the Indian missions within the Nebraska-Dakota area and proposed to General Convention that a "missionary jurisdiction" be created that was just for the Indians, with a missionary bishop provided for them—in short, a racially defined mission. In 1871, with little discussion of whether a racially defined missionary district was appropriate or in any way theologically complex—an issue that would be prominent for Black Episcopalians in a very few years—the General Convention approved the new missionary jurisdiction of Niobrara, to include all of the reservations in Nebraska and Dakota. This was the first time that the Episcopal Church had designated a missionary jurisdiction, complete with bishop, for a racial group rather than a geographic area, as had been the practice inherited from England.

Later in 1872 the House of Bishops, in special meeting, elected William Hobart Hare as its missionary bishop. In a sense, Nathaniel Harris's 1844 suggestion had been accomplished: a new diocese was created only for the Indians, with a white man as bishop and with sustained efforts to "raise up" ministry leadership among the Native Americans themselves. However, 1872 was not the 1840s in terms of American racial ideologies. The Niobrara jurisdiction was created with a strong aura of racial paternalism, supported by government policy and government money, and with a stated goal of fully "civilizing" the Indians, a goal that would be supported by the full force and power of the state and the threatened violence of surrounding white communities. Racial ideology was also growing more "scientific," incorporating the new ideas of evolution, competition, and survival of the fittest. While church leaders and missionaries generally rejected scientific racism in favor of the older, biblically based racial paternalism, the awareness of the possibility of Indians being actually physically exterminated by white people, and the idea that assimilation into "Christian civilization" would be their only hope for survival, shaped the intensity of attention to assimilative strategies. Harris's cheerful optimism about the future for indigenous people, happily assimilated into white communities, was transmuted into an almost fearful sense of the weight and importance of the mission and the danger which surrounded it.[41]

In his sermon at Bishop Hare's consecration, Whipple wrote:

> There is room for us to plant twenty Indian missions where we have one. Among our Christian Indians, schools and hospitals are to be builded. The rich stores of Christian history, or Christian songs and devotion are to be translated. The Church must send out brotherhoods to do what Christian men did for the Saxon race. Every Indian mission ought to have its sister-hood to train and mould Indian women to take a woman's rightful place as a helpmeet for many Christian men. A true Christian civilization must be the handmaid of religion. No true progress can be made until the Indian has a home, comforts for his loved ones. The tipi can never be a home. The follower and vassal of a wandering chief cannot be Christ's freeman. . . .
>
> The people who have no homes, no law, and no government, must always be the sons of Ishmael. The Home, the Church, and the State are institutions of God, and if you take one away, humanity is a wreck. . . . You have solved the Indian problem when you have made the home the centre of a man's in-terest, by giving him personal rights of property, Christian training, and the protection of law. The Church, the School, and the Government are teachers for this end, and the Gospel of Christ hallows and consecrates the work by blessing life here, and by giving hopes for the life beyond the grave.[42]

Whipple's emphasis on the lack of a home, and the lack of law among the Indians, reflects his own culturally and theologically limited sense of what these things could be. For Whipple, law resided purely in the government of white people. The laws and customs by which the indigenous people governed their lives were invisible to him. As Tinker notes, this lack of un-derstanding led to Whipple's belief that Indians' salvation lay in their submis-sion to a "true" government, connected to the plan of God for a benevolent hierarchy among human beings—similar, in the end, to the earliest ideas of English settlers in Virginia.[43]

Summary

In his closing peroration, Whipple told Hare, the new missionary bishop of Niobrara, to expect to be hated by his own people for his work to "save" the Indians: "The bad men of the border may excite savage hearts to deeds of blood. The Government may again forget its plighted faith. You may have to stand alone and breast the anger of the people in defence of the helpless. In the darkest hour look up to Christ your king. Better men than we have labored and died without seeing the harvest. . . . It is yours to work and pray and die."[44]

Realistically, it was the Indians who were in far more danger than the white missionaries. Because traditional religious ceremonies were illegal from 1883 to 1978, Christianity drew attention as the only option for a people who deeply valued a holistic spiritual connection and community. In 1890, the Ghost Dance reached its height—a messianic faith teaching kindness to all people until Jesus returned, who would usher in a new world with only Indians, the buffalo and dead relatives returning as well. The Indians, the prophet Wovoka said, would not crucify Jesus but welcome him. Sitting Bull allowed the Ghost Dance religion despite the fact that all Indian religious ceremonies had been illegal since 1883, and thus the Indian agent, who believed Sitting Bull to be an opponent of federal Indian policy (as indeed he was), decided to arrest him. Many of the older Indians had experienced white warfare before and recognized the signs of military buildup. Chief Gall offered to take the schoolteacher and all the mission staff and students to Fort Yates for safety, but she refused. The botched arrest of Sitting Bull, which killed him and eight others plus six Indian police sent to arrest him, was followed two weeks later by the massacre at Wounded Knee, where three hundred men, women, and children were killed by the Seventh Calvary on reservation land.

The pattern of Indian converts and missionaries coming out of the crucible of war and imprisonment was not universal—Enmegabowh, for instance, did not convert under wartime stresses—but was notable nonetheless. Elizabeth Amelia, the girl whose Baltimore baptism is described at the beginning of this chapter, was an orphan Ojibwa found by a white soldier on a battlefield as a child; she went back to her people with Minnegoshig, who had lost his own children, and served the church on the reservation with Enmegabowh, until her own death from sickness. The first ordained Cheyenne, David Oakerhater, was a Sun Dance war leader captured in war and imprisoned in Florida, where he met Colonel Richard Pratt, the founder of Carlisle School and the originator of the U.S. government Indian boarding school assimilation program, connected to the deliberate cultural genocide of Native tribes. Oakerhater converted to Episcopalianism, and after training at a small church in upstate New York, he returned to the Cheyenne-Arapaho reservation in Oklahoma, where he lived for decades and was the only Episcopalian clergyman among his people. Sherman Coolidge, a Northern Arapaho, was found as a child on a battlefield and adopted by a white soldier's family. Sponsored by Bishop Whipple, he was ordained in 1882 and returned to his tribe's reservation in Wyoming, where he had to relearn his own language in order to engage in missionary work.[45]

In this period, even when connections to the church did not grow out of direct experience of war, the reality that the people were surrounded by danger and mired in suffering, and that their future was in doubt, energized many converts and leaders to join the Episcopal Church in an effort to find a new way to be Native American, one based in holistic spiritual perceptions of the world, deep spiritual practice, and ties to community, as the old way had been.

The assimilationist goals of Native American Episcopalians themselves had never been as extensive as white missionaries and government workers had hoped. Indigenous Episcopalians worked to preserve their history and culture while critically engaging in the work of Christian life in their contexts. Ella Deloria, for instance, the daughter of Philip Deloria, became a noted anthropologist, recording the ways in which her people had lived both prior to and during the experience of colonization. Charles Alexander Eastman (Ohiyesa) recorded his family's experience of conversion and his childhood during the wars and after, becoming a culture broker between natives and whites. Sherman Coolidge, in his later years, turned away from assimilationist ideals and became a leader in the early Red Progressive movement in the 1920s, arguing that Native culture had something unique and valuable to offer to the world. The development of Native American Christian theology, and its responses to colonialism and assimilationism, continues into the twenty-first century.[46]

8

Emancipation and Exodus

Introduction

In 1843 in Baltimore, Bishop William Whittingham confirmed "half a dozen or more" enslaved people brought by their "master," who was himself an Episcopal priest. "Upon their confirmation they were set free, and, a few days later, sailed for Maryland in Africa"—that is, they were sent by the American Colonization Society to Liberia. This had been the primary answer of the Episcopal Church to free Black Episcopalians for much of the nineteenth century. Those free Black Episcopalians who insisted on their right to remain in the United States, the country in which they were born and to which they were deeply attached, struggled in many ways against racism and financial challenges to keep their congregations alive.[1]

In this chapter, I examine the missional work of the Episcopal Church with the Black community after the Civil War: the Freedmen's Commission and educational endeavors, Black congregations and leadership, the mission work in Haiti , and the development of relationships between white Episcopalian supporters and Black Episcopalian leaders and communities in the context of the racial paternalism of the church and the scientific racism growing in American society at large.

Following the Civil War and Emancipation, thousands of previously enslaved Episcopalians left the church, seeking a spiritual communal life which was "free"—not supervised or controlled by the planters or elite white leaders. In the time immediately after Emancipation, freed people sought to develop a life which was self-sustaining and self-governed, particularly by engaging in small-scale agriculture and by moving to towns and cities. However, the economy of the war-ravaged South was still a plantation economy, and plantation economies require labor that in some degree is unfree or coerced. Thus the white northerners responsible for reconstructing the South worked closely with the white southern leaders to develop a new system of coerced labor, insisting that Black people remain on plantations, developing a "pass system," and denying them access to agricultural land of

Mission, Race, and Empire. Jennifer C. Snow, Oxford University Press. © Oxford University Press 2024.
DOI: 10.1093/oso/9780197598948.003.0009

their own. While the white northerners insisted that the Black laborers now be paid wages, and thus were no longer enslaved, the freed population none-theless remained largely rural, impoverished, and controlled by the planters. A brief period of Reconstruction that saw the rise of Black political, religious, and economic leadership was crushed for decades under a new regime of racial terror, intended to keep Black people subservient and obedient to the white elite's need for labor, while racial hierarchy was enforced by legal segre-gation and lack of civil rights for Black people.[2]

In the brief period of Reconstruction, white northern Episcopalians worked with southern Episcopalian leaders to bring freedpeople back into the church, imagining that Black people after Emancipation were rudderless, unable to fend for themselves, and likely to be prey to false teachers, particu-larly teachers of their own race.

Black freedpeople who wanted to remain in the Episcopal Church also felt a missional intensity about this moment. For African American Episcopalians, the church's mission must encompass all the needs of the people: education, legal advocacy, farming, medical care, and spiritual life. Like free Black Episcopalians in the North before the Civil War, they believed that the Episcopal Church could be the best possible spiritual home for Black people, providing a beautiful and dignified liturgy, thoughtful preaching, and ordered daily prayer for ordered and dignified lives as free people. However, they faced the challenge—as Black northern congregations had—of how to demonstrate to their people that the Episcopal Church cared for and valued them. In the northern dioceses, congregations such as St. Thomas in Philadelphia and St. Philip's in New York had attained official participa-tion in their diocesan conventions only just before or even during the Civil War. In California, the missionary work of Peter Williams Cassey was unsup-ported by Bishop William Ingraham Kip's diocese, and he himself was never ordained to the priesthood.

For Black Episcopalian leaders—older free Black northern leaders such as Alexander Crummell, newly ordained southern freedmen such as James Solomon Russell and George F. Bragg, and the Black women such as Anna Haywood Cooper, who became teachers and organizers and deaconesses in this era—the church's gradual but hardening rejection of their ability to par-ticipate in the church as spiritual equals was symbolized by the figure of the Black bishop. The Episcopal Church consecrated two such bishops between the Civil War and 1890, but both James Theodore Holly and Samuel David Ferguson were consecrated as missionary bishops for dioceses outside the

United States (Haiti and Liberia). By the end of the nineteenth century, after decades of struggling for inclusion and being thwarted at every turn, many Black Episcopalian leaders asked instead for a "racial episcopate," an episcopate in which a Black bishop could lead Black Episcopalians as fully equal members of a multiracial national church.

Conventional Missional Response

Prior to the Civil War, Black Episcopalians were under the paternalistic control of white Episcopalians, either denied participation in diocesan governance in the North or relegated to slave galleries or segregated congregations under white control in the South. The Civil War had put more pressure on the Black northern Episcopalians. They were subject to antidraft mobs in New York City, while the congregation of St. Matthew's Detroit, a terminus of the underground railroad, was a frequent target of human traffickers dealing under the 1850 Fugitive Slave law.[3] There were no Black clergy in the South (aside from St. James in Baltimore) until after the Civil War. St. Stephen's Savannah was founded in 1856 for Black communicants from local white congregations, led by a lay reader, freeman James Porter, "a very intelligent and well-educated colored man." A church in Mobile, Alabama, was organized in 1857 but could not send delegates to convention. Calvary Church in Charleston, South Carolina, was made up overwhelmingly of enslaved people in 1860—fifty-five Black to eight white communicants. The occasional "mixed-race" congregation, such as St. Paul's of Wilmington, founded by the Bishop of North Carolina, became segregated after the war.[4] Despite a few outspoken white Episcopalian abolitionists, in general the silence of the church on slavery and on the Civil War meant that Black Episcopalians afterward were even more tenuously connected to the church, and their own efforts to bring other free Black people into their congregations were continuously undermined by the church's neglect.

In December 1865, General Convention organized the Freedmen's Aid Commission, which acted alongside the existing Domestic and Foreign Committees of the Episcopal Church and focused specifically on work among the freedpeople in the South. The pattern of expansion often built from schools—supported by and initially the main purpose of the Commission—which grew congregations. Thus in North Carolina, schools organized by the Freedmen's Commission included St. Cyprian's in New

Bern—where Peter Williams Cassey was called upon leaving California—St. Mark's Wilmington, St. Joseph's Fayetteville, and St. Ambrose Raleigh. In addition, the Commission established schools where Black freedpeople could be trained as teachers and later as clergy, particularly St. Augustine's, also in Raleigh.[5]

Most teachers in the Commission schools were northern women, supported by northern women's networks, but there were some men and southern Black and white women as well. For the southern white women, this work was a continuation of their projects of catechism and religious education of enslaved people before the war; one white woman in Mississippi noted that she had already been doing this work for thirty years, but before the war her teaching could only be oral. Pay was extremely low, and because of the poverty of the Black community in which the schools were located, the teachers frequently asked for donations of clothing and food to give to the students.[6] In 1869, the Freedmen's Commission was disbanded for lack of interest and funds, renamed the Commission on Home Missions to Colored People, which was formally reincorporated into the Domestic Committee in 1877, not coincidentally the close of the Reconstruction era. The interest of northern benefactors in supporting schools and missions among Black freedpeople had never been great, and waned quickly.

Bishops in the South had different attitudes toward the Commission. Bishop Thomas Atkinson of North Carolina was a supporter and indeed had helped to organize it, while Bishop Richard Hooker Wilmer of Alabama, the only bishop consecrated by the Episcopal Church of the Confederate States, did not permit the Freedmen's Commission to operate in his diocese, as he believed it "schismatic in nature," imposed upon the southern dioceses by the North. There was very little financial support for the Freedmen's Commission over time; by 1869, only 403 parishes out of over 2,400 contributed anything.[7]

The lukewarm attitude of the Episcopal Church toward Black Americans, compared to Methodists or Baptists, was criticized by white supporters of Black Episcopalians and the Black community in general. The white rector of a Black congregation in Baltimore wrote that on a visit to another southern city, he took a tour with a West Indian man who had refused to join the Episcopal Church, although a member of the Church of England, because of its racism. On the tour he saw a pitiful "shanty" school led by a well-intended but not educated Black man, begging for donations, and a huge, well-kept and -funded Methodist school, contrasting the two in terms of the interest and care of the Episcopal Church.[8]

The Black congregations established in the South began to flourish only when Black clergy leadership developed, but even being ordained priest was difficult for Black Episcopalians. Between 1866 and 1877, twenty Black men were ordained to the diaconate, but only six became priests; many were trapped in a permanent diaconate.[9] Peter Williams Cassey, for instance, the son of leading abolitionists, educated in Philadelphia and canonically fluent in Greek and Latin, served congregations in California (where he started a school under Bishop Kip but never received adequate funding to sustain it), North Carolina, and Florida, but was never made priest after being ordained deacon.[10] Similarly, despite the Bishop of North Carolina's frequent and passionate pleas to his diocesan convention to ordain Black clergy, he was stymied by the convention's rejection of local candidates. His first Black clergy in the diocesan rolls were brought from out of state, ordained in the North, until St. Augustine's began producing clergy graduates in the 1880s.[11] Even in Baltimore in the 1880s, the Standing Committee inexplicably refused, for years, to ordain a local Black candidate, always pointing to some mysterious lack in the paperwork. He was eventually ordained in another diocese.[12] Pierre Jones, a Haitian sent by Bishop James Theodore Holly to the Philadelphia Divinity School (founded by Bishop Alonzo Potter in 1857 to accept both Black and white candidates), was received with dismay by the white leaders and supporters of the Haiti mission as unsuitable for ordination. They thought that he was ignorant and possibly mentally deficient because he was so quiet, not understanding that he did not speak English and that he was terrified of the evils of the United States, which were legendary in Haiti.[13]

James Solomon Russell and Free Black Rural Congregations

North Carolina and Virginia were important centers for the early Black Episcopalian church in the post–Civil War South. George F. Bragg and James Solomon Russell were ordained in the same cohort in Virginia, but both came from Warren County, North Carolina, along with Thomas White Cain, the first and for many years only Black clerical delegate to General Convention, noted for public protests against racial discrimination. Cain was an elected delegate to the 1889 and 1892 Conventions from his church in Galveston, Texas; he was killed in the 1900 Galveston hurricane and memorialized by

Black Episcopalians with a chapel in North Carolina as an important member of the Black Episcopalian community.[14]

Russell's mother was enslaved on a Virginia plantation and his father enslaved on one in North Carolina; Russell himself was born into slavery in rural southwestern Virginia. The family was able to live together only after Emancipation, in great poverty, but Russell and his parents were determined that he would get an education. Attending first a Sunday school, then a private school run by an "aged white man" who accepted eggs and farm produce as tuition, Russell eventually went to boarding school at the Hampton Institute. When he graduated he returned home to begin teaching and used the Apostles' Creed to teach the children how to read. At that time he had no idea what the Creed was or where it came from; he had found it on a newspaper sheet and had "taken a fancy to it." As the children went home and recited it for their parents, a woman who had attended an Episcopal Church recognized it and told Russell what she remembered. "She told me all she knew about this communion, and the more she spoke, the more I became convinced that this was the church for me." After he found a whole, undamaged Book of Common Prayer, he wrote, "I then and there became, spiritually, a member of the great Episcopal Church."[15]

Knowing no other way to pursue this connection, Russell reached out to Pattie Buford, a local white woman known for her interest in missions to "the colored people," who arranged for him to meet with representatives of the Diocese of Virginia. Since a Black man was not eligible to attend Virginia Seminary, the diocese organized a "branch" theological school in Petersburg, Virginia. There in 1878 Russell went, the only student, under the tutelage of Reverend Giles Cooke, a Confederate officer who was dedicated to his vision of producing schools for the freedmen. Cooke would later expel Bragg for "insufficient humility," but he and Russell had an excellent relationship.[16]

Upon graduation and ordination, Russell was sent to Lawrenceville, Virginia, where the local white Episcopal church had about twenty Black communicants, for whom Russell was meant to establish a separate mission. Both he and his wife, Virginia Michigan Morgan, whom he married in 1882, were dedicated to education as well as church work, and together they began a school in the vestry room of the church; as the school outgrew this and even additional space, he decided to spend his life achieving his dream of a boarding and day school that would provide Black children "a good English education, coupled with a trade of some kind, and both rooted in thorough

Christian training." This became St. Paul's Normal School, and eventually St. Paul's College, which continued to serve students until 2013.

Russell began this work completely on faith and without any money in hand, but as he was able he bought up small plots of land, quietly so that no "speculator," or someone hostile to his dream, would get in the way. The very first time he made a deal with a white landowner, word got around that the "colored preacher" had bought land, and the white landowner immediately received an offer for twice as much as Russell could pay; luckily, the man kept his word and sold it to Russell regardless.[17] The land on which the school was built, once a plantation belonging to an absentee landlord, still had the "mud houses" of the enslaved people on it. Russell described them as built in the African traditional manner, which, after whitewashing, soon looked like "beautiful stone structure[s], the illusion being most effective on moonlit nights." The children's parents and grandparents were welcomed to night classes while the children came during the day.[18]

Russell loved his work for the school, and spent much of his life fundraising for it, running it, and teaching in it, but he was also dedicated to the Episcopal Church. In his work for the church, he noted near the end of his life, he had founded and "father[ed]" many churches—twenty-eight where there had been one—and seen the number of Black Episcopalian communicants increase from twenty to over two thousand. His most directly critical words in his generally charitable autobiography are directed not at the white rural population he worked among but at his beloved Episcopal Church, which left the African Americans after Emancipation "unserved and unwanted" and did not provide either enough monetary support or enough support for developing Black clergy to serve the missions and churches that it could have. When Emancipation freed the Black enslaved population and they were able to freely choose their Christian homes, they often chose to leave the Episcopal Church, and the church failed to support either white or Black missionaries for them.[19]

George Freeman Bragg and Free Black Urban Congregations

Bragg was born to previously enslaved parents just after Emancipation; his family founded and sustained the Black congregation of St. Stephen's Petersburg, Virginia, and were instrumental as well in the establishment of Bishop Payne Divinity School, named for Bishop John Payne, the white bishop of Liberia. Bishop Payne Divinity School provided education for the ministry for Black theological students, who were not permitted to register at Virginia Theological Seminary. In the long tradition of free Black urban congregations, such as St. Thomas in Philadelphia and St. Philip in New York City, Bragg organized the church not only as a spiritual center but to take care of the poor and to provide education and community.[20]

Bragg was interested not only in the work of his own congregation but in how Black Episcopalians were being received and supported—or not—by the Episcopal Church as a whole, and he developed literature and a net-working program to support and uplift Black clergy. He chronicled the lives of his people as part of the genre of African American histories that emphasized the worth, dignity, and accomplishments of Black leaders. One of his works remembered the first pre–Civil War Black missionary to a southern city, William Leavington of Baltimore, who had founded St. James Baltimore. As noted in a previous chapter, Leavington's community included both enslaved and free Black people and endured tensions both within and without due to racism. Leavington died so impoverished that there were no funds for a funeral; the expenses were paid by a white clergy friend. After Levington's death, his ministry was taken over by a white "missionary," Joshua Peterkin.[21]

From Bragg's work we have information about Harrison Webb, ordained priest in 1857, the second African American rector of St. James, Baltimore. The white churches which had previously paid the salary of white priests who served St. James in the interim between Leavington and Webb now refused to support a Black rector; the members of St. James, living where slavery was legal (and where at least some of them were enslaved), had little ability to financially support their church. Bragg took over St. James in 1890 and brought it back to a thriving congregation, governed by the Black commu-nity with the support of white friends—but emphasizing as well that it was only Black leaders who could truly do the work of leading the Black com-munity. He established a mutual aid society and other organizations to help those in need, as well as a home for "friendless colored children" in 1899, with a board of directors and staff completely composed of African Americans.[22] The spiritual lineage of St. James continued into the twenty-first century; it was the congregation in which Pauli Murray, a civil rights lawyer and the first African American woman ordained as a priest in the Episcopal Church, was baptized, and also the congregation where Michael Curry, later the first Black presiding bishop of the Episcopal Church, was serving when he was called as Bishop of North Carolina.

Black Bishop: James Holly and Haiti

In the late nineteenth century, the figure of the Black bishop was central to the Black Episcopalian resistance to racial paternalism and discrimination within the church. James Theodore Augustus Holly was born in 1829 to a Black family free for three generations, descended originally from an enslaved woman and a plantation owner, who freed his son in 1772. They lived in Washington, D.C., during Holly's childhood and suffered the growing discrimination and violence against the free Black community there, including a violent riot and stones thrown at the children in the street. The family was Catholic and attended church led by a white priest who had fled from Haiti. The family relocated to Vermont after the passage of the 1850 Fugitive Slave Act, which made free Black people vulnerable to kidnaping and enslavement.

Holly and his brother Joseph became active in antislavery work, but in different directions. Although both were abolitionists, Holly from an early age supported emigration as the best way for Black people to be truly free and to control their own destinies. He developed a plan to unite all Black people in the Western Hemisphere for mutual support, and envisaged Haiti as the most likely and hopeful place for Black Americans to emigrate and to help develop the Black Republic.[23]

Holly, like Crummell, believed in a great past as well as a great destiny for "the race." He interpreted biblical prophecy in accordance with the older racial biblicism that made white people the children of Japheth and Black people the cursed children of Ham. In his view, a great cataclysm would overthrow the oppressions of Japhetic society and churches, and the Black race, which had been trained in compassion, justice, and righteousness through suffering, would have a primary role in bringing about the millennial age of justice. For Holly, Haiti demonstrated the ability of Black people, enslaved, brutalized, and oppressed, to rise up and create their own society even in the continued oppression of white-led nations.[24]

Ironically, Holly's introduction to the Episcopal Church came at a confirmation of a white friend in Vermont, performed in 1851 by Bishop John

Henry Hopkins, who at that time was perfecting his pamphlet on the scriptural support for slavery. Hopkins's book on the Episcopal Church's "catholicity" (here meaning apostolic succession) convinced Holly to move toward it as a more "scriptural" form of Christianity than Roman Catholicism. He attended a Black Episcopalian congregation in Detroit and was ordained as deacon in 1855, the fourteenth Black ordinand of the Episcopal Church since Absalom Jones. Three weeks later, Holly was in New York City to ask the Foreign Committee to provide funds for him to go on an exploratory trip to Haiti. He ended up financing the trip largely through private means; the Foreign Committee, whose members were largely evangelicals, generally did not support "negro missionaries" and also distrusted Holly's high churchmanship and ritualism.[25]

In 1856 Holly was ordained priest by John Williams, Bishop of Connecticut, insisting on taking the Greek and Hebrew exams even when the bishop offered to dispense with them. He became the rector of St. Luke's in New Haven and an active and well-known figure in the community. Holly united his connection to the Episcopal Church and his desire to emigrate to Haiti, imagining emigration would be a way to bring far more African Americans into the church. He dreamed of an emigration specifically of African American Episcopalians to Haiti, envisioning the Episcopal Church as far better for the Black Republic than the Catholic Church, which continued to be run by white priests and was associated with the political elite.[26] In 1861, he brought a gathering of Black Episcopalians to emigrate with him to Haiti as the core of his visioned community, with a covenant of religious and communal life.

Holly may have underestimated the challenges of emigrating to Haiti, but he did not shrink from them, even when they became deeply personal. The colony, much like the Jamestown colony of English people coming to Virginia, was unprepared and poorly supported in their efforts to create an ideal agricultural society. Many of those involved were not even farmers—Holly himself showed no ability to farm throughout his life, despite many sincere efforts. They arrived in the middle of the rainy season, an unpropitious time to plant, and were not provided adequate shelter by the government, as promised in the emigration plan. Diseases became rampant. Dozens died, and some returned to the United States. Holly himself lost members of his family. However, as Holly noted, he had already lost two daughters in New Haven, partly due to the fact that even in the United States the situation of Black people was always far worse than that of whites; they drank tainted water, lived in polluted areas, and were not permitted to go into white hospitals. In New Haven, he argued, the death rate of Black people was twice that of whites.[27]

Holly begged General Convention for a bishop for Haiti from the 1860s onward. In fact there were few or no other options than Holly for this position, despite the fact that the Foreign Committee were unsupportive of the mission and not on good terms with him.[28] Holly was effectively the director of the mission and in charge of the new ordinands when they became priests, simply by dint of his seniority and organizational energy, but he could not do all that a bishop needed to do and the church could not function fully without a bishop. Haiti's need for its own bishop was far greater than that of most areas in the United States, where at least a bishop could theoretically visit every few years. In Haiti this was not the case. The death of Bishop George Burgess of Maine, the first bishop to visit Haiti at Holly's invitation, was well known. The vast majority of Episcopalian bishops who were requested to visit Haiti to confirm and ordain clergy candidates refused to do so. Bishop Kip of California, the retired missionary bishop of Liberia John Payne, the bishops of Connecticut, Delaware, Iowa, Rhode Island, and Minnesota all refused to visit Haiti. Though Holly's intense Anglo-Catholicism and his strong personality led to enmities with some white American leaders, nonetheless with this level of need, and an active and highly motivated clergyperson on the ground begging for consecration, it is hard to imagine any reason other than racism for Haiti's long neglect.[29]

At last Holly was consecrated bishop in 1874. Haiti would be a foreign national church, supported financially by the missionary program of the American church, but not a missionary district. This was important to Holly's dream of an autonomous national church, now named the Orthodox Apostolic Church in Haiti.[30]

Holly eventually chose to rely solely on native Haitian ministers, because those who were sent as missionaries from the United States, or even from other Caribbean islands who spoke English rather than French or Creole, tended to cause problems. Holly and his priests on their visitations and preaching in the countryside found unique difficulties. French white Catholic priests were connected with the elite and would tell the local peasants that Protestants were traitors to Haiti, while a Black priest was expected to perform the rituals of voudon rather than the official Catholic ceremonies, and it was not always easy to explain that the Black priests were not part of the voudon community.

Bishop Holly was constantly frustrated by the decisions of the Board of Missions regarding funding and programming. He longed to start a hospital and provide medical care, as he believed, like William Augustus Muhlenberg, that the healing of the sick was "an indispensable part of true gospel work." One of his sons, Alonzo Potter Burgess Holly, became a doctor, and Holly gave him charge of medical work. However, the Foreign Committee refused to fund the clinic and denied Alonzo's appointment. Similarly, Holly wanted to build a seminary for Haitian clergy so that they wouldn't have to go to a foreign land to be trained in an unfamiliar language and culture, but this was also scuttled by the Committee, which did not provide the funds. Instead of allowing some of the first ordinands to remain in the capital to staff the seminary, as Holly had planned, the Committee sent them to isolated mission stations.[31]

The Bishop of Haiti, and the mission as a whole, struggled with poverty. Holly was poor his entire life, and gave what little he had to the church; he had been taught the trade of shoemaking as a young person and sometimes supported himself and his family with this work, more than once turning down relatively lucrative, or at least better-paying, positions with the Haitian government. His position was similar to that of the clergy. Holly wrote:

> [C]lergy of the church in Haiti are workingmen in both the literal and spiritual aspects of that word. . . . [T]he aid thus given, while most gratefully acknowledged, in no case, except that of the Bishop, exceeds one third of the amount necessary to support themselves and their families; for the necessaries of life cost very dear in Haiti. Hence, they are obliged to follow secular occupations to gain the other two-thirds necessary to make out their livelihood. . . . [T]hey work every day in the week, like men of similar secular occupations, and devote Sunday and week-day evenings to the work of the blessed Gospel of Christ. Thus they have their full share of work—indeed, far too much for men to do in the exhausting heat of the tropics.

Lay workers, he noted, received no pay at all. Yet the land, volunteer hours, and buildings of the mission stations were all donated by local people despite their poverty.[32]

White Allies and Racial Paternalism

Holly was realistic in his understanding of the ability of American free Black people to organize and finance a mass emigration movement on their own. The resources simply were not there. He needed the support of white leaders, particularly financial support, to make this dream a reality. Before the Civil War, Holly was willing to attempt to build connections even with active slaveholders such as Leonidas Polk in order to pursue his dream. When challenged by a fellow emigration advocate about his connections to white leaders in his efforts to develop an emigrant program, Holly responded, "I am not opposed to pressing white men into our service so long as they fulfilled the behests of our race. The Anglo Saxon now predominates in this country because he presses all other races into his service. It will be mere folly and madness in us to refuse to do the same. I do not care for the persons of men so long as the cause of our race is subserved."[33] Holly believed that white people possessed skills and education that were worth having, and that Black people should learn from and take advantage of every educational opportunity offered to them, as well as seeking out white allies and supporters.[34]

The need for white allies in politics, internal church relationships, and financial resources was obvious to Black Episcopalian leaders in every pastoral situation and every part of the country throughout the nineteenth century. Black leaders were strategic in their efforts to reassure sympathetic whites that they were valued and their contributions were important, even when these contributions were attached to astoundingly blatant racism and condescension.

For instance, the introduction to Bragg's 1909 book on African American Episcopalian clergy was written by a white priest, Arthur Selden Lloyd. Lloyd was a Virginian, president of the Board of Missions, later coadjutor bishop of Virginia and suffragan bishop of New York, who argued that the problems encountered by competent and worthy Black people in achieving success and decent lives were not due to race prejudice but to their being "lost" in the "multitude" of bad Black people, who "had not been in America long enough to become civilized or to demonstrate the meaning of citizenship." The ludicrous nature of this statement—simply in point of basic facts, since the foreign slave trade had been illegal since 1808, all African American people in the United States in 1909 were descended from people who had arrived at least a century before—was offensive in every possible way. Lloyd continued that emancipation meant being "cast off to shift for themselves," as though this had been a catastrophe for the enslaved people, offered faint praise for those who were "competent" in "civilization," and claimed that Black people were unfit to govern or participate in governance. The church was called to work among them to prepare for "competent" citizenship in some distant future. Yet Bragg undoubtedly solicited this writing in an effort to ensure that the Board of Missions and the Episcopal Church were familiar with the work of the Black Episcopalian community, and hopefully to provide strategic support and resources to it.[35]

Bragg and other African American Episcopalian leaders often memorialized white Episcopalian supporters of the past. Alonzo Potter's efforts to bring St. Thomas into diocesan convention as a fully recognized Episcopal church was never forgotten; Bragg described Potter as "that great Bishop and ever-loving friend of the Black race," the most enthusiastic praise for any bishop or white priest in his writings. Bishop Holly named one of his children after Potter, and another after Bishop Alfred Lee of Delaware, who had ordained Crummell. Holly's address to Crummell on his ordination jubilee, the senior Black bishop of the Anglican Communion to the senior Black presbyter, described Bishop William White as "a Catholic-hearted prelate, in the person of the first Bishop of Pennsylvania, who had the Christian courage to ordain the Rev. Absalom Jones, a man of the Negro race, to the Sacred Ministry of the Church of Christ."[36] One purpose of these memorials was to remind white Episcopalians that they were not living up to the good work of their spiritual ancestors. Holly pointed out that fifty years after Jones's ordination, the "Christian spirit" of Bishop White "had unfortunately grown narrower and narrower."[37]

African American Episcopalian clergy were themselves portrayed as spiritual and communal heroes. Holly described Crummell as "a young Negro Levite, a candidate for Holy Orders, to vindicate the manhood of the race, in the very teeth and face of such ecclesiastical time-serving; and to claim the full acknowledgment by the Church of Christ, in his person of the equal Gospel privileges of men of every race around her altars." Bragg's books and writings chronicled the many Black Episcopalian heroes of the church while continually remembering the white supporters and advocates for the community. William Douglass's work on the history of St. Thomas in Philadelphia chronicled these leaders and activities, and their white supporters and opponents, from Absalom Jones onward. Russell's autobiography is full of praise for white Episcopalians who supported him and St. Paul's School, with relatively little written of the racism and obstacles he must regularly have encountered.[38]

Anna Julia Haywood Cooper, an internationally known scholar and teacher born into slavery and trained at St. Augustine's in Raleigh, North Carolina, described the faith of Black Episcopalians as the ultimate triumph of the catholicity of the church. Writing in 1886, she explained, "We believe in the Holy Catholic Church. We believe that however gigantic and apparently remote the consummation, the Church will go on conquering . . . till the kingdom of this world, not excepting the Black man and the Black woman . . . shall have become the kingdoms of the Lord and of His Christ."[39]

Instead of Black resistance to the claims of the church, Dr. Cooper placed the patronizing attitudes of white leaders and concomitant lack of resources as the heart of the problem. She noted, "[O]ur clergy number less than two dozen priests of Negro blood and we have hardly more than one self-supporting colored congregation in the entire Southland. While the organization known as the A.M.E. Church has 14,063 ministers, 4069 self-supporting churches, with property valued at $7,772,284, raising yearly for church purposes $1,427,000. Something must be wrong. What is it?" Cooper, the widow of one of the first Black clergy in North Carolina, supplied the answer to her own rhetorical question: "A conference of earnest Christian men have met at regular intervals for some years past to discuss the best methods of promoting the welfare and development of colored people in this country. Yet, strange as it may seem, they have never invited a colored man or even intimated that one would be welcome to take part in their deliberations."[40] The second oversight was a glaring lack of attention to raising up Black women as leaders, Cooper noting that in its first twenty years of existence, St. Augustine's had had only five female graduates.

At the heart of white Episcopalian views of Black people, particularly the refusal to recognize the wisdom and leadership of Black clergy and lay leaders in the mission of the church, was racial paternalism. Black people, in this view, were "children," not yet competent for the work of self-governance that adults could take on. The most important thing for the welfare of Black people was the "tutelage" of whites, a term used in the debate over inclusion of St. Thomas in diocesan convention. Under this "tutelage," eventually, at some long-deferred future point, Black people could be equals and Black Episcopalians could fully partake in the governance of the church. This paternalistic ideal, and Black Episcopalian resistance to it, was most clear in the proposal and aftermath of the Sewanee Canon.

The Sewanee Canon and the Racial Episcopate

In 1884, Calbraith Perry, white priest of a Black congregation in Baltimore, considered the reason that the "colored people" needed, for their own welfare, segregated churches and to be supported missionally by the whole Episcopal Church, rather than by the local parishes. After discussing the choice of the parishioners of St. Philip's to request a separate service and place of worship rather than attend the white congregation's services, Perry concluded, "They undoubtedly were right. However much any distinction in God's house or at God's altar as to race, color, or condition is to be condemned, it is practically necessary, at least for the present, that the Church should extend among colored people chiefly by getting them into separate congregations, or where that is not possible, by holding separate services for them."[41]

The realities of racism, which even for Perry himself led to social ostracism from other whites as he served a Black congregation, meant that while segregation was not what God wanted between the races, for the safety and well-being of Black people, and to give them space for their own leadership and places where they could worship together with self-respect and dignity, under the current racial regime of the United States it might be necessary:

> It is certainly the duty of clergy and congregations of all Christian churches to welcome colored communicants with that charity which bears in mind that God is "no respecter of persons," but where there are a sufficient number of colored people, it is no doubt, at least while prejudice remains so strong, best for themselves that they should have churches of their own. . . . As a part of a white congregation, they would remain an inappreciable element. There could then be no sphere of labor for the colored clergy. The colored people would not probably be found in choirs, vestries, or parochial societies, nor taking part in diocesan affairs. They would therefore have little personal interest in the Church's life and growth.[42]

This sense among Black leaders and their supporters that segregation of Black ministries might be required for the health of the Black Episcopal congregations was part of the debate around the idea of a Black missionary bishop. For Black Episcopalians, what would make this segregation different from that enforced by racist society at large was that it must be an equal partnership, a relationship of respect between Black and white leaders, with Black Episcopalians choosing their own worship communities and led by Black clergy and bishops who, within the church as a whole, were equal in authority to and respected by the white clergy and bishops.

Black Episcopalians—Holly, Bragg, Russell, Crummell, Cooper, and others—often used the ideal of "catholicity" in their writings, to mean the Episcopal Church's essential character in embracing equally all human beings regardless of race or language. "Catholicity" was a flexible term that could be used to advocate for racial equality or to cover a multitude of sins; it was quite possible for the Episcopal Church to be "catholic" while embracing slavery and discrimination. Bishop Levi Silliman Ives of North Carolina, for instance, a high churchman who deeply valued the ideal of the catholicity of the church and eventually converted to Roman Catholicism, in 1846 rejoiced in the image of the enslaved people attending services together with their masters on Easter. Being within the same church, regardless of the social domination of one group by another, was spiritually enough to argue against the claims of abolitionists.[43] Black Episcopalians, however, were clear that the "catholicity" of the church demanded quite specifically full equality of Black people in the life and governance of the church. This was the version of "catholicity" that lay beneath the agitation of Bishop Potter with the Church of the Crucifixion and St. Thomas in Philadelphia, striving for inclusion in diocesan convention, and with St. Philip's and John Jay in New York City.[44] In North Carolina, Bishop Atkinson's commitment to "catholicity" as an ideal meant that he insisted from the end of the Civil War that Black clergy and congregations were included in diocesan convention, and this remained the case in that diocese, even after the violent overthrow of North Carolina's state government by white supremacists in 1898. Nonetheless, the Black congregations were effectively segregated, underresourced, and ignored, and Black attendees at convention might have separate worship services from the white Episcopalians. In the Diocese of Virginia in 1886, and South Carolina in 1887, Black clergy had already been disenfranchised in their diocesan conventions.[45]

As Reconstruction drew to a close, legal and customary racial segregation at all levels became more entrenched, particularly in the southern states, in the Episcopal Church as well as secular society. In 1882, the Diocese of Virginia Council passed a canon "of mission churches," which permitted

African Americans to set up their own churches with their own vestries and "administer [their] own affairs," but without the right of lay representatives in Council, continuing the trend of slowly removing Black leadership from their post-Emancipation inroads into "white" authority spaces.[46]

In 1883, a gathering of bishops and clergy, all white, was called to Sewanee, Tennessee, in preparation for General Convention, where the bishops from the states with greatest experience with the "colored community" (namely, the former slave states) came together to recommend a strategy for missional outreach and governance of Black Episcopalians. This may have been the gathering Cooper referred to, though certainly there would have been many such all-white gatherings to discuss Black communities. The solution proffered was to organize "missionary districts" along racial lines, with a Black clergyperson or bishop at the head. However, this proposal was very different from the idea, suggested as early as the 1840s, of a "racial episcopate," where a Black bishop would have rights equal to all other bishops'. The Black bishop proposed by the Sewanee gathering would in fact be a subordinate to a white bishop, always under his governance and control and without the same rights in General Convention as other bishops.[47]

Black Episcopalians, led by Alexander Crummell, organized the Convocation of Colored Clergy in response to this plan to permanently deprive their clergy of any rights in the governance of the church. The proposed Sewanee Canon for creating racial missionary districts under the control of white Bishops did not pass in the House of Deputies of General Convention, and thus did not become a national church policy. Segregation along these lines was made reality nonetheless in southern dioceses. In Virginia in 1886, the Council created a diocesan Colored Missionary Jurisdiction, where Black clergy and laity could manage their own affairs under the supervision of the bishop and Council. They were expected to no longer send delegates to the Council itself. In 1889, since Black clergy were still coming to Council despite the Colored Missionary Jurisdiction, the Council passed a new canon, removing the right of attendance from Black clergy. The Colored Missionary Jurisdiction could send two lay and two clergy representatives to Council, but they could vote only on racial matters in order to avoid Black Episcopalians participating in the governance of white Episcopalians.[48] Russell refers to this as the "Black Canon," which he and other Black priests in Virginia regularly organized against, to no avail.

In 1886 the Convocation of Colored Clergy became the Conference of Church Workers among Colored People in order to include white people who supported Black rights in church and society. Perry, the white priest of Baltimore, suggested the strategy of memorializing General Convention. In 1889, the group presented—through William Reed Huntington, as there were no Black delegates at General Convention—a Memorial to General Convention requesting a clarification of the rights of Black clergy in the Episcopal Church, noting that in various dioceses they were being disenfranchised and segregated from diocesan councils. The Memorial stated:

> [There is] one great question, which we believe must have a satisfactory an-
> swer before the work of converting the Colored People can proceed with
> any prospect of success. The question which we would ask of the Protestant
> Episcopal Church of the United States of America, as represented in her
> General Convention, is this: What is the position of colored men in this
> Church? Is it in accordance with the real doctrines taught by this Church,
> that when men have once been admitted to the Sacred Ministry or
> Communion of the Church any restriction should be made in the spiritual
> or legislative rights of a colored man which would not be made in those of a
> white man? Does the action which has recently been taken in two Dioceses
> in the Church represent the true spirit of this Church? We ask the General
> Convention of the Church to give an emphatic and unequivocal answer to
> this our earnest and almost despairing inquiry.[49]

At Huntington's request, the Memorial was sent to a joint committee of the House of Bishops and House of Deputies, which produced a majority report and a minority report. Writing in 1904, Bragg noted that the majority report "told us to fight it out the best way we could in the various dioceses, for the General Convention had no power to act."[50] The minority report insisted that "every ecclesiastical privilege given to the white man must also be given to the Black," but proposed no way to ensure this principle was being honored in the church's life.[51] Both the majority report and the minority re-port said, in essence, the same thing: that the Episcopal Church was already "colorblind," having elected Black bishops (though only for Liberia and Haiti, not within the United States) and having received a Black delegate to General Convention in the past. Thus there was no need to do anything at all to safe-guard the rights of Black clergy. The situation was already fine.

In response, some Black Episcopalians developed a proposal to "adapt" the episcopate: permitting that where bishops agree, a missionary bishop may be elected for the Black congregations—a bishop with full powers and a vote like any other bishop, as opposed to a suffragan bishop who had no vote or right of succession and who depended completely upon the diocesan bishop. This missionary district would not report to any of the local diocesan conventions, and thus would not be supervised directly by a white bishop, but only by General Convention, and only General Convention could terminate or change the arrangement once made. Strategically, this plan would permit Black Episcopalians to have a Black bishop of their own supporting their interests, while diluting the control of white southern bishops by the entirety of General Convention, which would include more white allies. Bragg described this plan as avoiding the "vexation" of "negro domination" in dioceses where the number of Black congregations was increasing (apparently a serious fear of some white Episcopalians).[52]

For Bragg and other Black Episcopalians supporting the ideal of a "racial episcopate," this did not in any way threaten the unity or catholicity of the church.[53] Given that in 1873 the Episcopal Church had already created such a "racial" missionary district for the Sioux—though headed by a white bishop—the idea clearly was not theologically out of bounds for the Episcopal Church. Bragg wrote, "Separate jurisdictions and conventions do not imply separate and distinct churches. We are in the one Church by virtue of Holy Baptism; and the Episcopate, whether diocesan or missionary, constitutes the visible expression of the unity of all the parts in the one Catholic Church of Christ."[54]

In the end, the Episcopal Church adopted the plan of suffragan bishops as a compromise, allowing southern dioceses to appoint "racial bishops" that would be dependent upon and supervised by white bishops, and northern dioceses to have more help for the diocesan bishop in managing increasingly dense urban populations. This plan was not ideal from the point of view of white racists—the Bishop of South Carolina, William Guerry, was murdered by a retired white priest in 1928 partly as a result of his advocating for a racial suffragan in the diocese. Nor was it ideal from the point of view of many Black Episcopalians, since it made it all the more unlikely that they would have a bishop of their own who was ecclesiastically independent of white supervision. The two suffragan bishops elected under this plan in 1918, Henry Beard Delany of North Carolina and Edward Thomas Demby of Arkansas and the Province of the Southwest, both worked under conditions of disrespect and underresourcing. In 1932, after Delany's death, the new bishop dissolved the Colored Convocation and merged both white and Black mission work into one diocesan office under the banner of catholicity and abolition of "race self-consciousness" (i.e., colorblindness). While this worked well in the 1960s as there was not a segregated structure to dismantle during the civil rights era, but it did dismantle the structure that had supported Black ministry and congregations and had developed Black leadership, and put nothing in its place.[55]

Even in Haiti, the independent Black bishop disappeared after 1911. After Holly's death, the convocation of the church in Haiti petitioned the Board of Managers of the DFMS to dismantle the covenant Holly had made that created an autonomous church and to make Haiti a regular missionary district instead, due to the need for financial support. Because it became a missionary district, Haiti no longer had the right to elect its own bishops. White missionary bishops were sent instead from 1923 to 1970. It was not until 1971 that a native Haitian became a bishop.

Paternalism, Assimilation, and Scientific Racism

Whenever James Holly visited the United States at rare intervals he was reminded of why he had chosen to emigrate to Haiti. In Haiti he was a citizen and treated as such; he was a leading member of society, and his Black skin disqualified him from nothing at all. In the United States he was denied service at banks, restaurants, and other public places. He could not sleep in hotels and was forced to wait in line for the "colored car" when using the railway. Later in life, when Holly visited England, he experienced a completely different kind of society. Like Crummell, he found himself welcomed and celebrated as a person of accomplishments and intelligence, where in the United States his lifelong efforts to begin a church were only grudgingly recognized by the Episcopal Church as a whole.[56]

After the Civil War, racial ideologies began to develop in different directions among white Americans. One model replicated the older racial paternalism, idealized as "brotherhood," that could support white supremacy but rarely overtly supported the extermination of other racial groups. The racial paternalistic model, which was quite common among the white Episcopalian leadership, idealized racial hierarchy as "tutelage," claiming that while people of any race were able to become good Christians and good citizens, some would require supervision and oversight for the foreseeable future. They were like children, unable to fend for themselves, but all equally children of God, coming from the same creation.

Beginning in the 1850s, American racial ideology began to diverge from paternalism into scientific racism. Scientific racism saw races as distinct—sometimes with distinct biological roots—whose creations were not of God but simply of nature. Nature intended these races to be separate, as they were different and differently endowed with gifts, and to compete with one another in a Darwinian free-for-all that would eventually end in, at best, the servile obedience of weaker races to stronger ones, or the weak ones completely exterminated by the strong. While white scientific racists claimed that Anglo-Saxons were clearly the strongest race, they nonetheless evinced a great deal of anxiety that perhaps—if white supremacy was hampered by "charity" and "sentimentalism" toward the weak races—the white race might be overwhelmed. Despite enormous gaps in logic and fact in such a theory, it was prominent by the early twentieth century. It was used to justify Jim Crow laws, racial violence, and legal segregation as well as Asian exclusion, racist immigration policies, and eugenic sterilization of "unfit" women, often nonwhite women. Among many white Christian missional leaders, the old-fashioned racially paternalistic model remained dominant, but scientific racism did make inroads into the church as well.[57]

For racial paternalists, the solution to racial conflict was "assimilationism," the idea that the best option for nonwhite racial groups was to become as similar to whites as possible. This was the model which Henry Whipple depended upon in his work with the Ojibwa and Sioux, and which later the Japanese immigrants would adapt. In many ways, white leaders saw assimilation as at least partly an imposition required by racial hostility and necessary for survival rather than an unmitigated or natural good.

In 1884, the white priest Calbraith Perry mused about "assimilation" and "English virtues," writing that "the Englishman has little power of adaptation to the national peculiarities of other nations. Where he cannot convert to his own standard he tramples out. What he cannot assimilate he will not tolerate." Though the "American cousin" of the British is somewhat more flexible and adaptable, "we have not lost those English traits which serve to drive out and exterminate, instead of raising and assimilating, weaker races, as may be seen in our attitude toward the three of the great families of mankind in our land—the Indian, the Negro, the Mongolian. The presence of these alien races is an offense to us, largely because they are so dissimilar to ourselves, while their virtues—virtues which those who know them best testify are characteristic in each of these races—count for little because they are not English virtues."[58] Perry, like Whipple, understood assimilation not only as desirable but as the only alternative to total extermination. Support for cultural assimilation of racial and cultural minorities must then become the moral duty of the white Christian.

Assimilationism itself, however, gradually became a minority view in society at large as "extermination" and "competition" between races became a more popular way of understanding racial relationships. Given the scientific racist ideology that valued violence and competition and denied the possibility of racial assimilation or equality between races, white Episcopalian leaders who still held to a racial paternalistic model insisted all the more strongly on cultural assimilation and white "tutelage" for Black and Native Americans as the century drew to its close. White Episcopal leaders would idealize cultural assimilation and "tutelage" of racial minority groups in order to "save" them.

9

Westward the Course of Empire

At the turn of the century, American Episcopalianism expanded through a variety of colonial or empire-building processes beyond the continental United States. Hawai'i was annexed by the United States in 1898, and Puerto Rico, Guam, and the Philippines became American territories as a prize of the Spanish-American War shortly thereafter. While the United States had pledged not to annex Cuba after the Spanish American War, nonetheless Cuba's self-governance was limited by treaty with the US. The Panama Canal Zone became an American territory in 1904, permitting ships to avoid the long and dangerous journey around South America to reach California, the Pacific islands, and Asia. In all of these areas, Episcopalian mission either commenced or expanded as a result of this political expansion of the United States.

In this era, the intense focus on assimilation—civilizing and Christianizing—that characterized Episcopalian expansion among Native Americans and Black Americans was less total in the overseas missions, perhaps because American territories with people of different races and cultures were not seen as fully American, and therefore not requiring the total assimilation expected of those within the continental United States. These missional contexts, on the edge between what was seen as truly "American" and the "foreign," similarly were on the border between the total assimilationism expected of African Americans and Native Americans, complete with paternalistic racial oversight, and the more nuanced approach of missionaries in cultures that, while wrestling with colonialism, nonetheless were clearly too distant to ever be considered truly "American."

In some of these situations, such as the Philippines and Hawai'i, Episcopalian missionary practices were similar to those of foreign missionaries, who as small minorities within another culture's totality tended to develop skills of translation and attitudes of respect for local ways and other cultures, languages, and religions. These practices that began to move

Mission, Race, and Empire. Jennifer C. Snow, Oxford University Press. © Oxford University Press 2024.
DOI: 10.1093/oso/9780197598948.003.0010

away from total assimilationism in mission were part of a growing world Christian shift to a more morally questioning, nuanced, and self-reflective attitude toward racial, cultural, and religious difference among missionary practitioners and theorists. In contexts closer to "home," Episcopalian missions continued to work toward ideals of assimilationism couched in racial hierarchy.

Hawai'i

The Sandwich Islands, as they were known to English speakers from the United States and Great Britain, were one of the first mission locations for the Congregationalists and one of the first areas in which mission families rather than single men were sent. In Hawai'i missionaries first began to develop the ideology of the Christian Home, where missionary wives used the necessary toil of making a home and educating children in a strange ecology and culture as a tool of evangelism. Missionary wives invited native people to observe and learn the "Christian and civilized" methods of marriage relationships, child rearing, personal discipline, cooking, clothing, furnishing, and hygiene idealized by the Protestant missionaries.[1]

Arriving in 1820, the Congregationalist missionaries were quite successful even by their own standards. The Congregationalist expectations of Hawai'ians were almost Puritan in scope and put off-limits a wide variety of "entertainments," both Hawai'ian and white. In the early twentieth century, the first Episcopal bishop of Hawai'i described how the Hawai'ian Christians were confused when they took service on whalers and saw the white Christians casually doing things they were forbidden to do. When asked by a missionary what was the first Commandment, one Hawai'ian convert replied, "Do not smoke tobacco."[2]

In 1863, Rufus Anderson, the secretary of the Congregationalist mission society, visited Hawai'i and recommended that the missions be ended as the islands were "Christianized." The Hawai'ians, in his opinion, were at least as Christian and moral as the members of the early apostolic churches; they should be given their own way and ecclesiastical independence. The missionaries were thence retired from active service, but many, and their families, remained in Hawai'i as settlers, forming the core of what would later be called the "missionary party" in Hawai'ian politics. The missionary party would be pro-annexation in the political tensions surrounding the overthrow

of the Hawai'ian monarchy, the brief establishment of the Republic of
Hawai'i, and the islands' annexation by the United States in 1898.[3]

In this sea of Congregationalism, Episcopal or Anglican Christians were a
tiny minority, usually expatriate Americans or English settlers and diplomats
or visiting sailors, served by the occasional chaplain, if at all. However, the
royal family of Hawai'i began to develop an interest in the Anglican tradition in the 1850s, encouraged by both political and religious considerations.
Partly as a counterweight to pressure toward U.S. annexation, the Hawai'ian
monarch began cultivating stronger ties to England. This included a trip to
England to meet with the Queen and a request to Her Majesty to send an
English bishop to develop the Church of England in Hawai'i. In 1859, King
Kamehameha IV shot a friend who he believed had somehow betrayed him;
afterward he was drawn to spirituality to make up for his sin. Queen Emma
was an Anglophile, tutored by an Englishman and partly of English ancestry,
who also desired an Anglican establishment.

King Kamehameha IV offered to donate land for a church and provide
money for a salary for a clergyman and his family. This would be a personal
royal donation, as the Hawai'ian Constitution forbade the official establishment of a denomination, but clearly it would have political connotations.
Both King and Queen believed that Anglo-Catholic ritual in the practice
of the Church of England was most appropriate for the monarchy as well as
more attractive than the Congregationalist Christianity already in Hawai'i.[4]

As Hawai'i was an independent kingdom, logically this should not have
disturbed people in the United States, but since the United States had been
eyeing Hawai'i as a potential annexation site for some years, it did, in fact,
bother people. American journalists and politicians interpreted English involvement in Hawai'ian religion was as a political move to establish dominance in the islands. American Episcopalian leadership protested that this
was not the case at all. Bishop William Ingraham Kip of California supported
the mission, for which he came in for some criticism stateside. He defen-
sively reported that he had initiated the connection with England only after
receiving a request for clergy from Hawai'i that he was unable to fulfill. In addition, Bishop Kip and Bishop Horatio Potter of New York, who happened to
be visiting England when the request arrived, both firmly supported the idea,
and even imagined that there would be a joint American and English mission
to Hawai'i in the future.[5]

In responding to the Hawai'ian royal request, the evangelical English
Church Mission Society refused to support the mission, since Hawai'i was

already "Christian." However, Society for the Propagation of the Gospel in Foreign Parts was willing to do so even though Hawai'i was not a British colony, demonstrating the SPG's growing commitment to the idea of the missionary bishop as separate from the power of the state. The refusal of the Church Missionary Society to get involved meant that the chosen missionary bishop, and all of his chosen clergy, ended up being extreme Anglo-Catholics.[6]

The first bishop of the Church of England in Hawai'i, Thomas Staley, envisioned a church which would stand apart from the Congregationalist vision of Christianity, one which would welcome and include the "innocent amusements" of the native people rather than disciplining them, and could provide a more sacramental and beautiful way of spiritual worship than the more austere Congregationalist forms. However, he came unprepared for the actual complexities of Hawai'ian society, including the relationship between the monarchs and the existing white Anglican community, and between the nobility and ordinary Hawai'ian's.[7]

When Staley arrived in 1862, the King had already personally translated the services of Morning and Evening Prayer into Hawai'ian, and he now asked him to baptize the Queen and to confirm both of them. According to Staley, large numbers of Hawai'ians pleaded for a cathedral, where they could hear the services in Hawai'ian and be protected from the sun. The building of a cathedral became Staley's highest priority. This may well have reflected Staley's own preferences, or he may have been misled by the fact that most of the Hawai'ians he met were of the traditional nobility, a small slice of Hawai'ian society that was connected to the monarch and supported his religious reforms. The new bishop was intended both to baptize and to superintend the Christian education of the little prince of Hawai'i; Queen Victoria was to be the godmother. Unfortunately the prince died tragically just before Bishop Staley arrived in Hawai'i, but the royal couple nonetheless continued their determined support of the new Anglican mission.[8]

The depth of this commitment and King Kamehameha's seriousness about his new faith, the vision of a highly ritualized religious practice being brought to the islands, and Staley's desire to support and speak positively of Hawai'ian traditions, all are demonstrated in Staley's published journal of the baptism of the Queen immediately after his arrival:

> The whole occasion was most impressive, and I can never forget it. Two
> chiefs, fine men, above six feet high, bore the kahilis (long staves, at the top

of which were the yellow feathers of the royal bird, so much celebrated in the islands. The kahili is a symbol of royal authority). The King, said one of them, was deeply affected with the beauty of the service. The King, indeed, was engaged the whole of the afternoon in explaining to his courtiers the expressions in the service, and proving its truth by Holy Scripture. One of those with whom the King thus conversed said, "I felt as if angels were floating around me in the room." Two of them wanted to be baptized themselves forthwith; but the King found they had been so already by the Americans, and so he told them they must be confirmed.[9]

Later, Staley attended one of the "innocent amusements" of the Hawai'ians and wrote:

Friday, Oct. 31st—The King invited myself and clergy to go with him to a village feast, a few miles off. This feast is called a "Luan." . . . We first saw surf-riding on a small plank four feet long. An expert swimmer lies all his length on it upon his stomach, he paddles away to sea with his hands some three miles, and comes back upon the plank on the crest of a wave. . . . Then we had the banquet, in native style, under a room extemporised out of poles and the green leaves of tropical plants—cocoa-nut, palms, &c. The ground was covered with mats, and the food placed on them; no chairs. There was every kind of dainty—fish just caught, raw and cooked, of every sort; pork, half-roasted in the ground; poi (the prepared taro-root), like the paste we use for sticking bills to walls; and roast dogs upon dishes, all entire. . . . Much amusement was created when I took my first taste of dog (which was really capital), and when, in the national style, I dipped my fingers in the poi. We drank toasts, and I made a speech (which the King interpreted), telling them that He who was present at the marriage feast of Cana in Galilee was with them in their innocent mirth, as long as it was innocent; that it was the bounty of the great God which had provided their dainties for them so abundantly. There were some hundreds there. Odes were recited with a sort of monotone, in praise of the King and the young Prince just dead. National songs were sung, beautifully in chorus. Then began dancing, which was marked by grace and propriety.[10]

Staley was delighted by almost everything and eager to record his willingness to honor the hula, which had largely been forbidden by other white missionaries, as well as his own participation in local celebrations and foodways. He was not willing to be as flexible with the white Hawai'ian Anglican community, which did not share his love of Anglo-Catholic ritual, his theological understanding of the sacraments, his desire for a cathedral, or his views upon the authority of the bishop. The white American and English members of the church, aside from the clergy imported from England, disliked the bishop's high-handedness, refused to worship in Anglo-Catholic forms under his direction at the cathedral, and opposed his policies, while the Hawai'ian congregation remained relatively tiny.[11]

Nor did Staley's flexibility around "amusements" and Hawai'ian culture endear the new church to the mass of Hawai'ians, who most likely saw it as unfamiliar and a poor fit for their existing Christian identities. While royal and noble supporters found the church attractive for their own reasons, most Hawai'ians were already baptized members of Congregationalist, Catholic, or Latter Day Saints groups and were not attracted by Anglicanism. For those who did convert, often members of the alo ali'i (noble lineages), conversion matched the desire to assert the spiritual authority of the monarchy, similar perhaps to traditional religious ideals prior to Christianization. By the time of annexation and the arrival of the Episcopal Church to take over the mission from the English, the Reformed Catholic Church of Hawai'i had become firmly attached to the royal family, the noble elite, and the "royalist" party that opposed the "missionary" or annexation party during the political turbulence leading to the overthrow of the monarchy.[12]

Bishop Alfred Willis, Staley's successor as the English bishop of Hawai'i, was a Royalist and supported the monarchy against those who desired to overthrow it and set up a republic. Queen Liliuokalani had been a Congregationalist but converted to Anglicanism when she was held as a political prisoner in the palace, and Bishop Willis visited her there. The Queen eventually became a regular attendant at the Hawai'ian service at the cathedral and president of the Hawai'ian Women's Guild. After the overthrow, Willis believed that the royal family of Hawai'i had been denied their rights and spoke out against annexation, thus setting the Anglican establishment in Hawai'i firmly against American interests.

The brief Republic of Hawai'i came to an end as the white government requested annexation from the United States in 1898. Territorial government did not begin, however, until 1900, giving a two-year period of transition. Since part of the transition to U.S. authority would mean a transition in bishops—from the Church of England's Willis to an American missionary bishop—there would be a good many complications awaiting the Episcopal

Church in its new context, especially as most of the resident Americans attended other Protestant churches, the white members of the Church of England were largely English, and many native Hawai'ians who supported the monarchy saw Willis as their friend and resented the incoming American bishop.

That incoming bishop from the Episcopal Church was Henry Bond Restarick, stationed in San Diego for over twenty years before he was made the Bishop of Hawai'i. Restarick had developed a thriving congregation in San Diego and also had established several missions in the area which, by 1901, were all out of debt and healthy. This, plus his work at General Convention on the committee on the division of dioceses, may have brought his name to the attention of those who were electing a missionary bishop of Honolulu in 1902.

Restarick's history demonstrates an openness and interest in other races and cultures that would serve him well in Hawai'i. While in San Diego, he became interested in the problems of the California Indians, unlike Bishop Kip. He met Reverend Charles Smith Cook, a Lakota priest, when he visited San Diego with tuberculosis. Cook had been ordained by Bishop Henry Whipple and had been adopted by a white missionary. Writing decades later, Restarick remembered many details of Cook's life story, which must have deeply impressed him. He and Cook went together to Agua Caliente on Warner's Ranch to try to talk with the Indians there. Restarick wrote, "[Cook] was distressed by the degradation of these Indians and said he had never seen such conditions among any tribes known to him." Restarick took a leading role in trying to find the Indians a better place to live after they had been denied the ability to remain at Warner's Ranch by its owner, the governor of California, and congratulated himself that the place he had found for them was much better, with better soil and water.

Restarick recorded that these Indians were nominally Catholic, but he thought of the Indians in Minnesota who had learned to make lace through the mission agency there as a local industry, and brought a deaconess to teach lacemaking to the San Diego Indians. His work and attitude here are especially telling of his view of mission: while these Indians remained Catholic and under the supervision of Franciscans, Restarick brought the deaconess anyway to help them and promised that their faith would not be interfered with in any way (although he also told the Franciscans that the deaconess would teach them to recite the Creed, the Lord's Prayer, and the Ten Commandments). Restarick ends his story by noting that he visited the Indians at Pala in 1923 and "was delighted to find a prosperous and contented community. The houses were neat and the farms well tilled and a white man who lived near said they had better crops than anyone else in the district. It really was a providential thing that the Indians were moved from Agua Caliente."[13]

In all of this, Restarick demonstrated a clear and close attention to missional work through the Episcopal Church, a care for those who would not ever become Episcopalians, a long-term commitment in building relationships, and a willingness to go out of his way to develop respectful relationships with people of other cultures, religious affiliations, and races, though still working within the assimilative model of mission.

During his episcopacy in Hawai'i, Restarick's interest in missions among groups other than white settlers and native Hawai'ians led to growing congregations among Chinese and Korean Hawai'ians, some of which had begun under the Church of England in the 1880s. The first Chinese congregation included people who had had mission school training in China. They used the American Prayer Book from Shanghai, but they also had many German-style customs, particularly at Christmas, and hymns coming from the early training of several founding members at the Basle Lutheran mission in China (including Mrs. and Reverend Kong Yin-Tet, who was originally a Lutheran minister).

In China, Kong Yin-Tet had originally been very anti-Christian and had volunteered to give out Christian tracts with the intention of destroying them, but he decided to read them first and ended up going to the mission with questions. He was ordained deacon and then priest in Hawai'i, with the financial support of the SPCK, prior to U.S. annexation. Several of the Kong children attended school in the United States and China and became prominent leaders in both Hawai'i and China.

The congregation depended financially upon the Society for the Propagation of the Gospel and the SPCK, which ceased when the islands were annexed in 1898. Until Bishop William Nichols came to manage the transition, and then the arrival of Restarick in 1902, the Chinese missions suffered from lack of financial support. However, by 1913 the Chinese were able to fundraise from supporters in Hawai'i and the continental United States to build their own St. Peter's Church, fully furnished and without debt.[14]

In reflecting years afterward upon the establishment and flourishing of the Chinese Episcopal congregations in Hawai'i, as opposed to Kip's partly self-inflicted failure in the 1850s, Restarick wrote:

Californians have often said that the Chinese in Hawai'i were different from those on the mainland. One reason for this is that the Chinese, brought here by the Hawai'ian government for work on the sugar plantations, came from country villages and were an agricultural people, while so many in the states came from the city of Canton. Another reason for the difference is that having always been treated with friendliness, the best in them has been brought out; They have never been compelled to live in segregated districts but have developed side by side with the Hawai'ians and the Caucasians; Their children have been educated in the public schools of the territory and even in the more exclusive private schools when means would allow.[15]

Restarick drew attention to the dynamic of exclusion and oppression that existed for American Chinese communities from the 1850s onward, with the establishment of the Chinese Exclusion Act in 1882 and various anti-Asian laws, which were largely pushed forward by white Californians. The Chinese Exclusion Act, which forbade almost all immigration from China and was blatantly based in scientific racism, was later extended to include Japan through the 1905 "Gentleman's Agreement" and essentially all of Asia in the 1917 Barred Zone Act. Chinese Exclusion, and its preliminary anti-Chinese agitation and legislation on the West Coast of the United States, did not affect Hawai'i until after annexation, and thus the Chinese Hawai'ian community lived relatively unmolested until 1898.[16]

Bishop Staley had worked closely with an Anglo-Catholic sisterhood to run the Anglican schools, and from the American Episcopal Church now came deaconesses: women who had offered themselves to be "set apart" as religious workers and who remained unmarried. They were not considered equivalent to male deacons, who would normally become priests, as women could not be ordained, but from the mid-nineteenth century through the mid-twentieth deaconesses were central to many missionary efforts, including work on Indian reservations such as that supported by Restarick.

Deaconess Emma Drant of Cincinnati came on her own initiative to the Hawai'ian Islands, supported by the founder of Proctor and Gamble as "his own missionary." Drant worked among the Chinese in Honolulu, and with the support and guidance of Reverend Kong and his wife of St. Peter's, she organized a new congregation, St. Elizabeth's. Six months after arriving, she also began a "sewing school" for Hawai'ian and Chinese children and a night school for Chinese men at the same time, supported by a Chinese Christian leader who provided a room and furniture. Within ten months, over fifteen hundred men had attended. Drant had to leave Hawai'i by 1904 because of illness, but the work she had begun flourished with Chinese leadership.[17]

The mission at St. Peter's, which predated Drant's arrival, was completely Chinese-led from its beginning. Bishop Restarick memorialized congregant Yap See Young and his family of ten children, and how Yap, as a "progressive Chinese," cut off the queue required of Chinese male citizens and insisted that his wife walk next to him rather than behind him, according to Chinese custom. Because "he hoped to be on equality with his wife in heaven, he considered it right to treat her as an equal on earth." Yap thus demonstrated the monogamous, companionate marriage ideal which missionaries attempted to inculcate in cultures that had traditionally permitted polygamy. In the founding of St. Elizabeth's, Restarick noted that members from St. Peter's, especially the Kongs, were major contributors to leadership in the night school, making introductions in the community, and leading worship.

Drant's tireless and energetic colleague, Ng Ping, built up the Chinese missions over decades in Hawai'i and later in California. Ng Ping was the original name of Daniel Gee Ching Wu, who became one of the first Chinese Episcopal priests in the United States and led two Chinese congregations in the Bay Area. As a young child in Shanghai, he was kidnaped and effectively enslaved, but taught himself to read and write. He was then brought by his owner to Hawai'i to work on the plantations. While in Hawai'i he became active as an anti-Christian campaigner, one of the leaders of the Confucianist Club who preached against Christianity among the Chinese immigrants and workers.

When Deaconess Drant came to Honolulu to work among the Chinese under Restarick, she didn't speak Chinese and recruited Ng to teach her; he agreed in exchange for being taught English and for a promise that Drant wouldn't expect him to get involved in anything Christian. Nonetheless, within a few years he was baptized and became an active leader in the Chinese mission, St. Elizabeth's. According to his own account, he was attacked and beaten for this by his previous associates in the Confucian Club, but didn't fight back.[18]

While still in Hawai'i, Ng also became active in organizing Chinese against the Chinese Exclusion Act, which became effective in Hawai'i after annexation in 1898. In 1905, the U.S. Supreme Court ruled that a Chinese American was barred by the Exclusion Act from returning to the United States after leaving, setting off protests among the Chinese American community as well as in China. At one public protest, recorded in a local newspaper, Ng spoke on "how the Chinese should regard the Exclusion Act and how to urge the Chinese government to oppose it."

"After we have done so much," he said, "to open up the mineral wealth of America, and to develop the resources of the country, how unjust it is to cast us out. . . . Now that exclusion is in force and few Chinese are entering the United States, now that there is no danger of a deluge of Chinese laborers, the exclusion laws are being made stricter. Why should this be? It is claimed that there is an exempt class, but the officials are doing all they can to hinder it from entering. This policy is the rankest injustice. When these people get their passports, pass their medical examination, have their clothes disinfected, and take the steamer to the United States, they are turned back. Is this justice?"

"The boycott is quite justified if we have a grievance. It is not an extreme stand. By it perhaps we may bring the Americans to a realization of what they are losing. Let us all stand together and be firm." (Tremendous applause).[19]

Bishop Nichols of California called Drant to establish a Chinese mission in San Francisco in 1905. After the 1906 earthquake, many Chinese relocated from San Francisco to Oakland, and a new mission was begun there. In 1907 Drant requested Ng to come help, and he changed his name to Daniel Wu (Mandarin instead of Cantonese) because white Americans had so many problems with the sound of Ng. (Ng and Wu both mean "five" in their respective dialects.) In 1912 Wu was ordained and married Won King Yoak, an American-born Chinese woman who was active with Donaldina Cameron at the Presbyterian Mission in working with Chinese women who had been trafficked into sexual exploitation. Won lost her U.S. citizenship when she married Wu, who was still a Chinese citizen, another aspect of the restrictive citizenship and naturalization laws of the time. Wu was active in visiting Chinese immigrants held at Angel Island from 1910 to 1940, which was risky as it drew the attention of immigration authorities to himself and his family.[20]

Following the imposition of the Chinese exclusion laws upon Hawai'i after it became a U.S. territory, Koreans begin to arrive in 1902, and some came to the bishop requesting a ministry and a place to worship. The bishop recorded that most of those who came to see him in 1905 requesting ministry were not Christian, although some of the Korean immigrants were Presbyterian or Methodist. John Pahk attended Church Divinity School of the Pacific and became the first Korean priest in the United States. These missions used the Korean translation of the English Book of Common Prayer rather than the American version, but because the Koreans were transient in seeking work missions were often begun and then given up when the congregants left.[21]

In addition to successfully expanding mission work beyond the base of white settlers and native Hawai'ians, supporting mission work in multiple languages, and ordaining clergy from other racial groups, Restarick also increased the connection of the church to educational and medical work in Hawai'i. Unlike Bishop James Holly, Restarick had no problem raising funds to build hospitals and cathedrals and schools. This is a great difference between the missionary work in Haiti and the missionary work in Hawai'i, but it was not the result of greater support from the Board of Missions. Restarick himself had personal connections to generous donors and knew how to go about the process effectively. As in the days of William Augustus Muhlenberg, personal requests to wealthy supporters were the best and most efficient way to get money for missions, rather than a centralized process which seemed to rarely provide the needed resources quickly enough. This was one of the ways in which informal relationships played out in terms of differential access to resources for white and nonwhite Episcopalian leaders.[22]

The Philippines

At the same time that the United States was formally annexing Hawai'i, the nation had embarked on the exciting adventure of taking colonial possessions from Spain and making them American via the Spanish-American War. Initially inspired by Cuba's rebellion against Spain, and prodded to intervene by newspaper reports of Spanish atrocities and the sinking of the U.S.S. *Maine* in Havana harbor, the United States invaded both the Philippines (where there was also an anticolonial revolt in progress) and Cuba. Spain was unprepared and unable to defend its colonies, and its naval forces were resoundingly defeated. Though the United States had claimed prior to the war that it did not desire colonial possessions and would permit the local peoples to have autonomy and sovereignty, at the Treaty of Paris the Americans paid Spain $20 million and walked away with Puerto Rico, Guam, and the Philippines.

As the prospect of receiving the Philippines as U.S. territory became a public debate, American newspaper editors and politicians who were against annexation spoke out not in anti-imperialist but mostly in racist terms, echoing the fears of the "Mongolian horde" that had led to the Chinese Exclusion Act. Including these areas within American territory, with rights equal to other states, would lead to such ludicrous possibilities as Asian senators and tragedies such as leprosy, venereal disease, corruption, opium use, and increased competition for white workers against the cheaply working Asian. Thus, while annexation was pursued for reasons of "self-defense," creating military bases, or keeping competing European powers away from colonial possessions that could strengthen them, it was not initially expected that the population of the Philippines, in particular, would be American citizens with all the rights of white Americans.[23]

In this debate over the Philippines, Protestant missionary interests were supportive of annexation, seeing an opportunity never previously given for Protestants to enter an area which had been colonized and Catholicized by Spain. For centuries the Spanish government had forbidden any other religious organization to have contact with the native people, and so this debate echoed the historical tensions within the earliest English incursions into North America four hundred years before. But this period of the cultural high tide of scientific racism meant that many Protestant writers emphasized the importance of the "Anglo-Saxon race," rather than religion per se, in the carrying of "civilization and Christianity" to the far points of the world. Looking back on the decision to keep the Philippines, President McKinley, a devout Methodist, told a story of divine inspiration:

> I walked the floor of the White House night after night until midnight; and I am not ashamed to tell you, gentlemen, that I went down on my knees and prayed Almighty God for light and guidance more than one night. And one night late it came to me this way—I don't know how it was, but it came: (1) That we could not give them back to Spain—that would be cowardly and dishonorable; (2) that we could not turn them over to France and Germany—our commercial rivals in the Orient—that would be bad business and discreditable; (3) that we could not leave them to themselves—they were unfit for self-government—and they would soon have anarchy and misrule over there worse than Spain's was; and (4) that there was nothing left for us to do but to take them all, and to educate the Filipinos, and uplift and civilize and Christianize them, and by God's grace do the very best we could by them, as our fellow-men for whom Christ also died.[24]

According to the logic of racial paternalism and assimilationism, Filipinos were not "ready" for self-government or for equal relationships with and equal rights as white Americans. They would have to go through a period of "benevolent assimilation" first, just as African Americans and Native Americans required "tutelage" and "wardship."[25]

Unfortunately for American ideas of bringing welcome civilization to a distant people, the Philippines already had a highly educated, Christian, and "civilized" class of local citizens, some of whom had attended school in Europe, who were very familiar with the political reasoning behind the modern ideals of the sovereign nation-state and had already begun an insurgency against Spain before the American invasion. Annexation was a betrayal of the Filipino revolutionaries, and the war in the Philippines, so brief and easy against Spain, became a years-long bloody, atrocity-filled guerrilla war against Filipinos as the United States attempted to put down the "rebellion."[26]

Thus, when the Episcopal Church turned its attention to this new mission field, it came closely accompanying military force. When Admiral George Dewey destroyed the Spanish fleet and waited for reinforcements from San Francisco to take Manila, he offered a "sham battle" to the Spanish while insisting that the Filipino revolutionaries were sidelined outside the city and forbidden to participate until the treaty in Paris was decided. The chaplains on Dewey's fleet became the first Episcopalian presence in the Philippines. One of them, Charles Pierce, was actually sent by an American general to spy on the Filipino revolutionaries, believing, correctly, that they would not suspect a clergyman of such iniquity.[27]

Even after the war became one between the United States and the "insurgent" Filipino revolutionaries, military chaplains continued to develop relationships with Filipinos in Manila. The Brotherhood of St. Andrew, an organization of mission-minded Episcopalian laymen, sent representatives to the "Chaplain's Conference" to add missionary ideals to this work. At this time there were eight chaplains for 100,000 military Americans, so clearly they would not have much time to spend with Filipinos under such conditions; the Chaplains Conference thus welcomed the support of the Brotherhood and the Episcopal Church.

While initially Pierce resisted starting an Episcopal church in Manila, believing that because Catholicism was already Christian no missionary efforts were needed, local Filipinos encouraged him to do so by recalling the ways in which the local friars, usually Spanish, had taken advantage of the community.

The Chaplains and the Brotherhood of St. Andrew thus established Holy Trinity in Manila for the English-speaking civilians as well as the military. Despite his early use as a spy against the Filipinos, Pierce became extremely popular among the Filipino residents of Manila, for whom he became known as someone who would dispense medical care, arrange for funerals, and step in for families in need during the war. By 1899, a Manila Spanish-language newspaper editor wrote that "[Pierce's] sweet character, his generous heart, his eminently Christian soul take pleasure in well-doing; and the people, the poor, the helpless and the needy seek him because they see him [as] a true apostle of the Gospel . . . and a true son of Christ." Manuel Buirir, a member of Pierce's Filipino congregation, seconded the editor's assessment of the chaplain by sending a letter to the Episcopal Mission Board, saying, "Chaplain Pierce [is] a clergyman most exemplary, with a kind heart. . . . He understands how to secure the loyal friendship from all the Filipinos. We love him, respect him, and obey him." ' In 1899, Pierce confirmed fifty Filipinos when the Episcopal bishop of Shanghai came for a visitation.[28]

Despite these promising beginnings and the support of the Brotherhood of St. Andrew, Pierce struggled to raise the necessary funds for the burgeoning mission in the Philippines. The Episcopal Church, in nearly seventy years of financing foreign and domestic missions, was continually strapped and unable to provide resources; it had been true for California in the 1850s and it was true for the Philippines fifty years later. In 1900, when Pierce was in the United States trying to raise funds for the Philippines, the new director of the Board of Managers, the same A. S. Lloyd who would soon write the foreword to George Bragg's *First Negro Priest,* had been on the job for less than a year and was working through years of back-requests at the same time that American expansion had suddenly jumped into the Caribbean and the Pacific. Episcopalians continued to be apathetic in their financial support for missions, with only half of congregations giving for missionary purposes and less than 3% of the church's income earmarked for foreign missions. The canon law of the Episcopal Church also made developing new mission fields extremely cumbersome. Before any major expenditure in a new field, the mission board would first have to recommend that a missionary district be created, and in order to make such a recommendation, an endowment fund for the district and its bishop had to be established and money raised. Then the mission board's recommendation was sent to the General Convention for approval—and aside from the issue of raising the endowment, General Convention met only every three years.[29]

It was therefore only in 1901 that General Convention was able to establish the Philippines as a missionary district. Pierce was suggested as the first missionary bishop, but the high church party rejected him since he had originally been a Baptist minister. In any case, his health had been broken by illnesses in Manila and he could not return. Charles Brent, an Anglo-Catholic associated with the religious Society of St. John the Evangelist (the Cowley Fathers), and who had been involved in Anglo-Catholic social and religious ministry in Boston, drew from several strands of Episcopalian missional ideals: Anglo-Catholic ritual, Social Gospel activism, Broad Church incarnationalism and respect for science, and establishmentarianism. Like Pierce, Brent's original intention to "not raise an altar against an altar," and to accept that Roman Catholicism was working for Filipino Christians, was gradually undermined by his growing perception of the Catholic clergy as incompetent and inattentive to their people; he thus eventually gave permission for a chapel to be established in Manila, but by that time most of Pierce's converts had already left for other Protestant denominations.[30]

Bishop Brent's initial goal was to "Christianize" the American military, business interests, and diplomatic core in the Philippines in order to help protect the "benevolence" of American rule and ensure that Americans acted from Christian impulses rather than colonial exploitation. He built the Episcopalian cathedral in Manila and started a club for young people as well as two American schools in the mountains, so that Americans wouldn't have to send their children back to the United States for an education. Schools were characteristic of the Episcopalian missions in all communities, in Manila among the Tagalog, in Mindanao among the Muslims, and in northern Luzon among the Igorot, with an emphasis on the protective powers of education against the "vices" of civilization. Brent also drew on his experience in Boston to create a "settlement house" in the Manila slum area of Tondo—an area which had suffered greatly in the American-Filipino war—which included training in sewing, boys and girls clubs, an orphanage, and a medical clinic. Brent established a chapel there with a Filipino priest and welcomed any Filipinos who showed interest, but he was not willing to purposefully evangelize among the Catholic Filipinos and try to draw them away from the faith they already held. In his missional view, being present with the people in their sufferings was enough of a Christian commitment. Brent also became an international crusader against the opium trade, seeing the addiction and misery it caused in the Philippines.[31]

Bishop Brent chose to focus his attention on parts of the Philippines that had resisted Spanish-enforced Catholicization: the Chinese Filipino community, who lived in enclaves in Manila; the Muslim community in the southern island of Mindanao; and the mountain tribal communities of Luzon. His missionary episcopate was not hugely successful initially in terms of numbers, but demonstrated multiple models of mission work in different communities that took different approaches to "Christianizing and civilizing" through "benevolent assimilation." In the mountains, Brent sent missionaries to establish centers among the Igorot people, sensationalized as "headhunters" in American reports, one in the valley of Bontoc, which became a provincial capital, and one in the much more remote mountain village of Sagada. While both of the missionaries were Anglo-Catholics, they took very different approaches to their callings.

In Sagada, John Staunton, an engineer, immediately began developing a new industrial base for the town, including a sawmill, a quarry, a high school and hospital, and of course a church, while insisting on high Anglo-Catholic rituals, including the "silent canon" (wherein the priest whispers the words of eucharistic consecration), regular auricular confession (despite the fact that Staunton never learned to speak the local language), and withholding the eucharistic wine from laypeople. His wife was a nurse who did learn the language, and was much loved until her death from illness. Staunton's dedication and incredible skills in publicity and fundraising enabled him to remake Sagada as a town of Episcopalian Igorot developing a capitalist economy, but Sagada was too isolated to truly thrive under such expectations, and had been sustainable only with a vast influx of outside funds. Staunton eventually left his mission under duress for misappropriation of funds and disobedience to Bishop Frank Mosher, Brent's successor, but he is remembered in Sagada as the "venerable" founder of the church and community, which remains a stronghold of Filipino Episcopalianism.[32]

In the river valley of Bontoc, also an Igorot town, missionary Walter Clapp and a succession of single women missionaries and deaconesses, as well as clergy, developed a mission program centered around translation, learning the local language and translating the scriptures and prayer books into it. Bontoc eventually became a center from which even more isolated groups would request missionaries for their communities.[33]

The American Episcopalians were guided by local children and converts, who first were drawn to observe the liturgy and then began to develop relationships with the missionaries. The two initial "linguists," Clapp and

Deaconess Margaret Waterman, knew no Asian languages and undertook their translation work with no resources or books on any of the local languages, working from scratch and permitting themselves to be taught and their own understandings shaped by the children and converts around them. This strategy of mission encouraged mutuality and respect between the missionaries and the local community, and the missionaries' dependence particularly upon two children, Pitt-a-Pit (baptized Hilary Clapp) and Narciso, ensured that their own sense of superiority and control would be weakened in their work. While racial paternalism in this era led many white people to see nonwhite people as children in need of guidance, this experience led the missionaries to acknowledge their own "child-like" ignorance and dependence upon their teachers.[34]

Pitt-a-Pit, after his conversion and baptism, attended the Episcopalian boarding school in Baguio; he went to Canada, where he excelled at Greek, French, and theology, and returned to Manila to be trained as a doctor. He then returned to Bontoc and spent the rest of his life serving his people. During World War II, as the Filipinos were caught between the Japanese invasion and the U.S. battle for the Philippines, Hilary Clapp was executed by guerrillas as a Japanese collaborator. He had attempted to forestall Japanese reprisals against civilians by discouraging support for the guerrillas, although he was also in constant contact with the pro-American guerrillas and refused to divulge to the Japanese the location of American missionaries in hiding.[35]

Latin America and the Caribbean

The Panama Episcopalian mission was organized by the Board of Missions in 1854, in response to the opening of the gold fields in California in 1848. There was a sudden need to have an easy way to get from the Atlantic coast to the Pacific, and already a mostly overland route across the isthmus to ships waiting on the Pacific had become a favored possibility—this was how Bishop Kip reached California. At this time, Panama was part of Colombia, and American businesses invested there and imported workers from the West Indies and Asia to build first a railroad, and then the canal. These workers experienced a very high loss of life from tropical diseases and the harshness of their work demands. An Episcopalian business owner and investor, William Henry Aspinwall, wanted to at least provide for their religious needs, since the West Indian laborers were largely members of the Church of England, and he built and endowed a church for them.

The initial mission was planted in Aspinwall (a town on Atlantic Coast that was the eastern end of the planned railroad) in 1863. Bishop Alonzo Potter consecrated the new church during his final journey to San Francisco, where he died of "Panama Fever" on his ship in the harbor. Mission was thus developed in tandem with the business leaders investing in the railroad and in the growing American territorial interest in the West Coast and the Pacific.[36]

Aspinwall had great difficulty in keeping a priest in the beautiful church building due to the climate and health issues; the church was often without services. The second wave of immigration from the West Indies to work in the banana plantations was served by the Church of England, as Episcopalians withdrew for lack of funds. This situation continued until the United States took territorial control of the Canal Zone, and in 1904 the Episcopal Church took authority from the Church of England over the Anglican churches in Panama.[37]

One major contribution of the Episcopal Church to Panamanian Episcopalianism in this era was to move away from the Church of England's racially semi-integrated congregations (separate seating, same congregation) to fully racially segregated congregations. As the United States was nearing a high point of racial stratification, the Episcopal Church simply accepted the racial prejudices of white American immigrants to Panama as normative for the church. The U.S. government in Panama also instigated a racially stratified and segregated governance system, with Black employees being paid less than whites, and public facilities and residential areas were legally segregated.[38]

Puerto Rico and Cuba, won through the Spanish-American war, for the first time brought significant numbers of Spanish speakers into the church, although there had been missions previously in the American Southwest and a complicated relationship with the church in Mexico. The Mexican Episcopal church had begun independently after the Mexican Revolution and had requested a bishop to be consecrated, but the Episcopal Church was unwilling to do so due, in essence, to the late nineteenth-century racially paternalistic sense that the Mexicans could not be trusted to teach the correct doctrine and liturgical practice. After several decades of back and forth, in 1904 Mexico became an official missionary district of the Episcopal Church rather than an autonomous church.[39]

For the most part, the Episcopal Church had done little mission work in Latin America due to the general discomfort of the high church group, and particularly the late nineteenth-century Anglo-Catholics, with mission work among Roman Catholics. Most of the Anglican mission work in Central and South America had been undertaken either by an evangelical organization in the Church of England, the South American Mission Society, or by an independent voluntary evangelical Episcopalian missionary group, the American Church Mission Society, set up precisely because the Domestic and Foreign Missionary Society (DFMS) was unwilling to work in these areas, which were seen as Catholic and thus not an appropriate arena for proselytization. Early Church of England chaplaincies in Latin American nations tended to be set up with the reluctant permission of Catholic authorities and focused on providing spiritual care for expatriates and travelers. The evangelical societies were more ambitious and attempted to build relationships with indigenous peoples in isolated areas; Charles Darwin was an enthusiastic supporter of the mission to the Yahgan people of Tierra del Fuego. The Episcopalian Church in Brazil was initiated by graduates of Virginia Theological Seminary and included significant efforts to include Japanese Brazilians.[40]

In a similar pattern, the Episcopal Church in Cuba had begun with an evangelical Bible Society and Women's Guild in Philadelphia, which sent Bibles to Cuba in the 1880s. A few interested people, including a man named Pedro Duarte, began to organize and hold services, and Duarte eventually attended Philadelphia Divinity School to be ordained. He returned to Cuba, built a church, and worked with a second Cuban priest to organize an orphanage and several other congregations and mission stations, all with very little financial support. However, when Cuba became subject to American sovereignty, and the evangelical mission group gave its mission responsibility back to the Board of Missions of the Episcopal Church, instead of any of the local Cuban clergy an American clergyman was consecrated as missionary bishop. As more Americans entered Cuba after the Spanish-American War, the church began to see its primary responsibility as ministering to them rather than to the Cubans.

In Puerto Rico, as in the Philippines, the Episcopal Church came with the American occupying forces, and the first Episcopal services were offered by a military chaplain. Earlier work in Puerto Rico had been accomplished by the Church of England, which had active churches in the Caribbean, including occasional visits from the Bishop of Antigua in the 1870s. When a missionary bishop was elected from the United States, he saw his primary goal in mission to ensure that the Americans emigrating to Puerto Rico were "Christian," providing a salutary example to the native Puerto Ricans, particularly involving issues of the "Christian home."[41]

Summary

Long years after the events, the first American bishop of Hawai'i wrote, "Shortly before her death, [Queen Liliuokalani] said to me that she had come to the conclusion that things were best for her people as they were. . . . [T]he night before she died in 1917 I had prayers with her and she bade me goodbye."[42] Restarick's recollections did not seem to fully appreciate that "best for her people" could only be considered among the realities of unequal military power and violent expansion of American territorial sovereignty.

During this era, empire led to a growing pluralization within American territories and, in response, an intense emphasis on "Christianize and civilize" in places where the church was planted. In the next chapter, the early twentieth century will see the development of critiques of this missional racism and assimilationism in favor of supporting indigenous leadership with the ideal of a "national church."

PART III
MISSIO DEI

By the middle of the twentieth century, the previous understanding of mission, and the practices laid down by previous centuries, had completely dissipated. One can see the loss of focus even by the late nineteenth century when reading the 1921 history of the Episcopal Church's mission work, *A Century of Endeavor*. This chronological exploration of the work, practice, and funding of Episcopalian mission, written by a contemporary mission executive, simply falls apart in its later chapters in a flurry of funding, bureaucracy, General Conventions, reorganizations, personnel changes, and missionary bishops. The center does not hold. Thus, I have chosen to follow the thread of missional engagement at multiple levels, but not every possible one, in order to try to develop a focused and meaningful understanding of what happened in this crucial shift.

The paths I explore here are dictated by following the threads of "race," "postcolonialism," and "missiology." By examining this aspect of church history in this one denominational context, the twentieth century is seen as one of the turning points in world Christian history. In the twentieth century, Euro-American Christendom reaped the whirlwind of the centuries of colonialism and imperialism that had been seeded along with world Christian expansion.

Chapter 10 focuses on 1910 through the 1930s, tracing the shift away from traditional missionary ways of doing and thinking that occurred around World War I and the "Re-thinking Missions" report of 1932. The shifting patterns of thinking about other, non-European cultures and non-Christian religions, and of the need to address racism, animate the 1932 report and are already present in the global missionary movement of 1910. These shifts focus on the importance of justice as well as humanitarian action and foreshadow a missiology of partnership and mutuality that becomes prominent in the mid-twentieth century. In the specific context of the Episcopal Church, the chapter focuses on establishmentarianism as a missional theory and practice, both in the United States and in China, and on the Hocking Report, which was heavily inspired by the investigation into missions in China.

Chapter 11 focuses on the years around and following World War II, including the effect of the war on Japanese American Episcopalians and the loss of the Chinese missions, as well as the general turning away from "foreign missions" experienced by all denominations in this era. The experience of responding to Japanese internment was part of a growing attention to race as a justice issue in the church. Episcopalian expansion focused on suburban church-planting among white middle-class families, concomitant with a hollowing out of urban churches, traditionally the stronghold of Episcopalianism. The other side of the withdrawal of attention to foreign missions and a reluctance to support "segregated" or ethnic-specific congregations after the war was that the Episcopal Church became essentially identified with white, middle-class culture, and while there was an idealization of integration in some circles, this integration was assumed to include an assimilation to white, middle-class ways of being and thinking. Creative missional risk-taking that crossed boundaries of race and culture became a minority interest in the church's life.

Chapter 12 moves back to the global scene to trace the rise of *missio dei* theology and its connection to a mission of justice-oriented activism, exemplified in the United States by the movements around civil rights, gay rights, and the ordination of women. All of these things had their initial seeds of transformation in the earlier period of the 1940s and 1950s but were able to become central to the missiological practice of the church—controversially so—only with the rise of this new missiology that focused on bearing witness to and accompanying God's work in the world, letting the world set the agenda for the church. In the Episcopal Church context, I examine how the Anglican Communion's new missional focus, explicated in the 1963 document *Mutual Responsibility and Interdependence*, related to the Episcopal Church's civil rights work and the General Convention Special Program.

Chapter 13 connects these movements toward justice and the new *missio dei* theology to the changes in the Episcopal Church reflected in the 1979 Book of Common Prayer and the new baptismal covenant. Its language around service and human dignity—an important change barely reflected in the records of the decision-making around the language of the new Book of Common Prayer—became for many Episcopalians central to their sense of mission, and coincided with increasing attention to what is called "baptismal ecclesiology" and the belief that justice required that all people have access to positions of ordained leadership in the church.

Chapter 14 traces the consequences of this shift to missional inclusion, connected with shifts in ideals and practices around marriage and sexuality in the North Atlantic cultural contexts, as related to the ordination and consecration of openly gay or lesbian individuals and relationships with the global Anglican Communion. The combined weight of changes and shifts throughout the twentieth century in missional ideals and global relationships led to what is called "Anglican Realignment," schisms within the Episcopal Church and the Anglican Communion as a whole.

These chapters, taken together, offer a single argument, collecting the threads of mission, race, and empire traced throughout the book as a whole, placing contemporary issues within this context. This provides a new understanding of the state in which Episcopalians and global Anglicans today find themselves.

10

Mission to the World

Introduction

Coming out of the nineteenth century into the twentieth, American Christianity entered a brave new world of global connections built upon the "great century" of Christian missionary expansion from the North Atlantic churches. The ideal of "Christian civilization" as the basis of world society was at perhaps its greatest height of self-confidence and power, along with the height of imperial expansion of European and U.S. power over other parts of the world. This confidence is captured in the memory of Edinburgh 1910, the great global missions conference which led to the development of the modern ecumenical movement. Yet only a few short years later, Christendom collapsed in fire and blood in World War I. The ideal of a world Christian society had been a mirage all along, riddled with paradoxes and fatal flaws.

The Euro-American missionary movement that had both activated and critiqued this world expansion of Christian community was caught up in its own internal tensions and challenges. By the late 1930s, the nineteenth-century ideal of missional expansion would undergo a decisive shift affecting all Protestant denominations, Episcopalians most certainly included. For Episcopalians, the movement toward a shift in missional thinking included a particularly Episcopalian understanding of their church, known as "establishmentarianism." Within the United States, establishmentarianism led to a missional focus upon assimilationism; outside the United States, to a missional focus upon indigenization, or contextualization, in the service of creating a national church.

Ecumenicism and Establishmentarianism

The ecumenical movement of the twentieth century grew into being as the nineteenth-century missional movement reached its apogee, symbolized by the international, interdenominational missionary conference in Edinburgh

Mission, Race, and Empire. Jennifer C. Snow, Oxford University Press. © Oxford University Press 2024.
DOI: 10.1093/oso/9780197598948.003.0011

in 1910. For American Episcopalians, Edinburgh 1910 was a beautiful experience of self-confidence in the Christian work being done and joyous anticipation of the work in the future. Bishop Charles Brent of the Philippines was deeply involved in organizing the conference, and also led in the follow-up work that set the foundations of the global ecumenical movement with a series of conferences in the 1920s. But Edinburgh, with its global focus, was less consequential to Episcopalians at home than an experience ten years earlier. Americans had hosted their own global missions conference in 1900 in New York City, where over 200,000 people attended the exhibits and speeches, and keynotes were given by the president of the United States. This intertwining of the political establishment and the lauding of "Christianizing and civilizing" as the special task of missions in the world was the perfect representation of the late nineteenth-century Episcopalian missionary vision: establishmentarianism.[1]

An established church is one which is supported, legally or financially, or both, by the national government. After the American Revolution, in the new context of disestablishment, no denomination was an established church, and the new Episcopal Church had to develop its missional responses in its new context. However, the ecclesiological traces of establishment remained in Episcopalian polity: its governance structure similar to that of the nation itself, and intended to model democratic ideals; its diocesan structure, which originally was identical with the new states; its parish organization, which was geographically defined and was intended to include all people within that defined boundary. The realities of a voluntary, disestablished religious system sat awkwardly with this structure, and it set the Episcopal Church apart from other Protestant denominations.

The Episcopal Church's answer to this, also developing in the late nineteenth century, is sometimes called "establishmentarianism." Establishmentarianism is that aspect of the Episcopal Church's self-understanding where its role is to act as the conscience of the nation, guiding both ordinary people and political leaders, and speaking not only to and for Episcopalians but for the idealized well-being of all Americans. It built upon missional tensions to emphasize "comprehensiveness," a theological openness to diversity that could include, ideally, all other Protestant denominations in one "national church," moving toward an identity based in ecumenical relationships. Establishmentarianism also supposed that ideally other nations too would have "national churches" that would be the peers of the Episcopal Church and do the same work within their own contexts. More specifically in missional contexts, establishmentarianism idealized American-style democratic processes and governance, human rights, and a well-secured and stable social order. The National Cathedral in Washington, D.C., stands as the physical and tangible symbol of this missional ideology.

In order to act effectively as the conscience of the nation, there should ideally be one national church, not a multitude of denominations competing with each other. This position led to a set of late nineteenth-century developments that have usually been understood as primarily ecumenical in nature—particularly the Muhlenberg Memorial and the Chicago Quadrilateral—but this ecumenical project is at base missional, related to the church's sense of identity, self, purpose, and expansion.[2]

The Chicago Quadrilateral was written by William Reed Huntington in 1870 as a basis for future union of Protestants into one church structure, and in 1886 was adopted by General Convention as the basis for conversations about ecumenical unity. The Quadrilateral was inspired by Huntington's ideal of a "national Church," one united by simple shared commitments to four things. As adapted and resolved by the Lambeth Conference of international Anglican bishops, and recorded in the Book of Common Prayer, "in the opinion of this Conference, the following Articles supply a basis on which approach may be by God's blessing made towards Home Reunion:

(a) The Holy Scriptures of the Old and New Testaments, as "containing all things necessary to salvation," and as being the rule and ultimate standard of faith.

(b) The Apostles' Creed, as the Baptismal Symbol; and the Nicene Creed, as the sufficient statement of the Christian faith.

(c) The two Sacraments ordained by Christ Himself—Baptism and the Supper of the Lord—ministered with unfailing use of Christ's words of Institution, and of the elements ordained by Him.

(d) The Historic Episcopate, locally adapted in the methods of its administration to the varying needs of the nations and peoples called of God into the Unity of His Church."

It has become not only a proposed basis for church union between denominations but also a central point of identity for Anglican churches worldwide.[3]

Huntington, one of the most prominent Episcopalians of the late nine-teenth century, never held a position greater than rector of an ordinary New York City church. However, his writings on church unity, on the na-ture of the Episcopal Church and its relationship to other denominations, including a sense of its purpose as a future "national church," became central to the church's self-identity through the Quadrilateral. Huntington's initial idealism seems to have originally been inspired through his youthful deep emotional friendship with Francis Ellingwood Abbott, a leading Unitarian and later a philosopher of scientific theism, and the loss of that friendship due to theological differences.[4]

Throughout his life Huntington took every opportunity to broaden the boundaries of the church, corresponding with leaders such as Bishop Brent in the Philippines, and supporting the Conference of Colored Workers in the Church in presenting their 1899 Memorial to General Convention protesting racial exclusion in the church. Like African American Episcopalians, Huntington connected self-governance and participation in governance as important spiritual principles. In developing his ideas of the Episcopal Church as a national church, and of the ways in which Christian denominations could return to the unity necessary for effective mission, Huntington argued that the American nation had a particular spiritual gift in its freedom and self-government. Imperialism and colonialism by the United States undermined this deep spiritual principle and must be rejected. The principle must be that people may be trusted to govern themselves. Rather than colonial adventures, the spiritual goal of the United States must be to develop a national church which values and maintains the freedom of all its people; and every nation should have its own national church that demonstrated its own gifts and genius. Any international gathering of churches, to be a true council and a unified church, must be made up of na-tional churches—not of multiple denominations. Later in the twentieth cen-tury, this principle would underlie the modern Anglican Communion, a gathering of autonomous national churches.[5]

Within the United States, Huntington imagined God's Providence bringing all into the Anglo-Saxon inheritance of the white people of the United States. Huntington envisioned a national church that was culturally assimilative, if accepting of theological diversity, setting strict standards for difference. Even in the most charitable interpretation, Huntington, like many other white Christian leaders of the time, took a strongly assimilationist view of the solution to the challenges of religious and denominational and racial pluralism in the United States. The emphasis on cultural assimilation as solving racial tension and the continuing scars of colonization and enslavement—and as a response to the claims of scientific racism that only Anglo-Saxons had the genetic capability to embody Christian civilization—was demonstrated in practical terms by Episcopalian mission among Native Americans and Black Americans after the Civil War. Among white missionary supporters of the much-harassed Chinese and Japanese immigrant communities, cultural assimilation was seen as the best way to demonstrate their fitness for inclusion in the American project. Huntington's establishmentarianism thus implicitly included this racialized assimilationism.[6]

The final aspect of establishmentarianism that was particularly Episcopalian, aside from its internal self-confidence as the future container of all varieties of Christian practice and theology, was its social location. The Episcopal Church, despite its rather shocking frugality in terms of financial support of missions compared to almost any other Protestant denomination of its time, included some of the wealthiest men in the United States, and a disproportionate number of political and cultural leaders of the middle and upper classes. Among Black Americans, the Episcopal Church was known as the church of the elite as well.[7]

With such demographic specialization, it was easy for many Episcopalians to see their church as destined to lead the nation's conscience and lawgiving, not only through its theology but through beautiful rituals, the building of cathedrals, the support of the arts and culture, and providing education and uplift for the downtrodden and oppressed. Establishmentarianism, in the U.S. context, thus connected the theological, demographic, liturgical, and historical inheritance of the Episcopal Church with the governance ideals and elite leadership of the United States. Only such a church could be a national church, and the nation required such a church as this.[8]

Beyond the United States, ideals of democratic governance, a reformed and benevolent social order, high levels of education and literacy for all, and a national church as the guarantor of the nation's conscience were particularly noticeable in American foreign mission fields. Where the United States fell short, as it did in many of these ideals, the church's work was to guide both government and charity to move closer to the ideal. After World War I, the Wilsonian ideals of political self-determination of peoples and nations also became part of this mix of Episcopalian mission goals.[9]

Establishmentarianism and China

The Episcopal Church in China was a particularly vivid example of the work of establishmentarianism as a mission strategy. China was a major mission field for most American Protestant denominations, and for Episcopalians it was considered the jewel of the "century of endeavor." By the time that China was closed to missions in 1949 by the victory of the Communists in the decades-long Chinese Civil War, Episcopalians had well over a century of experience in the country. Henry Lockwood and Francis Hanson had been sent out in 1835 to learn Chinese in Java. William Boone joined them in 1837, and in 1844, as China was forcibly "opened" to Western missionary work, Boone was consecrated as the American missionary bishop of China and relocated the mission from Xiamen (known to the missionaries as Amoy) in southern China to Shanghai in the North. The first Episcopalian baptism of a Chinese person, Wong Kong Chai, took place in 1846, and medical missions began in 1866, demonstrating the development of missionary practice toward a more explicitly humanitarian focus.

As noted by scholar Edmund Xu, Chinese Christianity in the nineteenth century and the first half of the twentieth was not perceived as a gospel of liberation. It "bore a heavy cross for being closely identified with Western powers."[10] Missionaries and Christian Chinese were often caught in the crossfire of the violence of the first half of the twentieth century, beginning with the Boxer Uprising of 1900 and continuing through the Nationalist Revolution, the Sino-Japanese Wars, and the Chinese Civil War. Because of Christianity's association with the exploitation of China by Europeans—after all, missionaries were allowed in only after Britain had forced China to also swallow the importation of opium in two separate wars—Chinese anticolonial movements often characterized themselves as "anti-Christian." Ng Ping (Daniel Wu) had participated in nationalist movements in exile as part of "anti-Christian leagues" before his conversion, as had Reverend Kong Yin Tet.

Wong Kong Chai was one of only two clergy remaining to the Chinese Episcopal Church in 1864, when Bishop Boone died. In 1879, the second missionary bishop of Shanghai, Samuel Isaac Schereschewsky, established St. John's University.[11] As in other parts of the world, mission moved very slowly in the beginning, but then discovered a fruitful way forward that fit into the local culture successfully. For Episcopalians, the way forward was education. Education—medical, scientific, and literary—proved an ideal fit between Episcopalian standards for educated clergy and the traditional Chinese value placed on literary accomplishment, particularly for political leaders and officials. China's political turbulence and an elite population that highly valued literacy and education meant that Christian missions engaging in educational work would almost certainly become enmeshed in the national political leadership.[12]

While English Anglican missions were established mostly in southern China, radiating out from the English footholds of Hong Kong and Guangzhou (called Canton by the English), American Episcopalian missions were centered in Shanghai, closer than the English to the political and cultural heart of the Qing dynasty's imperial capital, with both risks and opportunities as a result. These missions developed close relationships with the political life of the country, and their educational efforts developed an elite that was literate in both English and Chinese. Chinese Episcopalian clergy were educated at the Episcopalian University in Shanghai, St. John's, which taught in English. Chinese Episcopalians had the Book of Common Prayer both in Mandarin and in *wenli*, the historic literary language of China.[13]

The Episcopalian mission in China was also closely tied to the United States through this value of education and social and political leadership. Sun Yat-sen, the leader of the Nationalist Revolution that overthrew the Chinese imperial dynasty in 1912, briefly attended Iolani School in Hawai'i during the time that it was a mission of the Church of England. Many of the Episcopalian Chinese in Hawaii sent their children back to China for education at St. John's, and many of these children became leaders in industry and education in China. Close ties between the Episcopal Church in China and the United States continued through immigration and transnational relationships until after World War II.[14]

The ideal of a national church, plus the sense that missions were at cross-purposes, led to the merging of the American, Church of England, and Church of Canada Anglican missions into one national Chinese church in 1912, immediately after the Nationalist Revolution and overthrow of the Qing dynasty. The Chung Hua Sheng Kung Hui, also called the Holy Catholic Church in China, included all Chinese Anglicans until 1958, when the Communist Party dissolved religious organizations.

Sun Yat-sen's brother sent him back to China, feeling that he was growing "too Christian," after his stint in Hawai'i. While in Hawai'i, Sun had already organized an anti-imperial organization agitating for political change in China. Christianity contributed to Sun's ideals for a new Chinese society, one where people would be democratically self-governing and would share resources; his conversion and baptism when he returned to China reflected his sense of Christianity as a revolutionary movement for the welfare of the people. In China itself, the "gospel of education" had similar effects on others. Mission-educated Chinese leaders became active in the Republican Revolution that overthrew the Qing dynasty in 1911, and during the later war against Japanese imperialism, leaders in the church became part of the war of resistance. A national church needed leaders of its own people, and this establishmentarian goal again fit well with new republican ideals in the Chinese Empire.[15]

The Rizhi Society, which contributed to the 1911 Revolution, was founded by a graduate of St. John's, Reverend Huang Ch-t'ing; he also protected and helped to hide revolutionary leaders when they were sought by the imperial government for arrest. The Rizhi Society was located in the Church of Our Saviour in Wuchang and then at St. Joseph's Chapel; Reverend Hu Lang-t'ing, also a St. John's graduate, transformed the Rizhi Society into a revolutionary secret society. The American bishop Logan Roots of Wuchang Diocese protected revolutionaries and developed a close friendship with Zhou Enlai, later a prominent Chinese Communist leader. Several Chinese Anglican clergy graduating from St. John were in the late 1940s and early 1950s members of the National Committee of the Chinese People's Political Consultative Conference, and originally had generally positive relationships with the Communist movement in China.[16]

Anglican Chinese leaders tended to be closer to the Kuomintang (Nationalist government) than to the Chinese Communist Party (CCP), but were able to maintain good relationships with both sides until the final chapter of the split. In this friendliness to both sides, including involvement and support for the incipient Communist government, the Episcopalian leadership in China did not differ from the American national civil service and diplomatic staff in the years running up to and beyond World War II. Many of them were the children of missionary parents and believed that China would benefit from a political revolution. Some later admitted that they saw the CCP as itself a missionary movement of transformation, much like Sun did.[17]

High-level ministers of the Kuomintang as well as radical young clergy connected to the CCP were both part of the Anglican Chinese community. After Shanghai was taken by the Japanese in 1937, St. John's became a center for the CCP; the YMCA and churches became part of the CCP underground guerrilla network. Clergy of the Chung Hua Sheng Kung Hui took significant roles in developing a new, state-approved Chinese Christian organizational structure after 1958, focused on removing imperialist and non-Chinese influences in the church's governance and severing all connection with missions or Western denominations. From the training program connected with the underground guerrilla network, K. H. Ting (Ting Kuang-hsun) developed the leadership cadre of the future Three-Self Patriotic Movement, the legally accepted form taken by the church after Western religious organizations were banned by the Communist government.

In 1955, as all Americans and other Western missionaries and religious organizations withdrew from China, Ting was consecrated as the Anglican bishop of Chekiang. However, after 1958 he could no longer exercise any traditionally episcopal functions in the new state church that he helped organize, an attempt to demonstrate to the CCP that Christianity was fully Chinese and free of foreign influence. This new structure, the Three-Self Patriotic Movement, was intended to be self-propagating, self-governing, and self-sustaining, representing the same three-self vision of the Church Mission Society's Henry Venn from the mid-nineteenth century.

Unlike Venn's ideas, and very different from the American context, this church was fully entwined with government—not as a guiding conscience but as part of the political structure. In an ironic sense, with the creation of the Three-Self Patriotic Movement establishmentarianism had indeed achieved its goal of creating a fully national, enculturated church, but this national church, and Chinese Christians, would be cut off from ecumenical relationships with other churches. Though Ting himself had been deeply involved in the global ecumenical and missions movement, studying at Columbia University and Union Theological Seminary as well as holding positions with the World Christian Student Federation, he and Chinese Christians would withdraw from these relationships as a result of the Communist Party's policies. The "loss of China" proved to be a turning point in ecumenical circles for global ideas about mission and one of the main events connected to the development of anticolonial *missio dei* theology.

Internal Tensions: Missional Critiques and Divisions

Within Christendom itself, other seeds of challenge were growing: fundamentalism on the one side, and an increasingly sophisticated critique of missions on the other. *The Fundamentals*, a series of essays defending the literal inspired interpretation of scripture and traditional doctrines such as the virgin birth, was published in 1910, the same year as the Edinburgh Conference. Episcopalians were relatively untouched by the fundamentalist movement. Other than welcoming a famous Presbyterian scholar who had been on the losing side of a heresy trial, and putting one ordinand through a heresy trial for denying the virgin birth, Episcopalians generally went about Episcopalian business. The cleavages and tensions in the Episcopal Church, which centered heavily around liturgy, ethical living, and sacramental theology, were quite different from those in other American denominations. Internal controversies over ritualism in the late nineteenth century had been resolved with an ideal of "Anglican comprehensiveness," which should be open enough to include diversity in theology and practice, and the growing Broad Church movement particularly valued its openness to science and the newest scholarship from Europe, which included the historical criticism of scripture that was so jarring to many believers and clergy.

In all Protestant denominations, the fundamentalist/modernist divide deeply affected, and was affected by, theologies and practices of mission. The split in missions practice originated in the 1890s with rise of premillennialism, which became connected to fundamentalism as it developed in the early twentieth century. Premillennialists rejected the optimistic, "progressive" faith of postmillennialists, who believed that the millennium would arise from the work of human beings to create God's kingdom on earth prior to the second coming of Christ. Premillennialists put the highest premium on immediate and universal evangelism in order to prepare for the "soon-coming" of Christ. Originally, these premillennialists were still connected to official denominational missions such as the Episcopal Church, but increasingly began to fund their own "faith missions," which were not under any denominational supervision. Premillennialist excitement led to the organizing of the Student Christian Volunteer Movement, yet its two most prominent leaders, John Mott and Robert Speer, were also leaders in the ecumenical group in the twentieth century. The split originating in the late nineteenth century thus continued to slowly develop, still retaining connections between the evangelical/fundamentalist groups and the ecumenical/mainline groups, until a final split in the 1970s.[18]

For most of the nineteenth century, despite denominational tensions, the vast majority of missionaries of all Protestant churches shared an understanding of what it meant to be Christian, of how to use scripture, of Christian

finality and superiority to other religions. Partly as a result of growing scholarship in scripture and church history, partly as a result of shifts in scientific
understanding undermining a literal interpretation of biblical creation, and
partly due to the experiences of missionaries with people of other religions
and cultures, this shared consensus was beginning to fray by the late nineteenth and early twentieth century. The new fundamentalist movement was a
response to these changes.[19]

Fundamentalists emphasized an ideal of mission that was focused on conversion and church-planting, often funded as "faith missions" by individuals
who felt the call and raised money on their own without the support or oversight of any denomination. Modernists focused their missional activities
on ecumenicism, developing relationships in the mission field that would
support Christian converts without the baggage of home-grown denominational boundaries, and on education, medical missions, social services,
human rights advocacy, and interfaith dialogue and cooperation. Modernist
missions continued to be staffed with relatively highly trained and educated individuals, both clergy and laypeople, who were chosen after a formal
process of application and investigation into their character and skills and
were paid by their denominational supporters; fundamentalist missions
were staffed by whoever felt the call of the spirit and was able to raise funds to
get them there.

This did not mean that fundamentalist missions were less (or more) effective than modernist ones. Each group had quite a different sense of what
constituted effectiveness. Modernist missions started to resist the idea that
their effects could be measured by the number of converts. After all, if a
woman who had had no chance at an education received one, was that not
God's work? If people who suffered from parasites and disease received
modern Western medical treatment, wasn't that what Christian mission
was also about? If people who were abused and sold into slavery were freed
and another economic system developed to support them in living freely—
surely that was also God's mission in the world. And if people who had
been exploited and oppressed by another nation had the chance to develop
their own leaders and to govern their own communities, either as churches
or as nations, that surely was part of the Christian mission. Such ideas and
practices had existed since the early nineteenth century, embedded in the
"Christianize and civilize" model, but now, as the modernist movement
diverged from the fundamentalist movement, these practices were given a
stronger humanitarian basis, even sometimes conceptualized as removed

from explicit connection with conversion, a priority on their own aside from the need to spread the gospel and make converts.

Other unexpected tensions within the missionary endeavor itself were beginning to bear rich and paradoxical fruit. The reality that missionaries were often people living between two cultural worlds meant that they were neither fully accepted nor part of either their "home" or their "missionary" culture, and thus engaged in both idealizing and critiquing both cultures, trying to find a central ground of compassionate and consistent Christian principle from which to do so. This led to growing criticisms not only of individual and specific abuses of human rights and sovereignty implicit in the imperial project, but also of the imperial project overall. What right did any human being have to exert domination over another, through either politics or culture? By extension, was "Christian civilization" truly what people believed it was? Was it truly the social life, mores, and expectations of middle-class white Euro-American Christians? Or was it something more radical, diverse, and unexpected? Within this growing critique and uncertainty came a stronger and more principled antiracism as well as the seeds of respect and interaction with non-Christian faiths. What constituted the true mission of the church, the question of its complicated relationship with race and empire, and what a missionary needed to do in this context, no longer seemed so clear and simple as obeying the Great Commission or "evangelizing the world in this generation."

While missional modernists generally remained committed to the finality of Christianity (the idea that even if other religions "prepared" for true knowledge of God, Christian revelation fulfills all religious impulses and is final in its completeness), they encouraged openness to what was good in all religious practices and cultural traditions. Some among this group of missionaries, particularly those working in India and China, began to doubt some of the traditional arguments for Christian superiority, even if still holding to Christian finality. They argued that there was much to be learned from non-Christian religions and to advocate for relationships of mutual dialogue and respect rather than militant opposition to non-Christian traditions.[20] Ritual practices and language might well be "Christianized" when they served positive purposes in a local context, for instance; philosophies and religious attitudes could teach Euro-American Christians about genuine spirituality. Under the influence of these ideas, some scholars of Christian theology and history began to question a variety of long-accepted doctrines that seemed to have little support in science or scripture as critically studied.

Speaking from their liminal position between two cultural and religious worlds, missionaries were able to perceive, gradually, that the values of their home culture might not make sense to Christians in another. Such examples were rife throughout the missionary world, in every context, culture, and continent. In China, for instance, conflict over "ritualism" and the choice of Boone's son as the replacement Bishop of Shanghai erupted around practices at St. John's Shanghai in 1883. A series of editorials, articles, and letters in the *Southern Churchman* pointed at a growing sense of the need for "contextualization" in mission:

> Christians take the sects of Protestant Christianity to the heathen, and with them their way of looking at things; but it is not likely that our way is going to be their way. They will work out for themselves their own forms. We must remember that theology is only our way of looking at the Bible. Theology, therefore, is not inspired; the Bible is inspired, but not our way of looking at it. Each Christian nation has its own theology, and the Chinese will have their way, when once they begin to think for themselves and read the Bible with their own eyes. Our Western modes of thought are not going to be their methods; but both will be true.[21]

This early attempt to nuance the assimilationist expectations of mission became stronger and more explicit in the early twentieth century. Bishop Frank Mosher, essentially firing John Staunton from his civilizing project in Sagada, the Philippines, charged him with having imposed foreign rituals and ideas upon the local people, denying them an opportunity to truly develop a lived Christianity from their own living world.[22]

Missionaries also began to criticize the lack of true commitment to indigenization in the sense of raising up "native" leadership and leaving the church to them. Among Anglicans, an English priest named Roland Allen, who had served as a missionary in China, wrote a book in 1912 titled *Missionary Methods: St Paul's or Ours?* in which he inveighed against the dependencies and lack of local initiative and leadership created by the traditional missionary structure of funding and foreign authority. He advocated for a fully "native-led" church.[23] The first American Episcopalian bishop of the Missionary District of Hankow, China, in 1902 reminded his clergy in his first pastoral letter that their goal was to raise up Chinese leaders and to ensure that, should they leave on a moment's notice, the church would be able to sustain itself quite well without them. He even explicitly told them to give some thought and planning to how they would support them-selves and contribute to China when they were no longer needed as church workers—an implicit acknowledgment of the deep love and commitment that many missionaries developed for the places and people among whom they ministered, and, often, an unspoken reason that they were reluctant to give up their work to local converts.[24]

While Allen was not particularly sensitive to the idea that local cultures and religions might have something good to offer as well as the leadership qualities of the people, other early twentieth-century missionaries very much were. One of the most powerful critics of mission as often practiced—as well as a passionate advocate for mission as practiced and understood differently—was Daniel Fleming, a Presbyterian who taught at Union Theological Seminary. He had experienced a religious awakening, which he termed a "reincarnation," as a missionary to India. He had gone to teach math and science with no real religious commitment at all, and was con-verted to a deep desire to engage in mission as he understood it: as a response to God's love for all humanity, expressed in growing relationships and care for all, in practical service, and in demonstrating the changed life from love of Christ. When he was forced to remain in the United States for the health of his family, he became a professor of mission at Union Theological Seminary. Episcopalians did not attend Union at this time, but it is quite likely that Episcopalian clergy were also affected by the teachings of Fleming, which were shared in YMCAs and popular writings rather than academic theolog-ical treatises.[25]

In 1919, Fleming published a nine-week course of daily scripture medi-tation and commentary titled *Marks of a World Christian*. While the book could have been used by English speakers anywhere in the world (and was published by the YMCA International Press), Fleming clearly had white Americans in mind as the audience that needed to be awakened to a sense of missional urgency and care for other peoples and cultures. He emphasized that the "world Christian," who had realized God's intention that human beings increase and expand their relationships and practices of love throughout their lives, would soon realize that God was at work in all reli-gious systems, and that there was much to admire of good in other cultures and much to critique in that of American Christians.

Among other things, Fleming wanted to warn white Americans:

[A]s Anglo-Saxons, we are especially subject to this ethnocentric pride. Constitutionally we have a high sense of racial superiority, and nothing would surprise us more than to have God turn to another race and give leadership to it. Would not many an Anglo-Saxon today thrust Jesus out of his cities and try to cast him headlong to destruction, if he should suggest that white civilization had refused to hear him and had after nineteen hundred years manifested so little comprehension of his principles that it would be necessary to turn elsewhere for leadership? May God help us humbly to reflect and examine ourselves.[26]

This realization that racial superiority complexes were, in themselves, impediments to mission was common among missionaries and missionary thinkers in the early twentieth century. In 1924, for instance, global missionary executive and ecumenical leader Robert Speer wrote about "race," a concept which in that time included what today would be called "culture" among English speakers: "In moral qualities we [white people] exalt energy, promptitude, exactness, veracity, readiness for progress, and so forth. These are good qualities, but, in the first place, are we sure that we individually possess them in sufficient measure to be entitled to racial self-satisfaction; and, in the second place, how shall we weigh them against the qualities of patience, long-suffering, considerateness, contentment, which are possessed by other races in a measure beyond us? If we were to judge each race by its possession of the qualities exalted by Jesus, especially in the Beatitudes, which races would rank highest?"[27]

Fleming went further, however, in explicitly denying the missional practice and ideal of assimilationism. Instead, diversity was divine. God had created human beings to be different from one another, with different "nations" offering different gifts and beauties. Just as Christians were all part of the Body of Christ, and within the Body the eye could not deny the worth of the hand, so within the world no American Christian should deny the worth and beauty and uniqueness of Japanese, Chinese, African, South American, Indian, or any other culture. "A Christian world democracy," he wrote, "must welcome the most diversely gifted peoples and have the conviction that a use will be found for every taste and every instinct and aptitude that God has given them."[28]

Rethinking Missions: The Hocking Report

As modernists and fundamentalists began to decisively divide after the early twentieth century, Episcopalians were firmly in the liberal or modernist camp. While not many Episcopalians may have taken seminary courses from Daniel Fleming, the Episcopal Church was one of the denominational sponsors of the bombshell Hocking Report published in 1932, which espoused many of Fleming's views and took them even further.[29] William Ernest Hocking, a philosopher of religion at Harvard, wrote the first four chapters of the report himself. Hocking was very interested in mission and had attended the International Missionary Council meeting in Madras in 1928. Baptist John D. Rockefeller, the funder of the investigation, chose Hocking to chair the Commission. The project was intended, as an almost business-efficiency operation, to determine what was going on with missions as funding and interest was beginning to dry up. The Commission interpreted the "fact-finding" group report, which was based heavily on visits to missions in China. Hocking's description of what was wrong, and what could be right, in mission was not exactly what the denominational supporters were expecting.

As scholars have noted, much of Hocking's critique was well-grounded in earlier missionary criticisms of the enterprise and its practice, particularly work by Fleming and Allen. Fleming and Allen differed theologically on many things, but they agreed on the need to encourage local Christians to develop their own Christianity unhampered and uncontrolled by missionaries. Hocking argued for "mutual partnership" between faiths, missionaries as "co-workers" or "ambassadors" with others seeking religious unity and shared truth. Evangelism was reinterpreted as "seeking together" with an emphasis on life and service, avoiding preaching. Hocking's emphasis on the missionary as an ambassador also meant that the missionary should be an expert at addressing social and economic problems. This foreshadowed the shift at midcentury to a secular humanitarian view of mission, such as the Peace Corps, which sent individuals to serve without any explicit religious agenda, and the later economic development movement which emphasized the importance of secular expertise in order to serve the "developing" nations.[30]

Where Allen, Hocking, and Fleming, along with many missionaries, would have differed was in the debate over humanitarian and social improvement, particularly providing hospitals and education, as an aspect of Christian mission work. Fleming and Hocking, along with most "liberal," "modernist," or "mainline Protestant" denominations, supported these aspects of mission work, while fundamentalists and Allen denied them as not only unnecessary but actually harmful if offered to non-Christians. (One scholar notes that Allen's hatred of missionary educational endeavors was almost "patholog-ical" in nature; in his view, education should never be offered by missionary societies to non-Christians.)[31]

Aside from theological disputes—Fleming was inflexibly a "Christian finality" person, a theologian committed to the idea that Christianity was a fulfillment of the best of other religions, which was not specified in Hocking's work—Fleming would have disagreed with the idea that missionary work should be left to only a few expert ambassadors. In his vision of mission one of its purposes was to change the missionary him-self or herself, growing behind the "crust of habit" into a wider sense of love and respect for God's people. In a practical sense, this had been well demonstrated by missionaries striving against colonial abuses of other people, by critiquing their home cultures, and by aligning themselves with those among whom they ministered, with many examples over the entire nineteenth century, in every part of the world, and in every Protestant de-nomination. While the alignment was certainly not perfect—there was no shortage of racist, imperialist missionaries, and different contexts produced different responses—there was certainly a strong pattern of missional attitudes that demonstrated that the foreign missionary was someone of neither the home culture nor the missionary culture, bridging the two, able to appreciate and critique both, however imperfectly.[32]

The experience of long-term missionary work, Fleming argued, was trans-formational *for the missionary*, and this transformation was central to the mission of God among human beings. The development of this larger self engaged in love beyond narrow vision and self-interest is a lifelong human work with God. As Fleming put it in 1919:

> *We rejoice to think that infinite reaches are ahead of us; that God has set no limit to the development of this capacity of going out to larger and larger ranges of interests and of entering into wider and wider relations with human beings.* Part of the process of becoming perfect as he is perfect is to attain range of love as well as quality of love. If any man would save his life, that is, if any one is going to hold on to his small self and try to wall in what he is at any point in his development, then Christ says he will lose the only thing that can be called life. But if any man will lose his self—if any man for

Christ's sake will break through the crust that habit is ever forming around a given self, he will find a new, richer, larger self—he will save his *life*.[33]

Summary

These missional critiques were the first hints of a deep missional shift that would come to a more explicit focus in the 1950s. For most Episcopalians, they were distant and unheard debates, not affecting the internal establishmentarian sense of the church as the "national conscience," the church of the "noble" and admirable in society, nor affecting the importance of ensuring that immigrants, Black people, and Native Americans were fully assimilated to the cultural and religious standards of the church if they desired to become part of it. Already by the late 1920s interest in foreign missions was waning, following the spectacular debacle of Christendom that was World War I.

In the 1940s, as World War II consumed much of the globe, the nineteenth century's casual attitude toward imperial expansion would collapse, just as the missionary consensus of the nineteenth century had collapsed in the era leading up to the Hocking Report. In response, establishmentarian Episcopalians began, like other mainline Protestants, to move even further away from "foreign missions" per se. A minority of mission-minded Episcopalians were drawn toward engagement in radical challenges to injustice in society, and became more willing to criticize the shortcomings of the United States and U.S. Christianity as much as or more than other religions and other nations. These mission-minded Episcopalians were often clergy leaders, and a growing gap developed, again as in other denominations, between these clergy leaders and many members of Episcopalian congregations.

The Episcopal Church's white leaders began, with difficulty, to attend to the challenges of racism within church and society. However, Fleming's challenge to the assimilationist project of the church would remain, for decades, unheard.

11

Turning Inward

Introduction

In 1937, Brooklyn priest William Howard Melish reported on General Convention, the triannual governing meeting of the Episcopal Church, with delight. Melish described the previous convention in the midst of the Great Depression as characterized by despair and weariness, and this one as much more energized, exhibiting a church on the upswing. Oriented toward social justice in his local congregation and a strong supporter of missions, he described the *Drama of Missions* play that was performed regularly to get people excited about supporting missions again, the Connections with Labor meeting, and ten thousand people attending the worship service. There was also special fundraising for China in response to the Japanese invasion.[1]

Melish's cheerful reporting on General Convention was, of course, premature. China was entering one of the worst periods of its modern history, and soon Chinese Christians would be politically separated from global Christian relationships by the rise of Communism. Japan would similarly be devastated, and the Japanese in the United States would suffer political persecution and internment. American Christianity would be in some ways invigorated by World War II, but its interest in foreign missions would continue its downward swing afterward, with attention given instead to missional expansion in the new suburbs. And Melish himself, with his sympathy for labor and lack of appropriate suspicion of Socialism and Russians, would be driven from his congregation in the 1950s as a minor casualty of the Cold War.[2]

Spirit of Missions, the Episcopalian mission magazine, ceased publication in 1939, reflecting the post–Re-thinking Missions era in the turn away from "missions" and loss of interest in international Christianity. This turn isolated those who had been part of the missions community, some of whom returned to the United States to pursue their commitment to international social and racial justice and missional expansion within a domestic context.

Mission, Race, and Empire. Jennifer C. Snow, Oxford University Press. © Oxford University Press 2024.
DOI: 10.1093/oso/9780197598948.003.0012

Missions to non-Christians became more of a minority interest within the American Episcopal Church, and at times such missions were undertaken on an individual rather than a corporate level, returning to the early days of Episcopalian mission work prior to 1835, when individual interests led the way into various areas of mission activity. Social justice work as mission in the domestic context began to focus on racism as a social evil, as well as class differences and the eradication of poverty, but often this, like foreign mission work, was taken on by a few individuals rather than as a true corporate commitment. Meanwhile, the expansion of the church took place largely in the context of the growth of the suburbs after World War II. While the "homogenous unit principle"—the idea that "men [*sic*] like to become Christians without crossing racial, linguistic, or class barriers"—would not become prominent until after 1970, it was already the basis of missional expansion in the United States well beforehand.[3]

During this time, there was still significant interest in foreign missions among a small minority of Episcopalians and other mainline Protestants, but after World War II church expansion became largely a domestic issue. Mission itself, as discussed in the next chapter, began to be more thoughtfully considered: not only the expansion of church planting and conversion but also reconsidering the deep purpose and meaning of the church in the world in which it existed. Thus the suburban expansion could be critiqued in terms of missional purpose and missional expansion of church members. The failure of the Episcopal Church to protest the internment of Japanese Americans gave rise to an increased awareness of the relevance of racial justice to the church's mission, and the importance of increased legal challenge to racial injustice would then become a more salient aspect of the church's mission in the early integrationist and civil rights work in the 1940s and 1950s. At the same time, an increased internal identification of the church with white middle-class culture strengthened the project of integrative assimilationism, bringing difference into the room and making it disappear.

World War II and Japanese American Internment

World War II brought many of the European colonies in Africa and Asia into the global violence, in addition to places such as China that had not technically been "colonized" but were centers of mission work for many European and American church organizations. Major shifts in mission organization and practice followed. The Japanese nationalist government expelled American Episcopalian missionaries in 1940, and after the victory of the Communists over the Nationalists in China in 1949, all Western missionaries, seen as agents of Western imperialism, were required to leave. With the end of World War II came a rapid unraveling of the colonial political order, and the Wilsonian ideals of "self-determination" of peoples that had been lifted up in World War I now became enshrined in ideals of international political relationships via the United Nations. "Self-determination" seeped into missionary understandings as well, and in the case of the Episcopal Church, this was a good fit with Episcopalian establishmentarian ecclesiology.

But what about situations where there was no clear, homogeneous "people" to be "self-determined," as in the racially and culturally pluralist United States? The experience of Japanese internment during World War II demonstrates that this problem was not an easy one for the establishmentarian Episcopal Church to deal with. The church struggled to find a response beyond obedience to the social order and cultural assimilationism.

The Episcopal Church had sent missionaries to Japan soon after Commodore Matthew Perry forced Japan to open its ports to foreigners in 1853. Channing Moore Williams, who had been a missionary in China since 1856, entered Japan in 1859 and was made missionary bishop in 1866. In the early years, Japanese eagerly sought Western education, cultural styles, and science in the hope of recovering their national prestige and ability to stand as equals with the American and European powers. In 1891, Bishop William Hobart Hare of South Dakota visited and wrote a report emphasizing that the missionaries needed to retreat and give leadership fully to the Japanese, but the missionary leadership was reluctant to give full power over finances, which were largely from the Episcopal Church, to Japanese leaders. It was not until 1923 that Bishop Henry St. George Tucker resigned his bishopric, believing this step was necessary for the Japanese to lead, and Japanese bishops were elected. However, that fall a huge earthquake and fire destroyed most of Tokyo and Yokohama, requiring much American financial support for reconstruction. Even with the Japanese bishops now consecrated, therefore, the American bishop John McKim remained, "feverishly" managing the finances.[4]

Japanese emigration to the United States had flourished after the Chinese Exclusion Act and the American-enforced "opening" of Japan in the 1880s, and when Hawai'i was annexed to the United States in 1898, Japanese Hawai'ians also began emigrating to the mainland. Like Chinese immigrants, Japanese were subject to extreme hostility and violence from the white American community, expressed in unofficial ostracism and in legal strictures forbidding Japanese immigrants to own land or to become naturalized citizens. After 1907, Japanese immigration of males was forbidden by the "Gentleman's Agreement" negotiated by Theodore Roosevelt with the Japanese government, though for a while afterward "picture brides" were permitted to enter the United States. These men and women were able to found a thriving Japanese American community in the early twentieth-century United States, mostly on the West Coast.[5]

The shift in U.S. immigration law in the 1920s that blocked all immigration from Asia, strongly favoring northwest European immigration and minimizing that from southern and eastern Europe, created a far more racially and culturally homogeneous U.S. population than had been the case either prior to the 1920s or after 1965, when immigration law shifted again. Because of the clear demarcations around immigration dates, rights, and cultural assimilation, the Japanese American community had clear generational markers: the Issei (immigrant generation, who spoke Japanese and were not able to own land or become citizens); Nisei (children born in the United States, who were able to own land and were American citizens); and Kibei (American-born Japanese children sent back to Japan for education). Each generation's experience of World War II was different, and in each generation some were Episcopalians.[6] The Issei generation were often laborers, gardeners, and farmers, beginning small enterprises or carefully managed fruit farms, and were strongly committed to their children's "Americanization."

As Joanne Gillespie notes in her close study of Japanese Episcopalian internment, the congregation of St. Mary's in Los Angeles was at worship when news of Pearl Harbor was announced. The church had been founded in 1907 by Reverend John Yamazaki, in a semi-segregated area surrounded by anti-Japanese signs. In the 1940s the church was flourishing, with about a hundred families. The congregation had many community-building and "Americanization" programs for young people, including English lessons, Boy Scouts, and missional organizations for both men and women, similar to those in white Episcopalian congregations. Reverend Yamazaki, an Issei, preached entirely in Japanese, but his son, who also became an Episcopal priest and later became the rector of the congregation, preached in English, reflecting the generational differences as well as the Japanese American commitment to cultural and religious assimilation as their best option for survival and prosperity. Nonetheless, no amount of assimilation was enough for the white neighbors surrounding them, and the younger Yamazaki remembers his father in the 1930s predicting that eventually the whites would drive the Japanese out because they hated them so much. The Japanese Episcopalian community thus experienced the Japanese attack on the United States as both utterly incomprehensible and terrifying in its likely consequences for them.[7]

In February 1942, Executive Order 9066 required the removal of all people of Japanese descent from the West Coast. When the Japanese American community was forcibly removed from their homes and interned in camps, the Episcopal Church had nine specifically Japanese congregations, eight on the West Coast and one in Nebraska. The Episcopal Church at the national level responded to Japanese internment orders largely without comment, moving from quiet resignation to individual and denominational acts of charity for the internees, then aid in resettlement afterward. At each step, there were roads not taken. For instance, when preaching to the Japanese internees at their transitional housing location in Los Angeles, before they were shipped out of state, Bishop William Stevens offered "regretful" words to the community, but there was no official criticism from the church politically, or any official condemnation or protest against the policy. Bishop Simeon Arthur Huston of Olympia, Washington, tried to find land where the two local Japanese congregations could be evacuated and cultivate together (since most were farmers) or have them placed in the Spokane area in Civilian Conservation Corps camps, but both efforts failed. Reverend Daisuke Kitagawa, who experienced these events and would later work in the national church office, noted that church representatives regularly appeared before the Tolan Committee, the congressional committee investigating the danger of Japanese communities to the war effort, to testify that there was no need for evacuation, but beyond this the church was silent and did not take action. The church building became a storage depot for those few belongings the Japanese Americans did not sell before being detained in the camps. When evacuation became enforced rather than voluntary, "to the astonishment of diocesan convention, the congregation of St Peter's made certain it had paid its annual assessment before leaving Seattle."[8]

It appears that many white Episcopalian leaders were troubled but unable to ascertain how to respond. The presiding bishop decided to provide a bishop for this exiled community, one who had been a missionary in Japan for forty years before being forced to leave due to the war in 1941. Bishop Charles Reifsnider became the de facto "missionary bishop" for the Japanese community in exile, describing the internment camps as "our new mission field" in 1943. This "mission field" was supported by the bishops of the dioceses in which the internment camps were located, and served by interned Japanese American priests.[9]

The Japanese American Episcopalians themselves, with their strong strategic commitment to cultural assimilation and a high value for social order, generally tried to demonstrate their patriotism and obedience to American authority, but the experience was extraordinarily bitter and painful. The loss of dignity and the right to live in their own communities and homes, in addition to the physical and emotional stresses of being piled into camps without adequate privacy, heating, or medical care, was remembered by Japanese Episcopalians throughout their lives. Reverend John Misao Yamazaki Sr. was beaten by a gang within the camp in March 1943, part of a pattern of violence against older Japanese leaders seen as supportive of the American administration. Yamazaki wrote that there were "radical Buddhists" who were saying they supported Japan in the war and demanding that the United States repatriate them to Japan instead of keeping them in the camps. A portrait of Yamazaki done immediately after the beating shows him bloodied against the fence, with his own theological reflection in Japanese: "When I received the blow I felt as if my own child was hitting me, for they were my own kind. Each blow reminded me of God's will teaching me of my own lack of suffering." Yamazaki was very dejected and isolated by the experience of being rejected by his own people and the Americans for exactly what he had striven to do all his life: he was too assimilated for the younger Japanese Americans, not enough for the white Americans; his seniority and wisdom, as that of the entire Issei generation, were rejected by both parts of society. From a culture that had deeply valued the leadership of older generations, this was an additional blow that was hard to bear.[10]

Bishop Stevens of Los Angeles, who had been not been able to protest politically against the executive order, nonetheless did not stop at preaching.[11] Stevens's daughter later remembered him in an "incandescent rage" over the evacuation order, but he was powerless to do anything to stop it and thus fell back on the strategy of trying to defend the property of the internees. With the help of Bishop Reifsnider, he developed a plan to create a property trust to hold the real estate and other assets of the internees safely for them—an important strategy as often the internees would lose their homes and other real estate assets. Reifsnider also advocated that the Episcopalian internees from San Francisco and Los Angeles be sent to camps together, instead of splitting up the communities.

One side effect of the Episcopalian attempt to support and protect the Japanese internees was a growing ability to speak about race and racism explicitly in terms of national policy and law. At the diocesan convention of 1942, Suffragan Bishop Robert Gooden of Los Angeles specifically called out the issue of "racial differences" as the reason for which the Japanese were singled out for this treatment and asserted that it was unchristian and unacceptable. Bishop Stevens cited racism as the cause of the relocation of the Japanese to "concentration camps"—a term not commonly used to describe the internment camps at that time, here used in an official publication of the Episcopal Church. Stevens also connected the exile of the Japanese to anti-Black racism, and condemned both.[12]

The annual report of the DFMS on "domestic mission" and the Japanese in 1945 saluted Japanese Americans for their Christian witness to other Japanese (not to all Christians) and for their helpful obedience to the U.S. government in wartime. Could they now be integrated into the white community as true Christian siblings? The author was uncertain as to whether this would actually occur and predicted that instead many Japanese would simply "be lost" to the church. At this time, the Episcopalian missionary strategy shifted to supporting the resettlement of the Japanese away from the West Coast as minorities in white communities. As the internees were relocated to unfamiliar cities in the Midwest, far from their original homes, Bishop Reifsnider was concerned that "too many" were concentrating in certain locations and wondered whether there should be mission funding for new Japanese congregations, or whether they should be forced to integrate into white congregations. The decision was for integration.

By 1945 Reifsnider envisioned a process by which a small group of Japanese, not too large to alarm the white community but large enough to provide internal support to the members of the group, would join white congregations. He envisioned this as "group integration" and was determined to avoid creating segregated Japanese churches despite the difficulties, which he foresaw, in integrating churches on a multiracial basis. These difficulties were not only about blatant racial prejudice but also about more subtle "unfriendliness" and cultural difference, whose language would be used, the race and culture of the clergy leader, and more.[13]

Despite good intentions not to replicate racial segregation in the church, this decision put the burden of change on the Japanese to continue to accommodate and assimilate, linguistically and culturally, to the Anglo-majority church. The Japanese now began to understand themselves as a "racial minority" like Black Americans in white America, and in some cases to question the anti-Black racism within Japanese communities as well. Some of the Japanese congregations that were rebuilt on the West Coast after World War II became multiracial in a way that was very different from majority-white churches. St. Mary's in Los Angeles, for instance, removed "Japanese" from the name of the church upon their return from the camps, to emphasize that now, with the shift from Issei leadership to Nisei, the congregation was English-speaking. The congregation became, unusually for an Episcopal church, an interracial one by late twentieth-century sociological standards, with 20% non-Japanese members, including in 1958 Filipino, Korean, Chinese, and white and Black Americans.[14] However, the question of race and cultural difference in the Episcopal Church was still largely answered by assimilative integration, and in the church at large this assimilationism was becoming even more narrowly focused in terms of race and class.

White Suburban Expansion

The postwar era was a time of significant suburban expansion for the Episcopal Church and other mainline Protestant denominations; the GIs returning from the war and starting their families looked to the stability and identity of a Protestant religious life. However, this expansion was demographically extremely specific. Looking inward, white American churches of the Protestant mainline become associated with middle-class culture and values in the growth of the suburbs, unable to deal with economic, social, or racial difference. The significant congruence between white middle-class identity and Protestant church membership led to a demographic expansion of the white middle class. The hidden cost was that all other paths to expanding the church's identity and membership were cut off. "Conversion" became a very specific type of assimilation, and "Christianize and civilize" took on a possibly more narrow identity than ever before in terms of congregational life, even as the global ecumenical theology of mission and church expanded and shifted toward increased commitment to anticolonial action.

These new congregations were often larger than the older ones, purpose-built to reflect the growing liturgical shift toward weekly Eucharist. For the

first time in Episcopalian history there were enough ordained clergy to provide a priest to each congregation, thus paving the way to a future centrality
of weekly Eucharist as an Episcopalian norm. These new congregations were
centered around supporting the life of the family in community according
to white middle-class expectations, with expansive Sunday schools, music
programs, and more; they became communal centers for the new suburban life.

In 1961, Episcopalian priest and social scientist Gibson Winter
published an analysis and critique of this new mode of suburban church
life. Winter argued that the result of this race and class stratification of the
churches—which included all white Protestant mainline churches, not just
Episcopalians—was twofold: an abandonment of the people and missional
responsibility in the central city, and a narrowing brittleness and shallow-
ness of the church's mission in the suburbs. Winter noted that Protestant
denominations saw the suburbs as "high growth potential—and they don't
mean potential for prayer." They were filled with affluent people who found
mainline Protestantism culturally attractive and had the space and energy to
build churches.[15]

Aside from the abandonment of the city, which, bereft of its wealthiest and
most politically connected citizens, was left to solve its problems on its own
without any involvement from the church, the actual life of the churches in
the suburbs was necessarily—and in Winter's view, tragically—spiritually
shallow. Despite their natural desire for comfort and safety, even the
suburbanites were looking for some deeper meaning and spiritual growth
from their church commitments, but there was not much to offer in the "organization church," which was focused only on its own survival. The minister in this church, too, in Winter's view, was in a rather pathetic situation.
Perhaps from personal experience, he wrote,

> The Protestant minister easily becomes the number-one victim of middle-
> class conformity. He feels his exclusion from the producing world and mis-
> sionary task principally as an enslavement to suburban children and the
> hypochondria which now characterizes the middle classes. He becomes
> a supplement to the didie [diaper] service. His scholarship, preaching,
> teaching, and even devotion are soon drained off into the great blob of
> middle-class culture, a culture which subordinates the depth and meaning
> of religious life to the middle-class preoccupation with children.[16]

These new suburban parishes were created by white flight from the inner cities, usually away from increasing racial diversity. Because the suburbs were insulated by distance from the more diverse and interdependent city centers, and because they were settled essentially all at once by people who chose their housing development in accordance with their social and economic status, often restricted to white people due to racial housing covenants, the suburban churches were from the outset extraordinarily homogeneous in every way. The congregation became an island of safety and stability in a changing world, a guarantee of membership in a social class, and a provider of supports to live the life they desired in terms of activity, meaning, child rearing, and social relationships. This stability and comfort was deeply important to the suburban parishioners. The congregation therefore could not manage disruption by those of different races or classes, or deal with social conflict, or take an activist role in metropolitan issues.[17]

As suburban areas grew, Protestant white denominations placed their energy there and abandoned the city. The remaining urban churches either depended on devoted commuters from the suburbs or closed. There were many other churches in the cities, but they were not mainline Protestant, and these remaining city churches, which often were Black churches or "sectarian" white fundamentalist churches, tended to be too small and have too few resources to really respond to the city's needs.

Aside from Winter's disdain for the rather crucial human task of continuing the generations, his missional critique centered upon this cultural and racial homogeneity, not upon the suburbs themselves, as a source of evil. There was every natural and unintended reason why, in this new situation of a communally insulated community in a pluralistic and tense world, a congregation would become homogeneous without even noticing it, and simply require assimilation to its norms or ostracize those who didn't match the standard. However, for reasons both practical and theological, this wedding of the church to the white middle class would ultimately be deadly. The total estrangement between white and Black Protestants, which had been increased to a great degree by the new suburban church dynamic, meant that even if denominational leaders encouraged racial integration, and even if they attempted it, the congregations would be completely unable to manage it. The suburban white Protestant congregations were too structured by and dependent upon homogeneity to welcome those who did not match their race and culture and class expectations. The suburban spirituality painted by Winter is thus the exact opposite of the missional commitment to expansive and boundary-crossing love that Daniel Fleming had described in 1919 as a "mark of a world Christian."[18]

The threat of a demographic and theological narrowing of the church was not reflected in the church's own sense of success. The Episcopal Church, and all mainline Protestant churches, exploded in numbers and financial support in this era. Church leaders could be forgiven, surely, if they thought that the path of least resistance—that of following the white middle class to the suburbs—was missionally appropriate. For many suburban churches with beautiful new church facilities, Sunday schools bursting, able to hire multiple staff and welcome full congregations each week, the 1950's seemed the best of times (and would be remembered as such for generations to come). Yet Winter argued that in fact the Protestant denominations had not really expanded at all; it was just that the white middle class had expanded with the postwar economic prosperity and the social supports offered particularly to white veterans. Protestant white mainline churches had largely shed their rural membership (which, in the case of the Episcopal Church, at least, had never been a strong point) and abandoned lower-class white Protestants who remained in the cities, thus focusing on the expanding white middle class at an ultimate cost in missional purpose and flexibility in the future. While the numbers of attendees, communicants, and churches made it appear that the denominations had gained in strength, truthfully they had only remained static in proportion to the population, gaining numbers through class expansion to make up for other losses. "The picture of a religious revival, however real it may be, should not obscure this factual picture of the development of the major denominations: they have been running full speed in order to stay in the same place; they have built and planned and schemed in order to remain at dead center."[19]

Even before the period of the postwar suburban expansion, this dynamic had been growing among the mainline and ecumenical Protestant denominations from 1910 through 1930: the lower-class and rural whites, as well as nonwhite Protestants, were gradually jettisoned for a narrowing of identity with the educated, white-collar, business-oriented class. Probably not coincidentally, this was also the era of growing professionalization and centralization, the idolization of business efficiency, among all white American Protestant denominations, and certainly as noted in most Episcopalian histories. In this period the Episcopal Church developed its National Council (Executive Council), an elected and then a full-time presiding bishop, increasingly efficient and centralized fundraising capacity, and greater bureaucracy for program management.[20] At all levels, the church was settling into a cultural norm and expectation for what "church" required and was unwittingly becoming less and less able to provide for or imagine other ways of being church in different contexts or among different people.

Aside from whether Winter's sociological analysis and statistics were accurate, like that of Muhlenberg in the 1850s, his very trenchant argument demonstrates a deep missional concern for a growing narrowness in the church's identity and mission, a move from inclusiveness—which Winter notes as a mark of the true church and its mission from the very beginning in the Acts of the Apostles—to exclusiveness, even if not consciously chosen; to a church that is for "people like us," a church which, because of the communal insulation of the suburb, never even has to realize that the church is so structured. In critiquing the suburban church, Winter echoes Fleming on the missional centrality of interdependence and inclusiveness from the early twentieth century:

> The real difficulty with denominational Protestantism is its arrested development as a form of the Church. . . . This [communal insulation] is pathology, because true identity cannot be achieved through insulation against others upon whom we are dependent. . . . [A] White man cannot discover his true identity in the United States if he insulates himself against contact with Negroes, for his own being is inseparable from theirs; personal identity emerges in dialogue with those to whom our lives are bound by common humanity and interdependence. *The churches can only embody or mediate a true identity to their members when the fellowship of members represents the interdependence of human life. Inclusiveness is intrinsic and not accidental to the nature of the church.*[21]

Instead of the freedom of the gospel, Winter argues, suburban congregations modeled the "iron law of conformity," excluded those who were different, and abandoned those who were less economically fortunate.

There was, in fact, a certain kind of religious revival going on in the suburbs, but it did not challenge the dominance of the white middle and upper classes in Episcopal congregations, nor the economic and racial stratification of society. An evangelical conversion while working for the YMCA in China—experienced through a one-on-one life-changing conversation—led Reverend Samuel Shoemaker to develop an evangelical ministry meaningful to the educated, affluent white Episcopalians he served as well as, ultimately,

to millions of people identifying as alcoholics worldwide. Shoemaker was religiously active in his youth, president of the Missionary Society in boarding
school, and met global ecumenical mission leaders John Mott and Robert
Speer at missionary conferences in 1911 and 1912. He initially went to serve
in British Army camp YMCAs during World War I, but feeling that there
was little actual ministry there, he then served in Beijing from 1917 to 1919,
where the Philadelphian Society of Princeton, his alma mater, ran a settlement house. Frustrated that he was unable to reach the Chinese students with
a religious message, Shoemaker met privately with Lutheran pastor and re-
vivalist Frank Buchman, who suggested that the problem was in himself and
that he needed to have time for introspection about his own spiritual life and
sinfulness. In Shoemaker's own memory, at least, this not only produced a
conversion experience for him, with a dedication to God's work, but the very
next day he had a successful religious conversation with a Chinese student,
his first "convert." This convinced him that personal, one-on-one evangelism
was crucial in spreading the gospel, and that this evangelism was based in
sharing honestly one's own spiritual life and experience.[22]

Shoemaker's first parish ministry coincided with the Great Depression,
and he felt that the solution to the appalling spiritual and physical needs of
the world was personal conversion. Only this would give the energy and motivation to live charitably and lovingly to help others. At no point in his life
did he espouse any sort of critique of the economic system; poverty was to
be fixed by personal conversion of the poor (to work harder) and personal
conversion of the rich (to share their wealth). He focused his parish ministry
around personal "interviews," sometimes three or four a day, lasting half an
hour to several hours, in helping individuals develop their sense of relationship to the divine toward a "decision" moment. His method, he observed,
was in "good taste" and adapted to the expectations of the educated, cultured,
upper- and upper-middle-class people of his congregation. It reassured them
that "vital Christianity" was not vulgar and crude and uneducated, like that
of the fundamentalists and evangelists caricatured in the journalism covering the Scopes Trial in 1925.[23]

In addition to the personal interview, Shoemaker used the "cell group"
method of developing spiritual life and commitment. His mentor Buchman
led the Oxford Group, a spiritual movement (later a nonreligious anti-
Communist movement that Buchman renamed "Moral Re-Armament")
which used "group guidance," essentially confessing sins to a small group.[24]
The dependence upon small accountability and confession groups was

similar to early Methodism; it was also similar to other revival methods that were spreading internationally at this time through networks of missionaries and students, for instance the Balokole/East African Revival practice of confessing sins publicly.

Working with "Bill W," or William Wilson, the co-founder of Alcoholics Anonymous, Shoemaker used Buchman's techniques to help develop the methods and "steps" of AA. The first AA meeting was an Oxford Group meeting at Calvary Church, which for a period of time was a base both for Wilson and Buchman with Shoemaker's support. While Shoemaker broke from Buchman permanently in 1941, and for a while was estranged from Wilson, after a time apart Shoemaker again became a supporter of AA in the 1950s, this time with admiration for its group democracy and shared unity in effort to help one another. The church, he argued, could learn from AA: its demands were "tougher, closer, more highly structured and demanding" than the church's way of being.[25] Wilson credited Shoemaker as the original source of the "twelve steps," and Shoemaker himself in a later speech instead credited Wilson, but it appears that at the very least both of them contributed to the twelve-step movement's structure and success. The movement itself was evangelical in form, involving shared testimony, personal accountability, witnessing and teaching through sponsorship, and a "conversion experience."

Occasional Radicals: Urban Ministry

While the suburban churches were growing, as Winter chronicled, inner-city churches were shrinking. This was a new situation for the Episcopal Church, which had historically been strongest in urban areas. But this new urbanization was different. The people living in the cities were now largely African American or immigrant, neither of which were groups that the Episcopal Church had historically been very successful in "reaching" and including in the church. Winter's study reflected upon why the churches were shrinking even in cities that were growing; he found that the class, linguistic, and cultural differences between the white Protestant mainline and the new immigrants were too great to be overcome, while the African Americans in the cities often were very highly churched already. In short, the Episcopal Church was not able to give what was needed: a commitment to the city's life and challenges rather than a commitment to worship in the inherited style, with those who historically had preferred it, continuing the Episcopalian attitude and practices critiqued by Muhlenberg a century before.

In response to this unease about the missional limitations of suburban expansion, some white Episcopalian clergy were drawn to the urban setting as a central locus of mission. Born to wealth, signed up for St. Paul's boarding school the day after he was born, with a summer house in the Adirondacks and winter vacations in a Florida mansion, Paul Moore was one such white Episcopalian. After graduating from Yale, Moore joined the Marines to fight in World War II and was wounded in the Pacific. When he returned, he decided to become a priest, having always felt a call to celebrate Eucharist; his spiritual piety centered around the liturgy, the sacraments, and their connection to justice in the world. Attending General Seminary, he found himself drawn to the ideals of urban ministry among the poor, like the Anglo-Catholics and Social Gospel workers of the late nineteenth century, and he, his fellow seminarian Bob Pegram, and his instructor C. Kilmer Myers developed a plan to ask several bishops to essentially give them a parish to revive in a "blighted" urban area. Most bishops turned them down, but the Bishop of Newark offered them Grace Van Vorst in Jersey City. After Moore was ordained a deacon in 1947, the three of them, along with Moore's wife and children, went there to live in an "open rectory," a space where they shared a common table and opened their home to the community, to try to make their ideals a reality.

Based on Moore's description of the area in his autobiography, Grace Van Vorst fit into Winter's schema perfectly: its white congregation of middle- and upper-class members had mostly fled to the suburbs, while the lower-class whites, Blacks, and immigrants remained. Writing years later, Moore remembered that when they arrived at the lychgate they saw a sign carved *Enter His Gates With Thanksgiving,* beneath which was a closed wrought-iron gate locked with a large KEEP OUT sign, a symbol of exactly what they hoped to change in the church by their work. Their intention was to minister to the community, physically and spiritually, but also to demonstrate to the church that parishes should not be closed when "Episcopalians" moved away. The church should remain in the community and become a church for those people who were not yet Episcopalian.[26]

Moore, Pegram, and Myers (in addition to Moore's children and his wife, Jenny, who was the provider of hospitality for the entire mission in the "open rectory"), moved immediately to build relationships with children in the area, and from there to relationships with their parents. Despite Winter's distaste for childcare as an important aspect of missional outreach, it was clear that even in "radical" urban missions the missionary families, like missionary wives worldwide, would provide much of the mission's creative ability to relate to local communities. Moore's memoirs indicate that their work was successful, moving from a few families to include over five hundred, with large-scale summer programs for children, projects with youth gangs, political activism and community organizing on neighborhood issues from police brutality to playground renewal and integrating housing, and of course regular eucharistic worship. Inspired as well by the liturgical renewal movement which would eventually result in a new Book of Common Prayer in 1979, the urban missionaries practiced innovations such as turning the altar so that the priest faced the people.[27]

The movement toward a "presence" among the people that included both children and family support and active political organizing and protests was new for the white Episcopal Church. While the "institutional church" as practiced by Muhlenberg and by the later nineteenth-century Anglo-Catholics and Social Gospelers had included clinics, education, and support for the poor, and in fact this had been common among foreign missions worldwide, the addition of political activism and civil disobedience moved the white Episcopal Church, very slowly, closer to the missional practice of the Black Episcopal Church. Black Episcopalian congregations, ranging from St. Thomas to the post–Civil War southern congregations, had always included all of these holistic supports for the community and had always engaged in and supported political activism and civil disobedience, from Absalom Jones's petition of 1797 through the mid-nineteenth-century work of the underground railroad and protests against the Fugitive Slave Act, and the early twentieth-century insistence on the rights of the people to political and educational opportunities and the right to shared and self-governance within the church's structure itself. In a foreshadowing of Moore's story of the Grace Van Vorst lychgate, James Solomon Russell, one of the first southern Black priests after Emancipation and a lifelong educator, had written, "Social service and community work are integral parts of the Church's Mission. . . . I have so often said that our churches should be the centers of community influence. Their doors should be open weekdays as buildings. . . . [I]f necessary, we should place a sign on the door bidding 'Welcome All' to the stranger within our gates, and then we should meet him and greet him with the hand of fellowship."[28] Ironically, however, the "new" urban ministry exemplified by Moore and his comrades was seen as an enormous and radical accomplishment.

Of the three founding clergy at Grace Van Vorst, Moore and Myers became bishops, and Moore became one of the best-known Episcopalians of the twentieth century. Yet the Black church leaders who had been doing this work for generations were, comparatively, ignored and unsupported.

Occasional Radicals: Racial Justice

The rise and dominance of scientific racism—teaching that races were immutable, separate, endowed with different and unequal abilities, that cultural habits were biologically inherited, and that races were in bitter, life-or-death Darwinian competition with one another—came to a crashing halt, at least temporarily, after the Second World War. It was clear that scientific racism underlay the eugenic atrocities of the Nazis; clearly scientific racism was "pseudo-science" as well as morally repugnant. Without the underpinnings of socially acceptable scientific racism, and with increasing demands for their rights as citizens and human beings from people of color in the United States, racial issues began to be far more prominent and connected to issues of morality and justice even in the eyes of white Americans. Moore, for example, was shocked in 1951 to be a near-witness to the public murder of three Black men in Florida by the local sheriff. It opened his eyes to a reality with which Black Episcopalians such as Thurgood Marshall, who had brought Moore there as a strategic white supporter, were quite familiar.[29]

Civil rights and race began to percolate as issues in white Episcopalian contexts during the 1940s. General Convention passed its first resolution on racial inclusion in 1943, establishing an "executive secretary for Negro work" in the national office and committing the church to "break through the encirclement of racial segregation in all matters which pertain to her program" (carefully avoiding breaking the encirclement of segregation in nonchurch issues). This deliberate effort to avoid the political sphere could not last, but within the church "program," the church closed the segregated divinity school in Virginia in 1949, and in 1952, responding to a crisis at the School of Theology at the University of the South (Sewanee), General Convention condemned any seminary that remained segregated. In 1955, General Convention was moved to Hawai'i to avoid holding a segregated meeting in Texas.[30]

Black Episcopalians, of course, were doing more than trying to desegregate the church. In the early 1940s Pauli Murray, a Black Episcopalian lawyer who would later become the first African American female priest, participated in antisegregation protests in Washington, D.C., and was arrested for breaking segregation laws in Richmond, Virginia. Like Alexander Crummell, Murray faced discrimination head-on and challenged it without cease throughout her life. She published *States' Laws on Race and Color*, an exhaustive compilation and analysis of all state-level legal strictures relating to race, urging that the NAACP shift its legal strategy from claiming that particular segregated facilities were not living up to the standard of "equal" to directly challenge the constitutionality of the "separate but equal" standard itself. Thurgood Marshall, also an active Episcopalian, called Murray's work the "bible of the civil rights movement."[31]

Women's Rights and Gay and Lesbian Rights

The post–World War II era also saw the beginnings of the gay rights or ho-mophile movement in the United States, further discussed in Chapter 14. The upheavals of the war, bringing young and single individuals together in urban contexts and offering to women the possibility of financial self-support in factories or even in the military, led to the development of gay and lesbian subcultures and relationships. As the mainline Protestant churches considered their missional outreach to urbanites, providing a safe and welcoming place for these people, and for their pastoral and spiritual care, became a particularly fraught issue discussed both in American and English church contexts. Certainly Episcopalians were among these gay communities, though almost always "closeted" (hidden) in church contexts. Those who knew them and provided pastoral care for them often began with a sense that homosexuality, if not sinful, was at least "sick," and thus best served by a therapeutic model. But some began to question what exactly was "sick" about the relationships they observed. Were the relationships them-selves wrong, or were these people suffering from the oppression and stigma of the world they inhabited—much of which came from Christian theology and institutions?

Among returned missionary activists, even those who were women or in-volved in same-sex relationships, there was far more energy for antiracism and anti-imperial work than for feminist or gay rights activism.[32] But the in-volvement of women in the church was also steadily increasing in the postwar years. In the U.S. context, women were first permitted to serve on vestries, and then to be delegates to General Convention. The first woman priest in the Anglican Communion was Florence Li Tim-Oi, ordained in Hong Kong in 1944. Her ordination by English Bishop Ronald Hall, to provide sacramental services during the war emergency, was challenged by other bishops in the Anglican Communion. In order to end the conflict Li agreed not to act as a priest. It was not until much later, as an immigrant to Canada, that she was able to once again engage in priestly ministry. The debate over Li's priesthood foreshadowed the debates about women in sacramental leadership that would become central in the United States in the late 1960s, and foreshadowed as well that these conflicts would be resolved not according to the needs of a local culture or context but the ability of globally distant leaders to accept it.

Summary

In the postwar years, the white Episcopal Church lurched towards a conformity with white middle-class values that built unconsciously upon establishmentarian mission and "proper" behavior. Confronted with the blatant reality of racism in the case of Japanese internment, the white church as an institution was largely helpless to respond, flailing for an appropriate theology and method of resistance which did not come to hand. Perhaps the experience of helplessness began to undermine, for some white Episcopalians, the trust in establishmentarianism which assumed that the rule of law was always just and to be obeyed. And for Black Episcopalians, inheriting a long tradition of political activism as well as the sense of the church as an inherently political and justice-oriented institution, this new awareness among white leaders may have helped in building some new, fragile relationships with white allies in the urban ministry work that would become stronger and more robust in the Civil Rights Era.

This gradual shift toward justice and activism in the white church's life was seen as central to mission in terms of celebration and energy and foreshadowed a shift in global Christian theology, ecclesiology, and missional thinking.

The actual missional practice and the bulk of resources of the white church, however, were more focused on church-planting, congregational leadership, Christian education, and liturgical renewal, as the church experienced an exhilarating period of growth within the United States. The best

Christian response to racism, as the white church saw it, was assimilative integration: people of other races should join the white communities and act according to the expectations of the dominant group.

The 1950s were a high point of Episcopal Church expansion in the United States. It was a short, fast flight with a hard landing. Just as the rise in parishes seemed to have a lot to do with demographics and cultural trends, not the church per se, so the post-1960s decline also had roots in these sources rather than any specific missional choices of the church itself. The church neither planned its blessing nor caused its own decline. The one very important exception to this was the largely unplanned and uncelebrated wedding of the suburban church to the white middle class. It set the church on a course difficult to correct. When that demographic no longer expanded, it became very difficult to change the cultural norms and expectations of cultural assimilation to white middle-class norms that the church now enshrined at every level.

The Episcopal Church in the United States thus struggled fiercely after the 1950s to expand missionally among people of color and the "new immigration" of the post-1965 era. The challenges of racism, and its missional response of working for justice, was often seen as something that existed *outside* of the church rather than something which had now become intimately and unconsciously intertwined with its congregational and organizational life.

12

Missio Dei

By the mid-1950s, following the Hocking Report of the 1930s and the dev-
astation of World War II, the Episcopal Church in the United States had
moved toward a sense of mission that diminished the uncomfortable activities around "foreign missions" in favor of what were once called "domestic
missions," meaning either suburban expansion or expansion within established dioceses rather than beyond the existing geographic or demographic
boundaries of the church. The remaining missionary districts within the continental United States were mostly among Native Americans or in the rural
West, where the church struggled desperately to provide religious services to
scattered homesteads and small towns separated by vast distances. Overseas,
in the missionary districts and missionary dioceses that were still part of
the Episcopal Church, including Liberia, Haiti, Puerto Rico, the Dominican
Republic, the Virgin Islands, Cuba, Mexico, the Panama Canal Zone, Alaska
and Hawaii (which did not receive statehood until 1959), Taiwan (the Chung
Hua Sheng Kung Hui, the United Anglican Church of China, which had
been officially driven from mainland China by the Communists), and the
Philippines, missionaries continued to be sent, including missionary bishops
elected by the House of Bishops rather than local Christians. The first "native" missionary bishops in some areas, such as Haiti and El Salvador, were
still decades away, as missionary bishops continued to be chosen from among
white American clergy rather than local clergy.[1]

On the global stage, shifts in missional theology and practice following World War II were ever more profound and challenging. These
shifts involved leadership within the Episcopal Church and the Anglican
Communion and were reflected in the Episcopalian responses to the specifically American cultural and social context of the civil rights movement as
well as the status of women and, by the 1970s, gay and lesbian people. Within
the United States, the demographically supported Episcopalian expansion
into the white suburbs was held in tension with a growing connection of

Mission, Race, and Empire. Jennifer C. Snow, Oxford University Press. © Oxford University Press 2024.
DOI: 10.1093/oso/9780197598948.003.0013

"mission" to social justice and humanitarian activity, particularly in terms of racism. Establishmentarianism took a new turn in the sense that the church, as the "conscience of the nation," was playing this new socially and politically active role as moral critic of the racial status quo, however awkwardly and uncomfortably.

It is important to note that in this context of global missiology and world Christian relationships, the terms "evangelical" and "ecumenical" have a very specific meaning. "Evangelicals" in this context are those churches, often nondenominational, that are not part of the World Council of Churches and have a missional orientation toward church-planting and conversion, often from a fundamentalist or charismatic background. "Ecumenicals" are those Protestant denominations which are part of the World Council of Churches, who may share a *missio dei* mission orientation. The terminology can be confusing because there are evangelical and charismatic individuals and movements among the ecumenical churches, and the term "evangelical" in particular has a long and complex history. But in this specific historical analysis, "evangelical" and "ecumenical" are shorthand terms used to trace the growing distinction between these two streams of modern missional thinking.

In this chapter, I trace the global developments first, followed by the American connections and contexts. The mid-1950s to late 1960s were a crucial turning point in world Christian missional theology and practice. By the end of this period, the Episcopal Church had become self-consciously part of a global ecumenical movement as well as a global Anglican Communion, and its leadership had taken steps toward trying to implement a radical and revolutionary version of the new *missio dei* theology of mission, not yet realizing that this new missional theology required greater depth of commitment and understanding within the church itself.

Global Contexts: The Rise of *Missio Dei* Theology

Edinburgh 1910 had not ended with the conference. Continuation Committees were set up to develop further relationships between the denominations, with an ultimate goal of church unity. In the 1920s, Episcopalian bishop Charles Brent was instrumental in organizing the continuation of global conferences regarding life and work (i.e., Christian practice, teaching, and humanitarian service) and faith and order (issues of doctrine and polity that currently separated the denominations). In addition, an umbrella organization for mission organizations was created, the International Missionary Council (IMC). The IMC was a "council of councils," including national councils of churches within many of the colonized and developing nations of the Global South, mission organizations and practitioners, and eclectic organizations such as Bible societies and student movement groups. With the IMC the Protestant world began to develop a theory and practice of ecumenical mission at almost exactly the same time that the missional world was splitting internally over the rise of fundamentalism and the ongoing internal critiques of mission.

The IMC included both traditional mainline Protestant groups and newer evangelical and charismatic bodies in addition to representatives from the "younger churches." It was thus more ecumenically comprehensive than the incipient World Council of Churches (known as the "WCC under development" until it was fully organized after World War II), which focused on institutional denominational leadership in an effort to bring denominations back into unity, and was initially strongly concerned with European church issues rather than global ones, considering the "younger churches" subsidiary to their European "sending churches."

Bishop Lesslie Newbigin, a British missionary to India, had helped to shepherd the development of the ecumenical union Church of South India, combining Anglican, Congregationalist, Methodist, Presbyterian, and others into one united church in 1947. To Newbigin's frustration, the Anglican Communion would not recognize the Church of South India as Anglican due to the opposition of Anglo-Catholics at Lambeth, who insisted on reordination for all the union ministers. Newbigin felt that the needs and priorities of the younger churches were being ignored by the historic denominations; they wanted only to preserve their own institutional priorities rather than permit themselves to be challenged and changed by Christians in other parts of the world. Partly for this reason, and partly because of his conviction that mission and church should not be separated, when he became the second president of the IMC in 1959 he advocated a radical solution: merging the IMC with the WCC, removing the distinction between the world mission and denominations.[2]

This project of integration was internally controversial for the IMC. While theologically everyone could agree that the churches should take responsibility for mission, in actual practice voluntary organizations seemed more effective: missionary work was done by those who were passionate about it, supported by a minority of churchgoers.[3] Bringing missionary work into the long list of things that denominations were concerned with risked making missionary work a very low financial and practical priority. While no one pointed to the Episcopal Church during this debate, they certainly could have—the integration of church and mission in the Domestic and Foreign Mission Society had led to a century of competing financial priorities and institutional needs. Limited resources within a denomination would naturally be used for the needs and sustenance of existing churches and institutions, not the creation or sustenance of new ones. Evangelicals in the IMC also were already beginning to suspect that the WCC was made up largely of Protestants who had embraced modernist theology and the theological critique of missions, and thus would not prioritize the work of conversion-oriented evangelization and church-planting, instead placing energy in humanitarian work, service, and ecumenical relationships.

When the final vote for integration was taken at the IMC meeting in New Delhi in 1961, all concerned recognized the tension between IMC and WCC goals. Anti-Western and antimissionary feelings from the younger churches were prominent in the discussion, and it was also clear that "the evangelicals" were uninterested in any kind of affiliation or sharing of mission responsibilities with "the ecumenicals," and would prefer instead to pursue mission on their own. According to reports at the time, only about 40% of North American Protestant missionaries in the field were associated with the IMC or WCC churches, and thus already a wide swath of Christian missionaries had no connection with the global ecumenical movement at all.[4]

After New Delhi 1961, when the IMC became the Commission on World Mission and Evangelism of the WCC, many evangelicals simply left and refused to take part in the WCC. This suspicion of the WCC became an important identity marker of evangelical denominations, churches, and leaders from this point forward. Evangelicals began to develop their own international organizations, though they were far more likely to simply work in an individualistic and noncoordinated manner than the historic denominations which were now officially part of the "ecumenical" missional stream. Later reflections on global Christian controversies pointed to the lack of relationships with ecumenical organizations, where churches and leaders were faced with different understandings of Christian polity, doctrine, and practice on a regular basis, as connected to deepening and polarizing divisions between evangelical and ecumenical Christians in their attitudes toward church identity and mission.[5]

Evangelical predictions proved correct: from the beginning, the WCC had very little interest in missions as traditionally conceived. Even when engaging in study of missions, as the IMC had done, the WCC did it differently, drawing on scholarly or academic expertise rather than missionaries in the field who had depended upon relationships and experience to know the reality of the Christian life in the younger churches.[6]

Missionary theology in the ecumenical stream continued to develop after the early twentieth-century critiques of Daniel Fleming and the Hocking Report, demonstrated in the meetings of the IMC between 1910 and 1961. These meetings gradually included a higher proportion of representatives from the younger churches, with Tambaram 1938 for the first time having a majority of its delegates coming from the Global South. The first post–World War II IMC conference, Whitby 1947, was marked by great optimism despite the carnage of the war. For the most part, the churches had not been divided against each other on any theological basis, while the younger churches had perforce been deprived of missionaries yet had thrived during their crisis.

Only three years later, at Willingen 1952, the entire attitude of the IMC had changed, particularly for Europeans and Americans. China had been "lost" to the Communists and all mission forces expelled, and as some IMC participants saw it, Chinese Christians had clearly been happy to see them go. The meeting was an "orgy of self-criticism," as the missionaries tried to understand where they had gone wrong and foresaw accurately a new world in which the age of colonialism would come to an end. What was mission *for* now? What was it going to do in the world, and why and how would it be done at all?[7]

From Willingen 1952 came the beginnings of a new theology and practice of mission, building upon the critiques of Hocking and Fleming, the experience of missionaries, the growing attention to local context, and an acknowledgment that the imbrication of mission with empire and colonialism had led to a situation where mission itself was discredited, a dangerous or harmful orientation and practice. The task of Christians in the world must be related to the rise of postcolonial nations in Africa and Asia, along with revolutions for human rights, self-determination, and dignity. This new ideal, identified in post-Willingen reports as *missio dei*, argued that God's primary arena of activity was not the church but the world.

These ideas became more radically challenging to the church as institution. Johannes Christiaan Hoekendijk, a mission theologian who had been born and raised in Indonesia in a third-generation missionary family, argued instead that there was no good thing inherent in a mission becoming a "church." Instead, mission should always be active, happening, central to the people of God who were aware of the world around them and its needs. Putting energy into the maintenance of institutional structures was a betrayal of the gospel. Mission occurs between the world and the kingdom of God; the church is thus an unsettled and shifting activity of mission, not a settled thing in any given context.[8]

The original *missio dei* terminology as used to describe the Willingen Statement held together three different views. Hoekendijk's understanding of mission as God's activity beyond the church in society was one of them. Another came from the German delegation, which was largely Barthian and located mission in the prophetic role of the church, which is active only in the unique revelation of Christ. The third was the North American delegation, which had an activist, Social Gospel orientation that fit well, though was not identical with, Hoekendijk's views, and which looked for God's activity in social and revolutionary movements. Thus two of the three delegations at Willingen described God's activity in the world as the nature of mission, rather than the church as central to that mission, or mission having anything essential to do with the church's institutional maintenance. The "messianic event" in the theology underlying these statements was one of revolution and liberation. It was this understanding of *missio dei* as both a revolutionary commitment to transformation of the world and a decentering of the church in mission that became prominent in the 1960s.[9]

This new missionary orientation in the global ecumenical setting certainly fulfilled all evangelical expectations of a withdrawal from traditional missionary work.[10] Rather than evangelism as conversion, missionary work was now seen as coming alongside the revolutionary and transformative movements in the world of social relationships, where the activity of God's spirit toward the establishment of the Kingdom of Heaven was at work in the world. Resources of the churches should be used to support these revolutionary movements and to provide humanitarian support for those who were suffering due to injustice and inequality. God's desire for all human beings to live in peace, prosperity, and dignity was the mission—sometimes called the mission of reconciliation or shalom—and all church resources should be used to support this mission in the world.[11]

The 1960s saw the most radical flowering of the implications of *missio dei* as combined with the new idea of "the church for the world" and a decentering of the church in the process of missional work. At Uppsala 1968, the WCC adopted a radical vision of mission which ran the risk of leaving no meaningful relationship at all between "church" and "mission," again led by Hoekendijk's views, which envisioned a church of flexible structures and contingent actions, responding to God's mission as the need arose. The traditional structures of the church and individual congregations became hindrances to this revolutionary work; instead the church should be an undefined, flexible, small group of people ready to attend to whatever needs they saw in the world as a result of God's activity in it. The *missio dei* orientation was exciting to younger Christians in particular. At Uppsala, the traditional representatives of mission and church were constantly interrupted by the student representatives. Only Hoekendijk's radically anti-institutional version of *missio dei* received a hearing among the young protesters who had come to Uppsala with plans for demonstrations, sit-ins, critical communications, and creative disruptions in an effort to see the church become radically active in the world. Whereas the *missio dei* could be interpreted as still having a place for the church, in the most radical 1960s version of a "church for the world," the primary missional activity was between God and world, and God's work was being done whether the church did anything at all.[12]

While Hoekendijk's theological version of a revolutionary, secularized mission of God in the world may not be well thought of by modern theologians and historians of mission—various scholars have argued that it leads to "absurdity" and is too deeply ecclesioclastic, too antichurch, too prosecular, to be tenable—nonetheless its general outline was and continues to be immensely influential. Versions of his anti-institutionalist, eschatologically and spiritually longing vision of the mission of the church in the world were shared by many Americans and Europeans in the 1960s, particularly young people. In his position as a professor of missions first at Utrecht and then at Union Seminary, Hoekendijk was able to share his views with students preparing for ministry both in Europe and the United States, expanding and normalizing this ideal among the ecumenical stream.[13]

Anglican Communion: Mutual Responsibility and Interdependence

As *missio dei* theology was still being developed in the WCC in the 1960s, within the Anglican Communion efforts were also being made to develop a new model of mission in the postcolonial era. Bishop Stephen Bayne of Olympia, Washington, an American and the first Anglican executive officer in the service of the Anglican Communion, traveled over 150,000 miles per year in visiting Anglicans throughout the world and developing his global consciousness of mission thereby. His writings in the early 1960s clearly demonstrate a *missio dei* orientation, consistently arguing against the idea that mission is about church extension or getting new people in the "club." In his view the traditional age of foreign missionaries was closing, and he adopted the "church-centric" view of mission advocated by the younger churches, that they themselves would be responsible for mission in their local contexts, only helped by and not directed by the older churches. Consistently as well, he reminded his readers and listeners that the mission did not belong to the church but to God, that mission was revolutionary, and that God was already present everywhere, even foreshadowing the "Church for Others" ideal. He wrote in 1961, "It would be better if church buildings were magically built for one generation alone, so that every generation had to face its own vocation."[14] Bayne added, in typical *missio dei* language:

> The mission is God's, not ours. He is the One who is at work out there. We go out to meet Him. We go out to encounter our blessed Lord. . . . Underneath all of the conditions of it and the hopes of it, underneath all the wisdom that you or I could bring to it, is the great simple truth that all this is His and not ours, that the mission is His because the world is His, the people are His, and the love is His. . . . And to us, less than the least of all saints, is this grace given that we are privileged to go where He is and for a minute to stand by His side.[15]

Bayne's passion for bringing this theology and a new commitment to mission in new ways was central to a major Anglican Congress organized in Toronto in 1963, which developed a statement titled *Mutual Responsibility and Interdependence* (MRI; most likely written by Bayne himself after consultation with others). The vision of mission in MRI begins with a "partnership" model, which at first replicates the practices of north-south transfers of resources but attempts to put the power of "asking" in the hands of those who are "receiving" rather than being a fully one-sided missional activity. Gradually, this would develop into greater appreciation for relationships over the long term, ideally each partner both giving and receiving.

As with *missio dei* orientations, the MRI ideals also had unintended consequences when taken in tandem with the anxiety about postcolonialism and the history of imperialism consequent upon it. Missionaries in the field shrank in number and were often development experts or else ordained people with specific sacramental roles in a community that lacked clergy. Fleming's early twentieth-century ideal of the Christian transformed by mission was limited to a very few individuals, including Bayne himself, who had the opportunity to develop relationships with Christians and non-Christians beyond their own local context, and even fewer of those individuals had a path or platform back into the "home church" where they would be able to share their transformational experience and affect local ideas about people of other cultures and religions. Whereas previously women had been very active in mission work, with fewer missionaries being sent and an emphasis on secular expertise or clergy status, there was no longer a clear path for women's involvement in mission work, as they still could not be ordained.[16]

The issues of financial resources and inequality were central in the problem that MRI was attempting to address. In the nineteenth-century *Spirit of Missions* periodical, money and personnel issues were front and center, and these resources were uncontroversially dedicated to the traditional church-centered mission: building and staffing churches, paying missionary bishops and clergy, and also building and staffing hospitals and schools in mission areas. With the development of the MRI and the *missio dei* orientation, decentering the church as an institution from mission, the immediate response was that significant resources should now go into supporting revolutionary transformation of societies and that a commitment to justice required that the transfer of resources from wealthy churches to impoverished ones be undertaken upon request—any request. As noted in the initial responses to the 1963 MRI document, this risked reinscribing inequalities of resources: the wealthy give to the poor, either as organizations or in interchurch development aid, in a way which remains paternalistic and encourages dependency. One helpful critic of the MRI as it was being understood and used globally in the 1960s Anglican Communion, Douglas Webster of the Church Mission Society, warned that equating the building of relationships with giving money would have dangerous consequences.[17]

The early missional critiques of Fleming had focused on the need for the missionary to be transformed through relationships, not the giving of money; Roland Allen had warned more explicitly that money would lead to both dependence and paternalistic control. Bayne similarly emphasized, consistently, the need for people to go and develop relationships, the requirement of better communication and better knowledge of one another, that money was not the central issue and that it was dangerous to focus on it. Indeed, in the postcolonial era, it was simply impossible and wrong to imagine that the church could still do mission by giving large sums of money to build institutions. Nonetheless, giving money was what many Episcopalians imagined mission was now, most easily, about.[18]

The Episcopal Church and Civil Rights: The General Convention Special Program

As Bayne was organizing the Anglican Congress in 1963 and promulgating the new MRI ideals, C. Kilmer Myers wrote, "There are many ways of not rocking the boat and no doubt Anglicanism has discovered them all. Among us Episcopalians not rocking the boat is called 'muddling through.'"[19] Myers was one of the urban mission pioneers, along with Paul Moore, and like Moore he would later become a bishop. His insight here, early in his career, poking at and challenging the Episcopal Church to become more involved and more meaningfully with the riskiness of mission, reflected the *missio dei* shift that would very soon become central in the church's life through engagement with the civil rights movement. This new approach deeply rocked the boat of Episcopalianism. During this era, the idea that God's redemptive mission in the world was connected to transformational and even revolutionary movements, which the church's mission was to seek out and support, took new shape in the General Convention Special Program (GCSP): a radical effort to give resources of the Episcopal Church directly to those most active in the struggle for justice, particularly Black-led empowerment and political action organizations.

Integration and racial justice had begun within the Episcopal Church in the early twentieth century, as some southern dioceses began to allow Black clergy to attend diocesan conventions. (The Diocese of Virginia reintegrated its diocesan convention in the 1930s.) Issues of racial justice and activism became more noticeable after the Second World War, and in the 1950s Episcopalians integrated two seminaries, Virginia Theological School and Sewanee. While the Bishop of Alabama was among those who wrote to Martin Luther King Jr. in a Birmingham jail, requesting that he stop his program of civil disobedience and obey the law, the Episcopal Church leadership had already, by 1963, come to the point of supporting King's demands for political access and civil rights for African Americans. The Episcopal Society for Racial and Cultural Unity, an organization of laypeople and clergy in the church, supported integration and civil rights by sending groups of clergy and students to take part in Freedom Rides in the South (often over the objections of southern diocesan bishops). Seminarian Jonathan Myrick Daniels was killed while trying to protect an African American woman from a white gunman. Many white laypeople, seminarians, and clergy were involved in this work, feeling deeply that it was part of the mission of all Christians. But many others either opposed it actively, unhappy that the church was taking "political" stances, or were quietly uncomfortable with this use of the church's resources.[20]

The church's involvement in civil rights, for those who were part of the *missio dei* theological stream, was so right and necessary and obvious that it went without question, and the need for a revolutionary commitment to social transformation was clearly part of the church's central mission. The church's validity would stand or fall on this commitment. Black Episcopalian Pauli Murray, for instance, had been involved in fighting against racism and sexism her entire life by the time that she was invited as a consultant on eliminating white racism to the WCC decennial conference in Uppsala in 1968. Initially reluctant to attend—she had become very weary of the racism and sexism of the Episcopal Church—she found that it was "one of those peak experiences seldom duplicated during a lifetime": "Uppsala fired me with a renewed determination to return to the United States and proclaim through my own life and work the universal sisterhood and brotherhood I experienced during those eighteen days, however transitory and incomplete that expression of solidarity may have been. . . . In fact, and perhaps paradoxically, Uppsala furnished both the inspired moments and the frustrating impediments that strengthened my resolve to remove all barriers to my full exercise of the Christian ministry of reconciliation."[21]

In 1967, Presiding Bishop John Hines, inspired by a visit to Bedford Stuyvesant with an Episcopalian African American layman, Leon Modeste, as his guide, proposed the GCSP. He envisioned it as a way in which the church could fulfill its mission of working for reconciliation and coming alongside God's revolutionary work in the world. Bayne, who was at that time on the staff of church headquarters, supported Hines's goal, and General Convention also agreed, setting a $3 million budget (out of a total denominational budget of $12 million) for this program, which would give grants, with no strings attached, to organizations supporting economic development and racial justice, led by minority groups themselves, with Modeste as the administrator of the grant fund. Modeste recruited staff and began grantmaking frequently to minority-led groups which were not church affiliated, some of which had reputations for recommending violent means of social change. Grants were sometimes made over the objections of bishops in whose dioceses the grants were given, and rarely supported the work of Black Episcopalians, who had a long history of struggling for justice and caring for their communities within the Episcopal Church.[22]

The controversy over the GCSP, from 1967 to 1974, was debilitating for the church as a whole, and for the church leaders of the time, both Black and white. Aside from the discomfort of many ordinary white Episcopalians with getting involved in controversial politics of race and class, at least some of the damaging aspects of the program, from the point of view of those closely involved, derived from the lack of a strong theological understanding of why it was being done, and how to do it with theological and missional integrity. The 1960s version of *missio dei*, de-emphasizing the role of the church in God's mission and without a strong basis for theological understanding shared among the clergy and laity, lent itself easily to a sense that the church's mission lay in monetary support for revolutionary political and economic goals. Divergent and unclear understandings of the church's mission meant that what some saw as a missional response of the church to God's work in the world, for others was a source of confusion, bitterness, and reproach.

Bayne wrote in 1967 that the civil rights movement was just the beginning. The church must respond to the poverty and inhumane conditions of many people, many but not all Black, in the cities of the North as well as the segregated and oppressed Black people of the South.[23] He was supportive of the GCSP and particularly understood the need for the grants to be without "strings," which he knew well from his experience as the global Anglican mission officer led too easily to paternalistic control. The entire structure of the church's staff had to shift in order to accommodate this new program. Bayne interpreted all this through his lens of *missio dei* and the MRI: the church was being restructured because of the need to respond to crisis in a flexible way, even though there would be other parts of the church's programs that would suffer as a result of this new orientation.[24]

As Bayne and Webster would have predicted, giving money without a relationship and without creating a shared missional basis between giver and receiver, as well as a shared missional understanding within the church, led directly to intense controversy, tensions among leaders, and a sense of being disrespected and ignored on every side of the issue. Sioux Episcopalian Vine Deloria Jr., at that time on the national church staff, recalled seeing things that were "not flattering" during the civil rights movement and protests: church diplomats trying to show themselves as socially activist, or paternalistically speaking "for" people of color, or telling Indian people what hymns they should sing to reflect the new turn of mission theology. "[These images] vividly chronicle an institution making up for lost time through the expenditure of vast sums of money and much personal energy and concern," he wrote.[25] However, without clear values or goals, these "uncontrolled emotions" meant that there were no guidelines in place, "and in this confusion The Episcopal Church authorized a major program with substantial financial commitment."[26]

Within the Episcopal Church itself, partly due to the ways in which the GCSP was staffed and structured to emphasize the mission of God as happening in revolution outside of the church, the witness and leadership of African American Episcopalians, lay and clergy, sometimes went unrecognized or was even treated with contempt by white leaders and liberals. Tollie Caution, the senior Black clergy leader of the church, was told to resign from the national church staff by the presiding bishop, as he was not considered radical enough. In 1969, the General Convention decided to give a grant of $200,000 to a nonchurch Black economic empowerment organization, yet no grants were given to the Black clergy and congregations who had been doing work in their communities since the American Revolution. One priest stood up in General Convention and protested, "I'm sick . . . I'm sick of you; you don't trust me, you don't trust Black priests."[27]

As he visited with those who were working on the GCSP as well as dioceses and bishops, Bayne realized that much of the division and controversy over the GCSP, both in its implementation and in its reception by the church, was because the missional theological shift toward *missio dei* arising from missional reflection in the modern era had not been adequately developed. Neither white supporters, who simply rubber-stamped anything that appeared to respond to social revolutionary transformation, nor white opponents, who argued that the church must stay out of politics, had properly understood the missional commitment that should be shared by all

Christians. For Bayne, it was only this missional shift that made perfect sense of the goals of the GCSP and would have provided a basis upon which to improve it: "The trouble with us is that we have failed to present the theological setting and foundation for the decisions we have made. The General Convention Special Program is a case in point. Whatever social or political justification this might have is really irrelevant; the Church has only one obedience which is to mission; and it was in the profound surge of obedience at Seattle that this program was undertaken. If it has lost that theological setting, the Church is lost; and we shall have nothing left to us but misunderstanding and suspicion and lack of confidence."[28] Bayne described the GCSP, both positively and negatively, in terms of its embodiment of the church's missional responsibilities. He saw the church's movement toward social justice as being the right one, but often done for "wrong or inadequate" reasons, particularly that it envisioned a false dichotomy between individual discipleship and social justice work.[29]

Like Bayne, Deloria argued in 1969, in private to the presiding bishop, that the church had no theology that would permit it to respond adequately to the crisis of racism in society and was just blindly reacting. Liberal white supporters of GCSP thought they were doing the right thing in demonstrating total commitment to this cause of justice, but this response was artificial and did not connect deeply with the true problem, with the people attempting to address it, or with the theological understanding of the church's role and mission. And like Deloria, Bayne continued to be troubled by the unmet need for theological reflection and understanding of mission as things became more and more tense. He proposed a theological process to "come to grips with our history theologically, and find the new and deeper level of obedience to mission which we lack. . . . [U]ntil systematic dialogue can be sustained so that the Church can find the degree of unity in mission and service we don't have and desperately need, we are simply not being true to our nature as His Body."[30] Bayne's proposals for creating a theological process of reflection were rejected; he was very worried by this, noting that tensions and divisions were constantly increasing because of the lack of shared theological conversation, insights, and sense of obedience to mission. In late 1969 he resigned from the Executive Council in frustration, just as did Deloria.[31]

In 1973 General Convention voted to discontinue the GCSP. Presiding Bishop Hines resigned in 1974, before his term was complete, and was succeeded by John Allin, a southern bishop who had something of a reputation as an obstacle to national church interventions around civil rights, but who was certainly seen as "safe" for those who had been uncomfortable with the direction the church had gone under Bishop Hines.[32] Allin would oversee the two major shifts within the church itself discussed in the next chapter, which also embodied the ideals and practices of *missio dei*, and which were similarly controversial.

The experience of the GCSP led to the church's turning inward, away from radical social change per se and toward internal, churchly justice issues, such as the ordination of women and the inclusion of gay and lesbian people within the church. The controversy also influenced the development of Latinx ministries, as documented by Carla Roland Guzman. Under Allin's leadership, and shying away from political intervention or controversial politics, the new Latinx ministry programs focused on more specifically ecclesiastical issues such as translating the Book of Common Prayer.[33] The lesson learned by most white Episcopalians was not that there was an intense need in the church for deeper theological engagement or relationship building among groups, or that there was not yet a shared sense of mission among all Episcopalians after the dramatic developments of the first half of the twentieth century, or that there was a deep history of race and empire waiting to be grasped and wrestled with together, but that it was better to not get involved in controversial political issues because people would be very upset, and that these people would then withhold their resources from the church.

This was certainly not all that could have been learned. Ten years after his resignation from the Council, Deloria reflected on the GCSP experience: "We badly need a consistent and comprehensive theology which relates human experiences of divinity in an intelligent context and speaks to the human conditions that the secularization of the old Christian worldview has created. We must understand our separate historical journeys and come to see ourselves as planetary peoples with responsibilities extending to all parts and beings of the universe. . . . If we can learn these lessons, GCSP will have been one of the most valuable experiences in the historical life of the church."[34] And Tollie Caution, the senior Black clergyman of the church, wrote after his dismissal from the national office, "But we are not discouraged. If there is any sense of failure, let it be among those whose racism is stronger than their commitment to the Gospel. Our witness for these 200 years has been steadfast, courageous and faithful. We will not become the evil that we deplore. We are responsible for what is *now*, and what *shall be*. Many chains are still to be broken; many shackles still to be unfastened."[35]

Summary

There is a clear parallel between the global Christian ecumenical transformation at the 1968 WCC Uppsala conference, attended by Pauli Murray and upended by student activism demanding change, and the 1969 Special Convention in the Episcopal Church, where radical racial justice activists took the floor and demanded that the church be not only responsive to but fully involved in and shaped by the needs of the world. The civil rights controversy also hinted at the first examples of resistance to change at the national church level expressed through the deliberate withholding of resources, keeping the diocesan contribution back from the national church budget, and at a congregational level, refusing to pay the diocesan assessment. Resistance to change for the first time also used the "dioceses' rights" argument that the national church cannot overrule a bishop's authority within their diocese.

The long-term consequences of the 1950s suburban captivity and assimilationist model meant there was a reluctance to become involved in controversial political issues rather than focusing on the "spiritual" life of a congregation. This is what most Episcopalians thought the church was for, and it had been a very successful model up to the mid-1960s in terms of church expansion among the white middle-class demographic. As the church began to lose members, this was blamed on the church's missional controversies and difficult politics, although in fact it was based largely in demographic shifts that had been predicted by Gibson Winter in 1961 and in the cultural shift toward noninstitutional structures for social engagement.[36]

The developing activism of clergy also produced an antagonist to the "people in the pew," as well as challenges to the traditional authority of diocesan bishops. Clergy could become "marching ministers" in a place distant from their home church without receiving permission from local bishops, indeed seeing their flouting of local diocesan authority as part of their commitment to risk-taking change in the service of God's mission. At the same time, this ability of clergy to mobilize nationally in support of distant issues was very important in transforming the church's sense of mission. In some cases, local laypeople who were devoted members of local congregations took great risks in trying to challenge the communities in which they lived. This demonstrates that even in the "suburban captivity," Christian formation was still deeply meaningful for many individuals and provided them with resources to challenge the status quo.[37]

The tendency to lionize white participation in the civil rights movement over the long work of Black clergy leaders in caring for their communities in the face of racism led to some of the misunderstandings and tensions in the later 1960s: a remaining paternalism even among white radicals. Repeatedly, white and Black activists sponsored by the Episcopal Society for Cultural and Racial Unity were not able to get local Black communities to come on board with their activities—not because they weren't working against racism but because their own interests and leaders hadn't been consulted, nor was their local reality understood.[38]

The goal of integration was radical in the 1950s, but when it was achieved technically in the Civil Rights Act, it was clear that communities of color were still not "equal," not able to be full participants in the social and economic world of the United States. This was the reality which Black leaders had been pointing to: that there was still a need after "integration" to hold a space in the church for Black leadership and Black communities as such. Ideologically this was not only about Black power but about the complicated relationship between equality and equity, integration and assimilation, which is still being worked out today. This issue had arisen in global Christian circles quite early on. In the postcolonial era, it became even more relevant. Racial and cultural diversity, perhaps even religious diversity, was gradually being seen as a positive good in the world; how could it be preserved without segregation and antagonism? How could diverse communities be autonomous and also in Christian relationship?

The divisions between evangelicals and ecumenicals also deepened and hardened in this era. A second WCC meeting, titled "Salvation Today," in Bangkok 1973, was considered by many evangelicals to be the nail in the coffin of ecumenical and evangelical relationships. Beginning in 1974, evangelicals began to hold their own international conferences, known as the Lausanne Movement. Evangelical mission work remained focused on conversion and church-planting, sending out long-term missionaries and focusing on the "unreached peoples." In the Anglican Communion itself, evangelical and ecumenical leaders began to go their own ways and develop different networks, with Stephen Bayne exemplifying the ecumenical missional understanding, and John Stott, English evangelical priest and active networking theologian, representing the evangelical. Stott was one of the main organizers of the 1974 Lausanne Conference, and his networks would later be central in the global controversy over sexuality.[39]

Moving forward from the postcolonial shift toward *missio dei,* the Episcopal Church came down firmly in the "ecumenical" camp in the continuously deepening twentieth-century cleavage between what had once been the "modernists" and "fundamentalists" and was now, in the global era, described as "ecumenical" and "evangelical." With other denominations that were part of the ecumenical group—generally the historic Protestant denominations that were members of the WCC—the Episcopal Church continued to give relatively less attention and resources to church-planting and conversion in the traditional sense, and more to social justice, humanitarian activism, and ecumenical relationships. Within the denomination, the shift to *missio dei* theology attended to practices of injustice within the church itself, seeing them as intrinsically connected to injustices out there in the world. As the liturgical renewal movement further developed a new version of the Prayer Book, movements within the church for justice and inclusion for those previously excluded from church membership and church leadership continued to gather steam, including for the ordination of women and the welcoming of openly gay and lesbian people to the church's communal and sacramental life. Deepening divisions within the church and in the global Anglican Communion between traditional missional understandings and the *missio dei* orientation had already led to some small schisms in the Episcopal Church, and this strategy of deliberate deepening of boundary markers based on competing missional visions would continue.

The rise of *missio dei* theology among ecumenical Protestants, despite evangelical critiques, did not reflect a simple "knuckling under" to modern culture; rather it was a long and serious engagement with mission work among the historic Protestant denominations. This reflection included a deep reckoning with injustice, exploitation, racism, and imperial power, as well as the reality, experienced by all missionaries, that non-Christian religions and cultures and people had much of good in them that needed to be acknowledged and honored in the development of genuine Christian commitment and communities. Theology and practice had thus changed for very good reasons, building on centuries of missional trial and error, decades of theological reflection, and wrestling with the failures of Christendom in the crises of two world wars. The experience of missional relationships changed the missionaries, who then imperceptibly changed the churches. Missionaries themselves were converted to a new way of thinking and being. The critique of traditional missions that lay beneath the *missio dei* shift was, in the end, one which could not be avoided forever.

13

The Church for Others

Introduction

In the 1970s, the Episcopal Church went through two major internal shifts: the production and revision of a new Book of Common Prayer, the document that delineates the practice of shared worship and a central identity focus of the life of the church, and the ordination of women, thus inviting a group of previously canonically excluded church members into the carefully bounded and disciplined world of church leadership. Scholarship on both the 1979 Book of Common Prayer and the debates and controversies over ordaining women in the denomination is well established. In this chapter, I argue that these two shifts, which fed into growing schism and controversy within the denomination and later within the global Anglican Communion, were both connected to the midcentury theological shift to *missio dei* described in the previous chapter.

At this time, the relationship of the Episcopal Church to the global Anglican Communion was not front and center in Episcopalian consciousness. Growing postcolonial awareness and the shift away from traditional foreign mission that had been building since the 1920s meant that, even though the Anglican Communion office was strongly connected to individual Episcopalian bishops, these important changes in the 1970s and 1980s appeared on the surface to be unrelated to international developments, and to even be a retreat from the radical commitment of the 1960s and the risky, messy experiment of the General Convention Special Program (GCSP).

In fact, however, the changes of the previous decades in missional life were now consolidated into a new guiding identity, worship practice, and rhetoric, cementing these shifts as the norm of the church's life for future Episcopalians. The liturgical renewal movement that led to the eventual creation of the 1979 Book of Common Prayer was intertwined with the shifts to the strengthened, family-oriented, and white-dominated suburban parishes of the 1950s, and the inclusion of social justice in the new baptismal covenant

Mission, Race, and Empire. Jennifer C. Snow, Oxford University Press. © Oxford University Press 2024.
DOI: 10.1093/oso/9780197598948.003.0014

of 1979 drew from the experiences of the 1960s with the civil rights movement and the ideals of radical urban ministry. The specific events that led
to the ordination of women were theologically shaped and interpreted by
supporters as a commitment to God's work as transformation, challenge, and
prophecy against the powers of social oppression: the ecumenical *missio dei*
understanding of the purpose and meaning of the church.

Thus, these seemingly unrelated changes internal to a single denomination were fruits of the global ecumenical Christian development that moved
mission and church identity from conversion and church-planting toward
justice and transformation in human relationships, envisioned as God's mission to the world. In turn, these internal denominational shifts would later
feed into controversy at the level of global Christianity as they strengthened
missio dei commitments within Episcopalian life and led to a more intentionally focused religious project that prioritized inclusion, justice, and challenge to inherited religious and social structures as missional practice. Those
individuals, congregations, and, at the global level, autonomous Anglican
churches that did not participate in the *missio dei* shift in the same way found
this new understanding of church and mission inexplicable and dangerous.
The lack of shared understanding of missional purpose, as Stephen Bayne
and Vine Deloria Jr. had warned, led to schisms that were at first small but
became potentially devastating to the Anglican Communion.

Liturgical Renewal, Mission, and the Baptismal Covenant

As one scholar notes, the liturgical renewal movement was "nothing less than
a paradigm shift from church as coterminous with society to church as set
apart from society in a post-Christian, pluralistic culture."[1] It was in its nature
a missional endeavor, adapting to a changed context as well as to a changed
understanding of what the mission of the church truly was. The Episcopal
Church's liturgical practice was bounded and set by the Book of Common
Prayer, and at various points in the church's history, the Prayer Book had
required revision to respond to a new missional context. In 1789, for instance, the first American Book of Common Prayer removed the prayers for
the monarch and balanced the high church demands of Samuel Seabury by
adding the Scottish eucharistic rite to the more low church orientation of the
originally proposed Prayer Book of 1785. Muhlenberg and others suggested
revisions in the mid-nineteenth century in order to make the Book more

accessible to those who were not already Episcopalian, and eventually the Book was revised slightly in 1892 and again in 1928. In all three revisions, however, despite more extensive suggestions from missionally oriented leaders, in the end the changes made were relatively slight, essentially tinkering around the edges with the 1662 Prayer Book inherited from the Church of England, which was used in most global Anglican churches. In essence, the 1892 and 1928 revisions caught up to previously existing changes in practice.[2] The Prayer Book revision that would issue in the final 1979 Book of Common Prayer was far different, encapsulating both a new liturgical understanding from scholarship and the shift into a *missio dei* missional theology.

Many denominations took part in deep and thoughtful revisions of worship practice in the twentieth century. The liturgical renewal movement bore its most obvious fruit in the Roman Catholic Church in Vatican II, and in mainline Protestant denominations in the 1960s through the 1990s. Among Episcopalians, its roots can be traced back into the early twentieth-century rediscovery by liturgical scholars of the worship practices of the ancient church, and the beginnings of critical historical study and theological revisioning attached to this scholarship. Liturgical renewal began to trickle into the actual life of the church in the 1930s and 1940s, captured in the 1942 publication of *Prayer Book Interleaves* by William Parker Ladd, dean of Berkeley Divinity School.[3]

Ladd's passion for liturgical renewal came from a sense that the church had lost its ability to relate to those who had been betrayed, lied to, or disappointed by Christianity, and particularly by the violence and hatred of Christians for one another in the bloody and pointless First World War. As noted in previous chapters, this attention to the failures of Christendom and rethinking of the church's role in the lives of individuals and society became pointed and urgent after the emptiness of Christendom was revealed in 1914. Like Muhlenberg, Ladd believed that changing worship styles, developing greater flexibility, allowing the liturgy to speak meaning to those in the culture, was central to the church's purpose. Unless the liturgy could speak to people in a meaningful way, they would find meaning elsewhere. The ideas gathered in Ladd's 1942 book were actually columns written throughout the 1930s, and after the Second World War they pointed the way forward for the church in its new missional context of suburban family churches.[4]

These suburban churches were larger, better funded, and more family-oriented than earlier Episcopal congregations, and since for the first time in

Episcopalian history there were enough ordained clergy to provide a priest for every congregation, the Eucharist could become more of a central part of the church's life.[5] In addition, the newly built churches could incorporate new liturgical architectural suggestions about the placement of the altar and where the priest would stand. At the time of Ladd's writing, Eucharist was normally offered once a month in most Episcopal congregations. For Ladd, Eucharist should ideally be frequent, a sacrament of unity, building a community together, and utterly anti-individualistic. Ladd suggested using this monthly communion pattern wisely to build a sense of mission among the congregation of work, witness, social celebration, adult baptism, and so forth, thus clearly connecting the sacramental life of the congregation to work out in the world. Although the Prayer of Consecration in the 1928 Prayer Book included the idea of self-offering, Ladd wrote, "[W]e seem to have little success in tying it up with the outgoing Christian life, e.g. with social service or missions." Making this connection was central to his vision of the liturgy. Similarly, Ladd's ideas about baptism were focused on initiation into a community of Christians who were committed to living out the gospel in the world. A spirituality of withdrawal from the world was an utterly false and mistaken one. With these two connections made—sacrament and unity/community, church as engaging in action and witness in the world—Ladd's 1930s writings demonstrated continuity with the path from Edinburgh 1910 through the Hocking Report to Johannes Christiaan Hoekendijk and the World Council of Churches, and connected as well with the centrality of the Eucharist to the missional ideals of the urban ministry practices described by Paul Moore in the 1950s. Within the context of the Episcopal Church, Ladd's view of the church, its worship, and its mission were congruent with the Broad Church movement, which became more ascendent as his ideas were put into practice.[6]

His student, liturgical scholar and seminary professor Massey Shepherd, continued the practice of writing such columns after his death, collated eventually in *The Living Liturgy*. It is worth noting that both Ladd's and Shepherd's column were published in *The Witness*, considered the most progressive of the Episcopalian periodicals. With a small group of clergy frustrated by the "dead" worship on Sunday mornings, Shepherd helped to form Associated Parishes for Liturgy and Mission in 1946, which aided in bringing liturgical renewal in practice to congregations, as well as leading in redeveloping the rites and language that became the 1979 Book of Common Prayer.

In 1950, as General Convention had rejected the 1943 suggestion of another Prayer Book revision to incorporate newer understandings of Eucharist and missional worship, the Standing Liturgical Commission began to publish *Prayer Book Studies*, a series of booklets about liturgical leadership and practice. These led clergy in parishes to begin trying out the new liturgical theology within the context of the existing 1928 Prayer Book, pushing its rubrics and language to their limit. After experimentation by the Associated Parishes for Liturgy and Mission, and much give and take among liturgical scholars, the process for a formal revision of the Book of Common Prayer began. Because of the Prayer Book's centrality to Episcopalian identity, this was a highly controlled process. General Convention allowed trial use of new liturgical forms as approved for a potential revision in 1964. In 1967, a new liturgy of the Eucharist was authorized for trial use, and the formal process of revision was outlined. The Standing Liturgical Commission created a drafting committee for each rite. These committees were tasked with creating draft proposals and experimental rites, receiving feedback from those who used the new version. The General Convention would need to approve the draft version of the Prayer Book in General Convention in 1976, leading to a final version for approval by General Convention in 1979. The entire process included ecumenical input and used an ecumenical lectionary, highlighting the importance of ecumenical amity to church and mission in the twentieth century.[7]

At the same time, the inward, Episcopalian-specific focus of the liturgical renewal movement and the writing of the new Prayer Book could not completely incorporate all contextual possibilities. Women still could not be ordained clergy, and the clergy-led process meant that the suggestions and involvement of women in the creation of the new Prayer Book were heavily limited, as was that of laypeople. Lay Episcopalian Margaret Mead, an anthropologist specializing in initiation rites, was named as consultant in 1967 for the drafting committee on Christian Initiation as an expert on ritual in human communities. She was a devoted Episcopalian who had found the church on her own and demanded baptism at the age of eleven in 1912, someone who had certainly experienced the church both as an insider and an outsider, and thus someone whose expertise could offer much to the process of creating a fully missionally oriented Prayer Book. However, her nonnormative experience—because of her own age and volition in the rite, Mead experienced what was essentially a "believer's baptism," not typical for the Episcopal Church—and her nonauthoritative status as a woman and a layperson meant that her suggestions were largely sidelined.

Writing to the task force in the pre-Stonewall era, Mead recommended, among other things, the creation of rites to bless same-sex partnerships. She also recommended the creation of diverse liturgies fitting the needs of different congregations, and rituals to mark life-cycle events beyond the traditional few: pregnancy, adoption, starting school, new career, divorce, retirement, elderly moving to children's home, "onset of a disability," and grief. Mead also suggested, to no result, that the revision process should include the voices and ideas of people under thirty. She and her daughter had written a liturgical rite to welcome someone into the church who had moved to a new parish or had just found the tradition; this was also rather rudely sidelined, so much so that a member of the committee later wrote her an apologetic letter.[8]

The committee members working on Christian initiation in Prayer Book revision were not interested in these questions or suggestions, which didn't fit their own sense of their necessary task, tightly focused on the baptismal rite and how it related to confirmation. While the revision of the Book of Common Prayer was thus extraordinarily missional and was undertaken in order to make the message of the church more meaningful and relevant in its cultural context, those who did the work were not necessarily committed to this as the guiding principle and did not undertake their work to wholly and consciously attempt it. Tellingly, the name of Massey Shepherd's organization, the Associated Parishes for Liturgy and Mission, itself demonstrates the intention for liturgical renewal to be explicitly connected to the church's mission, even though little or none of its program had to do with what had traditionally been considered "mission" in the nineteenth century. Despite the apparent inward, esoteric focus on worship practice and ritual language, the work of the Associated Parishes for Liturgy and Mission and Prayer Book revision did in fact represent a major missional innovation for the church and reflected this shift toward the *missio dei* orientation. This version of *missio dei* clearly saw a definite role for church in God's mission, a meaningful role to play, and it was accomplished through the liturgy.

The most important way in which this was expressed was via the new baptismal covenant in the 1979 Book of Common Prayer. This baptismal covenant is usually summed up in a set of questions and responses:

CELEBRANT: Will you continue in the apostles' teaching and fellowship, in the breaking of bread, and in the prayers?

PEOPLE: I will, with God's help.

CELEBRANT: Will you persevere in resisting evil, and, whenever you fall into sin, repent and return to the Lord?

PEOPLE: I will, with God's help.

CELEBRANT: Will you proclaim by word and example the Good News of God in Christ?

PEOPLE: I will, with God's help.

CELEBRANT: Will you seek and serve Christ in all persons, loving your neighbor as yourself?

PEOPLE: I will, with God's help.

CELEBRANT: Will you strive for justice and peace among all people, and respect the dignity of every human being?

PEOPLE: I will, with God's help.

In the 1979 version, the Apostles' Creed is included in the baptismal rite itself, and a set of questions renouncing sin and evil precedes the baptismal covenant questions. But it is not these things which demonstrate a significant change in understanding of sacrament and mission. The questions of the baptismal covenant in 1979 differ significantly from the 1928 version, which reflected both the older practice of the Episcopal Church and the older understanding of mission as conversion to true knowledge, ordered worship, and right living. In the 1928 baptismal rite, the candidate renounces the devil and all his works; states a belief in Jesus and desire to take Jesus as Lord, and states belief in "all the articles of the Christian faith, as contained in the Apostles' Creed." Finally, in the 1928 prayer book, the baptized person promises to walk in God's will and keep God's commandments.

The 1979 baptismal promises demonstrate a *missio dei* orientation in terms of the church's relation to God's purposes in the world, and the individual's role in it as a baptized believer. While "following" and "keeping God's holy will," the only hint at these things in the 1928 Book of Common Prayer, might have some missional and action implications, these are far more obvious and explicit in the 1979 version. The final two questions, about seeking and serving Christ in all persons, striving for justice and peace and respecting the dignity of every human being, are clearly more oriented toward the mission of the church and believer as active in the world, as well as right belief ("the teaching of the apostles" and "the prayers"). The 1979 baptismal covenant, as it became known in the Episcopal Church, reflected a new missional understanding which became foundational, inculcating this understanding of God, church, and mission in future Episcopalians through baptism, catechism, preaching, theology, and formation practices.

The process of creating this language seemed in some ways nearly accidental, perhaps reflecting how this missional orientation was already, by the late 1960s, widespread among committed and active Episcopalian clergy and scholars. In particular, the line about striving for justice and peace among all people was added without any documented discussion, simply suggested and then accepted at a committee meeting. Yet it is this question in particular that has become central to Episcopalian popular understanding of the meaning and practice of mission, and it makes the 1979 baptismal rite most distinct from earlier language.[9]

With the adoption of the 1979 Book of Common Prayer, deep missional shifts within Episcopalian practice and identity were cemented into normative expectations. While in 1950 only a tiny minority of parishes had Eucharist as the main Sunday service, the practice had increased even before the 1979 Prayer Book explicitly stated that Eucharist should be the main Sunday celebration, and after 1979 it expanded to near-universal practice in the church. The older forms of morning prayer accompanied by a long clerical sermon shifted to the "family service," also influenced by the 1950s development of the suburban church, which invited families and included singable congregational hymns as well as a shorter sermon. Laypeople became more active in worship-related roles.[10] The two shifts in sacramental practice, emphasizing the centrality of the Eucharist and baptism as complete initiation, echoed Ladd's earlier insistence that both of these sacraments were purposeful in creating a Christian community united in mission. These were radical changes from the 1928 Book, not only in language but in the underlying theology.

In Episcopalian practice, Eucharist became the center of the church's corporate life, not an individual pietistic practice. It was now open to all the baptized, even children. Historically it had been open only to those who had been confirmed, and denied to those who were "notorious" for evil living, according to the canon on repulsion from communion. The 1979 Prayer Book and the associated sacramental ecclesiology meant that most Episcopalians placed great importance on the Eucharist being offered to all comers without exception, and it became the symbol of relationship and "redemptive fellowship," following Ladd's ideal of Eucharist as the sacrament of unity and mission. This new practical understanding of the nature and purpose of the sacrament lay the groundwork for a shock among Episcopalians in the late 1990s with a "breaking of communion" in the Episcopal Church and the Anglican Communion over issues of sexuality, as discussed in the next chapter.

Mission, the Baptismal Covenant, and the Ordination of Women

The baptismal covenant of the 1979 Prayer Book reflects a "baptismal ecclesiology" which was, like *missio dei* theology, already in some ways practiced within the Episcopalian community before the Prayer Book was approved. Baptismal ecclesiology sees baptism as the "complete" sacrament of Christian initiation and as the initiation into Christian ministry; it is foundational and makes all equal in the community of Christ. Baptismal ecclesiology and *missio dei* ideals were prominent in the controversy, simultaneous with the Prayer Book revision process, over the ordination of women. Ruth Meyers notes, "Ordained ministries are particular expressions of the more fundamental baptismal gifts of ministry. So, for example, as the Episcopal church was considering the ordination of women in the 1970s, one argument advanced in favor of this step was 'ordain women or stop baptizing them.'"[11]

Women had always been central in the missional life of the church, actively engaging in missional expansion through funding congregations and church buildings as well as recruiting female missionaries, teaching, running Sunday schools, managing Altar Guilds, and even being "set apart" as deaconesses or members of female religious communities. Governance, however, was set beyond women as it had long been set apart from African American clergy. Women could not sit on vestries, hold formal leadership responsibilities within the church, or be ordained until the latter half of the twentieth century. In 1946 Elizabeth Dyers became the first woman elected as a deputy to General Convention, but women were not formally permitted to be seated with voice and vote until 1970.[12]

Traditionally in the threefold order of ministry central to Episcopalian polity, the order of deacon was considered to be temporary. Generally a man would be ordained deacon and then priest six months to a year later. This expectation hadn't always held, particularly in the case of men who were not white. (For instance, Cheyenne David Oakerhater remained a deacon his entire life, and many other Native American, Asian American, and African American men had to wait for extended periods or permanently in the diaconate.) But because of this expectation there had been a formal distinction made between deaconesses, who were "set apart," and deacons, who were "ordained." In 1964, the order of deaconesses was subsumed into the general category of "deacon," and in 1965 the controversial Bishop James Pike of California ordained a deaconess, Phyllis Edward, using parts of a new liturgy that were very similar to that for male deacons. He invested her with a traditional deacon's stole and listed her on the diocesan clergy roster, enraging opponents of women's ordination. If women could be deacons, they could eventually also be priests. Both Pike and Edward were well aware of the implications and wanted to make the point.[13]

In order to permit women to be ordained as priest, technically what was required (aside from resolving long-standing theological debates about the relationship between men and women) was a simple statement that the canons for ordination as already existing were all to apply equally to men and women. This had to be approved by General Convention. The change was narrowly voted down at the 1973 General Convention due to a parliamentary procedure, where the votes of dioceses that were split on the question were nullified. The presiding bishop asked all supporters of women's ordination to wait and see what would happen in the next General Convention, and some episcopal supporters in fact chose to do so, including Bishop Paul Moore. Being asked to wait yet again for their ministry to be recognized was something that some of the female priestly candidates and their supporters were no longer willing to do, especially as other parts of the Anglican Communion were already ordaining women priests and the world had not ended. Lambeth, the decennial conference of Anglican bishops, had approved the diaconal ordination of women in 1968, and in 1971 the Anglican Consultative Council, a new body made up of bishops and laypeople from throughout the Communion, stated that women could be ordained to the priesthood if approved by their province or synod. The Diocese of Hong Kong and Macao had already ordained two women in 1971, in addition to Florence Li Tim-Oi in 1944, and ordained yet another woman in 1973.[14]

In 1974, women who had been prepared for ordination and their supporters organized an "irregular" ordination service at the Church of the Advocate in Philadelphia. Three retired bishops ordained eleven women to the priestly order, leading to enormous controversy over the validity of their orders and what the church should do about the fact that there were now eleven female priests. Presiding Bishop John Allin and the House of Bishops declared the ordinations invalid, and even Bishop Moore, who strongly supported women's ordination, requested that Carter Heyward, a new woman priest from his diocese, refrain from exercising her orders until General Convention could settle things. (She refused.) Even after the General Convention in 1976 formally permitted the future ordination of women, women ordinands were subject to extraordinary hatred and threats of violence; the first woman ordained in the Diocese of Indianapolis in 1977, after General Convention had already approved it, wore a bullet-proof vest during her ordination, which was picketed by protesters from her own home congregation. Bishop Moore began to ordain women in January 1977, now that the approval from convention had come, including Pauli Murray, the first African American woman priest, and Ellen Barrett, the first openly lesbian priest.[15]

The actual ordination ceremony of the Philadelphia Eleven was held in a historically Black congregation, led by an activist Black priest who had previously been a missionary in Liberia, tying this history even more closely to the missional trajectory of the Episcopal Church.[16] In 1974, the Church of the Advocate was an urban church dedicated to its community, in the tradition of Jones, Williams, Bragg, Muhlenberg, and Moore. It had a day care center, community center, and summer camp for children, collected donations of food and clothing, and was a meeting place for Black Power activists and radical antiracist and justice work organizations, echoing the most challenging *missio dei* work of the Episcopal Church in the late 1960s. Paul Washington had previously been rector of Church of the Crucifixion in South Philadelphia, the same church that had fought for inclusion in the diocesan convention in the 1850s. He had then been a missionary to Liberia, where he helped found Cuttington College. On returning to the United States, he brought Church of the Advocate into the forefront of the struggles around race and justice in Philadelphia and nationally. The church hosted the Black Power Convention in 1968 and the 1970 National Convention of the Black Panther Party. The Church of the Advocate became known in Philadelphia as a place where the marginalized could be welcome, including poor people, Black people, activists, women, and gay and lesbian people.[17]

The Church of the Advocate held an anomalous position as a mission congregation despite the grandeur of its physical building. It had been established by a wealthy Philadelphian for poor and working-class people, and in class-conscious fashion he had stipulated that the church would be governed by a Board of Trustees appointed by the bishop, rather than a vestry. The supervisors of Paul Washington, the Black rector of the church in 1974, with power to fire him and to provide or stop financial support to the church, were all white suburban men. The rector's consistent taking of controversial stances on racial justice issues, even before the ordination of women, was thus a significant risk.[18]

Washington asked for congregational input—a very unusual move for him—about hosting the ordinations, because this was in direct contradiction of the wishes of the diocesan bishop that provided the church's funding. He had never asked the congregation's opinion or approval for his involvement in Black Power, although even some Black members of the congregation were uncomfortable with this. The congregation, however, strongly supported hosting the ordination ceremony. Renee McKenzie argues that the congregation was willing to support what appeared clearly relevant to traditional church identity and goals of mission, such as internal sacramental issues, and relatively clear-cut social issues such as housing, rather than the more amorphous, dangerous, and open-ended Black Power work, which reflected a more radical vision of the *missio dei* orientation.[19]

Murray, who attended the 1974 "irregular" ordination, described it in theological and missional terms as an exemplar of God's mission of reconciliation and "what the church *could* be": "I went to this ordination ceremony in fear and trembling, in almost panic, having the same fears and apprehensions as one about to break a tribal taboo. Therefore, I was completely unprepared for the resultant joy and sense of the Holy Spirit that I experienced." She described the fully integrated community, with little girls acting as acolytes and the "ghetto" church being the gracious and kind host to nearly two thousand largely white attendees:

> In an electrifying flash of insight, I saw the coming together of two groups who have been submerged in both our society and our church—no other two groups in the United States could have brought it about. . . . As I move closer to my ordained ministry, I find myself resolved to do all in my power to break down the barriers of race and sex between people. We can stand at the center of the ecumenical movement, drawing all communions closer together. We are the descendants of planters, slaves, immigrants, indigenous Americans, etc., etc., and if we are sufficiently creative, we will be flexible enough to reflect the range of our unique heritage, cross-fertilizing one another and breaking out of our cocoon into Christian joyousness.[20]

Early Schisms

Opposition to the ordination of women was widespread even after its approval by General Convention. Bishop Allin stated that he opposed the ordination of women and was willing to step down as a result. The House of Bishops, eager to find stability after the years of controversy following the GCSP and the ongoing process of Prayer Book revision, refused to accept his offer and instead designed a canonical solution in a special meeting, later known as the "conscience clause," forbidding any canonical penalty for any bishop or priest who refused to accept the orders of women priests as valid.[21]

In the history of the ordination of women, the role of bishops is central to the management and further extension of controversy, a pattern that became even more visible in the controversy over sexuality in the next decades. Bishops ordained women against the will of General Convention, but when General Convention then accepted women's ordination, partly as a result, some bishops refused to accept this decision. No bishop was disciplined as a result of any part of the process, and thus a sense of episcopal autonomy rather than synodical relationship was strengthened in the church as a whole. Certain dioceses continued to refuse to accept the orders of women priests even a quarter of a century later, and some of these dioceses would later attempt to leave the denomination.[22]

At this point, however, the main response of those who were deeply opposed to the ordination of women, and in some cases the new Book of Common Prayer, was to leave the church as individuals or as congregations and to attempt to set up new denominations. Because of the ideal of Anglican establishmentarianism, which expected that any valid church would be the only one within a geographical area, these denominations generally claimed to be the "true" Episcopal or Anglican church within the United States. They also placed a high premium on apostolic succession. In order to have sympathetic clergy ordained as their own bishops, a ritual which required the laying on of hands of three bishops in the apostolic succession, bishops from other churches whose succession they considered legitimate were invited, including the Philippine Independent Church and various Orthodox churches.

The earliest of these schisms, in 1962, was a response to the church's stance on civil rights (even before the GCSP). This early group was heavily evangelical in orientation, even fundamentalist; in the mid-1970s it stated its opposition to the new Prayer Book, to social involvement by the church, to women's ordination, to theological liberalism ("heresy"), to biblical criticism,

and to homosexuality. In this, it echoed the growing gap in missional orientation between the ecumenicals (the Protestant mainline churches) and
the evangelicals, who had withdrawn from the World Council of Churches
in order to focus on their own ideals of mission after the merger of the
International Missionary Council and the WCC. None of the schismatic
groups in this era were members of the WCC or the National Council of
Churches, and many of them specifically excoriated ecumenicism, again
marking their orientation as missionally conservative rather than *missio dei*.[23]

Several schismatic groups broke away even before the regular ordination
of women in 1976, and several afterward. These groups often fissured internally due to theological disagreements or internal personality conflicts, and
congregations regularly moved from one group to another. The pre-1976
groups tended to be more conservative and evangelical in orientation, and
the post-1976 groups tended to be more Anglo-Catholic and focused on a
high view of the episcopacy, reflecting a specific theological abhorrence of
women's ordination. The schismatic groups were often suspicious of and
hostile toward one another. Donald Smith Armentrout estimated a total of
perhaps thirty thousand members in all of the different schismatic groups
by 1985, and several had disappeared quickly.[24] However, the strategy of
schism as a response to differing missional views, the new idea of seeking
episcopal consecration from bishops outside the United States, combined
with the conscience clause, which permitted various dioceses to hold distinct
attitudes toward polity and orders, would provide a ground of experience
and personnel for later schismatic reactions to the issues of sexuality and sacramental leadership.

Mission as Justice, Mission as Inclusion

McKenzie's analysis of the church that held the ordination of the Philadelphia
Eleven is itself a theological document, demonstrating the importance of
the baptismal covenant and *missio dei* theology not only in the 1970s but its
growth and centrality to Episcopalian self-understanding in the twenty-first
century. McKenzie writes that the ordination of the Philadelphia Eleven was

> a movement of the spirit, as is true of most transformational moments,
> [which] required individual acts of bravery that coalesced into a mighty
> and definitive roar. For the larger Episcopal Church this roar proclaimed a

desire to live more fully into a calling where, "There is neither Jew nor Greek, Black nor white, male nor female; we are one in Christ." For the Advocate the roar affirmed its identity as a ministry of the Episcopal Church with sufficient outsider status to be transgressive and sufficient insider status to be the recipient of support, financial and otherwise, to nurture a radical ministry with extraordinary impact. The "irregular" ordinations were groundbreaking and so was the congregation whose arms opened in welcome.[25]

The implicit missional theology is important. The work of the Spirit is transformational, radical, transgressive, and inclusive, erasing boundaries between people and groups. This language reflects the *missio dei* shift of the late 1960s and is far different from the older, establishmentarian or missionary consensus understanding of mission and church.

Throughout the church, after the crisis of the GCSP, the most radical aspects of the *missio dei* ideals tended to be refocused on clearly church-related issues, particularly inclusionary sacramental practice and access to leadership roles. While Stephen Bayne's call for a theological reflection process on missional ideals had never borne fruit, in fact the Episcopal Church was dealing with the issues of *missio dei* through the development of baptismal ecclesiology and the revision of the Prayer Book. This would prove in the long run to be another kind of theological formation, one which would lead to a church shaped around the new baptismal covenant. In the early 1980s, however, for those who were not aligned with *missio dei,* the shift in both liturgy and practice seemed inexplicable and imposed upon them against their will and, they would argue, against the received tradition of Christianity as a whole.

The controversies and bitterness would thus continue, and expand globally as those feeling excluded from this new sense of mission sought new allies. In the next chapter, I examine the ways in which this new missional orientation around baptismal ecclesiology and *missio dei* played out in the context of sexuality in the church, and how the early schismatic practices around different missional orientations led to new strategies of Anglican realignment.

14

Sexuality and Schism

Introduction

The issue of sexuality, specifically that of sexual activity between two people of the same sex, has been at the forefront of global Christian controversy since the 1990s. Disciplining and guiding the sexual lives of lay Christians was complicated enough, but when openly gay and lesbian Christians began to be ordained in the Episcopal Church, the controversy was highly publicized and polarized. Within the United States, congregations and entire dioceses attempted to leave the Episcopal Church and bring church property along with them, and in the Anglican Communion, an "Anglican Realignment" continues to divide the global churches.

The high profile of this controversy, and its connections with larger cultural issues in the U.S. context, has drawn quite a few disciplinary gazes, from history, theology, sociology, anthropology, and gender and sexual studies. While each of these disciplinary approaches illuminates some aspect of the controversy well, in order to draw them together it is crucial to understand that at the center of the controversy is not only sexuality per se but the ongoing global shifts in practice and ideals about the mission of the church itself, playing out in a context shaped by the bitter inheritance of race and empire. In this chapter, I will examine this controversy as a meaningful endpoint—though, of course, not the end—of the trajectories of mission, race, and empire that have been the focus of this book as a whole.

The late twentieth- and early twenty-first-century controversy over sexuality in global Anglicanism, I argue, has its roots in the long history of colonialism and mission that shaped Christian disciplines of sexuality in certain ways in the Global South, and differently in the Global North. The shift in worship practice and ecclesiology in the U.S. Episcopal Church, including the new focus on Eucharist as the sacrament of unity, baptism as the sacrament of full Christian initiation, and mission as inclusion, justice, and prophetic risk-taking on social issues, all of which had flowered in the

Mission, Race, and Empire. Jennifer C. Snow, Oxford University Press. © Oxford University Press 2024.
DOI: 10.1093/oso/9780197598948.003.0015

mid-twentieth-century *missio dei* shift, meant that the understanding of many Episcopalians of the entire controversy was completely distinct from that of those on the other side. Not only did they disagree on fundamental issues, but they disagreed on what the fundamental issues even were. For those on both sides, what was at stake was the purpose and mission of the church.

In moving through this argument, I begin with the rise of Episcopalian concern for and with gay and lesbian people in church and society, which overlapped the work of the new Book of Common Prayer and the ordination of women. I then discuss issues of church discipline, marriage, and sexuality as they differed between North Atlantic churches and many church contexts in Africa and Asia, which led not only to different ideas about sexuality per se but about the role of the church in shaping it and, in the Anglican context, the uses of the sacrament in disciplining "Christian marriage." I then move to the actual events surrounding the rise of the controversy in the Episcopal Church and the Anglican Communion, and the movement toward schism within the Anglican Communion around issues of sexuality and gender.

Strangers in Our Midst

The first outreach to and concern for gay and lesbian people (with primary reference to gay men) in the Episcopal Church context began immediately after the Second World War. The mobilization of American men and women during the war, bringing large numbers of young people into cities and providing women with the ability to find jobs and support themselves, led to the beginning of a conscious, if not open, gay and lesbian subculture in the late 1940s and 1950s. Immediately after the war ended came a period of intense social conformity, pushing women away from their new jobs and toward traditional gender roles, as well as the Cold War conflation of homosexuality with the "Communist menace." Sexual intimacy between people of the same sex was a criminal act in many jurisdictions. Thus the gay and lesbian people of the 1940s and 1950s were closeted, stigmatized, and persecuted and often had to live in secrecy.

People with same-sex orientations and relationships had always existed in the church, even in leadership positions, but they were deeply "closeted," keeping their relationships out of the public eye and unacknowledged. In the period under discussion, lay theologian and activist William Stringfellow, for example, lived with his partner, Methodist poet Tony Anthony; laywoman

Margaret Mead lived with a female partner for the last decades of her life; returned China missionary and American radical Grace Hutchins lived with her lover, secret even from the leftist organizations she worked with; Pauli Murray, lay African American lawyer, civil rights activist, and poet, later ordained priest, was also involved in same-sex relationships, including her unacknowledged partner Irene Barlowe, with whom she regularly attended church. In these and many more such cases, individuals involved in same-sex relationships were very active in church and public life on justice issues in the twentieth century, but rarely on issues related to homosexuality, and rarely claimed an openly gay or lesbian identity.[1]

In her work as an anthropologist, Mead was an exception in advocating for the importance of raising these questions. As early as 1949, she wrote:

> Are such discussions [about gender and sexuality] querulous fiddling while Rome burns? I think they are not. Upon the growing accuracy with which we are able to judge our limitations and potentialities, as human beings and in particular as scientists, will depend the survival of our civilization, which we now have the means to destroy. . . . So, as we stand at the moment in history while we still have choice, when we are just beginning to explore the properties of human relationships as the natural sciences have explored the properties of matter, it is of the very greatest importance which questions we ask, because by the questions we ask we set the answers that we will arrive at, and define the paths along which future generations will be able to advance.[2]

Numbers of clergy and religious leaders in the postwar years were coming to agree with her. These questions of sexuality and marriage were important and required scientific attention as well as moral and theological investigation. In 1957, the Church of England, investigating the "moral welfare" of the British people, produced the Wolfenden Report, which recommended the decriminalization of homosexuality. This report was welcomed by those in the Episcopal Church, and other Protestant churches, who had been working with homosexual people in urban settings and recognized the damage from the criminalization and stigma of same-sex relationships.[3]

Efforts to provide pastoral care for homosexual people in the 1950s grew out of the urban mission ideals, serving those who had been cast out by society. Those involved in urban mission had a growing understanding of the role of stigma and ostracization as ways in which society oppressed and damaged people, and that the church had a responsibility to care for them and demonstrate God's love to them. In a 1962 book on the effort to care for gay people, *Strangers in our Midst,* the author quoted C. Kilmer Myers, one of the urban social missionaries in Paul Moore's cohort who would later become Bishop of California, on the fact that much of what was considered "anti-social" or problematic among poor Black or immigrant urban youth actually was due to their mistreatment by society and resulting lack of opportunities to develop a sense of self-worth and optimism about their own future. The same, Myers argued, was true of homosexual people. In 1950, already the ideals of a therapeutic model of responding to what had previously been considered criminal and sinful were well developed, along with the ideas of urban ministry to populations of those considered be-yond the pale of social norms. Acknowledging the spiritually and socially deforming effects of racism, poverty, and social exclusion on individuals led directly to perceive that the ministry to homosexual people, who also suffered exclusion and stigma, was an additional path of missional work in the city.[4]

Myers himself wrote the preface to *Strangers in Our Midst,* approving its work among homosexual people; indeed, among his many other projects he was the executive director of the Henry Foundation, the tiny Episcopalian organization that did this work. And this work was, in some ways, not yet "prophetic." The missional ideals of social revolution and transformation to-ward God's kingdom in the world were not yet present in urban ministry in the 1950s, the era represented in the 1962 book.

For Myers and other church leaders working with the gay community in the 1950s and early 1960s, the desire to "cure" or "repress" sexuality was not seen as desirable, but neither could the Henry Foundation encourage people, realistically speaking, to live their lives and relationships openly. Instead, the Foundation worked through the historic missional strategy of enforced assimilation, focusing on helping homosexuals to survive and ideally find some happiness, peace, and usefulness in a society that hated them.

Gay people were subject to arrest, criminalization, loss of jobs and families if they were found out. Many homosexuals experienced the church as a special source of contempt and hatred rather than help. Even psychiatrists were often hostile to homosexuals; one was recorded calling gay men "a choice collection of pleasure-loving psychopaths."[5] The goal of the Henry Foundation was to help people with this kind of sexuality to live without damage to themselves or others, and the role of the church in creating this hatred gave the church a special role in fighting it. In *Strangers in Our Midst*, Alfred Gross wrote:

> What is the responsibility of the church for those it has permitted to feel that their sins have cut them off from the life and work of the institution that calls itself the Body of Christ? . . . A bishop, when he pronounced sentence of deposition upon a homosexual priest, told him that he was not fit to walk on the same side of the street with decent people. Judgment is not enough. . . . [O]ught not the church inquire of itself what it had a right to expect from men it casts out when their problems obtruded themselves on the notice of its leaders? And, assuming there might be something to the indictment, what part have the church and society played in making the homosexual what he is?[6]

In considering the "practical aspects" of this ministry, Gross assumes a framework of legal danger and social condemnation that the homosexual must navigate daily and that the minister can only learn to navigate with him (or, rarely, her).

The Henry Foundation's work was apparently almost completely with male homosexual people, who were most likely to be caught by the police in criminalized sexual situations. The minister usually had the opportunity to step in at moments of crisis, when someone was going to jail, losing their job, losing their housing, or losing their family due to being caught in homosexual activity. The minister's role then was to help advocate for this person to retain what they needed to live and to reassure them that God did not condemn them and that they deserved to live a life of dignity and worth. *Strangers in Our Midst* noted that the minister himself was limited by what he could recommend and was also taking risks in doing this work, both in terms of his career and his family. Many clergy were incapable of doing the work or were too afraid of the social stigma involved.

This life of protective assimilationism might still be extremely closeted for those who did not wish or were unable to live in the "homosexual ghetto" of big cities, and sometimes the Henry Foundation's work included helping homosexual men remain in heterosexual marriages. Gross acknowledged that this intervention was successful only at keeping people out of jail, not necessarily at suppressing homosexual desires and behaviors. The "cure" or repression of these was not the goal. The goal was to help men in crisis to survive it.

The method encouraged secrecy and even, as Gross explicitly states, hypocrisy as a survival skill, something that in other ways would prove unhelpful to sexual ethics and lead to abuse.[7]

Acknowledging the evils of this kind of secrecy, Gross nonetheless argued that unless society and the church changed to permit people to live their sexual relationships in an open and honest fashion, there were few realistic options. He described the forces of social conformity with a sort of resigned despair:

> The fact remains that the people called normal make the rules. He who is able to make the greatest compromises is least likely to get into trouble with himself or those who disapprove departures from the accepted ways of doing things. The applicability of this home truth goes beyond sexual nonconformists. . . . Sooner or later, most of us come to realize the folly of beating our heads against stone walls. . . . In order to come to terms with himself, the homosexual has got to take the fact of the universe and its opinions into account. So long as he chooses to live in a private cloudcuckooland, he must remember that his is a glass house at which small boys and their unkind elders can be expected to throw stones.[8]

At various points Gross writes that the church must rethink its sexual behavioral ethics to reflect new understandings of human sexual nature, the scientific and ethical questioning Mead advocated in 1949. It is only in the very last chapter that he envisioned the decriminalization of homosexual acts between consenting adults, while retaining laws that protect children and adolescents, as well as laws against public sex that might be a nuisance to the community. However, Gross didn't expect either new ethics or decriminalization to happen anytime soon.[9]

Mission, Marriage, and Church Discipline

At the same time that urban missioners were discovering the need to serve a stigmatized and persecuted community, the Episcopal Church and the Anglican Communion at large were wrestling with other issues connected to the proper regulation of Christian sexuality in marriage. In the Episcopal Church throughout the nineteenth century, most marriage canons were related to divorce and remarriage. Marriage was to be monogamous, sexually exclusive, of course heterosexual, and indissoluble. Those who were not married according to the canons were supposed to be refused communion unless a bishop approved it, but it was not clear how often this was enforced; by the early twentieth century there was regular acknowledgment that most people were not paying attention and were getting divorced if they wanted to. In 1946, immediately after World War II and just as the gay community was being discovered by the church, General Convention changed the canons to allow for remarriage after divorce, without sacramental discipline, with the bishop's approval.

Heterosexuality and marriage—specifically divorce, polygamy, and contraception—were the pressing human sexuality issues for the Anglican Communion in the first two-thirds of the twentieth century. At the global level, the Anglican Communion debated marriage and issues relating to heterosexual relationships at Lambeth 1930, with a discussion about family planning, and in Lambeth 1948, 1958, and 1968 with a series of statements on sex, contraception, and marriage.

In 1948, the Lambeth Conference resolved that

> members of the Church who marry contrary to the law of the Church, as accepted in the provincial or regional Church to which they belong, should be regarded as subject to the discipline of the Church in respect of admission to Holy Communion. Their admission to Holy Communion lies within the discretion of the Bishop, due regard being had to their own spiritual good and the avoidance of scandal to others. It is important that the practice within each province or regional Church in this matter should be uniform. We restate Resolution 11 (b) of the Lambeth Conference, 1930, as follows: "That in every case where a person with a former partner still living is re-married and desires to be admitted to Holy Communion the case should be referred to the bishop, subject to provincial or regional regulations."[10]

Bishop Stephen Bayne, who was also working for the Anglican Communion on issues of mission and church relationships, chaired the committee that investigated marriage, and likely wrote the 1958 report. Among other things, the report emphasized that monogamy (without needing to specify that this monogamy was heterosexual) was the "greatest blessing of Christian life" and standard for Christians, while recognizing that this was difficult for those from non-monogamous cultures.[11]

This points to an additional, important facet of how the church related to human sexuality: it was disciplined primarily through the use or forbiddance of the sacrament of Eucharist, and in some parts of the world, through baptism (forbidden for polygamists in many cases) or through access to ordained status (forbidden for much of the church's history for those who were divorced or engaged in public immorality).[12]

Historically in Anglican congregations a minority of church members were "communicants," receiving the infrequent sacrament. In the missionary context of the eighteenth and nineteenth centuries, early missionaries and converts saw proper sexuality and marriage as a critical part of Christian life and identity, particularly regarding polygamy and premarital sex. Missionaries and early converts focused on the ideal of "Christian marriage": monogamous, companionate, heterosexual, indissoluble. In cultures that did not have a strong tradition approximating this monogamous, indissoluble marriage, "Christian marriage" became a major boundary marker of the Christian community, accomplished through church discipline around taking communion.

This affected indigenous communities in the context of the Episcopal Church's missions, since many Native American cultures permitted polygamy and divorce and had gender and sexuality concepts that did not fit European marital and gender ideologies. The Dine, for instance, traditionally had six genders rather than the European two. The Lakota had three genders, the third, *wi'n'kte*, being a biological male who took on certain women's roles, spoke women's language, and had a special status as a sacred mediator, and who might or might not be involved in same-sex activity. Missionaries, Martin Brokenleg notes, assumed that the *wi'n'kte* were "homosexual" and persecuted them mercilessly; they were unable to recognize that sexual activity and social role were far more complex than the simple Euro-American binaries.[13]

In African contexts, polygamy and various cultural practices around age cohort initiation, marriage, and premarital sexuality were heavily disciplined. African Christians had asked the International Missionary Council to investigate the basis of the requirement for monogamy for Christians as early as the 1930s, which finally resulted in a significant study of African marriage in the 1950s. One of the discoveries of the investigation was that in many parts of Africa significant proportions of Christian adults were permanently barred from the sacraments. Being a communicant thus came to signify someone who has lived up to the standards of the church, particularly in terms of sexual continence. This understanding of discipline around communion and sexuality became nearly universal across all denominations in Africa in the mid-twentieth century.[14]

Due to this missional history, many Christians in Africa and Asia continued to emphasize the connection of eucharistic discipline with Christian marriage as a communal commitment through the twentieth century. Within the Episcopal Church and other Global North church contexts, discipline around marriage and sexuality, including issues of cohabitation, divorce, and adultery, became rare and private by the nineteenth century and even more so in the twentieth.[15] This distinction between the Global North churches and the Global South churches regarding public eucharistic discipline around sexuality and marriage would become quite important as the controversy developed globally.[16]

Polygamy was not resolved officially by Lambeth until 1988. At that time, Lambeth declared that polygamists could be baptized, but could not take additional wives after baptism, nor could they "put away" any wife. In 2008, Lambeth clarified that polygamists should not be in positions of leadership within the church. This was already historically the practice—something that had led to various schisms and new denominational or congregational establishments within the African context, when polygamists did not feel that their married life required that they be disciplined by the church.

In 1973, General Convention repealed the canon that directed the minister to refuse communion to those whose marriages or sexual lives were canonically problematic, at the same time that the church was also struggling with the issues of revising the Prayer Book and women's ordination. In 1976, General Convention recommended pastoral care for "homosexual persons." While the rubric to repel from communion still existed in the 1979 Book of Common Prayer, it was very rarely used, and even more rarely was it used publicly. Once the eucharistic discipline was fully removed from issues of heterosexual marriage and divorce, the church's debate was no longer about heterosexuality and marriage, but about the access of homosexual people to ordination and, later, to marriage or a rite of blessing of same-sex relationships. The shifting understandings of sacramental discipline around sexuality in the global church at large would prove an additional source of mutual misunderstanding in the communion as the controversy grew.

Ordination and Consecration of Gay and Lesbian People

Within the American context, pastoral ministry to gay and lesbian people began to become more bold and "prophetic" in the later 1960s and early 1970s, moving away from the closet-supporting strategies of the Henry Foundation. Responding to the *missio dei* developments that emphasized the embrace of revolution and activism as transformational strategies in serving God's mission in the world, gay and lesbian individuals and their supporters began to agitate and protest within the church. Just as supporting civil rights had involved challenges to the system and taking great risks, so too, they argued, would the work of supporting the sacred worth of gay and lesbian people.

Gay and lesbian people in cities such as New York and San Francisco began to openly claim their status as citizens and even to publicly acknowledge their relationships. The first public same-sex relationship blessing was held in 1971 in New York City in the Episcopal Church of the Holy Apostles, for an African American lesbian couple. The rector had permitted a fully gay-affirming congregation to meet at the church—Church of the Beloved Disciple—and there was significant overlap between the Beloved Disciple and Apostles congregations, though they technically belonged to different denominations. The Episcopal rector performed blessings, while the Church of the Beloved Disciple performed marriages. Bishop Paul Moore stated that he thought the marriages were in "bad taste" but refused to discipline the rector despite an uproar from less accepting Episcopalians.[17] In 1976, General Convention passed a resolution affirming that "homosexual persons are children of God who have a full and equal claim with all other persons upon the love, acceptance, and pastoral concern and care of the Church." This resolution did not address ordination, but along with the change in the canons permitting women to be ordained in 1976, Bishop Moore was able to justify his decision to ordain Ellen Barrett in 1977.

Barrett was an openly acknowledged lesbian and one of the cofounders of Integrity, an organization advocating for gay and lesbian inclusion in the Episcopal Church and which exemplified the turn toward activism as mission that had developed in the Episcopal Church and the ecumenical world as a whole. In response, the House of Bishops, meeting at Port St. Lucie, Florida—the same meeting in which the "conscience clause" was developed, ensuring that there would be no canonical discipline for clergy or bishops who refused to accept the validity of a woman's orders—reasserted that homosexual activity was "condemned" by scripture, while heterosexual marriage was "affirmed." Structurally, "activity" (meaning sexual activity) for homosexual people was comparable to "marriage" for heterosexuals, though "marriage" was unavailable to gay and lesbian people. The House of Bishops also stated that that no bishop should ordain "in violation of these principles." The bishops at Port St. Lucie were uncertain whether a homosexual orientation was morally neutral or acceptable even if the individual was celibate.

C. Kilmer Myers, now Bishop of California, received Barrett into his diocese after her ordination and had to decide whether to relicense her. As he told the House of Bishops, he felt that she was well qualified and he would provide her with the license, although he would take no further steps toward new ordinations of openly gay people until the General Convention had discussed it at the planned 1979 meeting.

However, Bishop Myers wanted the House of Bishops to know the context and what society's hostility toward homosexual people meant in practice:

> Only a few months ago one of our most committed and effective priests in the mission district of the city was viciously attacked by hoodlums who called him "faggot" as they mercilessly beat him. His jaw was broken in three places and his left temple scarred for life. A few weeks later a young City gardener was stabbed to death, again reportedly with the cry of "faggot" ringing in his ears. He was buried from our cathedral with over 3000 people from all walks of life in attendance. . . . Since then there have been repeated firebombings in gay areas of our city and many gays feel forced to walk in groups armed with walkie talkies in order to protect themselves from possible assailants.
>
> Certainly homosexual behavior is sometimes sinful. But sometimes heterosexual behavior also is sinful. . . . If we say no to baptism and Eucharist and if we say yes to levitical penalty, we shall not be talking much about Jesus of Nazareth—at least as I through the years have come to understand his life, his message, his posture, his demeanor, and his end.[18]

The new Book of Common Prayer, with its new baptismal ecclesiology, was still on the way and wouldn't be officially accepted for another two years. Nonetheless, in defending his decision to relicense Barrett as an openly lesbian priest Myers was explicit in drawing direct connections between baptism and ordination as well as between this ecclesiology and the mission of the church:

The foundational sacrament of the Christian church is baptism. There is no Bishop in this house who has not baptized homosexuals or persons who later discovered themselves to be homosexual. . . . It is my conviction that *any* condition or circumstance which *ipso facto*, would bar *any* person from ordination would also make that person ineligible to receive the *primary* sacraments of baptism and Eucharist. All the other sacraments flow from these. Is it our intent then to "withdraw" baptism from such persons? To excommunicate them? If we cannot ordain them, then they should not seek baptism. . . . If a person can be baptized and admitted to the Holy Communion, he or she . . . can be ordained to the ministry of the Catholic Church. I see no alternative. Indeed, I welcome this new insight as yet another bold and Christian step towards the liberation of all God's people for humanness at its highest level.[19]

Finally, Myers's justification for relicensing Barrett's priestly ministry was explicitly, and passionately, rooted in *missio dei* principles and connected to the hope of the church's expansion and inclusion:

To stand up for the radically human, i.e. Christian, always is costly. . . . And yet there is a deep yearning in millions of human hearts that the Church of Christ return to its foundational beginnings. Those beginnings are rooted in the life, the teaching, the demeanor, the posture, the end, of the Jew, the man from Nazareth. This beloved founder did not declare himself on every human issue. But we do know what his directions were. They were to show us that God's cause is man's cause. And God's cause is our full humanisation. It is with that revolutionary matter—that revolution about God and about humanity—that we are called to struggle.[20]

Bishop Myers's plea to accept homosexual people as qualified for participation in all the sacramental life of the church, based in a sense of God's mission in the world as a literally revolutionary, countercultural, and risk-taking commitment to the value of the fully human person, was eloquent and also clearly missionally Christian in its underpinnings. Myers saw this mandate for the church as rooted in the person and work of Christ, and the response of the church as central to helping human beings know and respond to this love. However, it did not sway the House of Bishops. Far from accepting Myers's argument that homosexual people should be judged as candidates for ordination on the same standards as heterosexuals, the bishops at Port St. Lucie were not even sure they could accept that a celibate homosexual was morally equivalent to a heterosexual married person.

This demonstrates that while the *missio dei* orientation was prominent within the church, especially among those most concerned with missional outreach, it was not the dominant nor the only missional orientation. Many Episcopalians did not understand mission as commitment to radical social transformation or the transgression of social boundaries in the service of the gospel. As demonstrated first during the GCSP, and since then in the schisms and controversies surrounding the ordination of women, this reorientation of the church's missional self-understanding was not shared by all Episcopalians.

As the controversy over sexuality continued, these lines continued to be more clearly drawn. The rhetoric of transformation, revolution, change, and faithfulness to a God of radical love beyond social expectations continued to be part of the missional understanding of those advocating for the full inclusion of gay and lesbian people, while those in opposition held to a traditional view of mission that emphasized passing on and protecting the church's norms, particularly norms around sex and marriage.

In 1979, at the same convention that approved the new Book of Common Prayer, the House of Bishops chose between two resolutions on ordination of openly homosexual candidates. One was a "local option," permitting bishops to make this discernment themselves; the other stated that any candidate for ordination must be a "wholesome example" in their sexual lives and should not engage in any sexual behavior outside of marriage, thus ensuring that homosexual people could not be considered. The House of Bishops chose to insist on a "wholesome example." Several bishops, including Paul Moore and Edmond Lee Browning of Hawai'i, signed a protest statement pledging not to abide by the requirement that homosexual candidates be celibate in order to be considered.[21]

Bishop Browning, who would succeed Allin as presiding bishop in 1985, valued activism, transformation, and particularly "inclusion." The hallmark of his commitment as presiding bishop was that "there would be no outcasts" in the church. He had spent much of his life as a missionary in Japan or as a church executive dealing with ecumenical and Anglican Communion matters, both experiences which strengthened his *missio dei* orientation.[22] He made this explicit in an essay he wrote, "Our World Mission," for a volume edited by Presiding Bishop Allin:

I was not there to introduce God to the Okinawans or the Okinawans to God. I came to realize that he was there before I arrived—before any missionary reached those shores—and that I was there because he had called me to join him in one of the places in which he was already at work. Again, the key to understanding the Church's mission is to seek to discern in this confused, suffering, and starving world where God is at work and how we might join him. If we begin with this basic assumption—that God is at work within his creation seeking to free, to enable, to bring man to himself; that it is he who initiates this mission; that it is he who sets these concerns in our hearts and calls us to join him in these tasks—then, I think we can give thanks that the Episcopal Church has in the past few years responded in some significant ways to joining God in his mission.[23]

Browning's commitment to inclusivity and justice as a mark of the church's mission with God would soon be put to the test as the controversy around sexuality and ordination continued to heat up.

General Convention 1988 began a deliberate process of "dialogue" on human sexuality, in the midst of the AIDS crisis, as many Episcopalians became more aware of the gay male community, in particular, as one suffering deeply. In preparation for General Convention 1991, the Standing Commission on Human Affairs offered its report on this dialogue, in which it recommended accepting openly gay and lesbian noncelibate people as candidates for ordination and developing same-sex blessings for gay and lesbian couples. Bishop Jack Spong of Newark had ordained an openly gay man, Robert Williams, in 1989, who then made public statements deriding monogamy and describing monogamous gay people as traitors to the liberation movement. While Bishop Spong, Bishop Myers, and others argued that homosexual people who were living in committed, loving, and stable relationships should be considered for ordination without difficulty, no bishop in the church had advocated that monogamy should be displaced from its central role in the ideal Christian sexual relationship.[24] Thus, while Williams was removed from his role in outreach to the gay and lesbian community in the diocese, and later left the church, supporters did not see his remarks as evidence that gay people in general should not be ordained. The Diocese of Newark immediately began the process of ordination for Barry Stopfel, another gay man, although because of the controversy Spong did not ordain him personally. Bishop Walter Righter of Newark, Spong's assistant, ordained Stopfel in 1990. As a result, Righter was charged with heresy in a presentment endorsed by seventy-six active and retired bishops.[25]

The Internationalization of the Controversy: Anglican Communion and Schism

Opposition within the United States to granting homosexual people full access to the ordination process was strengthened by developments within American politics and culture as a whole, known as the "culture wars." These "wars," which at the time of this writing are still ongoing, polarized Americans over issues that could easily be used to encourage individuals to become politically active and demonize those who opposed them as existential dangers to the American way of life. For those who were motivated by religion in particular, these opponents were seen as spiritually polluting and damaging. Homosexual people and those who supported their rights were high on the list of these spiritually polluting dangers to the United States and to the church. The culture wars were not limited to any one denomination, but they became religiously as well as politically polarizing as they worked along the lines of the early twentieth-century modernist/fundamentalist split and became entwined in religious identities.

In the later twentieth century, these lines had become largely denominational, with the mainline, historic Protestant churches (including Episcopalians, though excluding Southern Baptists) on the modernist/ecumenical side, and the nondenominational, charismatic, and evangelical churches on the other. Within the Episcopal Church itself there were, in addition to those who were simply content with the church's traditional teachings on sexuality and marriage, a subset of active charismatic and evangelically oriented Episcopalians, as well as some Anglo-Catholics, who found aspects of the culture wars meaningful.

John Stott, an English evangelical priest, had worked for years to develop an international network of Anglican evangelicals, organizing support for theological education for Anglicans in Africa and Asia as well as networking with evangelicals of other denominations through the Lausanne Movement. His many books were shared with Anglican evangelicals throughout the world, and he helped to organize a new conservative evangelical Anglican theological seminary outside of Pittsburgh. At the same time that Bishop Bayne was traveling the Anglican world and developing relationships around the *missio dei* ideals that issued in *Mutual Responsibility and Interdependence*, Stott was doing the same in developing relationships with evangelical Anglicans, who often felt isolated and powerless in the Communion.

Sexuality was probably not initially a high priority for Stott personally (he himself was celibate), and he was much more oriented to the traditional evangelical priorities of teaching the Bible, encouraging conversion experiences and building churches. Only in 1994 did Stott first address homosexuality, not really considering it a major issue until it became so prominently connected to Anglican missional transformations. While Stott said that homosexuals deserved compassion, their proper course would be to embrace celibacy or pray for healing and conversion to heterosexuality.[26] Stott's statement was consistent with the theological and scriptural hermeneutic he had taught and espoused in the Anglican networks he had nurtured. His stature among global evangelical Anglicans ensured that his stance would be internationally supported.

In the United States, Bishop Righter was exonerated at a 1996 heresy trial when the court of eight bishops decided that he hadn't violated "core doctrines" but only "doctrinal teachings." Doctrinal teachings, which could change over time, would have to be made explicit via canon or General Convention resolution, and there was no such explicit doctrine on the ordination of homosexual people. This decision protected the autonomy of bishops in deciding who in their dioceses could be ordained, in the spirit of the "conscience clause," but continued the process of unpicking the connections between the General Convention of the Episcopal Church and the ability to discipline or require conformity from bishops.[27]

After the Righter decision, those who felt very strongly that the "embrace" of homosexual people by the Episcopal Church was theologically and morally indefensible began to argue that the church was beyond saving. They looked for other ways to maintain an Anglican identity which would continue to be, in their understanding, orthodox and free from such errors as liberal theology, social activism, and sexual diversity. Stott's network provided potential options. Many other parts of the Anglican world did not share the *missio dei* orientation of the inclusivist leaders of the Episcopal Church, and thus could be looked to as partners.[28]

Episcopalians from several small internal protest groups in the church began to cultivate relationships with some leaders from the Global South Anglican churches, many of whom also had connections with Stott. In 1997 they underwrote a meeting in Kuala Lumpur to help the bishops of these churches prepare for Lambeth 1998. Such preparation was desired by the bishops from the Global South, who felt that they didn't understand the Lambeth parliamentary procedures and hoped that they could learn to use the system as well as the European and American delegates so their voices would be heard. At this meeting, the northern participants emphasized the importance of sexuality and the ordination of homosexual people in the Episcopal Church as something on which the global Communion needed to discipline the Episcopal Church properly. This led to the Kuala Lumpur Statement, intended as a "study document" on sexuality and Christian faith, which was then used by northern conservative Episcopalians in their lobbying and advocacy efforts in the United States.[29]

The Kuala Lumpur Statement is brief and largely consists of emphasizing that the authority of scripture must not be questioned and that scripture is itself clear that the only valid Christian sexual option is sexual activity within the context of a heterosexual marriage. In addition, the statement expresses concern specifically about the ordination of homosexuals and same-sex blessings. "This leads us to express concern about mutual accountability and interdependence within our Anglican Communion"—language specifically echoing the MRI document, a reminder that in a postcolonial era missional relationships required respect for those with whom one is in relationship, namely the previously ignored churches of the Global South.[30] Returning from Kuala Lumpur, several leaders of the Episcopalian conservative groups organized an umbrella group, First Promise, which was explicitly intended to develop and cultivate these relationships with bishops from outside of the Episcopal Church, at this point Rwanda and Singapore.

Prior to the burgeoning international controversy, homosexuality per se was not a major issue in the African churches or in the Asian churches, though neither was it accepted or celebrated. The acceptance of people identifying themselves as "gay" or "lesbian," which were not usually "native" concepts about sexuality and sexual identity, was complicated by the history of colonialism, which in the postcolonial era made the idea of cultural imposition more sensitive. Were not these beliefs being "forced" on people by Westerners? Had not the Christian teaching always been about Christian marriage, and had not these ways been taken up at significant personal and social cost by the Christian converts and their churches? The history of complex and diverse sexual practices in precolonial cultures was not always available to be compared with the current situation, and in many previously colonized nations same-sex behavior had been criminalized by

British legal codes, which had not generally been challenged in the transition to independence.

In addition, personal sexual behavior and "Christian marriage" were often seen as very strongly connected to Christian identity—even for those who did not live up to its standards. As Kevin Ward notes, in East Africa it was common for well-respected members of the community to be refused communion because of their sexual history, but they nonetheless supported the church; when one bishop attempted to make communion available to everyone without distinction, the people were not supportive.[31] In the 1970s, Bishop Henry Okullu of Kenya wrote about church discipline and marriage primarily in terms of premarital sex and pregnancy, which were much more common, as the most pastorally complicated issues.[32] The focus on homosexuality was simply not the highest priority in the local context. It was, however, a point of connection and mutual agreement between some leaders in Asia and Africa and some American Episcopalians, in both cases because it matched their missional orientation.[33]

At Lambeth 1998, therefore, these leaders worked with American Episcopalian conservatives to put forward a resolution emphasizing that scripture condemned homosexual activity. At the conference itself, to the shock of American Episcopalians who were "progressive" and assumed that their concern for the economic development and human rights of the nations of the Global South would be a point of partnership, the vote for Lambeth Resolution 1.10 was a multiracial, international coalition of white conservatives and Global South leaders, while those who were working for the inclusion of gay people in the church, seen as an important aspect of God's mission in the world, were almost all white and from Global North churches.

While the issues of international debt did indeed show a Global South/ North progressive alliance, these issues certainly did not get as much press as the debate over human sexuality. Miranda Hassett notes that just as sexuality was a more interesting issue than debt to the media covering the Lambeth Conference, so too it appeared, to many individuals, to be more salient to the church. Sexuality is a personal moral issue that can be controlled by the individual and is traditionally connected to sin and purity, while perhaps poverty and debt relief are less so and certainly more difficult for an individual to take responsibility for.[34]

Both economic justice and sexuality, for both sides, were important in Christian mission. For one group, both were important because of a commitment to justice and inclusion as God's mission in the world; for the other group, the more important missional goal was for the church to discipline sexual behavior among Christians, thus protecting the traditions and teachings seen as central to God's commands and an individual's relationship with God.

In dry, formal language, Lambeth I.10 insistend upon sexual activity only within heterosexual marriages as the teaching of scripture, nonetheless expressed pastoral love and care to people who "experience themselves as having a homosexual orientation," "cannot advise the legitimising or blessing of same-sex unions nor ordaining those involved in same-gender unions," requested that the Primates of the churches and the Anglican Consultative Council "establish a means of monitoring" work relating to sexuality, and commended the Kuala Lumpur statement and the authority of scripture to the ACC to help in said "monitoring."[35] For many Episcopalians, who had begun to experience a church that welcomed gay and lesbian and trans people, Lambeth I.10, was bewildering and frightening, inexplicable in its dismissal of the missional values of love and inclusion. For other Episcopalians, Lambeth I.10 was a victory.

The Episcopal Church did not take Lambeth 1.10 as "binding," or as authoritative guidance to church decisionmaking. No resolution from Lambeth had ever been binding upon any Anglican national church, each of which was autonomous, and for which Lambeth was traditionally a council of bishops providing their thoughts on various issues, not a legislature or governing body of any kind. However, this led to Episcopalian conservatives striking out further away from the Episcopal Church.

In 1998, two American priests put their congregations under the oversight of a Rwandan bishop, thus deeply complicating traditional Anglican understandings of the geographical nature of a diocese and the authority of a bishop within it. A bishop could not operate in the diocese of another bishop without permission. However, under the premise that the local Episcopal bishop was invalid in his authority due to the Episcopal Church's continued insistence on the rightness of ordaining homosexual people and denying that they were inherently sinful and wrong in their sexual lives, this innovation was justified. Now there were two Anglican bishops, from different national churches, both in the apostolic succession, claiming ecclesial authority in the same geographic area.[36] In 2000, two American bishops from the First Promise network were consecrated in Kuala Lumpur by six bishops, including Bishop Emmanuel Kolini of Rwanda and Bishop Moses Tay of

Singapore, and a retired American bishop, Christopher FitzSimons Allison of South Carolina.

The involvement of the Bishop of Singapore in the proceedings, as well as the continued location of these meetings in Kuala Lumpur, points again to the complex role of global ecumenical networks in this story. The Singaporean church had been deeply affected by the American Episcopalian charismatic movement, which had begun in 1960 with Reverend Dennis Bennett's experience of speaking in tongues and his book about the experience of the Holy Spirit, *Nine o'Clock in the Morning*. The previous bishop of Singapore, Joshua Chiu Ban, had attended a World Council of Churches meeting in 1972 and received a copy of the book from a Fijian attendee. He then experienced a charismatic renewal and shifted his entire missional orientation from the ecumenical to the charismatic/evangelical, restructuring the church in Singapore around charismatic experience as well as biblical literalism. His candidates for ordination now attended a local evangelical Bible institute rather than the ecumenical seminary they had previously attended. Bishop Moses Tay, his successor and a consecrator of the American dissident bishops, was shaped by this context.[37]

Thus even before the watershed year of 2003, when the election of the openly gay priest Gene Robinson as Bishop of New Hampshire was confirmed by General Convention in Minneapolis, a strong infrastructure network was already in place to receive and encourage dissidents and defections from the Episcopal Church. This network claimed to be the true Anglican church in North America, with support and recognition from other members of the Anglican Communion (though not from the Archbishop of Canterbury, considered to be the validating point of membership in the Communion).

The Archbishop of Canterbury, Rowan Williams, responded to Bishop Robinson's consecration with anxiety and dismay, even though he personally was sympathetic to the argument supporting the ordination of gay and lesbian individuals. He anticipated, correctly, that there would be significant backlash from the Communion at large. As a result, the Anglican Communion needed to dive deeply into its own nature and the ways in which its churches would relate to one another: Through greater centralization or control? Or retaining provincial autonomy? There would need to be extensive work in building relationships across stated divides at all levels.[38]

Confronted with the hostility of other parts of the Anglican Communion, and accusations of causing schism, the Episcopal Church apologized for causing pain but would not withdraw its support of gay and lesbian people in church and society. Several bishops attempted to take their dioceses out of the Episcopal Church, and eventually a new united Anglican denomination was developed with dissident bishops consecrated by bishops from other parts of the Communion, bringing together the Anglo-Catholic groups that had left the church over women's ordination, and the evangelical groups protesting the new shifts in mission and understandings of sexuality. While evangelicals were prominent in the reaction to the sexuality debate, two of the bishops who attempted to take their dioceses out of the church were high Anglo-Catholics from dioceses that had refused to ordain women (Jack Iker of Fort Worth and John-David Schofield of San Joaquin).[39]

General Convention accepts dioceses who petition to join it and accept the constitution and canons of the Episcopal Church; can a diocese also vote to reject the constitution and canons and leave the church (as Pittsburgh and San Joaquin did)? The legal argument was that they could not, thanks to a piece of church legislation passed by General Convention in 1979 in response to the growing threat of schism over civil rights and women's ordination. The canon, sometimes called the Dennis Canon after its drafter, states that any parish or congregational property is held in trust for the Episcopal Church as a whole, and thus if individuals or even congregations leave the denomination, the property remains to Episcopalians. However, as some congregations and dioceses expressed their frustration with the full inclusion of LGBTQ people in the church by leaving and attempting to claim the property as well, state laws also came into play. A chaotic and complex series of lawsuits would greet the first female presiding bishop, Katherine Jefferts Schori, when she was elected in 2006. She was given the unenviable task of attempting to discipline errant bishops after a series of informal decisions stemming from the conscience clause made it ever more difficult to do so.[40]

American Episcopalians who held to a *missio dei* missional understanding and who, like Browning in the 1970s, rejoiced at the church's move toward inclusion and justice, were shocked by the rejection of the church's actions by other parts of the Communion, including the refusal of seven Anglican primates to take communion with Presiding Bishop Schori in 2007. Issuing a statement on the website of the Church of Nigeria, the Anglican bishops wrote, "We are unable to come to the holy table with the presiding bishop of the Episcopal Church because to do so would be a violation of scriptural teaching and the traditional Anglican understanding."[41]

Summary

The shift in missional orientation among Episcopalian "progressives" in the controversy over sexuality was prominent in the language used to describe the importance of "inclusion" as missional work, attending to God's work in the world as a *missio dei* church should. Those Episcopalians and global Anglicans who did not share the ideal of inclusion and social transformation as missional worked from a different missiological orientation, that of the planting of the true faith among people through conversion and church-building—and indeed, the new Anglican Church in North America (ACNA) denomination within the United States has focused on church-planting and expansion. Because of the emphasis on continuing the true faith, and different understandings of this within the ACNA churches—the Anglo-Catholic group still objects to the ordination of women, while the evangelical groups permit it at episcopal discretion—even within ACNA there have been threats of "impaired communion."

The ways in which the controversy over sexuality was internationalized were also structured by the global histories of colonialism and mission. Mission understandings of Christian marriage and sexuality were stamped upon converts and their churches via church discipline, so deeply that it became a central aspect of church life and identity. The legacy and bitterness of colonial exploitation transferred to the idea that homosexuality itself was a Western imposition upon other cultures (despite long histories of same-sex activity and relationships in non-Western cultures). On a very simple and practical level, the lack of "traditional" mission work in the Episcopal Church after the *missio dei* shifts, and even from the earlier period of mission critique in the 1930s and 1940s, meant that there were very few Episcopalians "on the ground" in other parts of the world building cross-cultural relationships of mutual understanding and transformation. Only those holding to the evangelical view of mission, who had not embraced *missio dei*, still sent traditional missionaries who could build these relationships and provide an opportunity for mutual learning about different ways of being Christian in the world.[42]

The missional shift in the Episcopal Church which began in the 1930s and gathered critical mass in the 1960s provided the internal engine for this developing mission of inclusion as a mark of justice, itself a mark of God's mission in the world to which the church must attend. The schisms and controversies within the Episcopal Church itself mean that at the time of this writing

(2021), it is likely that *missio dei* orientation is now the dominant mode of missional theology within the church, emphasized and formed with the support of the Book of Common Prayer and its baptismal covenant and ecclesiology. The controversy over sexuality may or may not have lasting results in terms of Episcopalian ability or desire to engage more substantially with the other members of the Anglican Communion, but it has certainly moved the church itself in a direction which will be explored in the conclusion's reflection, toward an effort to heal and respond to the scars left upon the church by its own history and involvement in racism and imperialism through its past missional practices.

Conclusion

In 2016, the presiding bishop of the Episcopal Church, Michael Curry, visited Standing Rock Reservation, a hub of Sioux Episcopalianism. He and many other Episcopalian clergy and laypeople had gone in support of a Native-led protest against the Dakota Access Pipeline, which had been planned to bring oil beneath the water and lands of the Sioux people, risking contamination and encouraging increased dependence upon fossil fuels. Care for creation had also become important in understanding God's mission and was a frequent topic of conversation among Episcopalians; an Episcopalian priest, Sally Bingham, had organized a national network of religious organizations striving to respond to climate change. The moment captured symbolically another extension of the *missio dei* orientation of the Episcopal Church as it attempted to come alongside God's mission in the world. This mission included racial reconciliation, as Curry was the first African American presiding bishop, fulfilling the dreams and hopes of the nineteenth-century African American Episcopalians for participation as equals in the governance of the church, and connections with the Sioux Episcopalian and non-Christian community in respect and with an attitude of listening and humility. The church has continued to reflect upon and to attempt to better understand its history in terms of racial and gender justice and inclusion in various ways, including by conducting a racial audit of the church.[1]

This study has argued that missional transformation has gone in multiple directions, to demonstrate that the "sending churches" of the "great century" were changed by mission just as the "younger churches" were shaped by it, and that in a sense the experience of colonialism itself has provided the context of a missional shift. This transformation didn't just happen in the late 1990s, as if the Episcopal Church suddenly woke up and discovered that there were Anglicans in other parts of the world. It developed over a centuries-long process of trial and error, tragedy, pain, reflection, and practice. The mainline Protestant denominations, including Episcopalians, are

Mission, Race, and Empire. Jennifer C. Snow, Oxford University Press. © Oxford University Press 2024.
DOI: 10.1093/oso/9780197598948.003.0016

what they are *because of* missional transformations in theology, practice, and identity since the settlement of North America by European Christians.

The history of missions shows that the process of *contextualization* occurs whenever Christianity moves from one culture into another. It is also sometimes called "syncretism" or "inculturation," and scholars have given much attention to how it occurred as European missionaries brought Christianity into non-European contexts, particularly in the nineteenth and twentieth centuries.[2] The study of contextualization has generally perceived the sending churches as stable sources of discrete practices and teachings, which are transformed in the receiving churches.

I have argued here that contextualization existed in Global North churches as well. It has not always been about things as simple as shifts in ritual practice or materials; there have also been theological and organizational pattern shifts less visible to the eye. In the American colonial period, this process of contextualization was largely unrecognized for its radical innovations and creativity—and those involved would have been deeply upset to think of themselves as innovators. They valued their historical and personal ties to the metropole, of which they saw themselves as the inheritors and teachers. Yet innovation occurred through trial and error: the establishment of educational institutions for "heathens" and enslaved people; the development of the theology of Christian slavery and mastery; new organizations intended specifically to expand the Church of England's reach in colonial contexts; baptism of adults from non-Christian backgrounds; catechisms and baptismal promises specifically designed for those in servitude; sacramental activities that took place in homes rather than churches; multicongregational parishes; growing churches through persuasion and argument with other varieties of Christianity; sustaining congregations through donations from voluntary organizations rather than local taxes and tithing; sustaining a church organization that required a bishop without one for almost two hundred years.

Training the lens on mission shifts our understanding of the narratives and personalities of church history; the "marginal" becomes central to the story. Relationships between people and groups, and how those relationships were shaped and perceived by those on all sides, are now the focus of the story rather than an aside. Mission history also demonstrates that contextualization is often resisted, seen as a devaluing of the inherited tradition and centers of authority, or as not being sufficiently theologically orthodox. The contemporary conflicts over sexuality are certainly one example of the hostile reaction to contextualization in this sense. The colonial history of the American church shows this resistance as well. The work of mission itself is an innovation, and resistance to some types of contextualization often, ironically, led to missional creativity and contextual developments. For instance, the development of the Society for the Propagation of the Gospel was founded in part to ensure that metropolitan expectations for religious life and leadership, particularly theological education, were not dropped to meet the new context. "Enthusiasm" was rejected as an innovation and as a threat to the developing values of order and control of the colonial church.

In other cases, the rejection of creative contextualization led to a cramping of potential missional paths. This is most obvious in the loss of the African American and Native American voices in the church's governance after the American Revolution. What would General Convention have been in the nineteenth century had Mohawk Anglicans been present in 1784 and their contributions to structures of decision-making and relationship building been placed in conversation with Bishop White's *Case of the Episcopal Churches Considered* and Bishop Seabury's insistence on episcopal authority? What would the Episcopal Church have become had Absalom Jones been welcomed to the diocesan and general conventions, if the church as a whole, and not only the Black community, had protested the Fugitive Slave Act and insisted on building relationships across racial boundaries? What if Bishop Kip had supported the Chinese and Black missions in early California and protested the murder of California Indians, instead of simply accepting violent racism and exclusion as natural to society? These missed opportunities can never be recovered and have shaped a church that still struggles to respond to the scars of race and empire.

In the continental United States, the Episcopal Church has an uncomfortable sibling relationship with the Anglican Church in North America (and vice versa). Global Christian debates over sexuality and gender reflect a deep and real missional split across which mutual comprehension is difficult. The ways in which this relationship plays out over the next decades remain uncertain. Presiding Bishop Curry has emphasized the importance of evangelism within the church, attempting to reincorporate the aspects of mission that had been set aside by the ecumenical movement in the mid-twentieth century. The theological work of truly grasping a full sense of mission, reconnecting the sense of mission as God's work with a love of invitation, incorporation, and sharing across difference, is still incomplete.

This struggle has taken place throughout the world Christian networks, transdenominationally as well as within the Anglican Communion. The *missio dei* orientation of the modern Episcopal Church arises from this struggle to come to terms with the complex and painful history of missional imbrication in colonialism and racism, as well as the experience of missionaries in discovering the goodness and worth of non-Christian religions and cultures. The modern controversies over sexuality and gender in world Christianity reflect this very real missional distinction. The missional orientation of twenty-first-century Episcopalianism is thus the result of a deep transformation and nuanced reflection on the costs and limits of a missional past practice. It is not a light shift or a recent one, nor is it about political correctness or taking Christianity or the Bible unseriously, as evangelicals sometimes accuse; it is deeply serious, centuries in the making, and now placed in the denominational heart through its liturgy and sacramental practice. The decades to come will show how deeply this missional commitment will affect Christianity and its life in the world.

Notes

Introduction

1. Katharine Gerbner, *Christian Slavery: Conversion and Race in the Protestant Atlantic World* (Philadelphia: University of Pennsylvania Press, 2018); David A. Hollinger, *Protestants Abroad: How Missionaries Tried to Change the World but Changed America* (Princeton, NJ: Princeton University Press, 2017).
2. George E. Tinker, *Missionary Conquest: The Gospel and Native American Cultural Genocide* (Minneapolis, MN: Fortress Press, 1993); Vine Deloria, "GCSP: The Demons at Work," *Historical Magazine of the Protestant Episcopal Church* 48, no. 1 (March 1979): 83–92.

Chapter 1

1. In this chapter, I deliberately use the word "English" instead of "British," as Jamestown was supported as an extension of specifically English power and influence.
2. The main binary categorization of peoples for early modern Europeans encountering non-European cultures was "heathen" and "Christian," a division that for some seems to have lasted until the late nineteenth century. Later categories of humanity built in complex ways upon these two categories in the development of racial ideology, with significant developments in the early colonial period around slavery. Katharine Gerbner, *Christian Slavery: Conversion and Race in the Protestant Atlantic World* (Philadelphia: University of Pennsylvania Press, 2018); Rebecca Anne Goetz, *The Baptism of Early Virginia*, reprint edition (Baltimore, MD: Johns Hopkins University Press, 2012). For later developments, see Jennifer Snow, *Protestant Missionaries, Asian Immigrants, and Ideologies of Race in America, 1850–1924* (New York: Routledge, 2006). Katherine Gin Lum argues that the category of "heathen" continues to underlie racial categories to the present: Katherine Gin Lum, *Heathen: Religion and Race in American History* (Cambridge: Harvard University Press, 2022).
3. Amos Yong and Barbara Brown Zikmund, eds., *Remembering Jamestown: Hard Questions about Christian Mission* (Eugene, OR: Pickwick Publications, 2010).
4. Rebecca Anne Goetz, "The Nanziatticos and the Violence of the Archive: Land and Native Enslavement in Colonial Virginia," *Journal of Southern History* 85, no. 1 (February 2019): 33–60.
5. Nicholas M. Beasley, "Ritual Time in British Plantation Colonies, 1650–1780," *Church History* 76, no. 3 (2007): 541–68; Nicholas M. Beasley, "Domestic Rituals: Marriage

and Baptism in the British Plantation Colonies, 1650–1780," *Anglican and Episcopal History* 76, no. 3 (September 2007): 327–57; Rebecca Anne Goetz, "'The Child Should Be Made a Christian': Baptism, Race and Identity in the Seventeenth Century Chesapeake," in *Assumed Identities: The Meanings of Race in the Atlantic World*, ed. John D. Garrigus and Christopher Morris (Arlington: Texas A&M University Press, 2010), 46–70; Gerbner, *Christian Slavery*.

6. Space does not permit an overview of the Reformation in any detail; for an introduction to this enormous historiography and an overview of the events, see Diarmaid MacCulloch, *The Reformation* (New York: Viking, 2004). The English Reformation has its own highly contested historiography, which again cannot be addressed here. For recent engagement with these issues, see Anthony Milton, ed., *The Oxford History of Anglicanism*, vol. 1: *Reformation and Identity c. 1520–1662*, reprint edition (Oxford: Oxford University Press, 2019).

7. The generalized distinctions between early Catholic and Protestant missions, and the conceptual/practical weakness of Protestant missions prior to the nineteenth century, are described in many works attempting to trace methods of Christian mission over world history, the most influential being David J. Bosch, *Transforming Mission: Paradigm Shifts in Theology of Mission*, 20th anniversary edition (Maryknoll, NY: Orbis, 2011). In addition, see Carlos F. Cardoza-Orlandi and Justo L. Gonzalez, *To All Nations from All Nations: A History of the Christian Missionary Movement* (Nashville, TN: Abingdon Press, 2013); Robert L. Gallagher, *Encountering the History of Missions* (Grand Rapids, MI: Baker Academic, 2017); Carla Gardina Pestana, "The Missionary Impulse in the Atlantic World, 1500–1800: Or How Protestants Learned to Be Missionaries," *Social Sciences and Missions* 26, no. 1 (2013): 9–39; Kristen Block, "Conversion as a Communal System of the Protestant Atlantic World," *Church History* 88, no. 3 (September 2019): 759–62.

8. Arthur Barlowe, 1584, cited in Michael Leroy Oberg, "Between 'Savage Man' and 'Most Faithful Englishman' Manteo and the Early Anglo-Indian Exchange, 1584–1590," *Itinerario* 24, no. 2 (July 2000): 146–69.

9. Alden T. Vaughan, "Namontack's Itinerant Life and Mysterious Death: Sources and Speculations," *Virginia Magazine of History and Biography* 126, no. 2 (2018): 170–209; Alden T. Vaughan, "Powhatans Abroad: Virginia Indians in England," in *Envisioning an English Empire*, ed. Robert Appelbaum and John Wood Sweet (Philadelphia: University of Pennsylvania Press, 2005), 49–67; David B. Quinn, *Set Fair for Roanoke: Voyages and Colonies, 1584–1606* (Chapel Hill: published for America's Four Hundredth Anniversary Committee by the University of North Carolina Press, 1985).

10. Increase N. Tarbox, *Sir Walter Ralegh and His Colony in America, Including the Charter of Queen Elizabeth in His Favor, March 25, 1584, with Letters, Discources, and Narratives of the Voyages Made to America at His Charges, and Descriptions of the Country, Commodities, and Inhabitants.* (Boston: Prince Society, 1884), 103, adjusted for modern spelling.

11. Thomas Hariot, "A Brief and True Report of the New Found Land of Virginia (1588)," ed. Paul Royster, *Electronic Texts in American Studies* 20, n.d., https://digitalcommons.

unl.edu/cgi/viewcontent.cgi?article=1020&context=etas, 36, adjusted for modern spelling.

12. Oberg, "Between 'Savage Man' and 'Most Faithful Englishman' Manteo." For additional information on the culture of the Roanoke and Croatan, and how the native people may have understood their interaction with the attempts to plant a colony at Roanoke, see Helen C. Rountree, *Manteo's World: Native American Life in Carolina's Sound Country before and after the Lost Colony* (Chapel Hill: University of North Carolina Press, 2021).

13. Helen C. Rountree, *Manteo's World: Native American Life in Carolina's Sound Country before and after the Lost Colony* (Chapel Hill: University of North Carolina Press, 2021), 94.

14. Avalon Project, "The First Charter of Virginia; April 10, 1606," March 1, 2005, https://web.archive.org/web/20050301092128/http://www.yale.edu/lawweb/avalon/states/va01.htm.

15. The general outline of events at Jamestown below draws heavily on Lyon Gardiner Tyler, ed., *Narratives of Early Virginia, 1606–1625*, Original Narratives of Early American History (New York: Barnes & Noble, 1959); H. C. Porter, *The Inconstant Savage: England and the North American Indian, 1500–1660* (London: Duckworth, 1979); Karen Ordahl Kupperman, *Pocahontas and the English Boys: Caught between Cultures in Early Virginia* (New York: NYU Press, 2019); Karen Ordahl Kupperman, *The Jamestown Project* (Cambridge, MA: Belknap Press of Harvard University Press, 2009); Bernard Bailyn, *The Barbarous Years: The Peopling of British North America: The Conflict of Civilizations, 1600–1675* (New York: Vintage, 2012).

16. James D. Rice, "War and Politics: Powhatan Expansionism and the Problem of Native American Warfare," *The William and Mary Quarterly* 77, no. 1 (2020): 3–32.

17. Bailyn, *The Barbarous Years*; Tyler, *Narratives of Early Virginia*. Kupperman in *The Jamestown Project* notes that the archaeological record demonstrates that in addition to the pressures of two cultures in conflict over land, the early years of the Jamestown settlement coincided with the worst local drought in centuries; thus the Powhatan and their allies were themselves short of food and reasonably resented the constant demands of the English to give up or trade their harvests.

18. On the role of young people in intercultural brokerage at Jamestown, see Kupperman, *Pocahontas and the English Boys*; Vaughan, "Namontack's Itinerant Life and Mysterious Death."

19. Tyler, *Narratives of Early Virginia*, 423–24.

20. Tyler, *Narratives of Early Virginia*, 20, 23, 109.

21. Philip L. Barbour, "The Riddle of the Powhatan 'Black Boyes,'" *Virginia Magazine of History and Biography* 88, no. 2 (1980): 148–54.

22. Helen C. Rountree, "Powhatan Priests and English Rectors: World Views and Congregations in Conflict," *American Indian Quarterly* 16, no. 4 (1992): 485–500.

23. Alexander Whitaker, *Good newes from Virginia: Sent to the Counsell and Company of Virginia, resident in England. From Alexander Whitaker, the Minister of Henrico in Virginia: Wherein also is a narration of the present state of that countrey, and our colonies there* (London: 1613), 24, 40. Available from Internet Archive, https://archive.org/details/goodnewesfromvir00whit/page/n5/mode/2up.

24. Oberg, "Between 'Savage Man' and 'Most Faithful Englishman' Manteo."

25. Tyler, *Narratives of Early Virginia*, 239.

26. For a detailed description of Pocahontas's experiences in England and how her presence was used for publicity purposes, see Kupperman, *Pocahontas and the English
Boys*. On the excitement generated in England on fundraising for Henricus College
and conversion of Powhatan children, see Porter, *The Inconstant Savage*, 434–50.

27. Kupperman, *The Jamestown Project*, 272.

28. "Letter from George Thorpe to Sir Edwin Sandys (May 15–16, 1621)," in *The Records
of the Virginia Company of London* (Washington, DC: Government Printing Office,
1906), 3: 446. Available from Internet Archive, https://archive.org/details/records
ofvirgini03virg/page/446/mode/2up, spelling modernized. See also Porter, *The
Inconstant Savage*, 453.

29. Tyler, *Narratives of Early Virginia*, 359–60.

30. William Strachey, *History of Travell into Virginia Britania*, 1612, quoted in Porter, *The
Inconstant Savage*, 333.

31. Tyler, *Narratives of Early Virginia*, 348.

32. Tyler, *Narratives of Early Virginia*; Porter, *The Inconstant Savage*.

33. Tyler, *Narratives of Early Virginia*, 359–61; Kupperman, *Pocahontas and the English
Boys*, chapter 6.

34. Edward Waterhouse, *Declaration of the State of the Colony of Virginia*, 1622, quoted in
Porter, *The Inconstant Savage*, 461.

35. Porter, *The Inconstant Savage*, 513–22. One instance of this oft-repeated pattern is
described in detail by Goetz, "The Nanziatticos and the Violence of the Archive."

36. Bailyn, *The Barbarous Years*, 169.

37. Bailyn, *The Barbarous Years*, 176–79; Ira Berlin, *Many Thousands Gone: The First Two
Centuries of Slavery in North America* (Cambridge, MA: Belknap Press, 1998). Goetz,
Baptism of Early Virginia, 57.

38. Gerbner, *Christian Slavery*.

39. Goetz, *The Baptism of Early Virginia*, 86–111.

40. "An Act Declaring That Baptisme of Slaves Doth Not Exempt Them from Bondage
(1667)," Encyclopedia Virginia, accessed March 19, 2020, https://www.encyclopediav
irginia.org/_An_act_declaring_that_baptisme_of_slaves_doth_not_exempt_them_
from_bondage_1667.

41. Gerbner, *Christian Slavery*, notes this interpretation among white planters in the
Caribbean, which is reflected in Godwyn's work in 1680.

42. Morgan Godwyn, *The Negro's [and] Indians Advocate, Suing for Their Admission to the
Church* (London, 1680); John Fout, "The Explosive Cleric: Morgan Godwyn, Slavery,
and Colonial Elites in Virginia and Barbados, 1665–1685," *Theses and Dissertations*,
January 1, 2005.

43. Samuel Purchas, *Hakluytus Postumus*, 1625, quoted in Porter, *The Inconstant
Savage*, 481.

44. For example, John Martin, "The manner howe to bring in the Indians into subjection without making an utter expertation," 1622, quoted in Porter, *The Inconstant*

Savage, 471. See discussion of Hakluyt's goals for colonizing in Michael Leroy Oberg, *Dominion and Civility: English Imperialism and Native America, 1585–1685* (Ithaca: Cornell University Press, 1999), 17.

Chapter 2

1. Andrew M. Koke, "Communication in an Anglican Empire: Edmund Gibson and His Commissaries, 1723–1748," *Anglican and Episcopal History* 84, no. 2 (June 2015): 166–202; Jacob M. Blosser, "Unholy Communion: Colonial Virginia's Deserted Altars and Inattentive Anglicans," *Virginia Magazine of History and Biography* 127, no. 4 (2019): 266–99.

2. John K. Nelson, *A Blessed Company: Parishes, Parsons, and Parishioners in Anglican Virginia, 1690–1776* (Chapel Hill: University of North Carolina Press, 2003); Daniel O'Connor, *Three Centuries of Mission: The United Society for the Propagation of the Gospel, 1701–2000* (New York: Continuum, 2000).

3. Thomas Bray, *Rev. Thomas Bray: His Life and Selected Works Relating to Maryland* (New York: Arno Press, 1972), 82.

4. O'Connor, *Three Centuries of Mission*; James Bell, *The Imperial Origins of the King's Church in Early America 1607–1783*, ed. J. C. D. Clark (New York: Palgrave Macmillan, 2004).

5. Bell, *Imperial Origins*; Bray, *Rev. Thomas Bray*, 85.

6. O'Connor, *Three Centuries of Mission*; Travis Glasson, *Mastering Christianity: Missionary Anglicanism and Slavery in the Atlantic World* (New York: Oxford University Press, 2017).

7. Bray, *Rev. Thomas Bray*; William Stevens Perry, *The History of the American Episcopal Church, 1587–1883*, vol. 1: *The Organization and Progress of the American Church*, 2 vols. (Boston: J. R. Osgood, 1885).

8. John Frederick Woolverton, *Colonial Anglicanism in North America* (Detroit, MI: Wayne State University Press, 1984); William Wilson Manross, *A History of the American Episcopal Church* (New York: Morehouse-Gorham, 1935).

9. Nelson, *A Blessed Company*; Edward L. Bond, "Anglican Theology and Devotion in James Blair's Virginia, 1685–1743: Private Piety in the Public Church," *Virginia Magazine of History and Biography* 104, no. 3 (1996): 313–40; Edward L. Bond, *Damned Souls in a Tobacco Colony: Religion in Seventeenth-Century Virginia* (Macon, GA: Mercer University Press, 2000).

10. Nelson, *A Blessed Company*.

11. Nelson, *A Blessed Company*.

12. Rebecca Anne Goetz, *The Baptism of Early Virginia*, reprint edition (Baltimore, MD: Johns Hopkins University Press, 2012); W. M. Jacob, "'In Love and Charity with Your Neighbours . . .': Ecclesiastical Courts and Justices of the Peace in England in the Eighteenth Century," in *Retribution, Repentance, and Reconciliation: Papers Read at the 2002 Summer Meeting and the 2003 Winter Meeting of the Ecclesiastical History*

Society, Studies in Church History vol. 40 (Woodbridge, NY: Ecclesiastical History Society, 2004), 205–17; Bond, "Anglican Theology and Devotion in James Blair's Virginia."

13. This development of distinguishing church participation between elites and enslaved people is further traced in Nicholas M. Beasley, *Christian Ritual and the Creation of British Slave Societies, 1650–1780* (Athens: University of Georgia Press, 2009).

14. Beasley, *Christian Ritual and the Creation of British Slave Societies*; Lauren F. Winner, *A Cheerful and Comfortable Faith: Anglican Religious Practice in the Elite Households of Eighteenth-Century Virginia* (New Haven, CT: Yale University Press, 2010).

15. Bell, *Imperial Origins*; Woolverton, *Colonial Anglicanism in North America*, chapter 4; Perry, *History of the American Episcopal Church*, 148–205.

16. Manross, *A History of the American Episcopal Church*, chapter 3 and 6; Perry, *History of the American Episcopal Church*, 247–55; Bell, *Imperial Origins*.

17. Manross, *A History of the American Episcopal Church*, chapter 5; Perry, *History of the American Episcopal Church*, 247–55.

18. Charles Woodmason, *The Carolina Backcountry on the Eve of the Revolution: The Journal and Other Writings of Charles Woodmason, Anglican Itinerant* (Chapel Hill: Omohundro Institute and University of North Carolina Press, 1969).

19. Katharine Gerbner, *Christian Slavery: Conversion and Race in the Protestant Atlantic World* (Philadelphia: University of Pennsylvania Press, 2018), 112–28.

20. Glasson, *Mastering Christianity*; Gerbner, *Christian Slavery*; John Fout, "The Explosive Cleric: Morgan Godwyn, Slavery, and Colonial Elites in Virginia and Barbados, 1665–1685," *Theses and Dissertations*, January 1, 2005; Morgan Godwyn, *The Negro's [and] Indians Advocate, Suing for Their Admission to the Church* (London, 1680).

21. Gerbner, *Christian Slavery*; Glasson, *Mastering Christianity*; O'Connor, *Three Centuries of Mission*.

22. Beasley, *Christian Ritual and the Creation of British Slave Societies*; Gerbner, *Christian Slavery*; Glasson, *Mastering Christianity*.

23. Lauren F. Winner, *A Cheerful and Comfortable Faith: Anglican Religious Practice in the Elite Households of Eighteenth-Century Virginia* (New Haven, CT: Yale University Press, 2010), 112; Gerbner, *Christian Slavery*. Glasson, *Mastering Christianity*, 116–17.

24. Annette Laing, "'Heathens and Infidels'? African Christianization and Anglicanism in the South Carolina Low Country, 1700–1750," *Religion and American Culture: A Journal of Interpretation* 12, no. 2 (2002): 197–228; Gerbner, *Christian Slavery*.

25. Glasson, *Mastering Christianity*; Rebecca Goetz, *Baptism of Early Virginia* (Baltimore: Johns Hopkins University Press, 2012); Gary Hart, "Virginia's Black Codes: Uncovering the Evolution of Legal Slavery," *OAH Magazine of History* 17, no. 3 (2003): 35–36.

26. Laing, "'Heathens and Infidels'?"

27. Gerbner, *Christian Slavery*; Glasson, *Mastering Christianity*, 78–80.

28. Glasson, *Mastering Christianity*, 128; Gerbner, *Christian Slavery*; Richard I. Shelling, "Benjamin Franklin and the Dr. Bray Associates," *Pennsylvania Magazine of History and Biography* 63, no. 3 (1939): 282–93.

29. "Letter from Virginia Slaves to Bishop Edmund Gibson (August 4, September 8, 1723)," Encyclopedia Virginia, https://www.encyclopediavirginia.org/_Letter_from_Virginia_Slaves_to_Bishop_Edmund_Gibson_August_4_September_8_1723.

30. Thomas Ingersoll, "'Releese Us out of This Cruell Bondegg': An Appeal from Virginia in 1723," *William and Mary Quarterly* 51, no. 4 (October 1994): 777–82.

31. Alan Taylor, *The Divided Ground: Indians, Settlers, and the Northern Borderland of the American Revolution* (New York: Alfred A. Knopf, 2006); H. Ward Jackson, "The Seventeenth Century Mission to the Iroquois," *Historical Magazine of the Protestant Episcopal Church* 29, no. 3 (September 1960): 240–55.

32. Timothy J. Shannon, *Iroquois Diplomacy on the Early American Frontier* (New York: Viking Adult, 2008); George E. DeMille, *A History of the Diocese of Albany, 1704–1923*, Church Historical Society Publication, no. 16 (Philadelphia, PA: Church Historical Society, 1946).

33. Shannon, *Iroquois Diplomacy*.

34. For more detail on the complex political situation within the Haudenosaunee and the development of the pro-English movement, see Daniel Richter, *The Ordeal of the Longhouse: The Peoples of the Iroquois League in the Era of European Colonization* (Chapel Hill: University of North Carolina, 1992).

35. Shannon, *Iroquois Diplomacy*; DeMille, *A History of the Diocese of Albany*; Jackson, "The Seventeenth Century Mission to the Iroquois." Daniel Richter, *The Ordeal of the Longhouse*, 230–33.

36. Taylor, *The Divided Ground*.

37. Shannon, *Iroquois Diplomacy*; Taylor, *The Divided Ground*.

38. Taylor, *The Divided Ground*. Richter, *Ordeal of the Longhouse*; Elizabeth Elbourne, "Family Politics and Anglo-Mohawk Diplomacy: The Brant Family in Imperial Context," *Journal of Colonialism and Colonial History* 6, no. 3 (2005): n.p. doi:10.1353/cch.2006.0004.

39. Taylor, *The Divided Ground*; Shannon, *Iroquois Diplomacy*. Isabel Thompson Kelsay, *Joseph Brant, 1743–1807, Man of Two Worlds* (Syracuse: Syracuse University Press, 1984).

40. Taylor, *The Divided Ground*.

41. Taylor, *The Divided Ground*; Shannon, *Iroquois Diplomacy*; Owanah Anderson, *400 Years: Anglican/Episcopal Mission among American Indians* (Cincinnati, OH: Forward Movement Publications, 1997).

42. O'Connor, *Three Centuries of Mission*.

Chapter 3

1. William Stevens Perry, *The History of the American Episcopal Church, 1587–1883*, vol. 2: *The Organization and Progress of the American Church* (Boston: J. R. Osgood, 1885), 335–60.

2. William Wilson Manross, *A History of the American Episcopal Church* (New York: Morehouse-Gorham, 1935); Robert W. Prichard, *A History of the*

Episcopal Church—Third Revised Edition: Complete through the 78th General Convention, revised edition (New York: Morehouse, 2014).

3. S. D. McConnell, *History of the American Episcopal Church, 1600–1915*, 11th edition (Milwaukee, WI: Morehouse, 1916), 142.

4. Stephen J Stein, "George Whitefield on Slavery: Some New Evidence," *Church History* 42, no. 2 (June 1973): 243–56.

5. Katharine Gerbner, *Christian Slavery: Conversion and Race in the Protestant Atlantic World* (Philadelphia: University of Pennsylvania Press, 2018); Stein, "George Whitefield on Slavery"; Philippa Koch, "Slavery, Mission, and the Perils of Providence in Eighteenth-Century Christianity: The Writings of Whitefield and the Halle Pietists," *Church History* 84, no. 2 (June 2015): 369–93.

6. Rowan Strong, *Anglicanism and the British Empire c. 1700–1850* (Oxford: Oxford University Press, 2007); Frederick V. Mills, *Bishops by Ballot: An Eighteenth Century Ecclesiastical Revolution* (New York: Oxford University Press, 1978).

7. Nancy L. Rhoden, *Revolutionary Anglicanism: The Colonial Church of England Clergy during the American Revolution* (New York: New York University Press, 1999).

8. Walter H. Stowe, "William White Ecclesiastical Statesman," *Historical Magazine of the Protestant Episcopal Church*, January 1953, 370–78; Rhoden, *Revolutionary Anglicanism*.

9. Walter Herbert Stowe, *The Life and Letters of Bishop William White: Together with the Services and Addresses Commemorating the One Hundred Fiftieth Anniversary of His Consecration to the Episcopate*, Church Historical Society Publication No. 9 (New York: Morehouse, 1937); Richard Salomon, "William White: The Case of the Episcopal Churches Considered," *Historical Magazine of the Protestant Episcopal Church*, January 1953, 433–506.

10. Salomon, "William White," 462.

11. Salomon, "William White," 465.

12. Salomon, "William White," 480.

13. Ross N. Hebb, "Bishop Charles Inglis and Bishop Samuel Seabury: High Churchmanship in Varying New World Contexts," *Anglican and Episcopal History* 76, no. 1 (March 2007): 61–88; Perry, *History of the American Episcopal Church*.

14. E. Clowes Chorley, "The Election and Consecration," *Historical Magazine of the Protestant Episcopal Church* 3, no. 3 (September 1934): 146–91.

15. Chorley, "The Election and Consecration," 148.

16. Hebb, "Bishop Charles Inglis and Bishop Samuel Seabury."

17. Perry, *History of the American Episcopal Church*; Manross, *A History of the American Episcopal Church*.

18. Chorley, "The Election and Consecration," 157.

19. William Douglass, *Annals of the First African Church, in the United States of America, Now Styled the African Episcopal Church of St. Thomas, Philadelphia, in Its Connection with the Early Struggles of the Colored People to Improve Their Condition, with the Co-operation of the Friends, and Other Philanthropists; Partly Derived from the Minutes of a Beneficial Society, Established by Absalom Jones, Richard Allen and Others, in 1787, and Partly from the Minutes of the Aforesaid Church* (Philadelphia, PA: King

& Baird, printers, 1862); "Giving the Full History: Who Owned Absalom Jones?," *Episcopal News Service*, February 11, 2008, https://episcopalchurch.org/library/arti cle/giving-full-history-who-owned-absalom-jones; George F. Bragg, *History of the Afro-American Group of the Episcopal Church* (Baltimore, MD: Church Advocate Press, 1922).

20. Douglass, *Annals of the First African Church*.

21. Douglass, *Annals of the First African Church*.

22. Douglass, *Annals of the First African Church*.

23. Douglass, *Annals of the First African Church*; Ann Conrad Lammers, "The Rev. Absalom Jones and the Episcopal Church: Christian Theology and Black Consciousness in a New Alliance," *Historical Magazine of the Protestant Episcopal Church* 51, no. 2 (June 1982): 159–84.

24. Lammers, "The Rev. Absalom Jones and the Episcopal Church"; Jennifer Snow, "The Altar and the Rail: 'Catholicity' and African American Inclusion in the 19th Century Episcopal Church," *Religions* 12, no. 4 (April 2021): 224.

25. Douglass, *Annals of the First African Church*; Snow, "The Altar and the Rail."

26. Douglass, *Annals of the First African Church*; Thomas E. Will, "Liberalism, Republicanism, and Philadelphia's Black Elite in the Early Republic: The Social Thought of Absalom Jones and Richard Allen," *Pennsylvania History: A Journal of Mid-Atlantic Studies* 69, no. 4 (2002): 558–76; Absalom Jones et al., *A Narrative of the Proceedings of the Black People, during the Late Awful Calamity in Philadelphia, in the Year 1793: And a Refutation of Some Censures, Thrown upon Them in Some Late Publications* (Philadelphia, PA: Printed for the authors, by William W. Woodward, at Franklin's Head, no. 41, Chesnut-Street, 1794).

27. Douglass, *Annals of the First African Church*, 82–84.

28. Absalom Jones, *A Thanksgiving Sermon, Preached January 1, 1808, in St. Thomas's (or the African Episcopal) Church, Philadelphia, on Account of the Abolition of the African Slave Trade, on That Day, by the Congress of the United States* (Philadelphia, PA: Rhistoric, 1966).

Chapter 4

1. Walter Herbert Stowe, "A Turning Point: The General Convention of 1835," *Historical Magazine of the Protestant Episcopal Church* 4, no. 3 (September 1935): 165.

2. Julia Chester Emery, *A Century of Endeavor, 1821–1921: A Record of the First Hundred Years of the Domestic and Foreign Missionary Society of the Protestant Episcopal Church in the United States of America* (New York: Department of Missions, 1921).

3. John K. Nelson, *A Blessed Company: Parishes, Parsons, and Parishioners in Anglican Virginia, 1690–1776* (Chapel Hill: University of North Carolina Press, 2003); William Wilson Manross, *The Episcopal Church in the United States, 1800–1840: A Study in Church Life*, Studies in History, Economics and Public Law, No. 441 (New York: P. S. King & Son, Columbia University Press, 1938), 39.

4. Manross, *Episcopal Church*, 144; William Stevens Perry, *The History of the American Episcopal Church, 1587–1883*, vol. 2: *The Organization and Progress of the American Church* (Boston: J. R. Osgood, 1885), 39, 64.

5. Caroline Baytop Sinclair, *Abingdon Church: A Chronology of Its History 1650–1970.* (Gloucester County, VA: n.p., 1972).

6. Sinclair, *Abingdon Church*.

7. Emma Jones Lapansky-Warner, "The Episcopal Church in Early Pennsylvania," in *This Far by Faith: Tradition and Change in the Episcopal Diocese of Pennsylvania*, ed. David R. Contosta (University Park: Pennsylvania State University Press, 2012), 39.

8. Walter H. Stowe, "William White Ecclesiastical Statesman," *Historical Magazine of the Protestant Episcopal Church*, January 1953, 370–78.

9. Charles D. Cashdollar, "New Growth and New Challenges, 1820–1840," in *This Far by Faith: Tradition and Change in the Episcopal Diocese of Pennsylvania*, ed. David R. Contosta (University Park: Pennsylvania State University Press, 2012), 113.

10. Lapansky-Warner, "The Episcopal Church in Early Pennsylvania."

11. Greenough White, *An Apostle of the Western Church: Memoir of the Right Reverend Jackson Kemper . . . First Missionary Bishop of the American Church, with Notices of Some of His Contemporaries; a Contribution to the Religious History of the Western States* (New York: T. Whittaker, 1900).

12. Stowe, "A Turning Point," 169; White, *An Apostle of the Western Church*, 25.

13. Perry, *History of the American Episcopal Church*, 2:238–39.

14. Divers Clergy to the Rev. Jackson Kemper (Committee/Supply of Vacant Churches), 1822, 1823 (n.d.), MISC: Incl: Committee to Supply Vacant Church, Diocese of Pennsylvania Archives, Lutheran Seminary, Mt. Airy.

15. John B. Wallace, "John B. Wallace to Jackson Kemper," September 20, 1824, MISC: Incl: Committee to Supply Vacant Church, Divers Clergy to Rev. Jackson Kemper, 1824, Diocese of Pennsylvania Archives, Lutheran Seminary, Mt. Airy.

16. White, *An Apostle of the Western Church*, 26.

17. George E. (George Edmed) DeMille, "The Recovery of the Episcopal Church in Up-state New York after the Revolutionary War," *Historical Magazine of the Protestant Episcopal Church* 13, no. 3 (September 1944): 236.

18. DeMille, "The Recovery of the Episcopal Church," 236.

19. George E. (George Edmed) DeMille, "Erie Water and the Episcopal Church," *Historical Magazine of the Protestant Episcopal Church* 39, no. 4 (December 1970): 383–88.

20. Manross, *Episcopal Church*, 114.

21. Robert Bruce Mullin, *Episcopal Vision/American Reality: High Church Theology and Social Thought in Evangelical America* (New Haven, CT: Yale University Press, 1986).

22. Manross, *Episcopal Church*; Charles R. Henery, *Yankee Bishops: Apostles in the New Republic, 1783 to 1873*, Studies in Episcopal and Anglican Theology, vol. 7 (New York: Peter Lang, 2015).

23. Mullin, *Episcopal Vision/American Reality*.

24. Manross, *Episcopal Church*; Henery, *Yankee Bishops*; Mullin, *Episcopal Vision/American Reality*.

25. DeMille, "The Recovery of the Episcopal Church," 246–47. Nash was eventually priested by Bishop Moore in 1801.

26. Manross, *Episcopal Church*.

27. Cashdollar, "New Growth and New Challenges."

28. John S. Stone, *Memoir of the Life of the Rt. Rev. Alexander Viets Griswold, D.D: Bishop of the Protestant Episcopal Church in the Eastern Diocese* (Philadelphia, PA: Stavely and McCalla, 1844); Henery, *Yankee Bishops*.

29. White, *An Apostle of the Western Church*, 45–47.

30. Quoted in Perry, *History of the American Episcopal Church*, 2:228–29.

31. Emery, *Century of Endeavor*; White, *An Apostle of the Western Church*; Philander Chase, *The Reminiscences of Bishop Chase (Now Bishop of Illinois)* (New York: A. V. Blake, 1844); Henry Caswall, *America and the American Church* (London: Rivington, 1839).

32. White, *An Apostle of the Western Church*, 62; Cashdollar, "New Growth and New Challenges."

33. Stone, *Memoir of the Life of the Rt. Rev. Alexander Viets Griswold*, 238–39.

34. Emery, *Century of Endeavor*, 34.

35. Emery, *Century of Endeavor*, 48.

36. Stone, *Memoir of the Life of the Rt. Rev. Alexander Viets Griswold*, 246.

37. Howard Greene and Elizabeth Pruessing, *The Reverend Richard Fish Cadle: A Missionary of the Protestant Episcopal Church in the Territories of Michigan and Wisconsin in the Early Nineteenth Century* (Waukesha, WI: Privately printed by Davis-Greene Corp., 1936), 77; Emery, *Century of Endeavor*.

38. I have not found any written record of the infraction for which the boys were punished.

39. Greene and Pruessing, *The Reverend Richard Fish Cadle*, 75–80.

40. Emery, *Century of Endeavor*; Manross, *Episcopal Church*.

41. Stowe, "A Turning Point"; Emery, *Century of Endeavor*.

42. Henery, *Yankee Bishops*.

43. Stowe, "A Turning Point," 178.

44. White, *An Apostle of the Western Church*; Walter Herbert Stowe, "Why Dr. Francis Lister Hawks Declined His Election as First Missionary Bishop of the Southwest," *Historical Magazine of the Protestant Episcopal Church* 9, no. 1 (March 1940): 90–92.

45. White, *An Apostle of the Western Church*, 156.

46. Emery, *Century of Endeavor*, 76.

47. White, *An Apostle of the Western Church*, 129.

48. Manross, *Episcopal Church*.

49. Perry, *History of the American Episcopal Church*, 2:257.

50. White, *An Apostle of the Western Church*.

51. Henery, *Yankee Bishops*.

52. Cashdollar, "New Growth and New Challenges"; DeMille, "Erie Water and the Episcopal Church."

53. Manross, *Episcopal Church*, 68.

54. My interpretation here follows the majority of early Episcopalian interpreters of this period of early expansion, including Emery, *Century of Endeavor*; Perry, *History of the American Episcopal Church*; Manross, *Episcopal Church*.

Chapter 5

1. Isaac DeGrasse's diary, cited in John Jay, *Caste and Slavery in the American Church*. (New York, 1843), 16.
2. Quoted in George F. Bragg, *History of the Afro-American Group of the Episcopal Church* (Baltimore, MD: Church Advocate Press, 1922), 38.
3. Episcopal Church, Diocese of Virginia, *Journal of the Convention of the Protestant Episcopal Church of the Diocese of Virginia [Serial]* (Richmond, VA: B. R. Wren, 1842), 7.
4. Bragg, *History of the Afro-American Group of the Episcopal Church*, 36.
5. Julia Chester Emery, *A Century of Endeavor, 1821–1921: A Record of the First Hundred Years of the Domestic and Foreign Missionary Society of the Protestant Episcopal Church in the United States of America* (New York: Department of Missions, 1921), 80.
6. Emery, *A Century of Endeavor*, 80.
7. N. Brooks Graebner, "The Episcopal Church and Race in Nineteenth-Century North Carolina," *Anglican and Episcopal History* 78, no. 1 (March 2009): 92; Tammy K. Byron, "A Catechism for Their Special Use: Slave Catechism in the Antebellum South" (PhD dissertation, University of Arkansas, 2008), 131; Erin Runions, "Keeping the Children Captive," SSRC, The Immanent Frame, September 5, 2018, https://tif.ssrc.org/2018/09/05/keeping-the-children-captive/. Thanks to Erin Runions for pointing me toward these sources on catechisms for enslaved people. The catechetical focus on the sexuality of African American enslaved people is echoed by obsessive attention to "Christian marriage" among Christian missionaries of all denominations in Africa itself. See Jennifer Snow, "The Troubled Knot: Tying Church Discipline to 'Christian Marriage' in African Contexts," *Journal of Ecclesiastical History* 71, no. 1 (January 2020): 135–53.
8. Emilie Amt, "Down from the Balcony: African Americans and Episcopal Congregations in Washington County, Maryland, 1800–1864," *Anglican and Episcopal History* 86, no. 1 (March 2017): 9.
9. Emery, *Century of Endeavor*, 80.
10. Emery, *Century of Endeavor*, 114.
11. "Negroes: Christian Instruction to Slaves," *Spirit of Missions*, May 1844.
12. Susan Markey Fickling, *Slave-Conversion in South Carolina, 1830–1860* (Columbia: University of South Carolina, 1924), 32. For more details on the ways in which white mistresses were involved in disciplining and controlling enslaved people, see Stephanie E. Jones-Rogers, *They Were Her Property: White Women as Slave Owners in the American South* (New Haven: Yale University Press, 2019).

13. Byron, "A Catechism for Their Special Use," 75.

14. Fickling, *Slave-Conversion in South Carolina*, 33.

15. "The Episcopal Church in Virginia, 1607–2007," *Virginia Magazine of History and Biography* 115, no. 2 (2007): 261; Byron, "A Catechism for Their Special Use." See also Runions, "Keeping the Children Captive."

16. Graebner, "The Episcopal Church and Race in Nineteenth-Century North Carolina," 89.

17. "The Episcopal Church in Virginia," 263; Diana Butler Bass, *Standing against the Whirlwind: Evangelical Episcopalians in Nineteenth-Century America*, Religion in America Series (New York: Oxford University Press, 1995), 147–48.

18. Quoted in Graebner, "The Episcopal Church and Race in Nineteenth-Century North Carolina," 91.

19. Craig D. Townsend, *Faith in Their Own Color: Black Episcopalians in Antebellum New York City*, Religion and American Culture (New York: Columbia University Press, 2005), 6–10.

20. Quoted in Bragg, *History of the Afro-American Group of the Episcopal Church*, 90–94.

21. The congregation appears to have been worshiping separately from Trinity Church in 1809, but the church was built and consecrated in 1819. See Townsend, *Faith in Their Own Color*.

22. Townsend, *Faith in Their Own Color*.

23. Townsend, *Faith in Their Own Color*, 53–59.

24. Townsend, *Faith in Their Own Color*, 68; J. R. Oldfield, *Alexander Crummell (1819–1898) and the Creation of an African-American Church in Liberia*, Studies in the History of Missions, vol. 6 (Lewiston, NY: E. Mellen Press, 1990).

25. Townsend, *Faith in Their Own Color*, 68. Philadelphia was also one of the northern cities least friendly to free Black people in this period. See Marie Conn, "The Church and the City, 1840–1865," in *This Far by Faith: Tradition and Change in the Episcopal Diocese of Pennsylvania*, ed. David R. Contosta (University Park: Pennsylvania State University Press, 2012), 155–77.

26. William Douglass, *Annals of the First African Church, in the United States of America, Now Styled the African Episcopal Church of St. Thomas, Philadelphia, in Its Connection with the Early Struggles of the Colored People to Improve Their Condition, with the Co-operation of the Friends, and Other Philanthropists; Partly Derived from the Minutes of a Beneficial Society, Established by Absalom Jones, Richard Allen and Others, in 1787, and Partly from the Minutes of the Aforesaid Church* (Philadelphia, PA: King & Baird, 1862), 142.

27. Townsend, *Faith in Their Own Color*, 180.

28. Douglass, *Annals of the First African Church*, 158–52.

29. Jennifer Snow, "The Altar and the Rail: 'Catholicity' and African American Inclusion in the 19th Century Episcopal Church," *Religions* 12, no. 4 (April 2021): 224.

30. John S. Stone, *Memoir of the Life of the Rt. Rev. Alexander Viets Griswold, D.D: Bishop of the Protestant Episcopal Church in the Eastern Diocese* (Philadelphia, PA: Stavely and McCalla, 1844), 244–46.

31. Oldfield, *Alexander Crummell (1819–1898) and the Creation of an African-American Church in Liberia*.

32. Oldfield, *Alexander Crummell (1819–1898) and the Creation of an African-American Church in Liberia*.

33. C. Peter Williams, "The Church Missionary Society and the Indigenous Church in the Second Half of the Nineteenth Century: The Defense and Destruction of the Venn Ideals," in *Converting Colonialism: Visions and Realities in Mission History, 1706–1914*, ed. Dana Robert (Grand Rapids, MI: Eerdmans, 2008), 86–111; Brian Stanley, *The Bible and the Flag: Protestant Missions and British Imperialism in the Nineteenth and Twentieth Centuries* (Leicester: Apollos, 1990).

34. Williams, "Defense and Destruction." For a twentieth-century example, see William L. Sachs, "'Self-Support': The Episcopal Mission and Nationalism in Japan," *Church History* 58, no. 4 (1989): 489–501.

35. Oldfield, *Alexander Crummell (1819–1898) and the Creation of an African-American Church in Liberia*.

36. Robert Bruce Mullin, *Episcopal Vision/American Reality: High Church Theology and Social Thought in Evangelical America* (New Haven, CT: Yale University Press, 1986).

37. Robert Trendel, "John Jay II: Antislavery Conscience of the Episcopal Church," *Historical Magazine of the Protestant Episcopal Church* 45, no. 3 (September 1976): 237–52.

38. Townsend, *Faith in Their Own Color*.

39. Ronald Levy, "Bishop Hopkins and the Dilemma of Slavery," *Pennsylvania Magazine of History and Biography* 91, no. 1 (1967): 56–71.

40. John Henry Hopkins, *A Scriptural, Ecclesiastical, and Historical View of Slavery: From the Days of the Patriarch Abraham, to the Nineteenth Century: Addressed to the Right Rev. Alonzo Potter . . .* (New York: W. I. Pooley, 1864), 17.

41. Levy, "Bishop Hopkins and the Dilemma of Slavery"; Hopkins, *A Scriptural, Ecclesiastical, and Historical View of Slavery*.

42. "The Episcopal Church in Virginia," 244.

43. Bass, *Standing against the Whirlwind*, 150.

44. Bass, *Standing against the Whirlwind*, 154.

45. Bass, *Standing against the Whirlwind*, 164.

46. Bass, *Standing against the Whirlwind*, 166.

47. "Pastoral Letter of the House of Bishops of the Protestant Episcopal Church," October 17, 1862, Anglican History, http://anglicanhistory.org/usa/mcilvaine/pastoral1862.html.

48. Douglass, *Annals of the First African Church*, 168–69.

49. Snow, "The Altar and the Rail."

50. Graebner, "The Episcopal Church and Race in Nineteenth-Century North Carolina," 93.

51. "Life and Letters of Phillips Brooks—1, Page Iii by Alexander V. G. Allen," Online Research Library: Questia, accessed June 20, 2020, https://archive.org/details/phillipsbrooksm00allegoog/page/135/mode/2up (p. 428 in book).

Chapter 6

1. Katherine Gin Lum, *Heathen: Religion and Race in American History* (Cambridge, MA: Harvard University Press, 2022).

2. Jennifer Snow, *Protestant Missionaries, Asian Immigrants, and Ideologies of Race in America, 1850–1924* (New York: Routledge, 2007).

3. Quoted in Alvin W. Skardon, *Church Leader in the Cities: William Augustus Muhlenberg* (Philadelphia: University of Pennsylvania Press, 1971), 154.

4. Skardon, *Church Leader in the Cities,* 113. Because of complications in the legal shifts, Holy Communion was not formally incorporated until 1867; it did not join diocesan convention until after Muhlenberg retired as rector in 1873.

5. Ann Ayres, *Evangelical Catholic Papers: Comprising Addresses, Lectures, and Sermons from Writings of Rev. W. A. Muhlenberg, D.D. during the Last Fifty Years,* 2nd Series (New York: St. Johnland Press, 1877), 79. For the general background of free churches and pew rents, see Skardon, *Church Leader in the Cities,* 106–13.

6. Skardon, *Church Leader in the Cities,* 115; Jacob M. Blosser, "Unholy Communion: Colonial Virginia's Deserted Altars and Inattentive Anglicans," *Virginia Magazine of History and Biography* 127, no. 4 (2019): 266–99.

7. Skardon, *Church Leader in the Cities,* 109.

8. Ayres, *Evangelical Catholic Papers,* 112–19.

9. Skardon, *Church Leader in the Cities,* 216.

10. Skardon, *Church Leader in the Cities,* 216.

11. Episcopal Church and Alonzo Potter, eds., *Memorial Papers: The Memorial: With Circular and Questions of the Episcopal Commission; Report of the Commission; Contributions of the Commissioners; and Communications from Episcopal and Non-Episcopal Divines* (Philadelphia, PA: E. H. Butler, 1857), 52–55.

12. Episcopal Church and Potter, *Memorial Papers,* 60.

13. Episcopal Church and Potter, *Memorial Papers,* 71–80.

14. Edward Lambe Parsons, "The Church Rush in the Gold Rush: The Beginnings of the Episcopal Church in San Francisco," *Historical Magazine of the Protestant Episcopal Church* 19, no. 2 (June 1950): 80–89.

15. John Edward Rawlinson, "William Ingraham Kip, Tradition, Conflict, and Transition" (PhD dissertation, Graduate Theological Union, 1981), 89.

16. Gregory Thomas Olson, "Civilizing Men: Protestant Religion in Gold Rush San Francisco, 1848–1856" (PhD dissertation, Claremont Graduate University, 2008), 61.

17. Olson, "Civilizing Men," 79.

18. Olson, "Civilizing Men"; Benjamin Madley, *An American Genocide: The United States and the California Indian Catastrophe, 1846–1873* (New Haven, CT: Yale University Press, 2016).

19. Rawlinson, "William Ingraham Kip," 93–107.

20. Douglas Ottinger Kelley, *History of the Diocese of California from 1849 to 1914* (San Francisco, CA: Bureau of Information and Supply, 1915), 39.

21. Rawlinson, "William Ingraham Kip," 108–26.

22. Rawlinson, "William Ingraham Kip," 180–201.

23. William Ingraham Kip, "The Chinese in California," *Spirit of Missions*, 1855; Rawlinson, "William Ingraham Kip," 123; "Proceedings of the Board of Missions," *Spirit of Missions*, 1854.

24. Rawlinson, "William Ingraham Kip," 142; Lionel U. Ridout, "The Church, the Chinese, and the Negroes in California 1849–1893," *Historical Magazine of the Protestant Episcopal Church* 28, no. 2 (June 1959): 115–38.

25. "Chinese in California," *Spirit of Missions*, 1855, 519.

26. "Chinese in California"; Ridout, "The Church, the Chinese, and the Negroes in California."

27. Rawlinson, "William Ingraham Kip"; Ridout, "The Church, the Chinese, and the Negroes in California," 128; Wesley Stephen Woo, "Protestant Work among the Chinese in the San Francisco Bay Area, 1850–1920 (California)," PhD dissertation, Graduate Theological Union, Berkeley, California, 1984, 87–88.

28. Ridout, "The Church, the Chinese, and the Negroes in California," 131.

29. Jennifer Snow, *Protestant Missionaries, Asian Immigrants, and Ideologies of Race in America, 1850–1924* (New York: Routledge, 2006).

30. Madley, *An American Genocide*.

31. Rawlinson, "William Ingraham Kip," 203.

32. Rawlinson, "William Ingraham Kip," 208.

33. Ridout, "The Church, the Chinese, and the Negroes in California," 134; "Peter Williams Cassey—St. Peter's Episcopal Church in Redwood City, CA"; Jerry Drino, "Sermon Honoring the Rev. Peter Williams Cassey and Annie Besent Cassey by the Rev. Jerry William Drino, June 7, 2009, Trinity Cathedral, San Jose," received via electronic communication from Lynn Hoke, archivist of the Diocese of North Carolina, September 15, 2020; Delilah L. Beasley, *The Negro Trail Blazers of California* (Los Angeles, CA, 1919).

34. Ridout, "The Church, the Chinese, and the Negroes in California," 134–35.

35. Ridout, "The Church, the Chinese, and the Negroes in California," 137; Rawlinson, "William Ingraham Kip," 237. On Cassey in North Carolina, electronic communication with Brooks Graebner, historiographer of the diocese, September 13, 2020. Bragg's list of African American ordinations in the nineteenth century includes Cassey's deaconing but no record of ordination to the priesthood. George F. Bragg, *History of the Afro-American Group of the Episcopal Church* (Baltimore, MD: Church Advocate Press, 1922).

36. Madley, *An American Genocide*. I am following Madley in using the term "California Indian" as the descriptor preferred by the native peoples of California.

37. Madley, *An American Genocide*.

38. Brendan C. Lindsay, *Murder State: California's Native American Genocide, 1846–1873* (Lincoln: University of Nebraska Press, 2012); Madley, *An American Genocide*.

39. Rawlinson, "William Ingraham Kip," 65.

40. William Ingraham Kip, "The Early Days of My Episcopate: By the Right Rev. William Ingraham Kip" (New York: Thomas Whittaker and Bible House, 1892), 133–34, https://tile.loc.gov/storage-services//service/gdc/calbk/062.pdf.

41. Rawlinson, "William Ingraham Kip," 153–57. On the development of scientific racism in California religious contexts, see Snow, *Protestant Missionaries, Asian Immigrants, and Ideologies of Race in America*. Kip's use of "Anglo-Saxon," "natives," and "mongrels" in other writings points to this particular ideology of racism. See his description of his journey through the Isthmus of Panama, and his denigration of Johann Sutter's inability to compete with "Anglo-Saxon" energy: Kip, "The Early Days of My Episcopate," 60.

42. M. A. DeWolfe Howe, *Memoirs of the Life and Services of the Rt. Rev. Alonzo Potter, D.D., LL.D: Bishop of the Protestant Episcopal Church in the Diocese of Pennsylvania* (Philadelphia: J.B. Lippincott Co., 1871), 15–22, 233; Jennifer Snow, "The Altar and the Rail: 'Catholicity' and African American Inclusion in the 19th Century Episcopal Church," *Religions* 12, no. 4 (April 2021): 224; Diana Butler Bass, *Standing against the Whirlwind: Evangelical Episcopalians in Nineteenth-Century America*, Religion in America Series (New York: Oxford University Press, 1995).

Chapter 7

1. Calbraith B. (Calbraith Bourn) Perry, *Twelve Years among the Colored People: A Record of the Work of Mount Calvary Chapel of S. Mary the Virgin, Baltimore* (New York: J. Pott, 1884), 133.

2. Perry's book does not specify—and perhaps Perry did not know—the tribal origins of one of the two Native American children who were brought to the Baltimore home for colored orphans, Albert Wazhewakka Morgan. Elizabeth Amelia (Chatry) returned with Minnegoshig to the Ojibwa.

3. Ibram X. Kendi, *Stamped from the Beginning: The Definitive History of Racist Ideas in America*, reprint edition (New York: Bold Type Books, 2017); George E. Tinker, *Missionary Conquest: The Gospel and Native American Cultural Genocide* (Minneapolis, MN: Fortress Press, 1993).

4. Episcopal Church, *Journal of a Tour on the "Indian Territory," Performed by Order of the Domestic Committee of the Board of Missions of the Protestant Episcopal Church in the Spring of 1844* (New York: Published for the Domestic Committee of the Board of Missions by Daniel Dana Jr., 1844).

5. Episcopal Church, *Journal of a Tour on the "Indian Territory,"* 4–5, 35. On the Christian Home, see Dana Robert, "The 'Christian Home' as a Cornerstone of Anglo-American Missionary Thought and Practice," in *Converting Colonialism: Visions and Realities in Mission History, 1706–1914*, ed. Dana Robert (Grand Rapids, MI: Eerdmans, 2008), 134–65.

6. Episcopal Church, *Journal of a Tour on the "Indian Territory,"* 18.

7. Carole A. Barrett, "'Into the Light of Christian Civilization': St. Elizabeth's Boarding School for Indian Children (1886–1967)" (PhD dissertation, University of North Dakota, 2005).

8. Episcopal Church, *Journal of a Tour on the "Indian Territory,"* 20; *Journal of the Proceedings of the Bishops, Clergy, and Laity, of the Protestant Episcopal Church in*

the United States of America, Assembled in a General Convention Held in St Andrew's Church, Philadelphia, from October 2d to October 22d, Inclusive, in the Year of Our Lord 1844 (New York: James A. Sparks, 1844), 179.

9. Thomas C. Reeves, "James Lloyd Breck and the Founding of Nashotah House," *Anglican and Episcopal History* 65, no. 1 (March 1996): 50–81; William P. Haugaard, "The Missionary Vision of James Lloyd Breck in Minnesota," *Historical Magazine of the Protestant Episcopal Church* 54, no. 3 (September 1985): 241–51.

10. Owanah Anderson, *400 Years: Anglican/Episcopal Mission among American Indians* (Cincinnati, OH: Forward Movement Publications, 1997), 47; Martin N. Zanger, "'Straight Tongue's Heathen Wards': Bishop Whipple and the Episcopal Mission to the Chippewas," in *Churchmen and the Western Indians, 1820–1920*, ed. Clyde A. Milner II and Floyd A. O'Neil (Norman: University of Oklahoma Press, 1985), 177–214.

11. Anderson, *400 Years*; Zanger, "'Straight Tongue's Heathen Wards.'"

12. Anderson, *400 Years*; Zanger, "'Straight Tongue's Heathen Wards'"; Haugaard, "The Missionary Vision of James Lloyd Breck in Minnesota."

13. Anderson, *400 Years*; Zanger, "'Straight Tongue's Heathen Wards,'" 179.

14. Zanger, "'Straight Tongue's Heathen Wards,'" 187.

15. Zanger, "'Straight Tongue's Heathen Wards,'" 185.

16. Zanger, "'Straight Tongue's Heathen Wards,'" 181–85.

17. Zanger, "'Straight Tongue's Heathen Wards,'" 196–99.

18. J. A. Gilfillan and Enmegabowh, *The Church and the Indians* (New York: Office of the Indian Commission, Protestant Episcopal Church, 1876), 4; Zanger, "'Straight Tongue's Heathen Wards'"; Tinker, *Missionary Conquest*.

19. Gilfillan and Enmegabowh, *The Church and the Indians*, 6.

20. Gilfillan and Enmegabowh, *The Church and the Indians*, 11.

21. Gilfillan and Enmegabowh, *The Church and the Indians*, 19.

22. Anderson, *400 Years*, 52–53.

23. Anderson, *400 Years*; William Joseph Barnds, "The Ministry of the Reverend Samuel Dutton Hinman, among the Sioux," *Historical Magazine of the Protestant Episcopal Church* 38, no. 4 (December 1969): 393–401.

24. Anderson, *400 Years*. On the history of missions among the Dakota prior to the Episcopalian presence, and the hostile division between traditionalists and farmers, see Daphne D. Hamborg, "The Impact of Dakota Missions on the Development of the U.S.-Dakota War of 1862" (master's thesis, Minnesota State University, Mankato, 2012).

25. Anderson, *400 Years*.

26. Hamborg, "The Impact of Dakota Missions on the Development of the U.S.-Dakota War of 1862"; Andrew Scott Brake, *Man in the Middle: The Reform and Influence of Henry Benjamin Whipple, the First Episcopal Bishop of Minnesota* (Lanham, MD: University Press of America, 2005); Anderson, *400 Years*, 56.

27. Anderson, *400 Years*, 58.

28. Anderson, *400 Years*, 59; Tinker, *Missionary Conquest*; Brake, *Man in the Middle*, 83–86.

29. Anderson, *400 Years*, 60.

30. Anderson, *400 Years*, 62.

31. Tinker, *Missionary Conquest*; Episcopal Church, *Journal of a Tour on the "Indian Territory"*; Brake, *Man in the Middle*, 86.

32. Brake, *Man in the Middle*, 108; Tinker, *Missionary Conquest*, 104.

33. Brake, *Man in the Middle*, 83, 209.

34. Barrett, "'Into the Light of Christian Civilization,'" 27. The standard work on the denominational division of reservation work, on which Barrett draws, is Francis Paul Prucha, *American Indian Policy in Crisis: Christian Reformers and the Indian, 1865–1900* (Norman: University of Oklahoma Press, 1976).

35. Brake, *Man in the Middle*, 97; Tinker, *Missionary Conquest*; Barrett, "'Into the Light of Christian Civilization,'" 32.

36. Zanger, "'Straight Tongue's Heathen Wards,'" 200.

37. Barrett, "'Into the Light of Christian Civilization,'" 30.

38. Anderson, *400 Years*, 68.

39. Anderson, *400 Years*, 85.

40. Barrett, "'Into the Light of Christian Civilization,'" 8–9; Anderson, *400 Years*, 97.

41. Lawrence L. Brown, "The Episcopal Church in the Arid West, 1865–1875: A Study in Adaptability," *Historical Magazine of the Protestant Episcopal Church* 30, no. 3 (September 1961): 142–72; Episcopal Church, General Convention, *Journal of the Proceedings of the Bishops, Clergy and Laity of the Protestant Episcopal Church in the United States of America* (Philadelphia, PA: S. Potter, 1871).

42. Henry Benjamin Whipple, *Niobrara, Sermon Preached at the Consecration of Rev. William Hobart Hare, S.T.D.: As Missionary Bishop of Niobrara* (Philadelphia, PA: M'Calla & Stavely, Printers, 1873), 12–13.

43. Tinker, *Missionary Conquest*.

44. Whipple, *Niobrara*, 15.

45. Edward S. Duncombe, "The Northern Arapahoe Experience of Episcopal Mission Work and United States Policy, 1883–1925," *Anglican and Episcopal History* 66, no. 3 (September 1997): 354–82; J. B. Wicks, "A Chapter from the Indian Territory: Story of the Indian Territory Mission," *Historical Magazine of the Protestant Episcopal Church* 3, no. 4 (December 1934): 262–69. On Oakerhater's training in upstate New York, I am grateful for the reports provided by Joan Green, archivist of the Episcopal Diocese of Central New York.

46. "The Soul of the Indian, by Charles Alexander Eastman (Ohiyesa)," Project Gutenberg, accessed October 15, 2020, https://www.gutenberg.org/files/340/340-h/340-h.htm; Duncombe, "The Northern Arapahoe Experience of Episcopal Mission Work and United States Policy"; Ella Deloria and Vine Deloria Jr., *Speaking of Indians* (Lincoln, NE: Bison Books, 1998).

Chapter 8

1. George F. Bragg, *The First Negro Priest on Southern Soil* (Baltimore, MD: Church Advocate Press, 1909), 23.

2. This interpretation builds on Eric Foner, *Reconstruction: America's Unfinished Revolution, 1863–1877*, revised edition (New York: Harper Perennial Modern Classics, 2014). On the exodus of Black Episcopalians, see Harold T. Lewis, *Yet with a Steady Beat: The African American Struggle for Recognition in the Episcopal Church* (Valley Forge, PA: Trinity Press International, 1996); J. Carleton Hayden, "After the War: The Mission and Growth of the Episcopal Church among Blacks in the South, 1865–1877," *Historical Magazine of the Protestant Episcopal Church* 42, no. 4 (December 1973): 403–27.

3. Robert A Bennett, "Black Episcopalians: A History from the Colonial Period to the Present," *Historical Magazine of the Protestant Episcopal Church* 43, no. 3 (September 1974): 238.

4. Hayden, "After the War," 408.

5. N. Brooks Graebner, "Historically Black Congregations in the Diocese of North Carolina, 1865–1959," Episcopal Diocese of North Carolina, November 15, 2018, 1–2, https://www.episdionc.org/uploads/files/_BOOKLET_-_Hist_Background_1865-1959.pdf.

6. Mary Sudman Donovan, "Educating the Former Slaves: Episcopal Freedom Schools, 1866–1877," *Anglican and Episcopal History* 87, no. 3 (September 2018): 295–306.

7. Hayden, "After the War," 419–21.

8. Calbraith B. (Calbraith Bourn) Perry, *Twelve Years among the Colored People: A Record of the Work of Mount Calvary Chapel of S. Mary the Virgin, Baltimore* (New York: J. Pott, 1884), 87–88.

9. Hayden, "After the War," 421.

10. Jerry Drino, "Sermon Honoring the Rev. Peter Williams Cassey and Annie Besent Cassey by the Rev. Jerry William Drino June 7, 2009, Trinity Cathedral, San Jose," received via electronic communication from Lynn Hoke, archivist of the Diocese of North Carolina, September 15, 2020.

11. N. Brooks Graebner, "The Rt. Rev. Thomas Atkinson (1807–1881): Advocate for an Apostolic and Catholic Church," *Anglican and Episcopal History* 86, no. 2 (June 2017): 148.

12. Perry, *Twelve Years among the Colored People*, 105–10.

13. David M. Dean, *Defender of the Race: James Theodore Holly, Black Nationalist Bishop* (Boston: Lambeth Press, 1979), 56.

14. Graebner, "Historically Black Congregations in the Diocese of North Carolina," 11.

15. James S. Russell, *Adventure in Faith* (Lawrenceville, VI: St Paul's College Museum and Archives, 2021), 16.

16. James Russell, *Adventure in Faith* (Lawrenceville, VA: James Solomon Russell–Saint Paul's College Museum and Archives, 2021), 16–19.

17. Russell, *Adventure in Faith*, 34.

18. Russell, *Adventure in Faith*, 39.

19. Russell, *Adventure in Faith*, 58–60.

20. Hayden, "After the War," 427.

21. Bragg, *The First Negro Priest on Southern Soil*, 18.

22. Rhondda Thomas, "'The First Negro Priest on Southern Soil': George Freeman Bragg, Jr. and the Struggle of Black Episcopalians in the South, 1824–1909," *Southern Quarterly* 50, no. 1 (Fall 2012): 79–101.

23. Dean, *Defender of the Race.*

24. J. Carleton Hayden, "James Theodore Holly (1829–1911) First Afro-American Episcopal Bishop: His Legacy to Us Today," *Journal of Religious Thought* 33, no. 1 (1976): 50–62.

25. Dean, *Defender of the Race*, 21.

26. Dean, *Defender of the Race*, 25–28.

27. Dean, *Defender of the Race*, 35–40.

28. William Hare was on good terms with Holly and very supportive of the mission when he was head of the Foreign Committee, but this was a very brief period as he was almost immediately elected missionary bishop of Niobrara.

29. Dean, *Defender of the Race*, 61.

30. Dean, *Defender of the Race*, 64.

31. Dean, *Defender of the Race*, 93; Hayden, "James Theodore Holly," 56.

32. "Facts about the Church's Mission in Haiti, by James Theodore Holly (1897)," Anglican History, accessed October 7, 2020, http://anglicanhistory.org/usa/jtholly/facts1897.html.

33. Dean, *Defender of the Race*, 28.

34. Hayden, "James Theodore Holly," 54.

35. Bragg, *The First Negro Priest on Southern Soil.*

36. Bragg, *The First Negro Priest on Southern Soil*, 18.

37. Holly quoted in George F. Bragg, *First Negro Priest on Southern Soil* (Baltimore: Church Advocate Press, 1909), 59.

38. George F. Bragg, *History of the Afro-American Group of the Episcopal Church* (Baltimore, MD: Church Advocate Press, 1922); George F. Bragg, *Afro-American Church Work and Workers* (Baltimore: Church Advocate Press, 1904); William Douglass, *Annals of the First African Church, in the United States of America, Now Styled the African Episcopal Church of St. Thomas, Philadelphia, in Its Connection with the Early Struggles of the Colored People to Improve Their Condition, with the Co-operation of the Friends, and Other Philanthropists; Partly Derived from the Minutes of a Beneficial Society, Established by Absalom Jones, Richard Allen and Others, in 1787, and Partly from the Minutes of the Aforesaid Church* (Philadelphia, PA: King & Baird, printers, 1862); Russell, *Adventure in Faith.*

39. N. Brooks Graebner, "One Great Fellowship of Love? Theological Convictions and Ecclesial Realities in the Racial History of the Diocese of North Carolina," Episcopal Diocese of North Carolina, November 16, 2017, 11, https://www.episdionc.org/uploads/images/one-great-fellowship-of-love-overview-of-racial-history_977.pdf.

40. Graebner, "One Great Fellowship of Love?," 7.

41. Perry, *Twelve Years among the Colored People*, 26.

42. Perry, *Twelve Years among the Colored People*, 30.

43. N. Brooks Graebner, "The Episcopal Church in Nineteenth Century North Carolina," *Anglican and Episcopal History* 78, no. 1 (2009): 91; Michael Taylor Malone, "Levi

Silliman Ives: Priest, Bishop, Tractarian, and Roman Catholic Convert" (PhD Dissertation, Duke University, 1970), 124–26.

44. Craig D. Townsend, *Faith in Their Own Color: Black Episcopalians in Antebellum New York City*, Religion and American Culture (New York: Columbia University Press, 2005); Douglass, *Annals of the First African Church*; Jennifer Snow, "The Altar and the Rail: 'Catholicity' and African American Inclusion in the 19th Century Episcopal Church," *Religions* 12, no. 4 (April 2021): 224; Bentley Manning, "The Rt. Rev. John Henry Hopkins: A Compromising Catholicity," *Sewanee Theological Review* 58, no. 2 (2015): 347–66; Graebner, "One Great Fellowship of Love?"

45. Graebner, "One Great Fellowship of Love?"; Graebner, "Historically Black Congregations in the Diocese of North Carolina"; Snow, "The Altar and the Rail"; "Confessions of the Diocese: A History of Race and Racism in the Diocese of Virginia (Draft)," 2012, https://71564dd6-a-62cb3a1a-s-sites.googlegroups.com/site/dovra cerelations/slave-trade-reports/DraftofA143ReportPDF1-1-12-12.pdf?attachauth= ANoY7cpTbSq5hQYmU5CuDEchsvA4CYAkgOPpRPM63e3IXgPmOQtHbr5CZJ llJf2zB7pRAHVaFK8xUCB1KPIkcXe4sTr2SWE4CKj_4iio2iJj7JD5qt1QywVre7dp 3XeDbvRLaXEr5yAStrPFePr5ySIfQNGMIJXiZU8xmr7ZcOqPld5UQ_OQXyqH4 nD8QFSiVVn1TI9Bw4im-PV1mJc9r1fKgTahNTrPgTNzBaAJe6FCbhedlgG7M- CHkSILzvg-b89GGLIMb5glRSXNK-IjOL-sDFdkbeokIA%3D%3D&attredirects=0.

46. "Confessions of the Diocese."

47. Lewis, *Yet with a Steady Beat*; Snow, "The Altar and the Rail."

48. "Confessions of the Diocese."

49. *Journal of the Proceedings of the Bishops, Clergy and Laity of the Protestant Episcopal Church in the United States of America Assembled in a General Convention, Held in the City of New York, From October 8 to October 24, Inclusive in the Year of Our Lord 1889,* 1890, 266. https://www.episcopalarchives.org/sites/default/files/publications/1889_ GC_Journal.pdf.

50. Bragg, *Afro-American Church Work and Workers*.

51. *Journal of the Proceedings*, 328.

52. Bragg, *Afro-American Church Work and Workers*, 18. Russell believed this was the case in his diocese; see Russell, *Adventure in Faith*, 63. Russell himself was not affected by the "Black Canon" as he had become a priest before it was put into effect, but he nonetheless excoriated it.

53. Bragg, *Afro-American Church Work and Workers*, 24.

54. George Freeman Bragg, *Afro-American Church Work and Workers* (Baltimore: Church Advocate Press, 1904), 30.

55. Graebner, "Historically Black Congregations in the Diocese of North Carolina"; Michael J. Beary, *Black Bishop: Edward T. Demby and the Struggle for Racial Equality in the Episcopal Church* (Urbana: University of Illinois Press, 2001).

56. David M. Dean, *Defender of the Race*, 62, 69–72.

57. For more background on missional racial categorizations and their shifts over time, see Jennifer Snow, *Protestant Missionaries, Asian Immigrants, and Ideologies of Race in America, 1850–1924* (New York: Routledge, 2006).

58. Perry, *Twelve Years among the Colored People*, 34–35, 37.

Chapter 9

1. Dana Robert, "The 'Christian Home' as a Cornerstone of Anglo-American Missionary Thought and Practice," in *Converting Colonialism: Visions and Realities in Mission History, 1706–1914*, ed. Dana Robert (Grand Rapids, MI: Eerdmans, 2008), 134–65; Dana L. Robert, "Evangelist or Homemaker? Mission Strategies of Early Nineteenth-Century Missionary Wives in Burma and Hawaii," *International Bulletin of Missionary Research* 17, no. 1 (January 1993): 4.

2. Henry Bond Restarick, *Hawaii, 1778–1920, from the Viewpoint of a Bishop* (Honolulu: Paradise of the Pacific, 1924), 54.

3. Restarick, *Hawaii*, 74; Merze Tate, "Early Political Influence of the Sandwich Islands Missionaries," *Journal of Religious Thought* 17, no. 2 (1960): 117–32; Merze Tate, "Sandwich Islands Missionaries and Annexation," *Journal of Religious Thought* 20, no. 2 (1963): 137–45.

4. Ralph S. Kuykendall, "Introduction of the Episcopal Church into the Hawaiian Islands," *Pacific Historical Review* 15, no. 2 (n.d.): 133–46; Andrew Forest Muir, "Edmund Ibbotson (1831–1914): S.P.G. Missionary to Hawaii, (1862–1866)," *Historical Magazine of the Protestant Episcopal Church* 19, no. 3 (September 1950): 214–41.

5. Kuykendall, "Introduction of the Episcopal Church into the Hawaiian Islands."

6. Kuykendall, "Introduction of the Episcopal Church into the Hawaiian Islands."

7. Henry Bond Restarick and Constance Restarick Withington, *My Personal Recollections: The Unfinished Memoirs of Henry Bond Restarick, Bishop of Honolulu, 1902–1920* (Honolulu: Paradise of the Pacific Press, 1938), 68–71.

8. "Extracts from a Journal of the Bishop of Honolulu, by Thomas Nettleship Staley (1863)," Anglican History, accessed October 7, 2020, http://anglicanhistory.org/hawaii/staley_extracts1862.html; Kuykendall, "Introduction of the Episcopal Church into the Hawaiian Islands."

9. "Extracts from a Journal of the Bishop of Honolulu," 11–12.

10. "Extracts from a Journal of the Bishop of Honolulu," 15–16.

11. Stewart J. Brown, "Sisters and Brothers Abroad: Race, Empire, and Anglican Missionary Reformism in Hawai'i and the Pacific, 1858–75," in *The Church and Empire*, ed. Charlotte Methuen and Andrew Spicer, Studies in Church History 54 (Cambridge, UK: Cambridge University Press, 2018), 328–44.

12. Sarah Mieko Tamashiro, "Seedtime and Harvest: The Establishment of the Hawaiian Reformed Catholic Church, 1855–1870" (MA thesis, University of Hawai'i at Manoa, 2018), 11–12; Restarick, *Hawaii*; Restarick and Withington, *My Personal Recollections*.

13. Restarick and Withington, *My Personal Recollections*, 309.

14. Restarick, *Hawaii*.

15. Restarick and Withington, *My Personal Recollections*, 332. Despite this statement comparing Cantonese in the mainland United States to non-Cantonese Chinese in Hawai'i, in another work Restarick notes that one of the main congregations in Hawai'i was also Cantonese.

16. Jennifer Snow, *Protestant Missionaries, Asian Immigrants, and Ideologies of Race in America, 1850–1924* (New York: Routledge, 2006).

17. "The First Fifty Years of St. Elizabeth's Church, Honolulu, by C. Fletcher Howe (1952)," *Anglican History*, 2, accessed September 11, 2020, http://anglicanhistory.org/hawaii/howe1952/; Restarick and Withington, *My Personal Recollections*, 320.

18. "In Search of Ng Ping," Free Online Library, accessed September 11, 2020, https://www.thefreelibrary.com/In+search+of+Ng+Ping.-a0425914639.

19. "In Search of Ng Ping." The "exempt class" referred to was scholars and wealthy merchants.

20. "In Search of Ng Ping."

21. Restarick, *Hawaii*, 322.

22. Restarick and Withington, *My Personal Recollections*, 337.

23. Stuart Creighton Miller, *Benevolent Assimilation: The American Conquest of the Philippines, 1899–1903* (New Haven, CT: Yale University Press, 1982).

24. "Manifest Destiny, Continued: McKinley Defends U.S. Expansionism," History Matters, accessed November 10, 2021, http://historymatters.gmu.edu/d/5575/.

25. Miller, *Benevolent Assimilation*, 16.

26. Miller, *Benevolent Assimilation*.

27. Mark Douglas Norbeck, "False Start: The First Three Years of Episcopal Missionary Endeavor in the Philippine Islands, 1898–1901," *Anglican and Episcopal History* 62, no. 2 (June 1993): 215.

28. Norbeck, "False Start," 216–20.

29. Norbeck, "False Start," 223–33.

30. Norbeck, "False Start," 233. On Brent's missional influences, see Mark Douglas Norbeck, "The Legacy of Charles Henry Brent," *International Bulletin of Missionary Research* 20, no. 4 (October 1996): 163–68; Arun W. Jones, *Christian Missions in the American Empire* (New York: P. Lang, 2003), 100.

31. Norbeck, "The Legacy of Charles Henry Brent," 166; Jones, *Christian Missions in the American Empire*, 100.

32. Jones, *Christian Missions in the American Empire*.

33. Marjorie Buslig, "A History of the Church from the Banao People: A Missional Perspective" (MTS thesis, Church Divinity School of the Pacific, 2019).

34. Jones, *Christian Missions in the American Empire*, 111.

35. Jones, *Christian Missions in the American Empire*, 130.

36. John L. Kater Jr., "The Beginnings of the Episcopal Church in Panama 1852–1904," *Anglican and Episcopal History* 57, no. 2 (June 1988): 147–51.

37. Kater, "The Beginnings of the Episcopal Church in Panama."

38. Kater, "The Beginnings of the Episcopal Church in Panama," 157.

39. Julia Chester Emery, *A Century of Endeavor, 1821–1921: A Record of the First Hundred Years of the Domestic and Foreign Missionary Society of the Protestant Episcopal Church in the United States of America* (New York: Department of Missions, 1921); John L. Kater Jr., "Through a Glass Darkly: The Episcopal Church's Responses to the Mexican Iglesia de Jesús 1864–1904," *Anglican and Episcopal History* 85, no. 2

(June 2016): 194–227. For more details on early Spanish-speaking work in the continental United States, see Carla E. Roland Guzman, *Unmasking LATINX Ministry for Episcopalians: An Anglican Approach* (New York: Church Publishing, 2020).

40. Kevin Ward, *A History of Global Anglicanism* (Cambridge: Cambridge University Press, 2006), 104–10.

41. "Handbooks on the Missions of the Episcopal Church: The West Indies (1926)," Anglican History, accessed October 7, 2020, http://anglicanhistory.org/wi/missions1926/.

42. Restarick and Withington, *My Personal Recollections*, 325–29.

Chapter 10

1. Ian T. Douglas, *Fling Out the Banner: The National Church Ideal and the Foreign Mission of the Episcopal Church* (New York: Church Hymnal Corporation, 1996); William R. Hutchison, *Errand to the World: American Protestant Thought and Foreign Missions* (Chicago: University of Chicago Press, 1987); Frank Eiji Sugeno, "Charles Henry Brent, Apostle for Unity," *Anglican and Episcopal History* 70, no. 1 (March 2001): 75–79; Frank Eiji Sugeno, "The Establishmentarian Ideal and the Mission of the Episcopal Church," *Historical Magazine of the Protestant Episcopal Church* 53, no. 4 (December 1984): 285–92.

2. Douglas, *Fling Out the Banner*; Sugeno, "The Establishmentarian Ideal and the Mission of the Episcopal Church."

3. Mark Chapman, "American Catholicity and the National Church: The Legacy of William Reed Huntington," *Sewanee Theological Review* 56, no. 2 (2013): 113–48.

4. Stuart H. Hoke, "Broken Fragments: William Reed Huntington's Personal Quest for Unity," *Anglican and Episcopal History* 69, no. 2 (June 2000): 211–41.

5. John F. Woolverton, "Huntington's Quadrilateral: A Critical Study," *Church History* 39, no. 2 (June 1970): 202.

6. Woolverton, "Huntington's Quadrilateral."

7. Harold T. Lewis, *Yet with a Steady Beat: The African American Struggle for Recognition in the Episcopal Church* (Valley Forge, PA: Trinity Press International, 1996).

8. Peter W. Williams, *Religion, Art, and Money: Episcopalians and American Culture from the Civil War to the Great Depression* (Chapel Hill: University of North Carolina Press, 2016); Thomas F. Rzeznik, "'Representatives of All That Is Noble': The Rise of the Episcopal Establishment in Early-Twentieth-Century Philadelphia," *Religion and American Culture: A Journal of Interpretation* 19, no. 1 (2009): 69–100.

9. Sugeno, "The Establishmentarian Ideal and the Mission of the Episcopal Church"; Douglas, *Fling Out the Banner*.

10. Edward Yihua Xu, "The Protestant Episcopal China Mission and Chinese Society," in *Christian Encounters with Chinese Culture: Essays on Anglican and Episcopal History in China*, ed. Philip L. Wickeri and Sheng Kung Hui, Historical Studies of Anglican Christianity in China (Hong Kong: Hong Kong University Press, 2015), 25–46.

11. David M. Dean, "Domestic and Foreign Missionary Society Papers: The China Papers: 1835–1951," *Historical Magazine of the Protestant Episcopal Church* 42, no. 3 (September 1973): 333–39.

12. Edward Yihua Xu, "Religion and Education: St. John's University as an Evangelizing Agency" (PhD dissertation, Princeton University, 1994).

13. Xu, "The Protestant Episcopal China Mission and Chinese Society"; Chloe Starr, "Rethinking Church through the Book of Common Prayer in Late Qing and Early Republican China," in *Christian Encounters with Chinese Culture: Essays on Anglican and Episcopal History in China*, ed. Philip L. Wickeri and Sheng Kung Hui, Historical Studies of Anglican Christianity in China (Hong Kong: Hong Kong University Press, 2015), 25–46. The secondary and primary sources here use different romanization systems for Chinese names and even when using Pinyin do not include tone marks; in order to avoid confusion, I will retain the form found in each source.

14. Henry Bond Restarick, *Hawaii, 1778–1920, from the Viewpoint of a Bishop* (Honolulu: Paradise of the Pacific Press, 1924); The Academic, "William Zu Liang Sung (沈嗣良)," *Boxer Indemnity Scholars* (blog), January 28, 2018, https://boxerindemnityscholars.wordpress.com/2018/01/28/william-zu-liang-sung-%e6%b2%88%e5%97%a3%e8%89%af/.

15. Henry Bond Restarick and Constance Restarick Withington, *My Personal Recollections: The Unfinished Memoirs of Henry Bond Restarick, Bishop of Honolulu, 1902–1920* (Honolulu: Paradise of the Pacific Press, 1938); Restarick, *Hawaii*; Andrew Forest Muir, "The Church in Hawaii, 1778–1862," *Historical Magazine of the Protestant Episcopal Church* 18, no. 1 (March 1949): 31–65.

16. Xu, "The Protestant Episcopal China Mission and Chinese Society," 25–41.

17. Xu, "The Protestant Episcopal China Mission and Chinese Society"; Xu, "Religion and Education"; David A. Hollinger, *Protestants Abroad: How Missionaries Tried to Change the World but Changed America* (Princeton, NJ: Princeton University Press, 2017).

18. Dana Robert, "'The Crisis of Missions': Premillennial Mission Theory and the Origins of Independent Evangelical Missions," in *Earthen Vessels: American Evangelicals and Foreign Missions, 1880–1980*, ed. Joel A. Carpenter and Wilbert R. Shenk (Grand Rapids, MI: Eerdmans, 1990), 29–46.

19. James Alan Patterson, "The Loss of a Protestant Missionary Consensus: Foreign Missions and the Fundamentalist-Modernist Conflict," in *Earthen Vessels: American Evangelicals and Foreign Missions, 1880–1980*, ed. Joel A. Carpenter and Wilbert R. Shenk (Grand Rapids, MI: Eerdmans, 1990), 29–46.

20. Lydia Huffman Hoyle, "The Legacy of Daniel Johnson Fleming," *International Bulletin of Missionary Research* 14, no. 2 (April 1, 1990): 68–73.

21. Cited in Starr, "Rethinking Church through the Book of Common Prayer in Late Qing and Early Republican China," 94.

22. William Henry Scott, "Staunton of Sagada: Christian Civilizer," *Historical Magazine of the Protestant Episcopal Church* 31, no. 4 (December 1962): 305–39.

23. Kevin Ward, "Roland Allen's Radical Missiology," *Ecclesiology* 15, no. 1 (February 6, 2019): 81–89.

24. W. Hamilton (William Hamilton) Jefferys and Domestic and Foreign Missionary Society of the Protestant Episcopal Church in the U.S.A, *James Addison Ingle (Yin Teh-Sen) First Bishop of the Missionary District of Hankow, China* (New York: Domestic and Foreign Missionary Society, 1913), 202–3.

25. Hoyle, "The Legacy of Daniel Johnson Fleming"; Hutchison, *Errand to the World*.

26. Daniel Johnson Fleming and Marjorie Quennell, *Marks of a World Christian*, Everyday Life Series (New York: Association Press, 1919), 28.

27. Robert E. (Robert Elliott) Speer, *Of One Blood, a Short Study of the Race Problem* (New York: Council of Women for Home Missions and Missionary Education Movement of the United States and Canada, 1924).

28. Fleming and Quennell, *Marks of a World Christian*, 31.

29. Patterson, "Crisis of Missions"; Hutchison, *Errand to the World*; Kenneth Scott Latourette, "Reassessment of W. E. Hocking's Rethinking Missions after Twenty-Five Years," *International Review of Mission* 46, no. 182 (April 1957): 164–70.

30. Patterson, "Crisis of Missions"; Ward, "Roland Allen's Radical Missiology"; Hoyle, "The Legacy of Daniel Johnson Fleming"; Hutchison, *Errand to the World*; Hollinger, *Protestants Abroad*.

31. Ward, "Roland Allen's Radical Missiology."

32. Brian Stanley, *The Bible and the Flag: Protestant Missions and British Imperialism in the Nineteenth and Twentieth Centuries* (Leicester: Apollos, 1990); Jennifer Snow, *Protestant Missionaries, Asian Immigrants, and Ideologies of Race in America, 1850–1924* (New York: Routledge, 2006); Robert D. Woodberry, "The Shadow of Empire: Christian Missions, Colonial Policy and Democracy in Postcolonial Societies," Academia, 2004, https://www.academia.edu/2128676/The_Shadow_of_Empire_Christian_Missions_Colonial_Policy_and_Democracy_in_Postcolonial_Societies; Hollinger, *Protestants Abroad*; Xi Lian, *The Conversion of Missionaries: Liberalism in American Protestant Missions in China, 1907–1932* (University Park, PA: Penn State University Press, 1996).

33. Fleming and Quennell, *Marks of a World Christian*, 15.

Chapter 11

1. William Howard Melish, "Episcopal Leaders Plan Expansion: General Convention Called to 'Responsibility and Service'—United Thank Offering—Drama of Missions,'" *Christian Century* 54, no. 42 (October 20, 1937): 1306–7.

2. Francis Henry Touchet, "The Social Gospel and the Cold War: The Melish Case," PhD Dissertation, New York University, 1981.

3. Donald McGavran, *Understanding Church Growth* (Wm. B. Eerdmans Pub. Co., 1970).

4. William L. Sachs, "'Self-Support': The Episcopal Mission and Nationalism in Japan," *Church History* 58, no. 4 (1989): 489–501.

5. Jennifer Snow, *Protestant Missionaries, Asian Immigrants, and Ideologies of Race in America, 1850–1924* (New York: Routledge, 2006); Ronald T. Takaki, *Strangers from a Different Shore: A History of Asian Americans* (Boston: Little, Brown, 1989).

6. For a general outline of legal strictures applying to early Asian immigrants in the United States, and their relationship with missionaries, see Snow, *Protestant Missionaries, Asian Immigrants, and Ideologies of Race in America.* See also Takaki, *Strangers from a Different Shore*; Andrew N. Otani, *A History of Japanese-American Episcopal Churches* (Minneapolis: Self-published, 1980).

7. Joanna Bowen Gillespie, "Japanese-American Episcopalians during World War II: The Congregation of St. Mary's Los Angeles, 1941–1945," *Anglican and Episcopal History* 69, no. 2 (June 2000): 136.

8. Linda Popp Di Biase, "Neither Harmony nor Eden: Margaret Peppers and the Exile of the Japanese Americans," *Anglican and Episcopal History* 70, no. 1 (March 2001): 101–17.

9. Gillespie, "Japanese-American Episcopalians during World War II," 137–41.

10. Gillespie, "Japanese-American Episcopalians during World War II," 157–59.

11. Gillespie, "Japanese-American Episcopalians during World War II."

12. Gillespie, "Japanese-American Episcopalians during World War II," 154–59.

13. Gillespie, "Japanese-American Episcopalians during World War II."

14. Otani, *A History of Japanese-American Episcopal Churches.* On the 20% statistic for nonmajority group in multiracial congregations, see Michael O. Emerson, *People of the Dream: Multiracial Congregations in the United States* (Princeton, NJ: Princeton University Press, 2008).

15. Gibson Winter, *The Suburban Captivity of the Churches: An Analysis of Protestant Responsibility in the Expanding Metropolis* (Garden City, NY: Doubleday, 1961), 30–32.

16. Winter, *The Suburban Captivity of the Churches*, 79.

17. Winter, *The Suburban Captivity of the Churches*, 71.

18. Winter, *The Suburban Captivity of the Churches*, 44.

19. Winter, *The Suburban Captivity of the Churches*, 55.

20. Winter, *The Suburban Captivity of the Churches*; Robert W. Prichard, *A History of the Episcopal Church: Complete through the 78th General Convention*, revised edition (New York: Morehouse, 2014); George R. Sumner, "What's Anglican about Mission," *Anglican Theological Review* 89, no. 3 (2007): 461–74; James Thayer Addison, *The Episcopal Church in the United States, 1789–1931* (New York: Charles Scribner's Sons, 1951).

21. Winter, *The Suburban Captivity of the Churches*, 77, italics in original.

22. Daniel (Daniel Edward) Sack, "Reaching the 'Up-and-Outers': Sam Shoemaker and Modern Evangelicalism," *Anglican and Episcopal History* 64, no. 1 (March 1995): 37–57.

23. Sack, "Reaching the 'Up-and-Outers'"; John F. Woolverton, "Evangelical Protestantism and Alcoholism 1933–1962: Episcopalian Samuel Shoemaker, the Oxford Group and Alcoholics Anonymous," *Historical Magazine of the Protestant Episcopal Church* 52, no. 1 (March 1983): 53–65. Shoemaker's approach to these "interviews" is summarized in Samuel M. Shoemaker, "Church Congress Syllabus 47: Personal Evangelism," *Anglican Theological Review* 100, no. 3 (Summer 2018): 481–91. The work was first published in 1947, at which point Shoemaker had many years of practice under his belt.

24. Woolverton, "Evangelical Protestantism and Alcoholism."

25. Cited in Woolverton, "Evangelical Protestantism and Alcoholism," 63.

26. Paul Moore, *Presences: A Bishop's Life in the City* (New York: Farrar, Straus and Giroux, 1997), 159.

27. Moore, *Presences*.

28. James Russell, *Adventure in Faith* (Lawrenceville, VA: James Solomon Russell–Saint Paul's College Museum and Archives, 2021), 66.

29. Moore, *Presences*, 120.

30. David E. Sumner, *The Episcopal Church's History: 1945–1985* (Wilton, CT: Morehouse-Barlow, 1987), 3; David Hein and Gardiner H. Shattuck, *The Episcopalians* (New York: Church Publishing, 2005), 123–25.

31. Pauli Murray, "Protest against the Legal Status of the Negro," *Annals of the American Academy of Political and Social Science* 357 (1965): 55–64; Thelma M. Panton, "Thy Rich Anointing: The Lives and Ministries of Pauli Murray and Barbara Clementine Harris," *Sewanee Theological Review* 51, no. 4 (2008): 386–404; Pauli Murray, *Song in a Weary Throat: An American Pilgrimage* (New York: Harper & Row, 1987). Throughout her life Murray worked passionately to emphasize intersectionality in identity and politics. On the complexities of Murray's identities, see Doreen M. Drury, "Boy-Girl, Imp, Priest: Pauli Murray and the Limits of Identity," *Journal of Feminist Studies in Religion* 29, no. 1 (2013): 142–47.

32. David A. Hollinger, *Protestants Abroad: How Missionaries Tried to Change the World but Changed America* (Princeton, NJ: Princeton University Press, 2017).

Chapter 12

1. Episcopal Church, ed., *The Church's Work in Domestic Missionary Districts and Domestic Mission Fields* (New York: National Council, 1948). For dates at which each missionary district received its first "local" bishop, see Robert W. Prichard, *A History of the Episcopal Church: Complete through the 78th General Convention*, revised edition (New York: Morehouse, 2014), 347.

2. Mark T. B. Laing, *From Crisis to Creation: Lesslie Newbigin and the Reinvention of Christian Mission* (Eugene, OR: Wipf and Stock, 2012); David P. Gaines, *The World Council of Churches: A Study of Its Background and History* (Peterborough, NH: Richard Smith, 1966).

3. Gaines, *World Council of Churches*, 905.

4. Gaines, *World Council of Churches*, 1032–33.

5. Leng Lim, Kim-Hao Yap, and Tuck-Leong Lee, "The Mythic-Literalists in the Province of Southeast Asia," in *Other Voices, Other Worlds: The Global Church Speaks Out on Homosexuality*, ed. Terry Brown (New York: Church Publishing, 2006), 57–76. The authors argue that the deliberate withdrawal from ecumenical relationships and conferences permitted the church in Singapore to develop an extreme conservativism.

6. Harvey Thomas Hoekstra, *The World Council of Churches and the Demise of Evangelism* (Wheaton, IL: Tyndale House, 1979); Jennifer Snow, "The Christian

Home in Missional Transition," *Studies in World Christianity* 25, no. 3 (December 1, 2019): 324–44.

7. Wolfgang Günther, "The History and Significance of World Mission Conferences in the 20th Century," *International Review of Mission* 92, no. 367 (October 2003): 521–37.

8. L. A. Hoedemaker, "The Legacy of J. C. Hoekendijk," *International Bulletin of Missionary Research* 19, no. 4 (October 1995): 166–70.

9. Wilhelm Richebächer, "Missio Dei: The Basis of Mission Theology or a Wrong Path?," *International Review of Mission* 92, no. 367 (October 2003): 588–605; Günther, "The History and Significance of World Mission Conferences in the 20th Century."

10. Hoekstra, *The World Council of Churches and the Demise of Evangelism.*

11. World Council of Churches, ed., *"You Are the Light of the World": Statements on Mission by the World Council of Churches 1980–2005*, Oikoumene (Geneva: WCC Publications, 2005).

12. World Council of Churches, ed., *The Church for Others and the Church for the World: A Quest for Structures for Missionary Congregations* (Geneva: World Council of Churches, 1967); Ans J. van der Bent, *From Generation to Generation: The Study of Youth in the World Council of Churches* (Geneva: World Council of Churches, 1986); World Council of Churches and Norman Goodall, eds., *The Uppsala Report 1968; Official Report of the Fourth Assembly of the World Council of Churches, Uppsala, July 4–20, 1968* (Geneva: World Council of Churches, 1968).

13. Hoedemaker, "The Legacy of J. C. Hoekendijk."

14. Jesse Zink, "Changing World, Changing Church: Stephen Bayne and 'Mutual Responsibility and Interdependence,'" *Anglican Theological Review* 93, no. 2 (Spring 2011): 243–62; Stephen F. Bayne, *An Anglican Turning Point: Documents and Interpretations* (Austin, TX: Church Historical Society, 1964), 219.

15. Bayne, *An Anglican Turning Point*, 207.

16. Zink, "Changing World, Changing Church"; Stephen F. Bayne, *Mutual Responsibility and Interdependence in the Body of Christ: With Related Background Documents*, Lambeth Conference (New York: Seabury Press, 1963); Ian T. Douglas, *Fling Out the Banner: The National Church Ideal and the Foreign Mission of the Episcopal Church* (New York: Church Hymnal Corporation, 1996), 269.

17. Douglas Webster, *Mutual Irresponsibility: A Danger to Be Avoided* (London: SPCK, 1965).

18. Daniel Johnson Fleming and Marjorie Quennell, *Marks of a World Christian*, Everyday Life Series (New York: Association Press, 1919); Bayne, *An Anglican Turning Point*, 207.

19. C. Kilmer (Chauncie Kilmer) Myers, "Episcopalians: Muddling through vs Creative Outreach," *Christian Century* 80, no. 48 (November 27, 1963): 1459–62.

20. Gardiner H. Shattuck, *Episcopalians and Race: Civil War to Civil Rights*, Religion in the South (Lexington: University Press of Kentucky, 2000).

21. Pauli Murray, *Song in a Weary Throat: An American Pilgrimage* (New York: Harper & Row, 1987), 381–85.

22. John Everitt Booty, "Stephen Bayne's Perspective on the Church and the Civil Rights Movement, 1967–1970," *Anglican and Episcopal History* 64, no. 3 (September 1995): 352–70; Shattuck, *Episcopalians and Race.*

23. Booty, "Stephen Bayne's Perspective on the Church and the Civil Rights Movement."

24. Booty, "Stephen Bayne's Perspective on the Church and the Civil Rights Movement."

25. Vine Deloria, "GCSP: The Demons at Work," *Historical Magazine of the Protestant Episcopal Church* 48, no. 1 (March 1979): 83.

26. Deloria, "GCSP."

27. Harold T. Lewis, *Yet with a Steady Beat: The African American Struggle for Recognition in the Episcopal Church* (Valley Forge, PA: Trinity Press International, 1996), 155–56; Deloria, "GCSP"; Shattuck, *Episcopalians and Race*.

28. Booty, "Stephen Bayne's Perspective on the Church and the Civil Rights Movement," 9.

29. Booty, "Stephen Bayne's Perspective on the Church and the Civil Rights Movement."

30. Booty, "Stephen Bayne's Perspective on the Church and the Civil Rights Movement," 27; Deloria, "GCSP."

31. Deloria, "GCSP"; Booty, "Stephen Bayne's Perspective on the Church and the Civil Rights Movement."

32. Joel L. Alvis, "Racial Turmoil and Religious Reaction: The Rt. Rev. John M. Allin," *Historical Magazine of the Protestant Episcopal Church* 50, no. 1 (March 1981): 83–96.

33. Carla E. Roland Guzman, *Unmasking LATINX Ministry for Episcopalians: An Anglican Approach* (New York: Church Publishing, 2020).

34. Deloria, "GCSP," 92.

35. John M. Burgess, ed., *Black Gospel/White Church* (New York: Seabury Press, 1982), 50.

36. Shattuck, *Episcopalians and Race*; Episcopal Church Foundation, *The Episcopal Church Today as Seen by Clergymen and Others: A Survey for the Episcopal Church Foundation* (Princeton, NJ: Opinion Research Corporation, 1964); Gibson Winter, *The Suburban Captivity of the Churches: An Analysis of Protestant Responsibility in the Expanding Metropolis* (Garden City, NY: Doubleday, 1961).

37. Shattuck, *Episcopalians and Race*, 79–99; Gardiner J. Shattuck, "William Stringfellow and the American Racial Crisis," in *Prophet of Justice, Prophet of Life: Essays on William Stringfellow*, ed. Robert Boak Slocum (New York: Church Publishing, 1997), 54–79; Laura R. Olson, "Mainline Protestant Washington Offices and the Political Lives of Clergy," in *The Quiet Hand of God: Faith-Based Activism and the Public Role of Mainline Protestantism*, ed. Robert Wuthnow and John H. Evans (Berkeley: University of California Press, 2002).

38. Shattuck, *Episcopalians and Race*; Lewis, *Yet with a Steady Beat*.

39. Caroline J. Addington Hall, *Thorn in the Flesh: How Gay Sexuality Is Changing the Episcopal Church* (New York: Rowman and Littlefield, 2013).

Chapter 13

1. Michael Moriarty, "William Parker Ladd and the Origins of the Episcopal Liturgical Renewal Movement," *Church History* 64, no. 3 (1995): 439.

2. I would like to express my gratitude to Dr. Ruth Meyers for clarifying for me the various historical processes by which the Prayer Book has been revised, and for her helpful conversations on liturgical history overall.

3. Michael Moriarty, "William Palmer Ladd and the Origins of the Episcopal Liturgical Movement," *Church History* 64, no. 3 (1995): 438–51.

4. Moriarty, "William Palmer Ladd and the Origins of the Episcopal Liturgical Movement," 441.

5. Robert W. Prichard, *A History of the Episcopal Church: Complete through the 78th General Convention*, revised edition (New York: Morehouse, 2014).

6. Moriarty, "William Palmer Ladd and the Origins of the Episcopal Liturgical Movement," 448.

7. Ruth A. Meyers, *Continuing the Reformation: Re-visioning Baptism in the Episcopal Church* (New York: Church Publications, 1997); Leonel Mitchell, "Episcopal Church and Liturgical Renewal: EBSCOhost," *Worship* 48, no. 8 (October 1974): 490–99.

8. Elesha J. Coffman, "Anthropology Meets the Book of Common Prayer: Margaret Mead's Role in Revising the Liturgy of Baptism," *Fides et Historia* 51, no. 1 (2019): 131–32. On the need for Prayer Book revisions which in some ways track Mead's suggestions, the creation of "Enriching Our Worship" and other additional liturgical resources have made some leeway. See, among others, Sylvia Sweeney, "Future Directions in Liturgical Development," *Anglican Theological Review* 95, no. 3 (Summer 2013): 517–24; Stephen Burns and Bryan Cones, "A Prayer Book for the Twenty-First Century?," *Anglican Theological Review* 96, no. 4 (Fall 2014): 639–60.

9. Meyers, *Continuing the Reformation*.

10. Leonel Mitchell, "The 1979 Prayer Book and Liturgical Change in the Episcopal Church," *Liturgy* 19, no. 2 (March 1, 2004): 41.

11. Ruth A. Meyers, "The Baptismal Covenant and the Proposed Anglican Covenant," *Journal of Anglican Studies* 10, no. 1 (December 2011): 31–41.

12. Sheryl A. Kujawa-Holbrook, "Women and Vocation in the Episcopal Church: Reflections on Our History," *Anglican and Episcopal History* 79, no. 2 (June 2010): 101–23.

13. Pamela W. Darling, *New Wine: The Story of Women Transforming Leadership and Power in the Episcopal Church* (Cambridge, MA: Cowley, 1994), 111.

14. Darling, *New Wine*, 117–22.

15. Jason S. Lantzer, "Hoosier Episcopalians, the Coming of Women's Ordination, and the 1979 Book of Common Prayer," *Anglican and Episcopal History* 72, no. 2 (June 2003): 229–54; Carter Heyward, *A Priest Forever: One Woman's Controversial Ordination in the Episcopal Church* (Cleveland, OH: Pilgrim Press, 1999).

16. Renee McKenzie, "Being the Advocate," *Anglican and Episcopal History* 83, no. 2 (June 2014): 165–76. McKenzie herself is an African American Episcopal priest and the previous rector of Church of the Advocate.

17. "The Reverend Paul Washington, 1921–2002," Episcopal Archives, accessed October 26, 2021, https://episcopalarchives.org/church-awakens/exhibits/show/leadership/clergy/washington.

18. McKenzie, "Being the Advocate," 166–67.

19. McKenzie, "Being the Advocate."

20. Pauli Murray and Anthony B. Pinn, *Pauli Murray: Selected Sermons and Writings* (Maryknoll, NY: Orbis Books, 2006), 193–95.

21. John Maurice Gessell, "The Iker Consecration, the 'Conscience Clause,' and the Function of the Law," *Sewanee Theological Review* 38, no. 4 (1995): 363–66; Darling, *New Wine*, 140–41.
22. "Compliance Sought on Women's Ordination," *Christian Century* 118, no. 7 (February 28, 2001): 11.
23. Donald Smith Armentrout, "Episcopal Splinter Groups: Schisms in the Episcopal Church, 1963–1985," *Historical Magazine of the Protestant Episcopal Church* 55, no. 4 (December 1986): 295–320.
24. Armentrout, "Episcopal Splinter Groups."
25. McKenzie, "Being the Advocate," 165.

Chapter 14

1. Heather White, "William Stringfellow and Anthony Towne: 'The Block Island Two,'" *OutHistory*, April 13, 2020, https://outhistory.org/exhibits/show/stringtown/stringtowne2. Troy R. Saxby, *Pauli Murray: A Personal and Political Life* (Chapel Hill: University of North Carolina Press, 2020); David A. Hollinger, *Protestants Abroad: How Missionaries Tried to Change the World but Changed America* (Princeton, NJ: Princeton University Press, 2017); Elesha J. Coffman, "Anthropology Meets the Book of Common Prayer: Margaret Mead's Role in Revising the Liturgy of Baptism," *Fides et Historia* 51, no. 1 (2019): 124–34. There are certainly hints that many other Episcopalian clergy and laypeople of earlier eras were involved in same-sex relationships, but due to the need to keep these relationships secret the written historical record is rarely explicit.
2. Quoted in Alfred A. Gross, *Strangers in Our Midst: Problems of the Homosexual in American Society* (Washington, D.C.: Public Affairs Press, 1962), 105. The quote is taken from Mead's 1949 book *Male and Female*.
3. Heather Rachelle White, *Reforming Sodom: Protestants and the Rise of Gay Rights* (Chapel Hill: University of North Carolina Press, 2015).
4. Gross, *Strangers in Our Midst*, 99, citing Myers, *Light the Dark Streets* (1950).
5. Gross, *Strangers in Our Midst*, 194.
6. Gross, *Strangers in Our Midst*, 98.
7. Gross, *Strangers in Our Midst*, 125.
8. Gross, *Strangers in Our Midst*, 147.
9. Gross, *Strangers in Our Midst*, 165.
10. *What the Bishops Have Said about Marriage: A Resolution Adopted by the Bishops of the Lambeth Conference 1968 Together with the Report of Committee 5 to the Lambeth Conference 1958 THE FAMILY IN CONTEMPORARY SOCIETY and the Text of Certain Relevant Resolutions Passed by the Conference* (London: SPCK, 1968), 40.
11. *What the Bishops Have Said about Marriage.*
12. Robert W. Prichard, *A Wholesome Example: Sexual Morality and the Episcopal Church* (Alexandria, VA: Charter Printing, 1991). See Prichard's article in this collection for

a clear outline of the history of the disciplinary canons relating to marriage in the Episcopal Church.

13. Martin Brokenleg, "Lakota Hca," in *Other Voices, Other Worlds: The Global Church Speaks Out on Homosexuality*, ed. Terry Brown (New York: Church Publishing, 2006), 5–14.

14. Natasha Erlank, "Strange Bedfellows: The International Missionary Council, the International African Institute, and Research into African Marriage and Family," in *The Spiritual in the Secular: Missionaries and Knowledge about Africa*, Studies in the History of Christian Missions (Grand Rapids, MI: William B. Eerdmans, 2012), 267–92; Adrian Hastings, *Christian Marriage in Africa: Being a Report Commissioned by the Archbishops of Cape Town, Central Africa, Kenya, Tanzania and Uganda* (London: SPCK, 1973); Kevin Ward, "Same-Sex Relations in Africa and the Debate on Homosexuality in East African Anglicanism," *Anglican Theological Review* 84, no. 1 (n.d.): 81–111.

15. Prichard, *A Wholesome Example*; William Paret, *The Pastoral Use of the Prayer Book: The Substance of Plain Talks Given to His Students and Younger Clergy* (Baltimore, MD: Maryland Diocesan Lbrary, 1904).

16. Jennifer Snow, "The Troubled Knot: Tying Church Discipline to 'Christian Marriage' in African Contexts," *Journal of Ecclesiastical History* 71, no. 1 (January 2020): 135–53; Ward, "Same-Sex Relations in Africa."

17. Heather Rachelle White, "Gay Rites and Religious Rights: New York's First Same-Sex Marriage Controversy," in *Queer Christianities: Lived Religion in Transgressive Forms*, ed. Kathleen T. Talvacchia, Mark Larrimore, and Michael F. Pettinger (New York: NYU Press, 2014), 79–90.

18. C. Kilmer Myers, "Statement on Homosexuality to the House of Bishops by C. Kilmer Myers, Bishop of California," typescript memo, House of Bishops meeting, October 1, 1977, 5, 6.

19. Myers, "Statement on Homosexuality to the House of Bishops," 3–4, emphasis in original.

20. Myers, "Statement on Homosexuality to the House of Bishops," 5.

21. Robert W. Prichard, *A History of the Episcopal Church: Complete through the 78th General Convention*, revised edition (New York: Morehouse, 2014), 323; Caroline J. Addington Hall, *Thorn in the Flesh: How Gay Sexuality Is Changing the Episcopal Church* (New York: Rowan and Littlefield, 2013), 59–60.

22. David Hein and Gardiner H. Shattuck, *The Episcopalians* (New York: Church Publishing, 2005), 144; David E. Sumner, *The Episcopal Church's History: 1945–1985* (Wilton, CT: Morehouse-Barlow, 1987).

23. Edmond L. Browning, "Our World Mission," in *Realities and Visions: The Church's Mission Today*, ed. Furman C. Stough and Urban T. Holmes (New York: Seabury Press, 1976), 8–15.

24. Prichard, *A Wholesome Example*; Addington Hall, *Thorn in the Flesh*.

25. Hein and Shattuck, *The Episcopalians*, 144. Hein and Shattuck note that this number comprised a quarter of the bishops of the church at that time.

26. William Sachs, *Sexuality and Anglicanism*, ed. Jeremy Morris (Oxford: Oxford University Press, 2017), 93–116; Addington Hall, *Thorn in the Flesh*, 63–69.

27. Hein and Shattuck, *The Episcopalians*, 144; John Maurice Gessell, "The Iker Consecration, the 'Conscience Clause,' and the Function of the Law," *Sewanee Theological Review* 38, no. 4 (1995): 363–66.

28. Miranda Hassett, *Anglican Communion in Crisis: How Episcopal Dissidents and Their African Allies Are Reshaping Anglicanism* (Princeton, NJ: Princeton University Press, 2007).

29. Hassett, *Anglican Communion in Crisis*, 58.

30. "The Kuala Lumpur Statement on Human Sexuality—2nd Encounter in the South, 10 to 15 Feb 97," *Global South Anglican*, accessed November 3, 2021, https://acl.asn.au/old/news/KLStatement.html.

31. Kevin Ward, "Same-Sex Relations in Africa and the Debate on Homosexuality in East African Anglicanism," *Anglican Theological Review* 84, no. 1 (Winter 2002): 104.

32. Henry Okullu, *Church and Marriage in East Africa* (Nairobi: Uzima, 1977).

33. Ward, "Same-Sex Relations in Africa"; Hassett, *Anglican Communion in Crisis*, 88–95; Kapya Kaoma, *Christianity, Globalization, and Protective Homophobia: Democractic Contestation of Sexuality in Sub-Saharan Africa* (n.p.: Palgrave Macmillan, 2018).

34. Hassett, *Anglican Communion in Crisis*, 95.

35. https://www.anglicancommunion.org/resources/document-library/lambeth-conference/1998/section-i-called-to-full-humanity/section-i10-human-sexuality.

36. Sachs, "Sexuality and Anglicanism."

37. Leng Lim, Kim-Hao Yap, and Tuck-Leong Lee, "The Mythic-Literalists in the Province of Southeast Asia," in *Other Voices, Other Worlds: The Global Church Speaks Out on Homosexuality*, ed. Terry Brown (New York: Church Publishing, 2006), 57–76.

38. Sachs, "Sexuality and Anglicanism."

39. Angela Gayle Guida, "We Remained Episcopal: Stories from before, during and after the Split in the Episcopal Diocese of San Joaquin" (2010) Master Thesis, Church Divinity School of the Pacific, 2010; Gessell, "The Iker Consecration, the 'Conscience Clause,' and the Function of the Law."

40. Harold T. Lewis and Mark Hollingsworth, *The Recent Unpleasantness* (Eugene, OR: Wipf and Stock, 2015).

41. Addington Hall, *Thorn in the Flesh*; Hassett, *Anglican Communion in Crisis*; Lewis and Hollingsworth, *The Recent Unpleasantness*; "Anglican Leaders Refuse Communion with U.S. Bishop," CBC News, February 16, 2007, https://www.cbc.ca/news/world/anglican-leaders-refuse-communion-with-u-s-bishop-1.635953; "Episcopal Bishops Remain Defiant on Gay Bishop's Election," EBSCOhost, accessed December 1, 2021, https://web.s.ebscohost.com/ehost/detail/detail?vid=0&sid=6e5de490-c98b-4f7b-942c-1155007125b8%40redis&bdata=JkF1dGhUeXBlPWlwLHNzbyZzaXRlPWVo b3N0LWxpdmU%3d#AN=ATLA0001457028&db=lsdah.

42. Willis Jenkins, "Episcopalians, Homosexuality, and World Mission," *Anglican Theological Review* 86, no. 2 (2004): 293–316.

Conclusion

1. M. Macdonald, "Presiding Bishop Tells Standing Rock Protectors 'the Way of Jesus Honors the Water,'" *Episcopal News Service* (blog), September 27, 2016, https://www.episcopalnewsservice.org/2016/09/27/presiding-bishop-tells-standing-rock-protectors-the-way-of-jesus-honors-the-water/.

2. The idea of contextualization as systematized theologically is often credited to Stephen B. Bevans, *Models of Contextual Theology*, revised and expanded edition, Faith and Cultures Series (Maryknoll, NY: Orbis Books, 2002). In terms of practice, even if not fully systematized, both Protestant and Catholic missionaries and their converts had been developing contextualization throughout the modern era. Other models of this shift are sometimes focused on translation, as in Andrew F. Walls, *The Missionary Movement in Christian History: Studies in Transmission of Faith* (Maryknoll, NY: Orbis Books, 1996); Lamin O. Sanneh, *Translating the Message: The Missionary Impact on Culture*, 2nd edition, revised and expanded, American Society of Missiology Series, no. 42 (Maryknoll, NY: Orbis Books, 2009).

Index

For the benefit of digital users, indexed terms that span two pages (e.g., 52–53) may, on occasion, appear on only one of those pages.